PRACTICING
WHAT WE PREACH

Sᴏᴜʀᴄᴇ Bᴏᴏᴋs ᴏɴ Eᴅᴜᴄᴀᴛɪᴏɴ
VOLUME 56
GARLAND REFERENCE LIBRARY OF SOCIAL SCIENCE
VOLUME 1193

PRACTICING WHAT WE PREACH

PREPARING MIDDLE LEVEL EDUCATORS

SAMUEL TOTTEN
CHARLENE JOHNSON
LINDA R. MORROW
TONI SILLS-BRIEGEL

FALMER PRESS
A MEMBER OF THE TAYLOR & FRANCIS GROUP
NEW YORK & LONDON / 1999

Published in 1999 by
Falmer Press
A Member of the Taylor & Francis Group
19 Union Square West
New York, NY 10003

10   9   8   7   6   5   4   3   2   1

Library of Congress Cataloging-in-Publication Data
Practicing what we preach : preparing middle level educators /
    Samuel Totten . . . [et al.].
        p.   cm. — (Garland reference library of social science ;
    1193. Source books on education ; vol. 56)
      Includes bibliographical references and index.
      ISBN 0–8153–3166–5 (alk. paper)
        1. Middle school teachers—Training of—United States.
    I. Totten, Samuel.   II. Series: Garland reference library of social
    science ; v. 1193.   III. Series: Garland reference library of social
    science.   Source books on education ; vol. 56.
    LB1735.5.P73   1999
    370'.71'1—dc21   99–32545
                                                                    CIP

Printed on acid-free, 250-year-life paper
Manufactured in the United States of America

Charlene Johnson dedicates this book to her family, especially her husband, Michael Carter, and son, Damani Carter. Without your patience and support, I could not have done it! In addition, this book is dedicated to all the multifaceted early adolescents who are our future leaders—may this book contribute to your positive growth and development as you prepare to take on the task of managing and furthering the world!

Linda McElroy Morrow dedicates this book, first, to my husband, Ron, for his continuing patience and support in my professional endeavors and, second, to my three coeditors, Charlene, Sam, and Toni with whom I continue to laugh and learn, for inviting me on this journey.

Toni Sills-Briegel dedicates this book to the thousands of students both in middle school and in university classes who have shaped her practice over the years and to the mentors who have guided her in her growth as a middle level teacher and college professor: Christine Cochran (retired teacher, London, Arkansas), Jerry Sills (counselor, Lonoke, Arkansas), Dr. Rebecca Fewell (Director of the Debbie Institute, University of Miami), and Dr. Samuel Totten (University of Arkansas).

Samuel Totten dedicates this book to the teacher educators he has had the great pleasure to study under who modeled hands-on/minds-on instruction: Dr. Art Costa (California State University, Sacramento), Dr. George Hallowitz (San Francisco State University), Dr. Ann Lieberman (Teachers College, Columbia University), and Dr. Karen Zumwalt (Teachers College, Columbia University).

Contents

Chapter 6: Technology   **177**

Chapter 8: Multicultural Perspectives   **243**

Practicing What We Preach: Preparing Middle Level Educators

The genesis of this book, *Practicing What We Preach: Preparing Middle Level Educators*, is rooted in three of the editors' efforts, all of whom teach in the College of Education at the University of Arkansas, Fayetteville, to support one another's pedagogical approaches in our middle level principles and methods courses. Respecting one another's passion for teaching and commitment to middle level education, we frequently sought out each others' advice as we attempted to strengthen various aspects of our middle level courses. At first, we began sharing our teaching strategies and assignments, particularly those that were designed to invoke thought, commitment, and understanding in regard to what it means to meet the unique needs of early adolescents. More often than not, the discussions revolved around the challenge of introducing and familiarizing preservice and inservice teachers to hands-on, minds-on instruction and the efficacy of such an approach in reaching early adolescents. Throughout our discussions, we found ourselves in constant agreement that our own credibility demanded that we implement and model the same learning strategies in our methods classes that we were advocating for use with middle level learners. The more we shared our ideas and borrowed or adapted each others' strategies and activities, the more we came to appreciate each others' strengths. Ultimately, our collegial discussions, which we believe to be largely an anomaly in university settings, led to key changes in both our curricular and instructional practices.

The various strategies and activities that the three shared were written up and published in a two-part series in *Current Issues in Middle Level Education*. When the fourth editor, who teaches at Southwest Missouri State University, was approached to contribute to a third article along the same lines, she suggested the idea of reaching out to middle level teacher educators across the country in order to ask them to contribute to a book whose purpose was to highlight minds-on, hands-on teaching strategies and learning activities for use in middle level teacher education programs. Thus was born the idea for *Practicing What We Preach: Preparing Middle Level Educators.*

For several months, we, the four editors, worked and reworked a tentative table of contents and developed a proposal for the book. We were intent on including practices in the book that addressed the unique needs of early adolescents, key components of middle level education (e.g., interdisciplinary teaming, advisor/advisee, exploratory), major instructional concepts and components (interdisciplinary instruction, movement in the classroom, classroom management), and field experiences (preservice and internships).

Calls for contributors were sent to a host of regional and national journals and newsletters (*The Chronicle of Higher Education, Journal of the New England League of Middle Schools, NASSP Bulletin: The Journal for Middle Level and High School Administrators, Action in Teacher Education,* and *Current Issues in Middle Level Education*), every state middle level journal in the nation, a group of individuals whom the editors designated as "pioneers and/or giants of middle level education," middle level teacher educators across the country who are known to be active in the National Middle School Association and/or actively engaged in writing for middle level journals, colleagues at other colleges and universities, and pertinent listserves. Interested parties were asked to submit a succinct description of a strong strategy, activity, or assignment and to follow that with a succinct commentary that addressed such issues as the students' reaction to the activity, particular strengths of the strategy in conveying a concept or topic, and any other pertinent information that other instructors might find useful. Every entry but two followed the aforementioned format. "Doing Service With Young Adolescents: The Lessons of Recent Research" and "Constructivism/Non-Directive Teaching: Some Thoughts on Developing Independent Learners" use an alternative format, but we felt that both of these pieces warranted inclusion in the book because of their significance.

Over a two-year period, the editors received 198 submissions. Close to 100 of those were accepted for inclusion in the book. Most of the 100 pieces were revised at least once, and some were revised up to three times.

The contributors to *Practicing What We Preach* are an eclectic group. They represent public and private colleges and universities in 27 different states (Arizona, Arkansas, California, Colorado, Connecticut, Florida, Georgia, Indiana, Illinois, Iowa, Kentucky, Louisiana, Maine, Massachusetts, Michigan, Missouri, New Jersey, North Carolina, New York, Ohio, Oklahoma, Pennsylvania, South Dakota, Tennessee, Texas, Virginia, Wisconsin) and three countries (Australia, Canada, and the United States). Professors, instructors, graduate students, teaching fellows (middle level teachers on sabbatical and teaching at a college or university for a short period of time), educational researchers, and directors and co-directors of middle level centers are also represented. One of our goals in developing the book was to solicit and include pieces from a diverse population of teacher educators. To a large extent, we have accomplished this goal.

As mentioned previously, our major goal was to include descriptions of strategies, activities, and assignments that are comprised of both a hands-on *and a* minds-on approach. A "hands-on" approach was only one half of the equation. When all is said and done, we are in basic agreement with O. L. Davis (1998) when he notes that:

> Hands-on activities simply focus on pupils' *doing,* on their action. Further, the term excludes too much. Very importantly, the activities do not explicitly require that pupils *think* about their experience. "Hands-on," simply, can be "minds-off." Raw experiences comprise the grist for thinking. They are necessary, but not sufficient, instructional foci. For the most part, hands-on activities must include *minds-on* aspects. That is, pupils must think about their experiences. They must, as Dewey noted, reflect about what they have done. Consciously, they must construct personal meaning from their active experience. Indeed, for hands-on activities to qualify as educationally appropriate tasks, teachers must work with pupils before, during, and after these engagements so that pupils maintain a minds-on awareness of their unfolding experiences. "Hands-on" offers an incomplete and often superficial vision of rich possibility. It stops short of a reasonably appropriate goal. Only as teachers stress minds-on dimensions will these activities edge closer to their bright intentions. With inadequate provision for minds-on opportunities, the activities become a type of fool's gold. (pp. 2–3)

Most submissions received were in the following three categories: needs of early adolescents, developmentally appropriate instructional strategies, and field experiences. The fewest submissions garnered were in the areas of advisor/advisee, exploratory, and scheduling. In fact, only a total of four pieces were submitted for the exploratory chapter, and only three pieces were submitted for the chapter on scheduling. As unscientific as it may be, it does lead us to surmise that many teacher educators are either shying away from teaching about exploratory programs and flexible and block scheduling or, more likely, teaching about such topics in a traditional manner (e.g., having the students read a chapter and conducting a class discussion around the subject matter).

This collection of activities, strategies, and assignments is not offered as an exhaustive collection for educating preservice and experienced educators about middle level learners and programs. Rather, we hope it will serve as kind of a tip of the iceberg in regard to the eclectic and diverse ways there are to teach various middle level concepts and practices.

For two years we read, discussed, critiqued, edited, recritiqued, and re-edited manuscripts. Throughout this period we were delighted with the many creative ideas to which we were being introduced. Indeed, the ingenuity and creativity evidenced in many of the pieces were a joy to come across.

The process of editing and selecting manuscripts has strengthened our own professional and personal relationships and pedagogical efforts. It is our hope that this account of our most rewarding experience will serve as a catalyst for discussions on other campuses about "practicing what we preach."

Although we now celebrate the conclusion of the project, the discussions among middle level teacher educators must continue. We believe we need to live the model of collaboration ourselves as we prepare middle level educators to work closely with their colleagues to meet the needs of their middle level students.

We hope that our readers will find the ideas in the book as stimulating and useful as we do.

Editors:
Samuel Totten
Charlene Johnson
Linda R. Morrow
Toni Sills-Briegel

REFERENCE

Davis, O. L. (1998). Beyond beginnings: From "hands-on" to "minds-on." *Journal of Curriculum and Supervision,* Winter, 13(2), 1-3.

CHAPTER 1

Foundations/Philosophy

The School Board Project:
In Defense of Middle Level Philosophy

ALISON BROOKE BUNTE
University of Wisconsin–Platteville

WILLIAM C. McBETH
University of Wisconsin–Platteville

STRATEGY/ACTIVITY/ASSIGNMENT

It's the first night of class. Students anxiously await the arrival of their professors. Instead, "Superintendent" Stone—spectacles dangling from a cord around his neck, dressed in a three-piece suit, and carrying a brief case—enters the room. To their amazement, Superintendent Stone addresses them as the faculty of Ben Franklin Junior High, welcomes them back to school, and identifies their task for the coming semester.

Superintendent Stone informs the "faculty" that the "school board" has voted to explore the process of transitioning to the middle school concept. The faculty is charged with the task of investigating the characteristics of young adolescents and exploring the recommendations made in *Turning Points* (Carnegie Council on Adolescent Development, 1989). Superintendent Stone explains that at a school board meeting to be held in December, they will present their proposal and must be prepared to defend their recommendations using their knowledge of the young adolescent and research findings. As the students sit with mouths open and looks of confusion on their faces, Superintendent Stone introduces the Ben Franklin Junior High "principal" and "curriculum director" who will lead them in their exploration. He thanks them for their dedication and commitment and exits the room. Superintendent Stone is played by a colleague of the instructors and the principal and curriculum director are the course instructors themselves.

This scenario describes the first night of class for students enrolled in Middle Level Block One at the University of Wisconsin at Platteville. Block One is composed of two courses, Characteristics of Adolescents and Key Concepts in Middle Level Education. This team-taught course is a simulation of a process that a faculty might go through in transitioning from a junior high to a middle school.

Each student is placed on one of seven teams as a result of an informal teaming profile (see appendix for TEAM Profile) given the first night of class. The profile is used to identify various roles that may strengthen a team, such as leader, motivator, detail person, and energizer. Heterogeneous groups are formed based on the characteristics identified in the profile. The use of the profile is an attempt to create a balance of personality types among team members. Teams are then assigned one of seven topics to research and prepare a written recommendation on for the school board meeting. Topics include:

- Curriculum A - integrated curriculum and service learning
- Curriculum B - instructional strategies and assessment
- Advisory programs
- Exploratory
- Student transition
- Professional development
- Interdisciplinary teaming

Throughout the semester students are exposed to a number of activities designed to increase their knowledge, understanding, and positive attitudes concerning middle level concepts. Teams are provided weekly planning time and access to the library at the Center of Education for the Young Adolescent. The task of each team is to develop a proposal for their topic based on current research and practice. The role of the instructors is to facilitate the process by identifying resources and serving as consultants. Teams share and consult with each other during the course of the project.

The final product of the course is a unified proposal outlining the transition plan to be presented to board members prior to the school board meeting. The week before the school board is to meet, the transition plan is submitted to the instructors and a dress rehearsal of the presentation is conducted. The culminating activity of Block One is the presentation of the proposal to a school board made up of volunteers from the local community. The instructors contact the volunteers and provide them with a copy of the transition plan prior to the meeting.

During the school board meeting students present their proposals using a variety of presentational styles. In the past, students have elected to use overheads, computers, posters, and role playing to convey their message. Each team determines how they will present their topic. As a class, the students decide on room arrangement, the order of presentations, and the form that the introduction and closure will take.

Superintendent Stone instructs the school board to hold all questions until the end of the presentation. The true test for the students occurs when the school board asks for further information, explanation, or research support for the proposal. Although questions may be addressed to specific groups, all students are encouraged to participate. As with any school board, there are varying degrees of acceptance of the proposal, which requires students to think on their feet and apply their learning in unanticipated situations. The school board then votes to reject the proposal, accept it in total, or accept it with modifications.

COMMENTARY

The key to this project lies in the authenticity of the task. Students participate in a simulation modeled after a process used by many school districts when exploring transition to the middle school. The act of developing, coordinating, and presenting their transition plan helps develop student ownership in the process. This is evident in students' passionate defense of their positions during the question and answer period. It is clear from their performance at the meeting that students have acquired the knowledge, understanding, and positive attitudes necessary to serve as future leaders in a middle school setting. On several occasions, students have reported that they have obtained positions or assumed a leadership role in their school as a result of this experience.

During post-project interviews, students have identified this project as one of their most worthwhile learning experiences in the School of Education. They are able to verbalize the transition from disequilibrium at the beginning of the project to equilibrium as a result of practice and the actual meeting. These two events appear to bring the concepts together for them.

REFERENCE

The Carnegie Council on Adolescent Development (1989). *Turning points: Preparing American youth for the 21st Century.* New York: Carnegie Corporation of New York.

APPENDIX
T.E.A.M. Profile

Place the appropriate number that best describes you next to each descriptive phrase.

Most   4   3   2   1   Least

A___True to Friends

B___Innovator

C___Thinks Things Through

D___Energetic

A___Thoughtful of Others

B___Daring

C___Wants All Information

D___Laughs Easily

A___Will Do as Instructed

B___Risk Taker

C___Wants Things Exact

D___Persuasive

A___Listens and Remains Calm

B___Wants to Win

C___Deliberate and Cautious

D___Enthusiastic

A___Hides Feelings

B___Courageous and Unafraid

C___High Standards

D___Likes to Talk

A___Friendly to Others

B___Results-Driven

C___Wants Order

D___Outgoing

A___Understanding

B___Takes Charge

C___Accurate

D___Achiever

A___Giving

B___Doing It Your Way

C___Deliberate

D___Articulate

A___Interested in People

B___Refuses to Give Up

C___Humble

D___Leads the Pack

A___Flows with the Crowd

B___Strong Personality

C___Dependable

D___Interesting Person

A___Doesn't Rock the Boat

B___Speaks Openly/Boldly

C___Plays by the Rules

D___Gets Others Involved

A___Wants Others Involved

B___Results-Driven

C___Difficult Time Deciding

D___Optimistic

Totals: A=_____   B=_____   C=_____   D=_____

Developing a Handbook of Key Middle Level Articles, Essays, and Research

SAMUEL TOTTEN
University of Arkansas, Fayetteville

STRATEGY/ACTIVITY/ASSIGNMENT

In the graduate course I teach, Middle Level Principles and Methods, each student is required to develop a handbook of key middle level articles, essays, and research on various facets of middle level education. The main rationales for such an assignment are to: (a) provide the student with an opportunity to conduct a thorough search of middle level articles, essays, and research on various middle level concepts and practices; (b) enable the student to become familiar with the work of key middle level educators, authors, and researchers; and (c) allow the students to develop a resource that can be used in developing and assessing new programs in his or her classroom, school, and/or district.

The directions for the assignment are as follows: Each student-researcher will search for, select, and design his or her own compilation of readings on a topic germane to the "analysis of teaching." To accomplish this, the student will need, at a minimum, to do the following: (a) select and narrow a topic; (b) establish a clear and thorough set of criteria for the article/essay selection; (c) search, locate, and read a host of articles (many of which will not likely meet the criteria set and thus will not be included in the compilation of readings); (d) place the articles/essays in a logical order; (e) develop a table of contents; (f) bind the work; and (g) write an introduction to the booklet (7–10 pages, double-spaced, typed).

The introduction must delineate (concretely and with a good amount of detail) the following: (1) why and how the topic was selected (one can include both personal as well as professional reasons); (2) a rationale regarding the criteria that were established (e.g., the "why" behind each component); (3) a discussion as to how the criteria were actually applied in selecting pieces for the compilation (e.g., Were the criteria too limiting? Too broad? Did the criteria have to be redesigned? If so, how?); (4) a discussion of the various journals that were examined in order to search out key articles and why those journals were used (It is assumed that a good number of research journals versus practitioner journals will have been consulted and used); (5) a discussion as to how the articles were placed in their particular order in the booklet; and, finally, (6) a thorough discussion of what was learned from this project regarding: (a) the topic itself; (b) key research related to the topic; (c) debates (if any) surrounding the topic; (d) whether this was a worthwhile project or not, and a discussion as to why this is so; and (e) anything else that one might consider pertinent. Also, if works or research findings are cited, then one must follow proper scholarly procedures in acknowledging them.

COMMENTARY

In the past, one of the assignments for this course was to develop an annotated bibliography of key works on a particular aspect of middle level education. Even though some students took the assignment seriously and genuinely attempted to gain as much as possible from the assignment, others were more inclined to simply select anything that they could find in a journal on a library shelf and write it up. These students were engaged in a perfunctory assignment bereft of much (if any) analysis. It was an assignment merely to get through. In that sense, once it was completed, it was forgettable—including any information that they could have possibly gleaned about middle level education.

The development of a middle level handbook requires a totally different level of commitment. Many students have commented on the value of developing a handbook that they will be able to refer to in the future and share with colleagues. Others have commented on the amount of thought that went into both the selection of the articles and the order in which they were placed. They said this was particularly true in light of the fact that they were required to develop criteria for selecting the articles. Finally, in a course evaluation, a student stated that she greatly appreciated the opportunity to study a single issue in great depth and that the development of the handbook on a single topic left her with a feeling of expertise that she didn't think she would have gained otherwise.

What Makes a Middle School a True Middle School?

SHERRY CARTER
William Woods University, Fulton, MO

STRATEGY/ACTIVITY/ASSIGNMENT

There are several schools in our area that call themselves "middle schools" but are much more like junior highs. In order for students to understand that schools can be "middle" in name only or be called a "junior high" but adhere to middle level philosophy, we take a field trip to various middle schools during the course of the semester. Prior to the field trip, we discuss Romano and Georgiady's (1994) "Fourteen Criteria for Evaluating the Middle School," which they list in their book, *Building an Effective Middle School.*

During the course of the tour and visit with the principal and other faculty and staff, students are expected to ask questions to find out if the school meets each criterion. When they return to the university classroom, the students discuss their findings, write an evaluation on the school, and ultimately decide whether the school adheres to the middle level philosophy. After they have visited all three schools and evaluated them, students design a rubric for rating future middle schools by deciding which of the fourteen criteria are the most crucial. For example, if students found that teaming was a more important middle school component than flexible class schedules, then they should rank it higher.

After students have developed their own ranked list, they get into small groups to compare and discuss their results. Following the discussion, the students, as a group, rank the components. Next, each group reports a consensus of their rankings to the large group, which then comes up with a class ranking. The class then develops the ranked list into a rubric that assigns a point system for each criterion. The students are then asked to individually evaluate another local middle school. The data may be gathered through interviews with administrators, teachers, staff members, or students (they must have at least two sources) and can be done via telephone, mail, e-mail, or site visits. Because I have small classes, no two students are allowed to evaluate the same middle school. They sign up as they select schools. The evaluation is written in terms of action research findings.

COMMENTARY

This activity can serve as a performance evaluation of the students' knowledge of middle school philosophy and curriculum. Students enjoy the action research approach. I do have to warn them that they cannot make evaluative statements or ask questions in a negative tone, since most administrators, teachers, and staff are loyal to their schools and expect the students to obtain the information in a professional manner.

REFERENCE

Romano, L. G., & Georgiady, N. P. (1994). *Building an effective middle school.* Madison, WI: Brown and Benchmark.

A Close Encounter: Interviewing a Middle Level Teacher or Administrator

SAMUEL TOTTEN
University of Arkansas, Fayetteville

JON E. PEDERSEN
East Carolina University, Greenville, NC

One of the more enlightening assignments our students undertook in the undergraduate middle level principles and methods course that we co-taught at the University of Arkansas at Fayetteville was the interview of a middle level teacher or administrator. It was an excellent way for preservice teachers to gain the undivided attention of a middle level professional and to glean answers to questions that he or she truly desired answered.

Each student was required to develop ten to fifteen questions for the express purpose of interviewing a middle level professional. The student was encouraged to develop questions on any concept, topic, or issue germane to middle level education, such as the educational philosophy of the interviewee; the interviewee's opinions about middle level philosophy; whether middle level philosophy and concepts truly meet the unique needs of young adolescents better than the junior high concepts do, and why that is so; what it takes to be a top-notch middle level teacher; the most difficult aspect of being a middle level teacher; the pros and cons of teaming; and what the interviewee perceives as the primary distinction(s) between middle level and junior high programs. The proposed topics were the result of an initial brainstorming session conducted by the professors and preservice students.

In order to develop their questions, students were required to take into consideration the information and insights they had gleaned from class discussions, activities, and readings (including *Turning Points* and *Fateful Choices*). Every question needed to have an open component to it. In other words, while a student could ask a closed (yes/no) question, he or she had to follow it up with an open question. Prior to having the students develop their own questions, examples of closed and open questions were discussed, and students were asked which type of question they thought would be more likely to elicit the greater amount of detail and why.

Students were required to submit copies of their questions to their professors for feedback. In certain cases, particularly where questions were either unclear, too limited in focus, or too far afield, students were required to revise their questions. In all other cases, the students were given the green light to contact a potential interviewee. The students were provided with a list of recommended schools (those schools noted as having top-notch middle level programs), and the name of a contact person who would assist them in arranging an interview (generally a principal or vice principal).

Prior to conducting the interview the students were also required to send the interviewee the set of questions that were to be asked. This was to ensure that the interviewee was given ample time to consider and ponder the questions prior to the interview. This was done in the hope that the answers would be more detailed and in-depth than if the interviewees were simply hit "cold" with the questions.

Students were required to conduct the interview using a tape recorder. Once the interview was completed, students were obligated to transcribe (verbatim) the tape of the interview. They were to include the interviewee's name, position (if the interviewee was a teacher, then the grade level was to be included), place of employment, location of interview, and date and time of the interview. Students were required to ask the interviewee if his or her name could be included in the write up. If the interviewee requested anonymity, then that was to be noted in the write up and a pseudonym was to be used in place of the person's name and place of employment.

Once the interview was transcribed, students were to submit a copy to the interviewee. The purpose of this requirement was twofold: First, it was a courtesy to allow the interviewee to see how the interview had been written up, and, second, it provided the interviewee with an opportunity to correct any errors in the interview, to fill in critical information, and/or to excise anything he or she deemed "unfit," for whatever reason, to print.

Finally, students were to write up a two- to three-page (double-spaced, typed) paper in which they delineated how they had personally benefited from the interview. At a minimum, students were required to address the following issues in their papers: (1) the most enlightening information they gleaned from the interview; (2) the most surprising or disturbing piece of information they learned from the interview, and why; (3) anything they gleaned that they wished we had studied in more detail in class, and why; (4) anything the interviewee said that called into question or contradicted what had been said or discussed in class; (5) anything in the interview that prompted them to look at young adolescents or middle level education with "new eyes," and why; and (6) whether the assignment was worth their time and effort, and why. They could also address any other issues or share any insights that they wished.

COMMENTARY

On the whole, students were very enthusiastic about this activity. They appreciated the fact that they were able to speak one-on-one with someone "in the trenches." Many also stated that they wished they had had more opportunities in other courses to meet face-to-face with teachers in order to obtain answers to "burning questions" they had about the day-to-day realities of teaching, and, particularly, the mesh between philosophy and reality. Concomitantly, many commented on how much they appreciated being able to raise those questions they *really wanted answered* and could do so without the pressure of asking them in front of their peers.

Some complained about the difficulty of arranging a time that was mutually convenient for the teacher and themselves or the difficulty of simply finding the time to get out to a school to interview a teacher or administrator. Also, some complained that their interviewee didn't seem to be as forthcoming as some of those interviewed by their peers. Even these students, however, found the assignment worthwhile.

Establishing Credibility for the Philosophy and Practices of Middle Level Education: Guest Speakers

LINDA R. MORROW
University of Arkansas, Fayetteville

STRATEGY/ACTIVITY/ASSIGNMENT

I invite middle level administrators and teachers to my undergraduate middle level methods classes to share their experiences as a means of establishing credibility for the philosophy and practices that we read about and discuss. These middle level educators demonstrate the importance of implementing a middle level philosophy that meets the unique needs of early adolescents and early preparation for developing an effective middle level program.

One of the first guest speakers is an associate superintendent in a district that opened two middle schools in the fall of 1995. Her detailed and honest explanation of her district's journey to middle level education is a testimonial to the fact that in order to implement change, all stakeholders must be fully informed about middle level philosophy and practices and be actively involved in the change process.

Because middle level practitioners pack such power in the credibility area, I also arrange visits from middle school principals and teachers. Recently, a new middle school principal shared the school's program and her experiences in moving to middle level education and in opening a new school.

During a recent summer session, a new middle level principal who was awaiting the construction of his building described the process of planning the schedule for his school and selecting interdisciplinary teaching teams. The information was presented as a problem-solving model so that class members could wrestle with the same issues that the principal must face.

COMMENTARY

These guest speakers are not only well prepared to share their various middle school experiences, but they also bring along documentation to support their practices in the form of middle level articles and publications from the National Middle School Association. Thus, the university program is supported by practitioners.

The undergraduate students typically ask thought-provoking questions to clarify their understandings of the connections between the middle level theory they've read about and the realities of actual practice. One of the most important results of this discussion is the realization that middle level philosophy must be implemented to fit the needs of the local student population. University students enjoy the informal interactions with these guest speakers following the class session because this affords the opportunity for additional personal learning as well as making professional connections.

Cooperative Logic:
Which School Is a "True" Middle School?

M. GAIL JONES
University of North Carolina at Chapel Hill

STRATEGY/ACTIVITY/ASSIGNMENT

After students have had a chance to read about and discuss the developmental characteristics of early adolescents as well as middle school philosophy, this logic activity can be used to assist them in applying their knowledge to descriptions of schools.

Students should be assigned to teams made up of 4 to 6 students and given an envelope containing the six clues to the logic problem. The directions are:

> You and your teammates should work together to figure out which school includes most of the characteristics typical of a "true" middle school. Inside the envelope are six sets of clues. When we begin, one person should open the envelop and pass out the clues so that everyone has one to two clues each. You may read the clues aloud to your group as many times as needed, but you may not show your clue to another person. Once you think you have reached consensus about the identity of the "true" middle school, reread your clues aloud within the group and check your evidence again. Be sure to discuss your ideas throughout the process with your teammates.

Instructor Information: The information given in the problem includes information that is useful as well as information that is extraneous to the problem-solving process (just as problems in "real" life include aspects that are not critical to the problem-solving process). In this activity students are asked not to show their clues to another person, in order to make the problem cooperative by ensuring individual accountability and positive interdependence. If students are allowed to show their clues to another person, often the result is that one person in the group will pull all the clues together and solve the problem for the group. The goal is to get the group to discuss their ideas and to share their perspectives and interpretations with other students.

Information Given in the Problem:

West Lake School
- All the sixth-grade students at West Lake have their classes in one wing of the building.
- West Lake School uses QUEST as their advisor-advisee program.
- Allejandro works at West Lake, an inner-city school.
- Josh tried out for the football team at West Lake, but was not selected.

Summary: West Lake groups students by grade level into "houses," or areas, and has an advisory program. West Lake continues to have competitive sports, which is seen by some middle school advocates as developmentally inappropriate.

Yancy School
- Sam teaches at Yancy.
- Yancy School is known for having the best math department in the area.
- All the teachers on a team have common planning time at Yancy.
- Yancy School assigns a guidance counselor to work with each student.
- The language arts teachers have departmental meetings once a week, and Sam hates to go to these meetings.
- The principal at Yancy goes to all the National Middle School Association conferences.

Summary: Yancy teachers have common planning. However, Yancy maintains content area departments, an organizational structure not recommended by some middle school advocates.

Randolph School
- Betty, Jane, and Mike teach on an interdisciplinary team together at Randolph.
- The area Association of Accreditation rated Randolph as having an outstanding academic program.
- Randolph School has grades 8, 9, and 10.
- Randolph School has an excellent self-contained gifted education program.
- Randolph School had the highest achievement scores in the state.

Summary: Randolph includes grades 9 and 10, an organizational pattern not considered ideal in meeting the needs of early adolescents. The self-contained gifted program is also not recommended by some middle school advocates.

Eastern School
- Eastern School has 84 teachers and 1,003 students.
- Tom's mother wishes that Eastern had an advisor-advisee program.
- Ms. Sink is the president of the State League of Middle Schools. She is the principal of Eastern.
- The teachers at Eastern did a great interdisciplinary unit on Native Americans.

Summary: Eastern teachers use interdisciplinary instruction.

Mountain View School
- Maria teaches at Mountain View School.
- Mountain View School contains grades 6 to 8.
- Maria spent a lot of team planning time working on a great interdisciplinary unit on ecology.
- Michelle teaches exploratory programs and plans the advisor-advisee program with Maria.

Summary: Mountain View has exploratory programs, an advisor-advisee program, includes grades 6 to 8, and involves students in interdisciplinary studies.

Of all the schools evaluated, Mountain View includes most of the components recommended for middle schools.

COMMENTARY

This activity can serve as an excellent vehicle for discussion about characteristics of effective middle schools. Students often find themselves debating whether effective middle schools should have high academic standards, such as Yancy School. The logic problem also highlights that some principals and schools may call themselves "middle schools" but their practices demonstrate more of a commitment to the junior high school model.

Directions: You may read this card as many times as needed, but you may not show your card to another person. Your goal is to work with your team to figure out which school includes most of the components of a "true" middle school.	**Directions:** You may read this card as many times as needed, but you may not show your card to another person. Your goal is to work with your team to figure out which school includes most of the components of a "true" middle school.
• Betty, Jane, and Mike teach on an interdisciplinary team together at Randolph. • The teachers at Eastern did a great interdisciplinary unit on Native Americans. • Mountain View School contains grades 6–8. • Ms. Sink is the president of the State League of Middle Schools. She is the principal of Eastern.	• Maria spent a lot of team planning time working on a great interdisciplinary unit on ecology. • The principal at Yancy goes to all the National Middle School Conferences. • All the sixth grade students at West Lake have their classes in one wing of the building. • The area Association of Accreditation rated Randolph as having an outstanding academic program.

Directions: You may read this card as many times as needed, but you may not show your card to another person. Your goal is to work with your team to figure out which school includes most of the components of a "true" middle school.

- Michelle teaches exploratory programs and plans the advisor/advisee program with Maria.
- West Lake School uses QUEST as their advisor/advisee program.
- The language arts teachers have departmental meetings every week and Sam hates to go to these meetings.
- Tom's mother wishes that Eastern had an advisor/advisee program.

Directions: You may read this card as many times as needed, but you may not show your card to another person. Your goal is to work with your team to figure out which school includes most of the components of a "true" middle school.

- Maria teaches at Mountain View School.
- All the teachers on a team have common planning time at Yancy.
- Yancy School assigns a guidance counselor to work with each student.
- Randolph School has grades 8, 9, and 10.

Directions: You may read this card as many times as needed, but you may not show your card to another person. Your goal is to work with your team to figure out which school includes most of the components of a "true" middle school.

- Alejandro works at West Lake, an inner-city school.
- Yancy School is known for having the best math department in the area.
- Randolph School has an excellent self-contained gifted education program.
- Sam teaches at Yancy.

Directions: You may read this card as many times as needed, but you may not show your card to another person. Your goal is to work with your team to figure out which school includes most of the components of a "true" middle school.

- Judy coaches intramural sports with Michelle.
- Eastern School has 84 teachers and 1,003 students
- Randolph School had the highest achievement scores in the state.
- Josh tried out for the football team at West Lake, but was not selected.

National Middle Level Education Month

LINDA R. MORROW
University of Arkansas, Fayetteville

STRATEGY/ACTIVITY/ASSIGNMENT

In recognition of March as National Middle Level Education Month, I arrange an evening meeting of middle level practitioners and graduate and undergraduate university students. Fliers advertising the meeting are posted in classroom buildings to alert students and faculty. I send invitations to middle and junior high schools in the northwest Arkansas area, students and faculty in the College of Education, and to the Middle Level Coordinator in the Arkansas State Department of Education. My goal is to strengthen university ties with area middle level educators and to recruit students to our middle level teacher education program.

The program consists of greetings and statements of support from university administrators and approximately an hour of speakers focusing on middle level programs in our area. Following the program is a more informal reception that consists of visiting and exchanging information.

COMMENTARY

As a result of such meetings, I am convinced that we are making a difference in the middle in northwest Arkansas. This is evidenced by the enthusiasm of the participants during this meeting, despite other such pressing matters as spring break plans and March collegiate basketball madness. Granted, I did guarantee a portion of the audience because the meeting occurred during my graduate-level middle level methods class time (a three-hour evening class), but my students were enthusiastic about the speakers and especially the potential employment contacts they made at the reception. Another very positive result was the increased visibility of the university's middle level program and the growth of middle schools in our area.

Student as "Leading Authority": Using Panel Discussions in the Middle Level Education Course

DAVE S. KNOWLTON

University of Memphis, Memphis, TN

STRATEGY/ACTIVITY/ASSIGNMENT

This assignment works especially well with graduate students in a middle school general methods course, but it could work equally well in any course where students need to be exposed to theoreticians and experts in the field. Students are asked to select a "leading authority" in the field of education from a list provided by the instructor. Some of these authorities should be people who are known for their middle school and early adolescent work (such as William M. Alexander or other authors who publish regularly in leading middle school journals). Other authorities should include those who aren't necessarily known for their middle school theories but do have theories or philosophies that are relevant to middle level education (such as Kohlberg, Piaget, and Erickson). Included with a list of these names is a list of the seminal works by each author or philosopher.

Over the course of two months, students are responsible for reading seminal works in an effort to become intimately familiar with "their" authority's philosophies and writings and how his or her work pertains to middle-level education. Students are given a list of middle level topics and told that they should be able to discuss their author's position (whether stated or inferred) on those topics, but students should also understand that they should be prepared to discuss topics that extend beyond the ones included on the list. (You could even reinforce students' studies of these authors by assigning several brief reports about the authors' positions or "summary/reaction" papers dealing with the authors' writings.)

This assignment culminates towards the end of the semester with a panel discussion in which the students "become" their assigned author and engage in discussions with other "authors" about the "hot" topics in middle level education. The role of the instructor is to moderate the discussion so that every student has a chance to make a statement on a relevant topic.

Students can be evaluated on the basis of the following criteria questions: (1) Did the student refer to specific parts of the author's writings to justify his or her position? (2) Was the student familiar enough with his or her "authority" to discuss the seminal works in a fluent and professional way? (3) Was the student able to connect his or her author's theories with those of the other authors represented?

COMMENTARY

Keys to making this assignment work include a well thought-out reading list and selection of "authorities." A selection of topics that are general enough to allow each student the opportunity to discuss them is also recommended.

While this assignment is designed to be "fun," it is important that the serious goals of this assignment be emphasized: (1) students will become familiar with leading authorities in the field, and (2) students will understand the "consensus" of knowledge and the growth of knowledge about middle school students.

Initially, this assignment will strike students as "a lot of work." They will often claim to feel "overwhelmed" by the breadth of the assignment and ask for a more narrow focus and clearer scope. After the semester-end panel discussion, they should see more clearly the value of the assignment and be able to recognize the progress they have made as middle level educators. Specifically, it becomes easier for students to see middle level education theory as an integrated whole. They better understand a theory/practice dichotomy since they have seen the theoretical basis for the structure and functions of middle schools. Frequently, students gain a stronger interest in middle school history as a result of studying various experts and theorists.

Historical Giants in Middle Level Education

MELANIE W. GREENE
Appalachian State University, Boone, NC

STRATEGY/ACTIVITY/ASSIGNMENT

In May 1992, the *Middle School Journal* launched its Founders Series to highlight educators who have made significant contributions to the middle level movement in the United States. To date, five revolutionaries—

William Alexander, John Lounsbury, Gordon Vars, Donald H. Eichhorn, and Conrad F. Toepfer—have been featured. Knowledge of these historical giants can provide undergraduate students with an understanding and an appreciation of the past as well as an incentive to advance confidently and intellectually in the future. Initially, teams of five preservice teachers should investigate the multifaceted role one of the revolutionaries played within the historical movement. Next, each team should create a skit that portrays the contributions made by these educators who have changed the course of American schools. The skits should be presented to the entire class.

COMMENTARY

Evaluation criteria include evidence of research, team planning, and creativity. A debriefing session following each skit allows for clarification and further discussion of the historical developments made in middle level education. Students have responded positively to this strategy with such comments as, "Role playing and skits are an interesting and enjoyable way to discover information," and, "It got us more involved than the lecture approach could have." It is essential that learning objectives are met, and as one preservice teacher noted, "The teacher must make sure that the content is coming through in the finished product."

CHAPTER 2

Needs of Early Adolescents

Reinforcing Comprehension of Adolescent Development

MAUREEN REILLY LORIMER

California State University, San Marcos

STRATEGY/ACTIVITY/ASSIGNMENT

A major component of any credential program with a middle level emphasis is the instruction of the physical, intellectual, and social/emotional aspects of adolescent development. In the Learning and Instruction in Middle Schools course, students are asked to read text with detailed information about early adolescent development. They are also required to participate in school-site observations and report their findings in a paper that focuses on early adolescent development. This complex topic, however, necessitates a variety of approaches for maximum comprehension. In order to reinforce this knowledge another assignment is required.

During one class session, students are required to create a paper doll that depicts the physical, intellectual, and social/emotional domains of their early adolescence. The instructor models this assignment. By sharing a photo of herself as a middle school student, she sets the tone for this activity. Next, she presents a paper doll of herself as a young adolescent, revealing her physical characteristics (glasses, acne, short stature, and long hair). In addition to the doll, the instructor arranges three speech balloons above the paper doll (similar to those used in comic strips). One balloon contains thoughts from the paper doll about the intellectual concerns of her early adolescent years ("I remember being an 'A' student in elementary school, now I don't know anything"). Inserted within the second balloon are thoughts about her memories of social/emotional scenarios ("Nobody likes me . . . I want to be part of the 'in crowd' "). The third balloon describes her thoughts about adolescent physical changes ("I'm so small and that girl is so beautiful . . . I wish I looked like her").

Students use this model to create their own paper doll and speech bubbles. Paper, markers, yarn, and other materials are available and allow for creativity. Upon completion, students display these projects around the room. Next, students form small groups and, one at a time, standing next to their doll, describe insights and connections between their adolescent experiences and those of the students they will teach. Prior to these presentations students are reminded to make connections with theoretical underpinnings of early adolescent development from previous readings and observations. The closure for this session is a whole-class debriefing consisting of questions that elicit student insights and understanding about adolescent development.

COMMENTARY

Preservice teachers generally enjoy this assignment even though self-reflection can sometimes be a sensitive situation for a variety of reasons (painful memories or difficulty in recalling details). It is imperative that the climate set by the instructor provides a safe place for disclosing personal information and reinforces the fact that positive learning experiences occur when we can remember ourselves as the students we wish to teach. Creativity is encouraged and, once this begins, students become engrossed in the development of the paper doll. Students truly want to create an accurate representation of their former selves. The most powerful aspect of this assignment is the oral sharing in class.

Although designed as an oral activity, this activity could certainly be augmented as a written paper to coincide with the art project. Instructors of preservice teachers will find that this meaningful strategy supports middle level education curriculum in that students: (1) can visually see the relationships between their own experiences as an early adolescent and those whom they will teach and (2) will link this experience with previous readings and observations, thereby reinforcing critical learning.

Students have commented that this resurgence of adolescent memories was valuable and enabled them to develop new empathy for middle level students. A quote from a former student illustrates this point: "My middle school years were awful. This activity helped me remember these feelings and consider that the students I'll teach may have the same attitude toward school. With understanding and sensitivity, I will provide a learning environment which will promote positive experiences for all students."

Picture It—Early Adolescence

CHARLENE JOHNSON
University of Arkansas, Fayetteville

STRATEGY/ACTIVITY/ASSIGNMENT

Understanding early adolescence and its unique qualities is an important focus of my undergraduate course on middle level philosophy and methods. When working with educators who already work with middle level learners (graduate students and/or inservice educators), it is equally important to gauge their understanding of early adolescent development. That said, this activity has been used with my preservice teachers who are striving to conceptualize early adolescence and its multifaceted qualities/dimensions and with inservice teachers receiving additional training on middle level programs. With both groups, the emphasis is on how early adolescence is conceptualized and understood.

The educators are divided into groups of four or five. When doing this activity with inservice teachers from different schools, the educators remained with others from their school. In the undergraduate course, preservice teachers voluntarily group themselves. The group is then instructed to brainstorm qualities of early adolescents and list them within the group. Rules of brainstorming (i.e., everything is accepted without criticism or qualifiers) are reviewed when these directions are given. This part of the activity usually takes from ten to fifteen minutes. The group is then given a large piece of paper and markers to decide how they would depict these qualities *without words* (i.e., sentences, paragraphs, or anything else that involves formal writing). After given sufficient time to finalize this depiction, each group then presents its portrayal and explains what it is and why it characterizes or reflects middle level learners. Questions and comments are offered after the presentations. Although clarifying questions or comments are welcomed, it is understood that there will be no negative comments or criticism.

Discussions about the process, expressing themselves outside of formal writing, group consensus of best depiction, brainstorming, variety of ideas, and so forth follow the presentations. Most agree that middle level learners would benefit from a similar activity on different topics because of its active nature and that it requires different intelligences to complete. Multiple intelligences and its relevance for middle level learners are often highlighted in these discussions.

COMMENTARY

This activity is usually met with resistance and concern when initially explained because participants are not allowed to use words. But as soon as the groups become engrossed in the activity, reservations are quickly dispelled.

Inservice teachers are often amazed at what they create and its significance and relationship to early adolescents. Based on the presentations, the instructor is given an indication of the knowledge base of the participants about early adolescents and can build on it rather than repeat it. What becomes evident when this is done with inservice teachers is that they have an understanding of who their learners are, but they may not have given it terms or definitions to date. From this, the instructor recognizes the strengths and understandings of the teachers and builds on them. Conversely, misconceptions often surface, and these can be addressed in future inservice sessions.

For university courses, this activity is often done either before or after addressing early adolescent development or just prior to it to ascertain how early adolescence is perceived and understood by the class. By working with peers, perceptions are monitored by peers as well as by the instructor. The activity is a favorite among those who have done it. Preservice teachers often remark about the relevance of this activity for making them think and grapple with the meaning of early adolescent development as opposed to just regurgitating the words they have been given to explain this phenomenon.

Introduction to "Who Are the Kids in the Middle?"

NORMA J. BAILEY
Central Michigan University, Mt. Pleasant

STRATEGY/ACTIVITY/ASSIGNMENT

This is the first activity administered on the first day in the first course to our students in middle level education (although the activity has also been implemented for teachers at staff inservices, graduate students in middle level education courses, and parents at parent meetings). Students are asked to write down, in brief form, incidents or memories they have about being 10 to14 years old or in the 6th, 7th, or 8th grade, be they incidents or memories from school, home, church, with friends, or with family. Several examples are given by the instructor to stimulate students' thought processes, such as the devastation of always being chosen last in gym class, crying to parents over being unable to memorize all the plant and animal kingdom names for a science test and worrying that everyone was going to think she was stupid, or picking out a dress for a first dance. This can be done as either a take-home assignment or in class (at least 15 minutes should be allocated to this activity). Then students are asked to get in small groups (3 to 4 students) and share their stories, one story at a time. There is generally a great deal of laughter and also piggybacking of stories during this sharing time.

The instructor then reminds the students that human beings develop in a number of domains and, for the purposes of this activity, they are going to look at this development in three areas: physical (P), cognitive (C), and social/emotional (SE) ("social" being defined as how one relates to others, and "emotional" being defined as how one relates to self and others). After the instructor models the process of labeling each of his or her examples with a P, C, SE, or any combination of the letters, the students then mark a P, C, SE, or combination of letters, by each of the incidents or memories that they have written down. The instructor then asks students, by a show of hands, to identify their markings and then creates a rough graphic of the results. "How many of you have a fair number of C's? How many a fair number of P's? How many of you a fair number of SE's?" Invariably, the resulting graphic is one with very few C's, a fair number of P's, and a vast majority of SE's.

At this point, the instructor pulls the introduction together. In doing so, he or she may also use various visual or descriptive examples to further illustrate the point (e.g., a slide presentation of young adolescents in the sixth, seventh, and eighth grades or a verbal description of six very different sixth, seventh, and eighth graders). The first comment is that this is the reality of young adolescence; it was the same thirty years ago (relate it to the age of the audience members), it is the same today, and it probably will be the same thirty years from now. The unique reality of young adolescence is that these youngsters are going through enormous *changes*, more rapid and profound than at any other time during their lives. In addition, this is a period of tremendous *variability*, with dissimilar rates of growth in every area of development, and yet every young adolescent is trying to figure out "Am I normal?" (thus, comparing himself or herself to everyone else). These areas of development are *inexorably intertwined* so that, for example, how a student achieves in class on any given day might be dependent upon what happens in the hallway with friends (National Middle School Association, 1995). This unique reality doesn't mean that young adolescents can't be taught during this time but rather that we can't reach them cognitively unless we recognize the impact of all the other developmental areas in their lives.

COMMENTARY

This activity serves as an excellent introduction to the needs and characteristics of young adolescents. Invariably, it begins to open people's minds to, or reminds them of, the uniqueness of young adolescents. First of all, it is an introspective activity: it "gets inside people" and reminds them of what it was like to be a young adolescent, with all its newness and confusion and excitement and insecurity, and young adolescents indicate that one of the best signs of a good teacher is that "they remember what it was like . . . " Second, it is an interactive activity, allowing people to rediscover all the similarities, uniquenesses, and differences they possess, even when sharing with only a few colleagues. Most importantly, it is an activity that begins to break people of the mindset of "I am a math teacher" or "I am a seventh grade teacher," because, as one student wrote in her reflective journal, "I immediately began to realize that I have a responsibility to get to know each and every one of my students individually in all ways—physically, cognitively, socially, and emotionally."

REFERENCE

National Middle School Association (1995). *This we believe: Developmentally responsive middle level schools*. Columbus, OH: Author.

Designing the Developmentally Responsive Middle Level Program

TRUDY KNOWLES
Westfield State College, Westfield, MA

STRATEGY/ACTIVITY/ASSIGNMENT

Following a class session on the developmental changes in the young adolescent and one in which middle school students are interviewed, the class breaks into small groups to design a developmentally responsive middle level program.

Students are divided into four groups. Each group is given a large sheet of paper that lists either physical, cognitive, social, or emotional developmental issues for the young adolescent. (See the list of issues below.) These issues had been identified during the previous class as having possible implications for middle level education. Students are asked to discuss the issues and list their ideas for responding to them in a developmentally appropriate way. In analyzing appropriate responses to the issues, the students need to consider the curriculum, extracurricular programs, instructional strategies, classroom management, special subjects, organization of the school, the physical plant, and even miscellaneous topics such as the cafeteria foods and type of furniture. The college instructor circulates throughout the groups to facilitate the discussions.

After twenty to thirty minutes, groups exchange papers and begin to work on another area of development, either expanding on the ideas already on the paper or presenting new ideas. This process continues until all groups have considered all four areas of development.

In the following class period, each idea or response is analyzed in terms of the appropriateness of that idea for middle level students. We refer back to developmental changes in determining the appropriateness. We accept, reject, or modify the ideas in order to come up with a list of suggestions that are developmentally appropriate. It becomes a work in progress.

This list is referred to throughout the semester. We compare the list to the middle level concept; statements from middle level organizations; readings in different areas; and information gained through observations and interviews with principals, students, parents, or students. As new ideas are examined and explored, additions and modifications are made to the list. The end product is a thoughtful description of a developmentally responsive middle level program designed by preservice teachers.

Following are examples of developmental issues presented to the groups and the initial brainstorming that resulted.

1. **"The young adolescent experiences the emergence of primary and secondary sex characteristics."**
   - Middle schools should have a comprehensive health education curriculum.
   - Middle school students should have access to community health services.
   - Every school should have a school nurse.
   - Teachers should help young adolescents understand what's going on with their bodies.

2. **"Some students are developing abstract thinking while others are thinking at a concrete level."**
   - Students should experience hands-on activities.
   - Activities should be designed to reach all levels.
   - Students should be allowed to help design the curriculum.

3. **"The young adolescent vacillates between dependence and independence."**
   - The school should provide increased counseling services.
   - Teachers should really get to know their students.
   - There should be increased use of humor in the classroom.
   - Let students choose a mentor.

COMMENTARY

This activity is presented in a class called "The Middle School and Its Students." It is a class designed to provide an introduction to the young adolescent and to issues related to middle level education. This activity allows preservice students to synthesize the knowledge they accumulate on the developmental needs of the young adolescent and fashion that into an analysis of how those needs can best be met through an appropriate school environment.

This lesson is sometimes difficult. Many preservice teachers have a mind-set about what the middle school is and how it should be organized. They come to class thinking along strict subject-discipline lines with a six-hour day broken into fifty-minute periods. Suddenly, they are confronted with the task of designing a school that truly meets the developmental needs of this age student, and they find it difficult to change their thinking about what a middle level program is or should be. This lesson, however, forces students to expand their thinking about what is possible in middle level education.

Following this lesson we analyze the middle school concept and talk about the similarities and differences between the various recommendations made in *Turning Points* (Carnegie Council on Adolescent Development, 1989) and what we have designed. This lesson also becomes a starting point for talking about curriculum design and appropriate instructional strategies.

When asked to evaluate the activities done in class, students ranked this experience high because it opened their minds to new ideas about what constitutes an appropriate learning environment. One student commented, "This made me think about what is done and why some of it is ridiculous." The appropriateness of what we had designed was apparent in the comment, "Just wish we could implement it too!"

Another side benefit of this activity was brought to light by the student who commented, "I think by having the students work in groups at the beginning gave us a chance to get to know each other. It created a very calm environment." The class truly became a community of respect in which students felt safe to question old assumptions and explore new ideas. This activity allowed students to experience the evolution of knowledge, the benefits of risk taking, and the power of student-centered learning. It is a model I hope they will carry into their classrooms as they implement their own design.

REFERENCE

Carnegie Council on Adolescent Development (1989). *Turning points: Preparing American youth for the 21st Century*. New York: Author.

Student-Produced Pamphlets

LINDA R. MORROW
University of Arkansas, Fayetteville

STRATEGY/ACTIVITY/ASSIGNMENT

After reading various sources on the rationale for middle schools and the developmental needs of early adolescents, preservice teachers in my middle level methods class work in groups to produce pamphlets that focus on the developmental stages of social, emotional, physical, and intellectual growth of students. The information must be presented succinctly in text and graphics in order to fit the 8 1/2" x 11" dimensions of a trifold pamphlet. The purpose of the pamphlets is to educate a particular audience such as parents, teachers, school board members, or middle level students about the developmental stages of early adolescent development and the need for middle level schools committed to meeting those needs. The process of producing this document gives university students the opportunity to consolidate and publish their learning regarding middle level philosophy and practice.

This assignment models teamwork, synthesizes information by teaching others, uses writing as a learning tool, and uses word processing and graphics to produce a group project. The pamphlets are evaluated on accuracy and depth of information, professional references, creativity, and mechanical correctness.

COMMENTARY

This project works well after students have been introduced to content information regarding the developmental needs and characteristics of early adolescents and functions as a means of solidifying a solid understanding of middle level philosophy. It also emphasizes the importance of teamwork and of building a sense of community. The trifold pamphlets, complete with graphics, have become treasured items in student portfolios. Because much of the work has to be done outside of class, students have to arrange times for group meetings and access to computer labs.

"Getting to Know Me" Project: Creating a Safe Learning Environment for Students and Teachers

NANCY L. BRASHEAR
Azusa Pacific University, Azusa, CA

MARGARET E. ALBERTSON
Azusa Pacific University, Azusa, CA

STRATEGY/ACTIVITY/ASSIGNMENT

On the first day at Main Street Middle School, USA, girls and boys enter their new classrooms with intermingled feelings of hope, fear, and in some cases, apathy. They come speaking English, Spanish, Mandarin, and other languages. Their clothing styles reflect a continuum of statements about themselves and society. Many are strangers to each other. The challenge for their teachers is to make personal connections with and between these students and then to form them into cohesive groups that will work together in whole-class units as well as in small-group formations.

How the classroom teacher lays the groundwork for creating a "safe environment" during these beginning days will most likely determine the general tone of the class throughout the remainder of the year. Students need to know that making mistakes is a natural part of learning and that their classmates will support them in setting new goals as well as in celebrating successes. Establishment of this base of trust is paramount for the young adolescent who often feels awkward, self-conscious, and self-critical. Indeed, it is necessary for optimal cognitive, affective, and social learning to take place in subsequent lessons.

The needs of teacher education candidates for understanding and accepting the similarities and differences of each other are similar. In addition, education students need tools for working with young students in these affective domains. Professors may find it useful to repeat the following activity later during the course to extend the personal level of trust that has been established.

Students decorate a "container" of some kind, as an at-home or in-class project, that depicts them in a *public* manner, as well as a *private* one. Shoe boxes are readily available and hold up well as they are transported; paper bags are plentiful and inexpensive. Students are told that they will be displaying their "Getting to Know Me" projects in class. In addition to featuring their names somewhere on the containers, students decorate the outside with personally created pictures, symbols, or words (with original drawings or cut-and-paste clippings from magazines and newspapers). The items on the outside of their containers should contain information that they want to share with *all* their classmates. For instance, examples may include printed words that describe their personality or hobbies, or pictures of sports heroes or nature scenes with special meaning. The inside will contain items that represent the "private" person. Students may wish to include souvenirs, words, pictures, a secret wish or goal, or other carefully selected representations of their lives. They will share these items selectively with one or two partners.

On the day that students bring their projects to class, the professor directs them to share a few of the symbols on the outside of their containers in groups of two or three, allowing a total of approximately ten to fifteen minutes. Next, students select an item from inside their containers to share. Approximately five to seven minutes per person is usually sufficient time for students to talk about the item. If a student feels uncomfortable sharing personal information, it is acceptable to say "I pass" or to focus on another public symbol. After sharing, the student who has just presented receives a verbal affirmation from group members, i.e., "Thanks for your commitment to preserving our environment."

At the conclusion of the small-group discussions, the professor leads a discussion about what the participants experienced, thus introducing and expanding the concept of how building classroom rapport within the parameters of a "safe environment" promotes a positive learning environment. By closely examining the process in which they have just participated, education students will articulate linkages between meeting affective and social needs of adolescents and promoting respect-based learning environments in their classrooms. This may take the form of classroom discussion, small-group debriefing, or personal journaling.

A practical extension for education students is to actually implement this activity in a classroom. When used with middle school students, the education student and host classroom teacher will need to determine whether to place students into predetermined groups or to let them choose their own. By quietly and respectfully listening in on student responses (an action that is announced in advance), the teacher can learn about individual students as well as observe small-group dynamics.

COMMENTARY

This activity is highly effective in getting education students to experience firsthand the bonding process that occurs when structured activities allow for trust building. By actually participating, they are more likely to reenact this activity in middle school classrooms.

When used during the opening weeks of school, this activity has been especially effective in helping adolescents and their teachers to get to know each other quickly. If students have rotating schedules and change classrooms during the day, the teacher may want to provide a storage place in class or ask students to bring their containers with them as directed. This project can serve as a basis for future classroom discussion and writing activities as well as facilitate conversations at home between children and their family members. Most importantly, this activity gives children an opportunity to make personal connections in the classroom. This is vitally significant, as no child should feel isolated from his or her peers.

The Shadow Study

MELANIE W. GREENE
Appalachian State University, Boone, NC

STRATEGY / ACTIVITY / ASSIGNMENT

A shadow study is a systematic plan for observing and recording the events in a young adolescent's daily school routine (Stevenson, 1992). It may well serve as one of the most insightful, in-depth investigations into the developmental levels and interests of our constituents. Results from a shadowing activity can also provide middle school educators with a rationale for planning and presenting a developmentally responsive curriculum.

The following steps are recommended for conducting a shadow study. When the school site is selected, permission should be sought from the administration to conduct the study. It is mandatory to request parental permission for students selected to participate in the investigation; however, individual students must not be informed of their involvement. Confidentiality is essential throughout the study and in reporting the conclusions. The preservice teacher must secure a schedule of the subject's school day as well as a map of the school campus. The investigator should discreetly follow the student and record anecdotal notes at short intervals, preferably every ten minutes throughout the school day. Notes should focus on the physical, social, emotional, and cognitive aspects of the subject. Leading questions for physical aspects would include approximate height and weight as well as general observations about the appearance of the subject. Social aspects might include interactions with peers, teachers, parents, coaches, and other adults in various situations. Emotional characteristics may be observed as social interactions occur and may be better described following a more lengthy investigation. Questions to address in the cognitive arena should include preferences between core curriculum courses, levels of participation in classes, types of questions asked and responses given during instructional time, task commitment, and so forth.

At the conclusion of the shadowing, a brief and informal exit interview between the young adolescent and the investigator should take place. Here, the student can be given an opportunity to respond to specific questions that might have arisen during the observations. The student could also share opinions about core curriculum, extracurricular activities, peer interactions, preferred teaching strategies, and attitudes about school and society. This conversation will likely provide further insight into the life of the young adolescent. A written narrative is required following the shadowing activity. The narrative should include a summarization of the observations and conclusions drawn from the study.

COMMENTARY

An examination of the unique cognitive, social, emotional, and physical development of the young adolescent is integral to the training of middle level educators. The shadow study requires preservice teachers to observe the events in the life of one student for an entire day within the context of middle school activities. The interactions with peers, teachers, and administrators can also be observed. Since the data generated pertain to the individual selected for the study, global conclusions cannot be generalized for the entire population; however, preservice teachers can glean much insight from the results of such an assignment. This insight can provide the stimulus for understanding the value of planning curriculum tailored to meet the unique needs of this population. One prospective teacher reacted to the study with the following comments:

I was surprised at how much I learned from this assignment. No two young adolescents are alike. Each one is unique and has special strengths and weaknesses. It was amazing to see how these strengths and weaknesses influenced their interactions with peers, teachers, and even the school principal. Now I understand why teachers must plan lessons that are appropriate for this age.

REFERENCE

Stevenson, C. (1992). *Teaching ten to fourteen year olds.* White Plains, New York: Longman.

Learning About Early Adolescent Learners

PATRICIA H. PHELPS
University of Central Arkansas, Conway

STRATEGY/ACTIVITY/ASSIGNMENT

In order to become effective middle school teachers, preservice teachers need deep knowledge and understanding of early adolescents. Knowing what middle level students are like will help prospective teachers decide whether they actually wish to teach at this level and will provide a more realistic view of their future students. One way to achieve the level of understanding needed for effective middle school teaching is to provide preservice teachers with real data gathered from early adolescents for comparison with readings on early adolescent growth and development. As a field experience assignment, teacher education students can survey middle school students. Also, former students who are now teachers can be enlisted to gather data from their own students. For example, a survey of seventh graders could be constructed for anonymous completion. Such questions as the following may be posited:

1. Briefly describe yourself in one paragraph.
2. What do you like *most* about being your age?
3. What do you like *least* about being your age?
4. What advice would you give to someone preparing to teach middle school students?

Once the completed surveys have been collected, a small-group learning activity can be structured whereby teams of preservice teachers complete the following assignment:

1. Read the results of the seventh-grade surveys.
2. Examine and discuss the characteristics of early adolescents as presented in the textbook, article, handout, etc. (The instructor can identify the appropriate source(s) of information.)
3. Find examples of each attribute listed in the text or article in the surveys.
4. Identify the implications of your findings relative to curriculum and instruction. (i.e., What meaning does your knowledge of early adolescents have for middle school teaching and school organization?)
5. Prepare to share your findings with the class by summarizing what you have learned and its implications. Use the flip chart or transparency provided in Figure 2.1, below.

Note: This activity could easily be "jigsawed" by giving each team a different aspect of development on which to focus—physical, intellectual, emotional, or social.

Figure 2.1

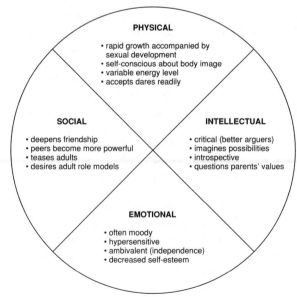

COMMENTARY

Increased sensitivity relative to the needs and characteristics of early adolescents is a primary result of this activity. Students remark how enlightening the exercise is; they particularly enjoy being able to read the words (and handwriting) of seventh graders. Reading "advice" from actual students allows prospective teachers to begin to value students' voices in improving their own instruction. By stressing the *implications* of developmental characteristics, future teachers are encouraged to become more student-centered as they apply their knowledge of learners toward the creation of learning experiences.

Middle-Years Ways of Representing Learning: Newspapers and Group Skills

DAVID W. FRIESEN
University of Regina, Regina, SK, Canada

STRATEGY/ACTIVITY/ASSIGNMENT

I teach a middle level foundational course in the second year of our preservice program (middle level track). The focal activity of this course is an inquiry project into the lived experiences of young teens outside of school. Initially, groups of six students formulate some general concerns they want to explore that relate to the lives of middle level students. Some examples of the concerns that have been explored in this course are: the influence of popular media on young teens; the trends in young teen culture; and the selection of heroes and their effect on young teen identity. Each student develops a plan to pursue specific questions related to the group's general concern and then spends considerable time over the semester with an individual or group of young teens involved in various activities. The students volunteer at a variety of sites that give them access to teens, such as places involved in community sports and arts programs. They also make contact with young teens informally at young teen events, hangouts, and shopping malls. The inquiry involves observing, interviewing, video and audio recordings, keeping a journal, and collecting various artifacts from their experiences. The method is dependent on the particular site chosen by students.

Towards the end of the semester, each group plans a presentation of their experiences and what they have learned about young teens. In the first part of the presentation exercise, each group is given responsibility for a section of a middle-years newspaper. Groups choose the front page, sports page, editorial page, teen culture page, letters to the editor, advertising section, and so on. The newspaper is written from a young teen's perspective incorporating the learnings from the intensive study done over the semester. Each group writes out its part of the paper on large newsprint, taking care to use color and design appealing to young teens. After all the parts are completed, the paper is assembled and then displayed in the middle-years university classroom.

The groups also present skits to demonstrate their understandings of teens from their inquiry project and from readings done over the course of the semester. They select a particular theme that runs throughout their individual studies and design a skit to portray that theme. Past groups have presented skits on teen relationships, tattooing, dress, music trends, substance abuse, hangouts, language, socioeconomic comparisons, and so on. The students are expected to integrate their understandings into a creative and young teen–oriented production, complete with props, music, and dress. Before the skits are presented, the students develop criteria for assessment such as the following: the depth and breadth of the content; use of multiple intelligences; and creativity. After the presentations, students assess the presentations using the agreed upon criteria.

COMMENTARY

The course aims to help the students become oriented to young adolescents. The newspaper project and skits are designed to help the student teachers become teacher researchers of the lived experiences and culture of this particular group of people. This beginning middle level course is always rated highly by the students partly because of the use of these unique ways of representing their learning. I am never disappointed with the newspaper produced or the skits presented.

Students learn much about the characteristics of young teens from the newspaper and the skits. They are able to make the connection between these activities and their responsibility as teachers to enhance learning at the middle level. The inquiry projects also tend to represent the diversity that is found in the teen population with respect to development, ethnicity, socioeconomics, and gender. Students learn what is really important to these young teens and what this might mean for teaching. The students are able to relate these characteristics of young teens to the readings they have been exposed to during the semester.

These activities engender group cohesiveness along with reflection on pedagogy that is responsive to the middle-years level. The lived experience of this research project integrates experiential learning, problem-based learning, and thematic planning. The project allows the modeling of these middle level appropriate approaches without reducing them to decontextualized techniques. Later in the program, students learn to enact these forms of teaching, and they often refer back to their own experiences with these approaches in this initial middle level course.

Middle School Students Speak Out

TRUDY KNOWLES
Westfield State College, Westfield, MA

STRATEGY/ACTIVITY/ASSIGNMENT

Twenty middle school students—grades 6 to 8—arrive in a class entitled "The Middle School and Its Students." Members of the college class divide into four groups and each group takes five students to interview. For fifteen to twenty minutes they ask the middle level students open-ended questions about their development and their experiences at school. Questions include: What advice would you give to someone wanting to be a middle school teacher? Describe a teacher that you think is great. Now describe one that is terrible. What is it like being in middle school? If you could change anything about yourself, what would it be? How have you changed in the past year? Describe an ideal middle school.

The college students follow the lead of the middle school students, probing for more information when appropriate. Sometimes the questions are more direct, such as "What do you think of school dances?" or "Do you date?"

After fifteen to twenty minutes, a short break is taken, cookies and juice are offered to the middle school students, and they switch to a new group. This procedure continues until each group has had a chance to talk to all of the students.

Prior to this class session, the parents or guardians of each middle school student have been sent an information letter describing the purpose and structure of the interviews. Parents are assured that anonymity and confidentiality are respected. They are also advised that, should they agree to have their child interviewed, the results of the interviews will be used in class discussions at the college and may be used in other professional presentations or publications. A parental consent form is attached. To be interviewed, students must bring in the signed form. Students are also asked to sign a consent form agreeing to be interviewed.

Following the session, all students are sent thank-you notes on college letterhead.

COMMENTARY

My college students learn more about the development and needs of the young adolescent from listening to middle school students than from any other method I have tried. The young adolescents provide insights about development, preferred instruction, classroom management, how to maintain the boundary between being a teacher and being a friend, relevant curriculum, and what they view as important issues in the young adolescent's life. As one college student commented, "I was amazed at the variety of the students and yet the inner innocence they still had deep inside. . . . The thing that I loved the most was their honesty to the particular questions. They were very insightful. The knowledge they possess is incredible. . . . The two hours that the students were here gave me a better integration of knowledge than any textbook I've ever read. It was definitely a worthwhile experience."

During class sessions and through readings assigned prior to these interviews, the college students have investigated the physical, intellectual, social, and emotional development of the young adolescent. Following the interviews, my students are asked to reflect on what they learned from these middle school students. We then compare what these students have said with our previous knowledge on young adolescent development. This analysis leads us into creating, as a class, a developmentally responsive middle level program. Students look at what would be appropriate based on certain physical, emotional, social, and cognitive changes as well as young adolescent feedback.

The interviews with the middle school students become the foundation for everything else we do in the class. Class discussions about any topic are tied to what we have learned from the young adolescent. My students' ability to respond and understand speakers, readings, videos, observations, and so forth is enhanced by their firsthand experience of listening to these middle school students.

I am fortunate that I teach this class in the evening in a two hour block of time. This time gives me access to middle school students. If the class were to be taught in a one-hour block during the day, modifications could be made. The college class could go to the middle school or a middle school class could take a trip to the college.

Middle school students find this activity empowering. They comment that it is a chance for them to influence future teachers as well as to be listened to. Finding young adolescents willing to come is never an issue. Principals also feel that this is a valuable activity and most are willing to work out arrangements.

Permission slips signed by parents and students are necessary. Also, the thank-you notes sent to students following the sessions give them a sense that they have done something important—which they have.

Guest Speakers—Middle Level Teacher and Students

SAMUEL TOTTEN
University of Arkansas, Fayetteville

STRATEGY/ACTIVITY/ASSIGNMENT

At least once a semester, a middle level teacher is invited to bring five to six of his or her students (between the ages of 10 and 15) to speak on a given topic to my undergraduates in "Middle Level Principles and Methods." In the past, topics have ranged from life as a middle level student (which included a host of issues, such as male/female relationships, the school curriculum, extracurricular programs, the students' perspective of "good" and "not so good" teachers, and so forth) to service learning projects, and from student perspectives of advisory/advisee programs and/or interdisciplinary teams to the transition from an elementary school to a middle school.

In a panel format, the middle level students are each asked to provide an opening statement in regard to what they like best and least about being a young adolescent and/or their school life. Following this opening, the university students ask virtually any questions they wish, both from the lists they have been required to individually generate as well as anything that comes to mind during the course of the panel's presentation. The middle level students are not privy to the questions prior to the session and that is due to the fact that the university students are not required to develop the questions until the week of the actual presentation.

Initially, many of the middle level students are tentative about giving detailed answers, but when they discover that the university students are genuinely interested in what they have to say, the middle level students become more spontaneous and provide more in-depth answers. Generally, the middle level students spend two to three hours with us and are happy to answer most of the questions posed to them.

COMMENTARY

The key reason for inviting young adolescents to class is to provide ready access for the members of the class to the unique words and insights of young adolescents. To come face to face with young adolescents is generally much more meaningful than reading about them in a book and/or seeing them on a video. It also allows the university students to recognize and appreciate (a) the radical differences in physical size among young adolescents; (b) how serious, articulate, and humorous young adolescents can be; (c) the unique concerns and issues with which young adolescents are dealing; and (d) their unique perspectives on the middle level programs that are ostensibly in place to meet their needs.

A major benefit of having young adolescents come to the university classroom is that public school schedules are such that it is often difficult to arrange mutually convenient times for discussions sessions like these between university and middle level students. Indeed, during the day, middle level students are usually engaged in work germane to their own education, and so it is not fair or pedagogically sound to pull them away from such concerns.

The visit by the students is always a great hit with both my undergraduate and graduate students. The university students are often quite amazed at the perspicacious insights of the middle level students. Some university students always comment on what a wonderfully educative session the visit was, particularly due to the fact that the middle level students raised issues that some of them (the university students) had not thought about or considered since their days as young adolescents.

Middle School Student Panel: Interviewing Young Adolescents Through Panel Discussions

SANDEE SCHAMBER

Black Hills State University, Spearfish, SD

STRATEGY/ACTIVITY/ASSIGNMENT

This activity involves bringing a panel of six to twelve middle school students to an integrated class session of two middle level courses for the purpose of a panel discussion. The courses focus on the characteristics of young adolescents and the principles and practices of teaching in the middle school. These are taken by both preservice teachers and teachers who are already in the field and who are seeking a middle school endorsement for their teaching certificate. For this activity, middle school students are invited and ushered to class by the participants in the courses. Sometimes they are the sons and daughters of class members and their friends; other times they are students of those class members who are already teaching.

At the advent of the discussion the students are told that they have been invited in order to help the college students become better teachers. It is emphasized that it is necessary for good teachers to understand their students, and that they, the students, have valuable suggestions regarding the best teaching practices for students in the middle school. After introductions are made, the college students are free to question the students regarding their thoughts and feelings about being an adolescent or about middle level practices.

COMMENTARY

This activity provides many preservice teachers with their first glimpse into the lives of today's young adolescents. The middle school students' responses are extremely informative. Questions flow freely from the college students, and members of the panel are eager to talk about themselves and their situations. The panel presentation offers middle school students the opportunity to tell their side of the story of life, and tell it they do—with vigor and pride! Rarely do panel members exercise their option to pass on a question. This activity provides preservice teachers with an opportunity to hear about young adolescence from young adolescents. As one preservice student stated: "The live action panel of students was about the best combination of theory and practice you could get. The young adolescents were candid and honest. They even followed theory perfectly. . . . The panel made all of the lectures and reading come alive."

Creating Opportunities to Learn About Early Adolescents: Real Questions from Real Teachers

DOUGLAS HAMMAN
Merrimack College, North Andover, MA

STRATEGY/ACTIVITY/ASSIGNMENT

Studying Adolescent Development: Making Preparation Relevant to Practice

College-level course work offers an important opportunity for the preservice teacher to learn about theories of human development. Successful middle level educators, however, need more than a passing knowledge of early adolescent development and a familiarity with some theories. They need an understanding of development that transcends neatly contained chapters on identity, peer relations, or biological changes.

The assignment described herein is intended to help preservice teachers broaden their practical understanding of their college-based knowledge about early adolescent development. In order to do this, preservice teachers use their knowledge of early adolescent development to address real questions from real teachers (Collins, Brown, & Newman, 1989).

Procedures for creating the opportunity: Role of the cooperating teacher

The college instructor extends an invitation to middle level educators via electronic mailing lists (e.g., Middle-L). In the invitation, middle level educators (cooperators) are given specific instructions about how to participate. First, cooperators submit a question for the student researcher (i.e., preservice teacher) to investigate. There are some limitations on the type of question that can be submitted. For example, the question must have at least some connection to theories of adolescent development. Also, the question should not serve as a test for the preservice teacher but rather provide a focal point around which mutually beneficial discussion may occur.

Second, via e-mail, the cooperator responds to a student researcher's request for a discussion of the question. Discussion should focus on the context from which the question arose (i.e., "What made you think of this question?"). By discussing the context, student researchers are more likely to understand the value of pursuing their studies in adolescent development. In addition, the student researcher witnesses firsthand an actual teacher asking a real question about real early adolescents' development.

Third, via e-mail, cooperators receive updates from the student about their progress with the research. At best, this correspondence provides an opportunity to foster a mentoring relationship between student and cooperator. This correspondence at least provides a way for student researchers to monitor his or her progress toward the goal of responding to the cooperator's question.

Finally, the cooperating teacher receives (via post) and reviews (not "grades") a hard copy of the student's research findings. Comments about the paper are then sent via e-mail to the course instructor, who then relays the comments to the student researcher. Cooperator's comments should provide the student researcher with feedback regarding the feasibility or practicality of their interpretation and findings.

Responding to the opportunity:
Role of the student researcher

Student researchers are shown all the questions that educators have submitted and are then asked to select one question for their own project. Students are given instruction regarding the use of e-mail (as needed) and provided some opportunity during class meetings to access Internet resources and communicate with their cooperating teacher.

Student researchers gather and review available literature aimed at addressing their cooperating teacher's question. At three different points during the course of the project (i.e., at the beginning, mid-point, and when submitting the review) student researchers are required to communicate with their cooperating teacher. Additional e-mail correspondence is encouraged but not required. Upon completion of the written projects, the reports are disseminated in three ways: (1) the report is submitted to the cooperating teacher, (2) a copy of the report is submitted to the course instructor, and (3) a 120-word summary of the report (along with the author's e-mail address) is posted on a Web page created for other interested educators (e.g., http://chasm.merrimack.edu/~dhamman/Projectframes.html).

The core presentations: Role of the collegial community

Finally, the college instructor arranges for students to meet with other classmates who were researching similar topics. Group members jointly identify a core issue to which all their research is relevant. Once a core issue has been identified, students plan and deliver a theme-based presentation. Classmates and all members of the college-community are invited to attend the presentations, which take place at the end of the semester. Themes of past core presentations have included vulnerability of adolescents to eating disorders, adolescent sexuality, and management and discipline in the classroom.

COMMENTARY

Like most assignments that are long-term, involve collaboration, and require a good deal of effort, students are somewhat overwhelmed when they first encounter this assignment. For many, the mention of e-mail and the Internet are nearly paralyzing. Organization on the part of the instructor, however, is key to helping students overcome many of the obstacles that arise. For example, instructors can provide class time, supervision, and tutoring for those who are unfamiliar with e-mail. A predetermined structure and explicit guidelines for the written report are also beneficial for many reluctant writers.

The moment of triumph (from the perspective of both the instructor and the student) is the core presentation (Sizer, 1996). Through their research, students have become real, local experts in their field of interest. The presentation is made to class colleagues and members of the academic community (e.g., other college faculty, administrators, local practitioners, peers), thus heightening the value for clear communication and relevant information.

Alternatives

The assignment as described can be easily modified to fit a variety of situations. For example, teachers' questions might be drawn from a local school community. If too few questions are identified, students could collaborate on the projects or investigate different aspects of one question. Presentations could be videotaped and shown to cooperating teachers as a means of creating a larger audience. Any alteration, however, should retain the essential nature of the assignment, which is identifying and responding to a real question from a real teacher for a real purpose.

REFERENCES

Collins, A., Brown, J. S., & Newman, S. E. (1989). Cognitive apprenticeship: Teaching the crafts of reading, writing, and mathematics. In L. B. Resnick (Ed.), *Knowing, learning, and instruction: Essays in honor of Robert Glaser* (pp. 453-494). Hillsdale, NJ: Erlbaum & Associates.

Sizer, T. R. (1996*). Horace's hope: What works for the American high school.* Boston, MA: Houghton Mifflin.

Using Literature to Explore the Unique Needs and Developmental Characteristics of Young Adolescents

SANDEE SCHAMBER
Black Hills State University, Spearfish, SD

STRATEGY/ACTIVITY/ASSIGNMENT

This culminating activity in a course on adolescent development gives students the opportunity to identify, through literature, the needs and developmental characteristics of young adolescents that have been discussed throughout the course. Students are asked to select a children's or early adolescents' literature book in which the main character is between the ages of ten and fourteen years. They are then asked to locate specific passages that reflect the unique needs and/or developmental characteristics of young adolescents. For example, the following passage from Judy Blume's *Are You There God? It's Me, Margaret* (1970) reflects the ever-present peer pressure to conform, which most, if not all, young adolescents experience: "Oh, listen . . . on the first day of school wear loafers, but no socks . . . if you're wearing socks the other kids might not want you" (p. 13).

When time is short these selected passages are submitted in writing, but when time allows they are presented in class. These presentations offer the opportunity for further discussions relating to the identification of the needs and characteristics of young adolescents.

COMMENTARY

The ability to recognize the needs and characteristics in the daily thoughts and actions of middle school students is critical to responsive teaching. This activity provides students with an opportunity to hone these recognition skills. As one former student commented, "I do not like to read novels, but when given the opportunity to discuss the books from a student's perspective, it definitely made me a better teacher."

REFERENCE

Blume, J. (1970). *Are you there God? It's me, Margaret.* New York, NY: Dell Publishing.

Getting to Know Young Adolescents Through Young Adolescent Literature

SAUNDRA BRYN
Arizona State University West, Phoenix

STRATEGY/ACTIVITY/ASSIGNMENT

If teachers are to teach middle level students successfully, practicing and preservice teachers must understand the developmental characteristics and needs of young adolescents. This assignment is based on the belief that university students can obtain insight into the lives of contemporary young adolescents through the reading and discussion of well-written young adult literature.

MAJOR OBJECTIVES

1. The students will examine the characteristics of early adolescents through young adult literature.
2. The students will consider the implications of early adolescents' characteristics for middle level programs.

3. The students will examine the diversity found among early adolescents and consider its impact on middle level classrooms.

RATIONALE

The college of education does not offer an adolescent literature course. Elementary education students complete reading courses that focus on children's literature; only secondary education students with English majors are required to take any literature courses. The instructor expects that introducing preservice and practicing teachers to young adult literature will encourage them to use it with their own early adolescent students as well.

PROCEDURES

1. Just prior to the end of the first class, the instructor provides students with copies of Avi's *Nothing but the Truth* with the instructions to read it and respond to the issues raised in the book in a short (no more than two pages) paper. Students are *not* to report on the events in the book but rather to reflect on key issues the book raises in their minds.
2. During the next class period, the students divide into groups of three or four with the simple directions, "Talk about the book."
3. The instructor reconvenes the whole group and elicits from class members the topics discussed in their groups. As students respond, the instructor lists the topics on chart paper and puts checks by the issues that need further discussion. These issues include the major themes of the book as well as common concerns of adolescents.
4. After directing students' attention to the quote in the front of the book ("I swear to tell the truth, the whole truth, and nothing but the truth") and its subsequent question ("Does anybody ever lie?") and, through discussion, bringing out the idea of people's varying perceptions of truth, the instructor assigns students to small groups to discuss the quote and its question from the various characters' points of view. The focus: Are this person's actions consistent throughout the book? True to life? What would you have done as this person?
5. Each group presents its conclusions, then each student spends five to ten minutes writing additions to his or her response paper,

indicating any changes or confirmations to his or her view of the characters and issues in the book.

6. The students do a "blind" selection of one of four books—Cooney's *Drivers Ed*, Myers's *Scorpions*, Philbrick's *Freak the Mighty*, or Soto's *Taking Sides*—to read and respond to for the following class.

7. After an initial small-group discussion in which the students who read the same book meet to talk about it, students move into groups composed of people who have read different books. The groups discuss their books and their characters, emphasizing the similarities and differences of the main characters.

8. Groups continue to examine similarities and differences by constructing Venn diagrams (interlocking circles in which the overlapping part of the circles shows similarities and the non-overlapping parts show differences). One group focuses on "the peers," another on "the families," and another on "the school personnel."

9. As each group presents its findings to the class, the class engages in discussion about the impact the other characters and the situations have on the main character(s).

10. Finally, students compare the characteristics of young adolescents listed in *This We Believe* (1995) with those of the fictional characters they've just read about, then list the implications these characteristics have for the school organization and curriculum of young adolescents.

COMMENTARY

Both graduate and undergraduate students love this assignment—and every single one of them completes it on time. In fact, many times students read more books than the ones they are assigned.

The assignment serves as a reminder of the importance of knowing the characteristics and needs of young adolescents and stresses the application of that knowledge in the middle level classroom. As a bonus, it introduces students to some wonderful young adult books that they can use with their middle level students. As one student said, "It was surprising to me: the abundance of good young adolescent literature—a sampling of which we looked at today. I don't know where I was during my middle school years, but we didn't read novels like these. It was fifteen, sixteen years ago . . . have things changed that much?"

These novels depict the lives of many young teenagers today. In two of the books the main characters are from two-parent suburban families. The others have only one evident parent. One boy lives with his grandparents. The characters also reflect the ethnic diversity of our society: some are Anglo, some Black, some Hispanic. In two of the books, gang influences are very evident. One of the main characters is highly gifted; another is tagged as learning disabled; one is an athlete; another is a "low achiever"; two are "pretty normal kids." All have strong friendships with peers. One student commented, "All these books show the way young adolescents are coping or responding to life—conflicts with peers . . . , showing parents' and teachers' concerns or lack of, . . . the accepting of responsibility."

The reflections of students support the value of this assignment: "I think the whole child has come more into focus for me with these books. Children have so many different issues that they deal with outside of school that [sometimes] school is just not as important to them. Just because a kid is acting up in class or is not the best student—there may be outside reasons the child is not performing the way he or she should."

Another commented, "After our discussion in class I can really see how important it is to *really* get to know the 'whole student.' So many things interfere or impact a young child's life. As an educator I will make a point of learning as much as I can about each of my students." Still another said, "The family and teachers play such a role in teens' lives. It is interesting to note that the characters all needed the same support in moral development and in emotional and social acceptance."

Several students addressed the implications for middle level classrooms, one saying, "I think that the implications we made in class regarding all of these books are that junior high [sic] students need someone to advocate for them. Many children do not have a complete family environment, an ideal social situation, or a good friend to guide them. I think it would be nice for these kids to know that they have someone on their side." A graduate student (a practicing teacher) expanded on the implications: "All of the novels we read struck me as having serious implications for teachers. The middle school child may need us to make a connection with them that no other adult in their life does. I have up to 160 students at any given time, and I must say that I have probably passed over hundreds of opportunities to connect with kids—simply because I know the kind of energy and risk that it takes. It is a risk. But we must be about the business of educating human beings in the middle school, not just [teaching] our disciplines. . . . It was a thoughtful discussion and made me do some soul searching. We are given moments to reach kids, and we pass over many of them."

REFERENCES

Avi. (1991). *Nothing but the truth*. New York: Avon Books.

Cooney, C. (1994). *Driver's ed*. New York: Bantam Doubleday Dell Books for Young Readers.

Myers, W. D. (1988). *Scorpions*. New York: Harper and Row.

Philbrick, R. (1993). *Freak the mighty*. New York: Scholastic Inc.

Soto, G. (1991). *Taking sides*. San Diego, CA: Harcourt Brace and Company.

Lounsbury, J. (Ed.) (1995). *This we believe*. Columbus, OH: National Middle School Association.

Middle Level School Counselors and Nurses: A Panel Discussion

SAMUEL TOTTEN
University of Arkansas, Fayetteville

STRATEGY/ACTIVITY/ASSIGNMENT

A panel of middle school counselors and nurses are invited to attend my undergraduate "Middle Level Principles and Methods" classes to address such topics as: emotional and health concerns/issues faced by young adolescents; working with teachers to address the social/emotional and health issues facing young adolescents; their interactions and interventions with young adolescents; and how the unique and diverse needs of their students are either met or not met.

Prior to the panel discussion, each counselor and nurse is sent an executive copy of *Fateful Choices* (the report on the health and social needs of young adolescents issued by the Carnegie Council on Adolescent Development) and informed that students are reading it in preparation for their visit. In addition, they are informed that at the outset of the panel discussion they will each be given time to provide an opening statement in regard to: what their job entails; the diverse needs of the students with whom they have daily contact; their interactions and interventions with young adolescents; their insights into the lives of young adolescents today; special programs in the school and/or community that are in place to meet the social/emotional and health needs of young adolescents; and what and how well middle schools in the area are doing in regard to meeting the unique needs of early adolescents in relation to health and social concerns.

They are also informed that each of the students will develop a list of three questions they would like them (the counselors and nurses) to answer and that they will each receive a list of the questions upon their arrival to class. Finally, they are told that the students and the instructor may have additional questions to ask.

Prior to meeting with the panel, the university students are required to read the executive summary of *Fateful Choices* and to generate a minimum of three questions based on his or her reading or to note any concerns he or she may have that are germane to the focus of the panel. Students are required to bring a set of questions—all of which must be typed—for each panelist, the professor, and one for themselves. Students are free to ask additional questions as the discussion unfolds.

COMMENTARY

This session always proves to be enlightening to preservice teachers. Through their stories, the panelists relate the diverse types of issues and problems faced by many of today's young adolescents. Such issues and problems often include: homelessness, improper hygiene, drug use, peer pressure, child abuse, lack of acceptance by peers and/or teachers, lack of parental involvement. Through these discussions, the preservice teachers gain unique insights into the complexity of a young adolescent's life and what it means to address the needs of the whole child.

The preservice students often express amazement at the problems faced by the young adolescents as well as to the types of situations teachers, administrators, counselors, and nurses attend to on a daily basis. They also express great interest in the various intervention programs available to meet the needs of young adolescents. At the same time, some find it heartbreaking that the schools and school personnel are limited in how much they can do to address the numerous and serious hardships faced by many young adolescents. Some also begin to appreciate the significant role that counselors and nurses play in the school setting and just how dedicated many are in their attempt to meet the unique needs of young adolescents. As a result of this session, many begin to truly appreciate for the first time that schooling involves much more than just teaching subject matter. Indeed, without fail, some preservice students note that this panel discussion, more than anything else that takes place during the course of the semester, makes them appreciate why a key aim of middle level education is to meet the various needs of young adolescents, not simply those in the cognitive domain.

REFERENCE

Hechinger, F.M. (1992). *Fateful choices: Healthy youth for the 21st century.* New York: Carnegie Corporation.

Pulling It All Together

ADELE B. SANDERS
University of Northern Colorado, Greeley

STRATEGY/ACTIVITY/ASSIGNMENT

Learning about early adolescent growth and development and the organizational structures that support young adolescents' needs is the focus of two different courses in the middle grades teacher-preparation program (one undergraduate, one graduate). One way for students to "summarize" (synthesize) their understanding of middle schoolers (growth and development) and appropriate learning environments (organization) is through this creative and open-ended activity.

I have used this activity in a second-semester middle grades teacher-preparation course (the second course in a five-course sequence) and in an introductory graduate middle level course for practicing teachers. Whatever the level of the course, however, the course's curriculum should be rich with information about early adolescents (their physiological changes, intellectual needs and capacities, emotional frailties and strengths, and social anxieties and behaviors) and the types of programmatic structures and instructional strategies most likely to invite the students' involvement and provide support. (It has also been used during the third-semester course for undergraduates in the program.)

Throughout the progression of both courses, the students read about and discuss the various changes that ten- to fifteen-year-olds experience on their way to adolescence. We discuss those changes and the kinds of environments and programs (e.g., teaching styles, variable assessment, exploratories, advisor/advisee, block scheduling) that are well-suited to the early adolescent's stages of development. In this way, the course attempts to provide a rationale for the whys of the middle school movement.

As a culminating activity students are asked to make some concrete representation of their learning about and understanding of the link between the early adolescent and the recommendations for their schooling environment. The only real guidance I give students is that their representation must include aspects of "middlers" and of the schooling environment that they believe are connected and, therefore, important to highlight. Not until the students are close to producing their representation do I show any examples of previous students' efforts.

When their representations have been completed, the students share them, one at a time, with the rest of the class. The students explain their representations, indicating why something was depicted or stated and the significance and meaning it has for them.

If this activity is done in class, markers, crayons, poster board or large paper for each student would be appropriate provisions. If this activity is to be completed at home, students will be able to use more innovative materials for creating the "map" of their middle school schema.

COMMENTARY

When I did this the first time, I had no examples to share. Nonetheless, I received some fine representations. The one example from that class (developed by a preservice teacher) that I used in the subsequent introductory graduate-level course is a wonderful picture of many truly significant elements for a positive middle grades learning environment. The upper three-fourths of the paper (done in various colors) has a balanced seesaw with "fun" on one side and "learning" on the other; "timing is critical" is written above an hourglass; three somewhat overlapping balloons have the letters A.D.D., L.D., and E.S.L. in them with "variety is a stimulating challenge" written underneath; and a globe is drawn with the words "apply everything to the real world" on it.

Across the bottom quarter of the page, below the words "The Foundation of a Strong School," are four boxes: Integrated Curriculum, Service Learning, Team Planning and Learning, and Advisor/Advisee. There are several other images on this "Middle School Mind Map" that indicate this student's comprehensive understanding of our discussions and of her readings and experiences.

Other examples of students' work include a recipe for "frog soup," a newsletter with brief "articles" about some of the important components of middle schools and teaching in them, an expository essay (written by a math teacher who didn't see himself as being very creative or artistic), and a two-foot by three-foot puzzle. The puzzle's images include a schoolhouse with windows written over with exploratories, advisor/advisee, teams of teachers and students, and interdisciplinary learning; a boy and girl holding hands (only one of them is smiling); a stick-figure teacher with a large red heart and big friendly smile; and a briefcase with the word "new" popping out of it and some kind of tool resting nearby.

The students' explanations of what these images mean to them provide a quality opportunity to learn about the students' deeper understanding of what they have been "studying." It works better than any paper-and-pencil test I might design.

This activity serves as the final "exam" for the second semester undergraduates and for the beginning graduate students. Although no rubric has been specifically designed, the students are advised, as indicated earlier, that middle school components discussed in class should be included. When this activity is used with the preservice teachers (in their third course), it is used halfway into the semester. This activity provides an opportunity for the instructor to assess what connections are being made (or not being made) as this course's content and instructional strategies are added to preservice teachers' schema.

Scenarios on Fostering Creativity

JONATHAN A. PLUCKER
Indiana University, Bloomington

STRATEGY/ACTIVITY/ASSIGNMENT

Recent research on creativity provides evidence that adolescents' affect (e.g., attitudes toward evaluation, self-efficacy) directly impacts the development of creative abilities (Isen, Daubman, & Nowicki, 1987; Shaw & Runco, 1994). At a time when social pressures often dominate early adolescents' lives, factors in students' environments—at home, in school, on the playing field—may impact their willingness to apply their creativity in any observable way. In a course or unit that deals with the impact of early adolescents' affective needs on their learning (in this case, their creative development), the following scenarios allow undergraduate preservice students in educational psychology courses to explore the environmental factors that either foster or inhibit creativity. The scenarios are distributed to students working in groups of three or four. They receive the following description:

> The following paragraph describes the situation of a specific student or teacher. For the purposes of this simulation, any details of the scenario that are not provided should be determined by your group. For example, if your group is interested in middle level science teaching, assume that the student being described is in your middle level science class.

As you read the situation description, consider:

- What is the main problem in the environment with respect to creativity?
- How can the environment be modified to ensure long-term success?

When answering these questions and the question asked at the end of the description, consider:

- the role of the student
- the role of family, teachers, peers, and other people directly involved in the student's life
- the role of advisors, school psychologists, administrators, and other people who may have contact with the student
- the role of assessment
- the role of learning-style differences
- the physical environment (e.g., in the classroom, on the playground, in the home)
- attitudes toward creativity and achievement
- the role of interdisciplinary and exploratory curricula and developmentally appropriate instruction
- resources

THE SITUATION

If you had to pick the ten most troublesome of your former or present students, Susan would be in the top three. She is always out of her seat, teasing her peers, talking, and being generally disruptive. But you learn through the grapevine that Susan loves to go to art museums with her family, frequently draws and paints at home, and takes painting and sculpting lessons after school and on weekends. When participating in these activities, Susan is much less disruptive.

THE QUESTION

How can you modify Susan's environment to help her further develop her creativity? Each group receives the same basic instructions, but "The Situation" and "The Question" differ from group to group. Other classroom-tested scenarios are included at the end of this article. After each group has spent roughly fifteen to twenty minutes developing their answer to the question, each group shares its scenario, identifies what the group members perceive to be the underlying issues, and shares the group's suggestions for addressing the situation. When appropriate (usually after all of the scenarios have been shared), the instructor reiterates the major issues raised collectively by the scenarios and emphasizes the aspects of early adolescence that are to be covered in the course or unit.

COMMENTARY

Reactions to the scenarios, both by inservice and preservice teachers, vary widely. Several people, having been in similar real-life situations, become highly focused, whereas others may question whether the scenarios are realistic in any way, shape, or form. The instructor can interject with, or ask others to share, some real-life examples when these teachable moments occur. Since the purpose of the scenarios is to create motivation for learning about early adolescence and not to supplant the detailed curriculum, instructors should not feel required to answer every skeptical comment with a detailed mini-lecture.

The instructor can easily develop similar scenarios to help introduce other middle level issues. The instructor should have a few colleagues and students read and attempt the scenario to be certain that the instructions, descriptions, and issues are clear.

The scenarios also make great "starter questions" for on-line discussions that can supplement classroom activities. For example, after discussing different models of adolescent self-concept development, the instructor could send a scenario to the class listserv and require the students to apply one or more of the models.

The temptation to use this type of scenario as a post-coverage assessment technique should be avoided; after covering aspects of early adolescence in significant depth, most short simulations will be far too simplistic to allow students to apply their knowledge. The instructor should also pursue the use of videotaped case studies, theatrical films (e.g., *Searching for Bobby Fischer*), or classroom observations whenever possible.

ADDITIONAL SCENARIOS

1. *The Situation:* Marika is a teacher's dream: quiet, well behaved, does whatever you ask without complaining. During a conference with her parents, you realize that Marika is very linguistically creative—always creating and telling jokes and stories, writing poems, and writing plays.
   The Question: What modification could you make to your classroom to help foster Marika's creative abilities?

2. *The Situation:* Juan enjoys his dance lessons immensely, and you are aware that he is very talented in this area (bodily-kinesthetic). But he is afraid to let others know about his dancing because he has been teased about it by his peers.
   The Question: How can you modify your classroom environment to value his creative talents (and those of all your other students)?

3. *The Situation:* Alan is a very creative student—artistically, linguistically, and with respect to problem solving. Yet you can tell from your interactions with Alan's parents that they do not think he is creative (or exceptional in any other way). They do not foster their child's creativity at home, and they do not see a need to do so.
   The Question: What can you do to help create more creative environments for Alan?

REFERENCES

Isen, A. M., Daubman, K. A., & Nowicki, G. P. (1987). Positive affect facilitates creative problem solving. *Journal of Personality and Social Psychology, 52,* 1122-1131.

Shaw, M. P., & Runco, M. A. (Eds.). (1994). *Creativity and affect.* Norwood, NJ: Ablex.

CHAPTER 3

Curriculum

Modeling an Integrative Curriculum Design

TRUDY KNOWLES
Westfield State College, Westfield, MA

STRATEGY/ACTIVITY/ASSIGNMENT

Students are involved in the development of the syllabus for a class entitled "The Middle School and Its Students." They design the class activities as well as the assignments they will be doing.

During the first two or three class sessions, the class explores four questions:

1. What questions do you have about middle school students or the structure of the middle school?
2. What concerns do you have about being a middle school teacher? What do you think you should know or be able to do to be effective?
3. How do you want to learn this knowledge or these skills?
4. How can we assess that you have learned the knowledge and skills?

The first question is posed to the entire class during the first class meeting. The class is broken into groups of four to five students. Together, they brainstorm and list on large pieces of paper the questions they have about middle school students or the structure of the middle school. The brainstormed lists are then shared with the entire class.

For the next class period, students are to bring in their individual responses to question 2. I then compile all the responses to the first two questions and categorize them in a way that makes sense (i.e., questions related to young adolescent development, curriculum, instruction, and so forth). I add to the list those topics that I feel are important for students to know and explain to the class why I feel they are important. For example, most students have not heard of "the middle school concept" and thus do not know to ask about what it is.

The next step is for the entire class to look at the questions and concerns that have been listed and engage in a discussion on how they would best like to learn about such topics. The suggestions then guide the development of the activities and lessons for the course. Throughout the semester, we frequently revisit the list of questions and concerns and make class decisions about what topics have the highest priority for them.

The assignment and assessment portion of the class is also designed on the basis of the individual interests of class members. I ask the class the final question and as a large group they brainstorm ideas. In general, the suggestion is made that students have the opportunity to learn and explore material in ways that are most valuable and interesting to them individually—whether it be reading, writing, interviewing, observing, analyzing case studies, viewing videos, or some other option.

COMMENTARY

In *A Middle School Curriculum: From Rhetoric to Reality*, Jim Beane (1993) favors an integrative curriculum design for middle school students that not only focuses on general education but helps the students explore themselves and their concerns about society. This design dissolves curriculum boundaries and focuses on major concepts that emerge from significant personal and social issues.

The middle school curriculum, according to Beane, should be embedded with the skills, knowledge, and democratic ideals that students need to function in society. As such, learning experiences are identified and developed by students in collaboration with their teachers.

If teacher educators believe in the integrative curriculum design, it should be modeled in the college classroom for future middle school teachers. By taking control of their own curriculum, preservice teachers will learn what it means to allow middle school students to take control of theirs. By answering their own questions about middle school students and how the middle school works, future teachers learn how to design a curriculum that responds to the questions and concerns of their students.

Some of my students have had difficulty with the idea of helping to design the course. Most college students have not been in a situation where they can choose those things that have meaning to them. One student was not pleased when we began to develop the syllabus. He commented, "I came here to have an expert tell me what I should know." In the evaluation at the end of the semester, however, he stated, "At first I didn't like the structure. I didn't think I would get much out of it. But I found out that many things I believed to be factual were not that simple. This class was very thought-provoking."

Another student commented, "I especially enjoyed the development phase of the course. It provided answers to a misunderstood subject."

In general, my students have opted for an assessment design in which they can choose the projects they want to do. My only requirement is that they do at least one project in each of the following areas: young adolescent development, the middle school concept, curriculum, and instruction. Options provided include such things as reading articles; writing research papers; interviewing teachers, students or parents; viewing videos; observing in the classroom; presenting an area of interest to the class; analyzing case studies; or developing their own project. I assign points to each option. If students accumulate a certain number of points, they receive an "A." What I have discovered is that most students go far and above what they need to do to get the "A." They get excited about reading articles, interviewing teachers, or researching instructional strategies, and because they are motivated, they keep working—long after they have accumulated enough points. No longer are they working just for the "A," but for knowledge as well. It is as powerful a curriculum model for them as it will be for their students.

Comments from students concerning the assessment portion of the course include:

- "I like the empowerment."
- "This was probably one of the best classes that I have taken. I was able to do what I wanted, when I wanted, and wherever I wanted. I liked being able to choose and do what is meaningful to me. I had the chance to do observations because I wanted to and not because I was forced to."
- "I liked being able to focus on my interests and concerns about teaching and not what you wanted me to learn about."
- "Creating how we wanted to learn this material was not only beneficial to what we learn but also in giving us some perspective as to how these kids are feeling."

I have found that the energy generated by my students during this course is very similar to the energy I feel when I visit middle schools. My students are involved in a variety of projects and are constantly checking out articles, books, videos, or case studies from my file box. Their energy drives their learning in much the same way self-directed learning drives the enthusiasm and learning of middle school students.

When asked at the end of the course what was the most important thing they learned, one student replied, "The most important thing I learned is that middle school kids need choices and some decision making power to make their learning more meaningful." Having college students be involved in the design and implementation of the syllabus provides both the experience of making choices for themselves and the model for providing this opportunity to their students.

REFERENCE

Beane, James A. (1993). *A middle school curriculum: From rhetoric to reality.* Columbus, Ohio: National Middle School Association.

Exploring Curricular Models

LINDA R. MORROW
University of Arkansas, Fayetteville

STRATEGY/ACTIVITY/ASSIGNMENT

As a means of learning about middle school curriculum, students in my preservice and graduate-level middle level methods classes are divided into three groups, each group focusing on the curricular model of James Beane, Heidi H. Jacobs, or Susan Kovalik. This learning activity is implemented near the end of the semester, after the students have had opportunities to learn about the social, emotional, physical, and intellectual characteristics and needs of middle level students as well as interdisciplinary teaming and flexible block scheduling.

Each group is given a packet of information describing the model of Beane, Jacobs, or Kovalik. Each student reads an article by the author on whom his or her group is focusing and then writes a summary that is shared with the group. The group then writes a summary of that particular model to share with the entire class. Groups have presented this information via the use of overhead transparencies, posters, and role playing.

In this manner, the entire class experiences an in-depth look at three curricular models. The presentations are evaluated on the basis of their accuracy of content, participation of all group members, and effectiveness of presentation format.

A lively discussion ensues as a result of these presentations, as students compare the pros and cons of the three models. Since this activity is completed just prior to the students' working in teams to write an interdisciplinary unit of study, there is a great deal of interest in determining the most effective model for writing middle level curriculum.

COMMENTARY

I've found this activity to be an efficient way to relay important information in an already crowded semester. Since curriculum often does not receive the attention it should and because of its importance, I feel that students need to take a serious look at the rationale for such recommended changes. Students are often surprised to find theorists who focus on the parallels between the needs of early adolescents and themes and topics explored through the lens of particular disciplines. It also gives students another opportunity to experience group inquiry focusing on higher-order thinking skills. This activity is completed during class time, when the class is scheduled as a three-hour evening class. For class periods of less time, students are asked to read the articles outside of class and come to the next class session prepared to share a summary with their group. The preparation of transparencies, posters, role playing, and so forth is completed during class time. Students respond positively to learning about these curricular models in such a succinct manner.

Examining Issues Surrounding Implementation of an Integrated Curriculum

SUSAN E. BRECK
Southwest Missouri State University, Springfield

INTRODUCTION/RATIONALE

Curriculum—what is taught and how it is taught in public schools—has been the topic of serious debate in the United States for decades. Even when a type of curriculum is identified as the most developmentally appropriate, as the middle school movement has done with integrated curriculum, discussion over the specifics continues. As is evidenced by the attendance at the debates about integrated curriculum between Drs. James Beane and Paul George at recent NMSA national conferences, this is a healthy and important discussion among a large and far-ranging constituency. Everyone from students and their parents to content-area college professors rightly has an interest in public middle school curriculum.

After reading Beane's (1993) *A Middle School Curriculum: From Rhetoric to Reality* (2nd ed.) for a middle school curriculum graduate class, students are given the following assignment to introduce them to the various perspectives on middle school curriculum and to help clarify their own professional perspective on middle level curriculum.

STRATEGY/ACTIVITY/ASSIGNMENT

The Everyville School district has decided to reexamine the curriculum model used in its middle school. As a result, several teachers have approached the school board with a proposal to implement a curriculum model based on James Beane's theories outlined in *A Middle School Curriculum: From Rhetoric to Reality.* The school board decides to establish a commission consisting of representatives of several groups who have expressed an interest in the outcome of the decision. The commission is formed with the following groups: teachers and administrators who currently staff Everyville Middle School; parents and students; and others with an interest in the middle school curriculum (composition of this group is to be determined by the class). The school district charges this commission with the task of selecting the most appropriate curriculum for Everyville Middle School. In order to gain widespread consensus, the board has arranged special meetings for members of the commission to express their support of, or concerns with, Beane's model.

After receiving this scenario, the class brainstorms a list of those who would be included in the "others with an interest" group and decides the specific composition for that group. The class is then randomly assigned to one of six groups:

1. teachers and administrators who currently staff Everyville Middle Schools and who support the implementation of Beane's curriculum model

2. teachers and administrators who currently staff Everyville Middle Schools and who oppose the implementation of Beane's curriculum model
3. parents and students who support the implementation of Beane's curriculum model
4. parents and students who oppose the implementation of Beane's curriculum model
5. others with an interest who support the implementation of Beane's curriculum model
6. others with an interest who oppose the implementation of Beane's curriculum model

Each group is assigned the task of developing and presenting a 20-minute position statement from the perspective of their assigned special interest group. Each statement must represent the researched position of their assigned special interest group. Students are given two weeks to complete this assignment. They are encouraged to include in their research the five articles in the "Focus Section: Curriculum Integration: Proceeding with Cautious Optimism" in the *Middle School Journal,* *28*(1), 3–26 (a section resulting from the first debate between Drs. Beane and George over integrated curriculum at the NMSA national conference in New Orleans, November 1995). It is also suggested, if possible, that students interview a representative of their special interest group.

EVALUATION

After all the special interest groups have presented their position statements to the class, each student is required to write a one- to two-page position paper outlining his or her own professional opinion on the appropriate curriculum model to be implemented in Everyville Middle School. The paper must include research supporting the position and discuss the perceived impact this decision will have on the school district.

COMMENTARY

I originally developed this assignment for a distance learning class with two sites. I assigned one site to represent the groups who supported Beane's model and the other site as those who opposed the model. The students seemed to enjoy the assignment and were very creative in their presentations. The assignment created an atmosphere of open professional discussion in which I learned as much as the students did about the effects of interdisciplinary teaching on those concerned.

Note: In 1997, Beane published a new text on curriculum, *Curriculum Integration: Designing the Core of Democratic Education*, which I will use in future classes.

REFERENCES

Beane, J. A. (1993). *A middle school curriculum: From rhetoric to reality.* (2nd ed.). Columbus, OH: National Middle School Association.

Beane, J. A. (1997). *Curriculum integration: Designing the core of democratic education.* New York: Teachers College Press

Developing Curriculum Themes

TRUDY KNOWLES
Westfield State College, Westfield, MA

ACTIVITY

"The Middle School and Its Students" is an undergraduate introductory class for preservice middle level educators. During our discussion about curriculum, middle level students are invited into the class and, during the two-hour session, are led through the process of developing curriculum themes using the model advocated by James Beane in *A Middle School Curriculum: From Rhetoric to Reality* (1993). The college students are involved in helping the students condense, refine, and choose themes for study. These themes do not focus on any one subject area but are based on the significant questions and concerns that young adolescents have about themselves and the world around them.

At the outset of the class period, a discussion is held with the middle level students about what types of things they learn in school and who is responsible for choosing those things. They are then presented with the idea of being able to choose what they would like to learn in school on the basis of the questions and concerns they have about their world.

In a large group discussion, facilitated by the college professor, the middle level students are asked to express their questions and concerns about the world (including school, family, friends, city, state, country, and so forth). Their comments are listed on large pieces of paper. They are then asked what questions and concerns they have about themselves. These are also listed. The college students are observers during this discussion.

The process of identifying questions and concerns takes from thirty minutes to an hour. Smaller groups are then randomly formed, with about four middle level students grouped together with four college students (depending on class numbers). The middle level students usually want to stay with their friends in the small groups but tend to be very flexible in terms of where they go and with whom they interact. Together, the middle level and college students look at the lists generated and begin to combine similar themes, group them in ways that make sense, and delete those that are redundant. When they have completed that process, each small group generates a list of the ten themes in which they are most interested.

Gathering in the large group again, each small group presents their ten with some explanation of how they combined or chose those ten. We analyze the ten that each group has come up with in order to ascertain if there are any that are common to all groups. As a large group we begin to delete, combine, and re-group.

Continuing either as a large group or breaking into small groups again, students choose their top and bottom three out of the latest lists. These are listed for whole group discussion, and the middle level students then pick the first theme they would like to study if given the choice. It is a process of discussion, thinking, compromise, and consensus.

Once a theme has been chosen, the middle level students talk about what they think would be important to learn about this theme and how they would like to go about learning it. If time permits during the two-hour class, college students ask the middle level students questions related to issues of instruction, curriculum, and assessment. The middle school students then give feedback on how they feel about this process of choosing curriculum themes.

COMMENTARY

In *A Middle School Curriculum: From Rhetoric to Reality*, Jim Beane (1993) advocates a middle school curriculum based on a curriculum integration model in which the students' exploration of themselves and society is an integral component. This design centers on major concepts that emerge from students' significant personal and social concerns. Beane does not advocate merely asking students what they are interested in or what they want to learn about but suggests providing students the opportunity to seriously study those issues that are personally and socially significant.

The middle school curriculum, according to Beane, should be embedded with the skills, knowledge, and democratic ideals that students need to function in society. As such, once themes are chosen for study, learning experiences are identified and developed by students in collaboration with their teachers.

This activity provides college students with an opportunity to implement Beane's model hand in hand with middle level students. The college students first listen to the questions and concerns that the middle level students have. They then participate with them in analyzing these questions. Through observation and participation, the college students begin to see the depth of understanding, concern, and knowledge that middle level students have. The whole process allows the college students to begin to develop the conceptual understanding and skills to implement a curriculum integration model in their classroom.

I have used this activity in an introductory class on the middle school. It followed class discussions of different curriculum models (i.e., single subject vs. curriculum integration), and it was followed by an analysis of the curriculum at the middle level and whether it meets the needs of the middle level student.

Although developing themes with a class of middle level students may actually take days to complete, by necessity this process has been condensed to about two hours for the purposes of the college class. I am fortunate that I teach the class in the evenings and have a large block of time to work within.

When we first began the process of identifying questions and concerns about the world, although not hesitant to give their ideas, the middle level students responded in what seemed to be a superficial manner ("Why is a quarter round?" "Why do locker rooms always smell?"). When they began to see that all of their questions and concerns were going to be taken seriously, the tone changed. Students began bringing up topics that were of concern to them. One student talked at length about his concern regarding genetic engineering and cloning. He was worried that parents would then have the ability to choose the type of kids they wanted, thus extinguishing diversity. Another student expressed concern about the powerlessness that young adolescents have.

"Without us, the schools wouldn't even exist," he said. "And yet they give us no input into what happens here."

What follows are some of the responses from one group of middle level students when asked what questions and concerns they have about the world (the groupings are mine):

- Technology of the future: cloning, anti-matter energy, space travel, genetic engineering, "designer children," life on other planets
- Pollution and other environmental problems
- Dating, making friends, peer pressure
- Power-hungry people
- Government, foreign policy: Why do politicians lie?
- Hanson and the Spice Girls: stupid music
- Subliminal messages
- Child pornography, manipulation, molestation, and abuse
- Stereotypes: Why do people judge you according to how you look?
- The Holocaust
- Cults, Satanists, the KKK
- Hypocrites
- Prostitution
- And the old standbys: racism, poverty, gangs, drugs, AIDS, sexism, discrimination, unemployment, teen pregnancy, violence

When the lists were compiled and analyzed, the middle level students overwhelmingly picked a unit on teen problems (including dating, teen pregnancy, gangs, peer pressure) as the one they would like to study first. The second and third areas of interest were discrimination and "back to the future" (a unit on technology issues of the future).

This activity can also be used in middle level curriculum classes. Initially, themes can be developed with middle level students. The college students can then take those themes and develop units of study that address them, embed necessary skills, and respond to any state or local curriculum mandates.

My college students were generally impressed with the maturity and the depth of questions and concerns from the young adolescents. The myth that middle level students are only concerned about how they look and who they date was dispelled, replaced by the idea that those personal concerns tie into much larger ideas.

Comments from my students included:

> "The best thing about this class was bringing in the middle school students. This was a great idea. It gave us an opportunity to learn about them and what they like and dislike," and, "They are so insightful. I was amazed."

In my introductory class, some of my students are already middle level teachers who need additional courses for new state mandates in middle level education. A few attempted this process in the regular classroom and were also amazed at the level of intensity and motivation that developed. One teacher in particular found that those students who had traditionally been uninvolved and mediocre students not only became responsive but the leaders of the class and "A" students.

Seeing the interests, enthusiasm, and energy of the middle level students has convinced some of my students that middle school is not where they should be teaching. One student commented, "I do not like teaming. . . . I don't think students have the right to tell us what to teach." Another said, "Through being around middle school students, I figured out that I'm not cut out to be a middle school teacher." Doing this activity has convinced some that middle level teaching is not where they should be. It has convinced many others that it is.

Understanding what is involved in being a middle level teacher requires analyzing developmental issues of young adolescents and relating those issues to creating a developmentally responsive curriculum with appropriate instruction and assessment. My goal is to assist preservice teachers in developing those understandings and to become committed to middle level education. This activity provides a mirror for developing those understandings and helping preservice teachers assess their commitment.

REFERENCE

Beane, J. A. (1993). *A middle school curriculum: From rhetoric to reality.* Columbus, OH: National Middle School Association.

Teacher–Librarian Collaboration: Selection of Appropriate Information for Resource Units

BARBARA R. SAFFORD
University of Northern Iowa, Cedar Falls

DONNA SCHUMACHER
University of Northern Iowa, Cedar Falls

STRATEGY/ACTIVITY/ASSIGNMENT

In the course "Middle Level Curriculum," university students develop thematic resource units appropriate for grades 4–8. Students form teams that approach the thematic unit holistically, from multiple subject areas. The unit contains a variety of introductory, developmental, and culminating activities. Required elements of the resource unit include a rationale for using the selected theme, semantic maps, concepts related to the learning objectives, outcomes (cognitive, skill, affective), activities, evaluation strategies for the teaching and learning processes, annotated bibliographies of teacher resources, and student resources and nonbook materials.

The initial phase in this thematic unit development project is the examination of the topic itself and the creation of a semantic map that might be based on subject areas, learning styles, multiple intelligences, or unit concepts. Preliminary research is conducted by the team of university students in the college of education's curriculum laboratory using texts, curriculum guides, scope and sequence charts, and commercial materials as the team refines themes and identifies grade-level appropriate outcomes.

At this stage in their planning, each student team then forms another partnership with a student from the Division of School Library Media Studies who acts as the librarian in support of the curricular plan. The teams (preteachers and prelibrarians) meet for several sessions in the university library's Youth Collection, which is a model school library. The librarian team members practice their roles as information specialists and curriculum consultants. The teacher team members refine their selection of themes, and the librarian team members conduct preliminary information searches for materials in a wide variety of formats within the range of subjects associated with the themes. The librarian team members are familiar with specialized search tools and strategies and can identify a wide range of book and nonbook sources that teachers might select for their units.

Partnership meetings between the teacher and librarian team members further explore the unit topics in order to determine viability in terms of available resources. The teacher/librarian team investigates the unit topic and explores the elements of unit design, such as the group and individual use of materials, opportunities for cross-curricular connections, multiple learning styles, and evaluation techniques. They discuss the objectives and outcomes and whether the topic is too broad or too specific. The librarian, using a specially created unit planning document that elicits information about the teachers' objectives, serves as a professional sounding board to help envision the unit concept. Such details as length of unit, its depth and scope, its grade level, and possible approaches to instruction might be discussed.

In the second stage, the teacher/librarian teams work together to establish plans to identify sources and types of information. These may include home libraries, public libraries, community resources, regional educational collections, the Internet (WWW, listservs, newsgroups), books, periodicals, reference materials, professional bibliographies, videos, CD-ROMs, and computer software. The materials are collected and evaluated for appropriateness. Criteria for inclusion are accuracy, recency, literacy-level, content, and authenticity.

During the third stage, all participants share the materials they have discovered. Methods for finding additional sources are also investigated. Student librarians prepare working bibliographies and communicate via e-mail with their teams. At this stage the unit may be restructured on the basis of the resources identified. The teaching team continues to explore resources as they work through the entire unit development process. They make final selection of those resources they feel are most appropriate for inclusion in their unit bibliographies. Librarians continue to be available to their teams for both resource identification and unit consultation.

COMMENTARY

This activity in itself models the kind of cooperative planning between teachers and librarians that make interdisciplinary instruction in middle schools more effective. Because the professor of curriculum and the professor of school library media studies work together with the class, a model of cross-discipline teaching is provided to both middle school and library-studies students. The opportunity for experiential learning that this activity provides both preteachers and prelibrarians is powerful; student reactions have been positive from both groups. The middle level curriculum students experience the value and pleasure of collaborating with a professional who has an extensive knowledge and awareness of both materials and children. The librarians discover the pleasure of matching information sources to instructional needs voiced by real teachers. Both groups of students learn to communicate and negotiate. The librarians learn to ask better questions about goals and objectives and about the kinds of materials teachers want. The teachers learn to articulate their unit concepts clearly and to be specific in their requests for information. Each group learns about the other's roles in a collaborative environment.

Analyzing the Presentation of Social Justice Issues in Middle School Literature

SHARON TOOMEY CLARK
Claremont Graduate University, Claremont, CA

MARGARET ALBERTSON
Azusa Pacific University, Azusa, CA

STRATEGY/ACTIVITY/ASSIGNMENT

In this activity, education students critically analyze the manner in which issues of social justice are presented in middle school literature. They prepare a presentation that critiques a selection of five or six books, specifically addressing an issue of their choice. In addition, they prepare a brief annotated bibliography of the books they critiqued to be distributed to their classmates.

This activity requires education students to consider one element of social justice and investigate the manner in which it is presented in several works of literature. The issue may be homelessness, the marginalization of language minority students, gender inequality, nontraditional families, and so forth. The student begins by identifying an issue of personal importance. While finding examples from professional journals might be one way to investigate this topic, a hands-on approach will expose the student to many books not necessarily cited in the journals. For this reason, the student next visits a large bookstore because the number

of current middle school books therein invariably exceeds those found in
school or local libraries. The student surveys the available books on the
topic, recording title, author, and a one- or two-sentence summary. (The
summary can even be the one written on the copyright page.) Although
the student may find books that he or she wants to add to his or her future
classroom library, purchasing books is not a requirement. Provided with
a sense of the breadth of available adolescent literature, the student next
makes a trip to a library to select books to read and analyze. For this activity, bad examples are as informative as goods examples!

Books are brought to class for the presentation. They are initially
displayed and later made available for interested students to examine.
Presentations should include the student's criteria for analysis and the
process that led to its development. Any particular difficulties related to
finding literature about the student's topic should also be reported.

COMMENTARY

Middle school students do not always have access to books that address
issues of social justice. In fact, outdated books with marginalizing messages are more likely to be available in many libraries. Education students need to become aware of current directions in literature for middle
school students in order to supplement their students' available literary
choices. Through this activity, education students can become familiar
not only with current books that have personal value to them but, by
sharing bibliographies, they can enhance their awareness of current middle school literature. More importantly, they will have an understanding
of the ways in which social justice issues are presented to their students,
and they will be able to make better choices about reading curricula.

Service Learning:
A Model of Democratic Education

WILLIAM C. McBETH
University of Wisconsin–Platteville

STRATEGY/ACTIVITY/ASSIGNMENT

At the University of Wisconsin-Platteville, students seeking middle level
teaching endorsement are required to take two team-taught classes. In

middle level block I, the focus is on characteristics of the young adolescent. Middle level block II (MLII) focuses on instructional strategies and classroom practices that are appropriate for the education of young adolescents. One of these instructional strategies is service learning.

During MLII, the instructors model good teaching practice by using the instructional strategies taught in this course, and service learning is one of the strategies. Through brainstorming sessions, aided by a perusal of newspapers and phone books, students identify organizations that might support service learning projects. Once identified, representatives from these agencies are contacted, invited to class, and asked to provide a brief presentation identifying what their organization does and how students could help them accomplish their mission. Students may choose a project on the basis of presentations made or select one of their own. Once a project is selected, students are asked to complete a contract (Appendix A) in which they identify and describe the service learning project, indicate how they will complete the required ten hours of involvement, and identify the expected outcomes of their project.

At this point, it is the instructor's responsibility to scrutinize the proposed outcomes to ensure that they are germane to the teaching of young adolescents. The learning outcomes must reflect sound educational philosophies and practices. For teacher educators, this piece is critical. We need to view the education of preservice teachers on two levels. The first level is as students in class who are there to learn about education. The second level is as potential teachers who must reflect on what they will do, how they will do it, and what the potential outcomes might be for their students. This second level is where our best teaching is conducted, and this is the level at which the engagement in a service learning project is aimed.

Once all parties have signed the contract, students arrange their personal schedules to accommodate the required ten hours. During the semester, students engage in general reflection by keeping logs or journals of their service learning experiences. They also reflect more specifically on how their experiences have affected them as teachers of early adolescents through guided in-class reflections.

While there were several service learning projects that were proposed and accepted, three were particularly noteworthy. The New Friends Club was organized by a group of six students in MLII. They worked closely with the local middle school on the identification of students in need of social support and skill development. These students worked one on one and developed group activities to help the middle school students with social skill development. Two MLII students who worked with a group of drama students from the local middle school organized the Reading Play. The goal of this activity was to create a play on the importance of reading to children and deliver it to participants in an adult literacy program. The adults in the literacy program were working on improving their levels of literacy as well as their parenting skills. The middle level librarian worked with the local community librarian by reading books to children during a youth reading time and shelving books that were appropriate reading for the early adolescents.

During structured in-class reflections, preservice teachers identified some of the effects of their service learning projects. These effects included learning about their potential students and about problems within the Platteville community, which they had previously thought existed only in urban communities. They also identified learning outcomes that are more difficult to structure within any particular class. These outcomes were intrapersonal in nature and included such things as persistence, tolerance, patience, self-esteem, and adjustment to personal philosophies of education.

COMMENTARY

Service learning is on the rise as a learning/instructional strategy. It is based on the democratic principles of schooling: students help to identify their project, develop project outcomes, and engage in reflective practice. Service learning differs from community service through its direct connection to the instructional outcomes.

There is a paucity of research directed at investigating the effects of service learning on student learning, skill development, and attitudes; more research has been conducted on the effects of community service. In her work, Hedin (1995) cited studies that indicated substantial gains in knowledge (when appropriate testing procedures were used), problem solving, open-mindedness, critical thinking, interpersonal skills, level of personal and social responsibility, civic involvement, commitment to basic democratic values, self-esteem, and moral and ego development.

The preservice teachers of MLII identified service learning as one of the most valuable components of the course. Prior to engaging in a project, they had trouble envisioning how to integrate their project with the curriculum. After the completion of the project, they were able to articulate how they could connect service learning to academic work in the classroom. Lastly, they identified intrapersonal understandings that can be developed through making a positive difference in the world around them.

REFERENCE

Hedin, D. (1995). Current research and methods of assessing community service. In R. W. Cairn & J. C. Kielsmeier, (Eds.), *Growing hope: A sourcebook on integrating youth service into the school curriculum* (pp. 109–119). St. Paul, MN: National Youth Leadership Council,

APPENDIX A

Service Learning Agreement
The University of Wisconsin–Platteville

This project requires a minimum of ten hours of service. The completion of this form identifies the project for your instructors. This form also indicates that you have contacted a site supervisor and have reached an agreement on the nature of your project (as indicated by the first signature of the site supervisor). The site supervisor's second signature indicates that you have successfully completed the required minimum of ten hours of service.

Name(s): _____ **Date:** _____

Work site: _____

Description of service learning project: _____
_____

Schedule: _____
_____

Expected outcomes: _____
_____

Signature of student: _____

Signature of site supervisor: _____
  (Signature one; agreement to participate)

Signature of site supervisor: _____
  (Signature two; project was successfully completed)

Looking at Curriculum

PATRICIA H. PHELPS
University of Central Arkansas, Conway

STRATEGY/ACTIVITY/ASSIGNMENT

There are numerous curricular materials for middle level students. Textbooks, curriculum guides, CD-ROMs, and trade books are widely available for classroom use. Prospective teachers need opportunities to examine such materials and evaluate their usefulness before being expected to implement middle level curriculum effectively.

Arnold (1985) presented the following characteristics of a responsive curriculum: (1) helps students make sense of themselves and their world; (2) uses appropriate methods and materials; (3) emphasizes knowledge and thinking skills over information; and (4) values concrete, real-world experience. After reviewing the principles of curriculum design relative to middle level education, students can be assigned the following task either as an individual activity or as a small group project: Students should locate a curricular resource in their particular subject area. The selected materials should be evaluated using Arnold's (1985) criteria (or some other criteria established by the instructor). Preservice teachers should also be encouraged to offer suggestions. A written and/or oral presentation can be required.

COMMENTARY

Beginning teachers are often reluctant to modify existing curriculum because they lack knowledge and experience. This activity is designed to equip prospective middle school teachers with the knowledge and skills necessary to evaluate and to enhance curriculum. Providing future teachers with the opportunity to suggest modifications helps to increase their self-confidence. As a result, their ability to create curriculum that is responsive to the needs of early adolescents is also improved.

Students enjoy the hands-on nature of this activity. They respond positively to it and appreciate the focus provided by having a useful framework. Having the opportunity to share their evaluations in class broadens students' awareness of available materials and helps them see possible interdisciplinary connections and resources.

REFERENCE

Arnold, J. (1985). A responsive curriculum for emerging adolescents. *Middle School Journal, 16*(3), 3;14-18.

Doing Service Learning with Young Adolescents: The Lessons of Recent Research

PETER C. SCALES
Search Institute, Manchester, MO

In recent years, there has been an upsurge of interest in youth and community service, particularly in the idea of integrating service within the middle level curriculum. More than the typical curriculum, the experiential nature of doing service is thought to be a form of authentic instruction as well as promoting authentic student performance and authentic assessment. For service to truly become service *learning,* there must be substantial and thoughtful student preparation before the service experience, a well-crafted service experience itself, and considerable student reflection about the meaning of the experience and its connection to the subject matter. According to Newmann, Secada, and Wehlage (1995), such authenticity is characterized by students gaining a deep knowledge of a subject by studying disciplinary content, experiencing a connection of the subject to the real world and appreciating its value beyond school, and engaging in substantive oral and written conversation and communication about their experience. It is expected that excellent service learning will better engage students than most of their other instructional and/or curricular school experiences and have positive effects on their social responsibility and academic performance.

The description of the structure that characterizes authentic curriculum—its positive student outcomes of school engagement, social responsibility, and academic performance—represents an ideal for service-learning programs. Research suggests that most service-learning programs do not attain that level of integration with the curriculum (Scales & Blyth, 1997). And yet, done well, recent studies indicate that service learning can have desirable effects on middle level students.

Search Institute (Scales, Blyth, Berkas, & Kielsmeier, 1998) studied more than 1,000 students in three sixth through eighth grade–configured middle schools. About half the students were enrolled in service-learning courses ranging from fewer than 10 hours to more than 31; the other half, acting as controls, were not. Findings indicated that over the course of the school year, service-learning students maintained their concern for others' welfare, whereas the concern of control group students dropped significantly. Moreover, service-learning students also declined far less than control students in their reported level of communication with parents about school—a finding never before reported.

Those findings may appear modest. They were not surprising given that, on average, students in the service-learning programs in this study had relatively little exposure to service learning, with most of the programs lasting only 10 hours over a several-week period. For most students, service learning was just a small part of one or two classes, not fully integrated across their entire curriculum. In addition, most of the teachers had very little prior preparation for implementing service-learning programs. Finally, only a minority of students experienced the ideal of considerable preparation and reflection surrounding their service experience; for example, just 14 percent said they did a lot of reflection.

In many respects, then, the programs studied were typical of service learning in middle schools today. And yet, when effects were examined as a function of the duration of the service-learning program, the degree of reflection experienced, as well as other features of the programs, other significant findings emerged.

Students who had more than 30 hours of service learning significantly improved their sense of efficacy in helping others and slightly improved their pursuit of better grades compared with other students. Students who said they had done a lot of reflection in service learning, compared with other service-learning and control students, significantly improved their sense of duty to help others and their pursuit of better grades, and declined less in their commitment to doing classwork. Pursuit of good grades is a measure of how important it is to the student to be well evaluated and get high marks in a course.

Commitment to classwork is actually closer to the idea of engagement than it is to the pursuit of good grades. Commitment to classwork is a measure of students' interest level about the classes they are currently taking, how bored they are, and whether they'd like to take similar courses again. One could be, in general, interested in working hard to get good grades, and yet find oneself quite uninterested in the specific classes currently taken. Finally, students who said they were motivated to do better in their other classes because of service learning significantly improved their sense of duty to help others and their sense of efficacy in helping others. They also maintained their belief that school provided plentiful developmental opportunities and encouraged their pursuit of learning for its own sake.

These rather impressive results suggest that if service-learning programs have particular key features, then they may have the positive impacts desired. In the Search Institute study, the most impressive results were seen among students who had more than 30 hours of service learning, had reflected a lot on the experience, and who felt motivated by service learning. Even more impressive results on school engagement and academic performance were observed by Melchior (1997) in a Brandeis University study of middle level programs that lasted, on average, more than 50 hours, or five times the average duration of the programs we studied.

Taken together, the results of the Search Institute and Brandeis University studies suggest that significant effects of service learning on academic success variables will most likely occur when:

- students experience more than 30 hours of service learning across the school year
- students have considerable time for preparation and reflection about the service experience
- teachers are formally trained in the standards and pedagogy of good service learning (beyond a one-day workshop, which was the most common training teachers in the Search Institute study had received)
- service learning is truly integrated across the curriculum
- academic achievement is explicitly named as an expected outcome (in our study, this was the least common student goal among service-learning teachers, whereas increasing student altruism was the most common goal)
- the potential effects on parent-adolescent communication about school—a powerful influence on academic success—are maximized by explicitly incorporating more intentional parent-student activities into the service-learning program

The debate on whether service learning can have important academic effects should be settled. Given the appropriate program features and commitment, it can be a stimulating part of the primary methods we use to engage and teach young adolescents.

REFERENCES

Melchior, A. (1997). *Interim report: National evaluation of Learn and Serve America school and community-based programs.* Washington, DC: Corporation for National Service.

Newmann, F. M., Secada, W. G., & Wehlage, G. G. (1995). *A guide to authentic instruction and assessment: Vision, standards, and scoring.* Madison, WI: Center on Organization and Restructuring of Schools.

Scales, P. C., & Blyth, D. A. (1997). Effects of service learning: What we know and what we need to know. *The Generator—Journal of Service-Learning and Service Leadership, 17*(1), 6-9.

Scales, P. C., Blyth, D. A., Berkas, T., & Kielsmeier, J. (1998). The effects of service learning on middle school students' social responsibility and academic success. Minneapolis: Search Institute (ms. under review).

CHAPTER 4

Developmentally Appropriate Instruction

Brainstorming and Developing Lists of Hands-On, Minds-On Activities That Preservice Teachers Experienced During Their Middle Level and Junior High Years

SAMUEL TOTTEN

University of Arkansas, Fayetteville

STRATEGY/ACTIVITY/ASSIGNMENT

In order to set the stage for discussing hands-on, minds-on learning activities, I always have the preservice teachers in my middle level methods and principles course brainstorm and develop a list of the most engaging learning activities they experienced when in middle school and/or junior high. The session serves four basic purposes: (1) to introduce students to the purpose and process of brainstorming; (2) to have them reflect on how thought-provoking and engaging their middle and/or junior high school courses were; (3) to encourage them to begin to think about that which constitutes an exciting, minds-on, hands-on class versus that which is not; and (4) to mull over what they can learn and take from their own learning experiences as they move from being a student of teaching to a teacher of students.

Prior to conducting the brainstorming session, we initially discuss the purpose of brainstorming, e.g., to generate as many ideas as possible about a topic. We also go over and discuss the rules of brainstorming: (a) "anything goes," i.e., it is fair game to broach any idea or issue; (b) no one needs to raise his or her hand during a brainstorming session, but should feel free to call out his or her ideas; (c) when calling out an idea, one should be as succinct as possible so that the person at the board does not become overwhelmed; (d) various people can "piggyback" or play off another person's idea; (e) no comments—positive or negative—about an idea should be made by anyone, including the teacher, during the course of the brainstorming session; and (f) following the actual brainstorming session the class should conduct a debriefing session to discuss the feasibility of the ideas. Finally, we also discuss the power and beauty of using brainstorming in a classroom setting.

Next, we conduct the brainstorming session, listing all the students' ideas on the board. In order to facilitate and expedite the brainstorming session, two student volunteers come to the board to write down the ideas as they are generated. They are told that they, too, should feel free to join in the brainstorming session as they write down the various ideas. As students call out their ideas, I repeat what has been said in order to assist the individuals at the board. This is a simple but important task, as the volunteers often fall behind as the class generates ideas.

After the brainstorming session, we discuss the types of activities the students have listed on the board. Individuals who have come up with examples may expound on them in much more detail, and others in the class can ask questions about the learning activity or teaching strategy.

At the conclusion of the discussion, I give the following assignment: Each student must type up three to five of the most thought-provoking and engaging learning activities or projects that they experienced while in middle school or junior high and succinctly list or discuss the following elements: grade level, course or topic, basic focus of the activity or teaching strategy, the various steps or task involved, the appeal of the activity or project, whether he or she would use the task in his or her own classroom, and if so, why, and if not, why not. Finally, they are to turn in a disk and a hard copy with this information on it.

After all of the assignments are submitted, the disks are given to a secretary who collates the files, cleans up the spacing, numbers each item, and prints out a copy. The instructor reviews the items one by one, striking those that are, for whatever reason, pedagogically questionable. The file on the disk is revised on the basis of the changes, and copies of the final list are provided for everyone in the class.

The lists are distributed at the next class session, which continues the focus on hands-on, minds-on instructional strategies. At the outset of the session, the instructor comments on the items on the list and then continues to focus on the cognitive traits and intellectual abilities of young adolescents and instructional strategies that are ideal and appropriate for use at the middle level.

COMMENTARY

This session serves several useful purposes. First, it serves as a stimulating anticipatory set to our sessions on cognitive development and middle level pedagogy. Second, it proves to be extremely useful in encouraging preservice teachers to begin to reflect on what they, individually, found exciting, stimulating, challenging, or boring at the middle or junior high levels. Third, it generally prods them to begin to think about how they are going to tackle instruction in their own classes. Fourth, it provides them with some solid ideas they can take with them into their student teaching or fifth-year internship.

Most students find this to be an engaging activity. It allows them to recall their middle and junior high years and to gain a new appreciation of those teachers who had a passion for teaching and reaching young people. It also gets them to reflect on those teachers who were innovative and really engaged them in learning something that was memorable. It also makes them reflect on the types of teachers they hope not to become—those that were "satisfied" with lecturing and giving staid assignments that simply involved looking up information in the chapter of a book or doing a host of worksheets. When examining all of the different activities on the list generated, it also makes them appreciate just how many teachers are attempting to reach their students in exciting and new ways. Finally, they are always impressed by how many different and powerful ways there are to teach lessons.

An Introduction to Multiple Intelligences

SAMUEL TOTTEN
University of Arkansas, Fayetteville

STRATEGY/ACTIVITY/ASSIGNMENT

In both my undergraduate and graduate middle level methods courses I introduce my students to the concept of multiple intelligences. I do so in three major ways. First, throughout the course and in almost every session I model the use of multiple intelligences and engage my students in activities that span the various intelligences. Second, all students are required to read and write a short-response paper on Thomas Armstrong's (1994) *Multiple Intelligences in the Classroom*. Third, about a quarter of the way into the course, by which time the students have read and responded to Armstrong's book, I conduct a more formal introduction to the concept of multiple intelligences. That is what will be delineated here.

At the outset of the class session I read three very short children's books or stories to the class. (Sometimes, for variation, I may ask different students to read different booklets or stories on their own, or I may use a poem. When I use a poem, I will generally place it on the overhead, read it to the class, and then leave the overhead up during the remainder of the class session.) After all three stories have been read, the students— either individually, in pairs, or in triads—are required to respond to and interpret one of the stories in an innovative manner. Although many of the stories are quite short and ostensibly simple, students are encouraged to listen very carefully to the story in order to recall the storyline, the personality, the words and actions of the various characters, and so forth.

Over the past several years I have used a number of different books and stories, including, but not limited to, Sam Swope's *The Araboolies of Liberty Street*, Eve Bunting's *Fly Away Home*, and Eve Bunting's *Terrible Things*. No matter which stories are selected, it is imperative that each be quite different in regard to storyline, characters, setting, and tone. It is also a good idea to select pieces that provide diverse cultural perspectives, thus modeling how one can and should address multicultural concerns in as many ways as possible in one's class. Reading such stories is also an excellent opportunity to introduce preservice teachers to literature that is ideal for use with middle level students.

Sometimes a provocative poem that most, if not all, of the students have never read is used. One particularly interesting poem is Dan Pagis's "Written in Pencil in the Sealed Freightcar." Although this poem is likely to be too complex for most middle level students, it clearly illustrates the process of how to engage students in a multiple-intelligences activity.

The reading of the stories generally takes about fifteen minutes. Afterwards, students select a story on which to focus. Once stories are selected, the students decide to work either individually, in pairs, or in triads in order to develop their response to their specific story. They may present their interpretation in any way they wish. In the vernacular of multiple intelligences, it may involve any of the eight intelligences frequently cited by Howard Gardner (1983, 1993): linguistic, logical-mathematical, spatial, bodily-kinesthetic, musical, interpersonal, intrapersonal, and natural-ist. Having already read Armstrong's book, they know this may involve, for example, composing and singing a song, creating and doing a mime, creating and conducting a simulation, creating and doing a dance, creating a piece of art or music, and so forth. They are encouraged to be as creative as possible and informed that if they choose to do something representing the linguistic intelligence, then it should not be a staid lecture.

In order to facilitate the students' work I always bring in a variety of materials: old magazines with lots of colored pictures, large pieces of poster board, magic markers, crayons, pencils, pens, scissors, construc-tion paper of various colors, tacks, a ball of string, scotch tape, masking tape, paper clips of different sizes, a stapler, ruled paper, white paper, and, periodically, clay and water colors.

Students are informed that on completion of their interpretation, each individual, pair, or triad are required to conduct, perform, or display their interpretation for the rest of the class. Following each presentation, the rest of the class is required to: (1) guess which literary work the indi-vidual, pair, or triad has interpreted; and (2) discuss the meaning behind the interpretation.

During the next class session, each individual, pair, or triad presents his or her creation. Then, the rest of the class, as a group and out loud, guesses the booklet or story being presented and discusses it. Playing off of each others' ideas, there is considerable interaction as students ques-tion, comment, or provide interpretive suggestions. During this class ex-change, the individual, pair, or triad that designed the response remains silent, while observing and carefully listening to what is being said.

At the end of each critique by the larger group, the individual, pair, or triad is asked to comment on the group's interpretation (e.g., whether it was accurate, inaccurate, new insights the creator(s) gleaned from the class' interpretation/discussion), explain their own interpretation, tell the class how they decided to approach the story in the manner that they did (e.g., using the intelligence(s) they did), and explain how they actually designed/developed their interpretation.

COMMENTARY

When students are initially introduced to this activity, many are wary about it because they are not accustomed to doing something of this na-ture. However, once they begin the process of interpreting their story and realize that they have the freedom to do so in any way they wish, most become engaged in the process.

For the students—whether preservice teachers or experienced teachers—the process is often revelatory for numerous and different reasons. First, almost everyone (including the instructor, and this is true no how matter how many times this session is conducted) is amazed at the varied, imaginative, and powerful interpretations of the different individuals and groups. Second, in the debriefing session following the entire activity, many comment on how the activity and the varied responses to it have prompted them to consider how they could use it with their own students and with the content they teach. Third, many also comment on the high levels of thinking that resulted in both the development of the responses to the stories as well as the subsequent whole-class discussion/interpretation of the stories. In fact, students often comment on how astounded they are that such an ostensibly simple activity could result in such creative and critical thinking. Fourth, some always comment on how the activity truly resulted in a class discussion involving a great number of the class members versus the typical recitation (where the teacher asks a question and generally receives a single answer or two from one or two students, and then moves on to his/her next comment or question) that one sees and experiences in many classrooms. Fifth, some invariably comment that a major reason certain interpretations were so interesting is because many presenters tapped some of the intelligences less commonly used in classrooms or used the more commonly used intelligences (e.g., linguistic) in extremely creative ways. And sixth, a vast majority of the students comment on how much fun the entire activity was and how it turned a typical exercise into something highly engaging.

REFERENCES

Armstrong, T. (1994). *Multiple intelligences in the classroom.* Alexandria, VA: Association for Supervision and Curriculum Development.

Bunting, E. (1991). *Fly away home.* New York: Clarion Books.

Bunting, E. (1993). *Terrible things: An allegory of the Holocaust.* Philadelphia, PA: The Jewish Publication Society.

Gardner, H. (1983). *Frames of mind: The theory of multiple intelligences.* New York: Basic Books.

Gardner, H. (1993). *Multiple intelligences: The theory in practice.* New York: Basic Books.

Pagis, D. (1995). Written in pencil in the sealed freightcar. In Hilda Schiff (Ed.) *Holocaust poetry.* New York: St. Martin's Press, p. 180.

Swope, S. (1995). *The Araboolies of Liberty Street.* New York: Dragonfly Books.

Multiple Intelligences: An Introduction

STEVEN A. GREENGROSS
Southern Connecticut State University, New Haven

STRATEGY/ACTIVITY/ASSIGNMENT

The theory of multiple intelligences, as developed by Howard Gardner (1991), has the potential to truly revolutionize teaching, particularly at the middle level. The purpose of this activity is to sensitize students to multiple intelligences—what they are and how they can affect learning.

The activity begins with an "ice breaker" in which each student must find other students, each of whom can do one of the following: recite a short poem; complete a number sequence; explain how an electric motor works; stand on one foot for five seconds; whistle a few notes from a symphony; tell about a recent dream; and tell about something he or she recently has done alone. The rule is that the person must actually be able to do the activity, not just say he or she can. The seven tasks are, of course, examples of seven of the eight multiple intelligences as identified by Gardner: linguistic, logical-mathematical, bodily-kinesthetic, spatial, musical, interpersonal, and intrapersonal.

At the conclusion of the ice breaker, there is a whole-class discussion of the theory of multiple intelligences. Emphasis is placed on the following: that each person possesses all seven intelligences; that each person has certain of these intelligences that are primary intelligences and others that are secondary; and that teachers subconsciously tend to develop learning activities that emphasize their own primary intelligences.

This leads to the next phase of the activity in which each student identifies his or her own primary and secondary intelligences. This is done with the use of a checklist and a scoring grid. The students are given a list of the major characteristics for each intelligence (i.e., "likes to read" is a descriptor for linguistic intelligence), and each student checks off the ones that apply to him or her. After completing the checklist, the student adds up the checks under each intelligence and puts the results on a grid. The intelligences with the most check marks are the student's primary intelligences, and the ones with the fewest check marks are his or her secondary intelligences (Gardner, 1983).

Next, the students are put into groups on the basis of their primary intelligences: all the students whose primary intelligence is linguistic are

in one group, all the students who are logical-mathematical are in another group, and so on. The students are then given the following task to
complete: Using a common theme such as food, each group is to develop
three activities for students to do using that group's primary intelligence.
For example, one activity the spatial group may develop is to create a
food collage; the linguistic group may want students to use food as a
topic or theme for writing a haiku.

Once this task has been completed, the students are then regrouped
on the basis of their lowest score, or least intelligence. Each group looks
at the three activities created by the primary intelligence group and rank-
orders them: Number one is the activity the group would do if it had to
choose one of the three; number three is the one the group would least
like to do; number two is somewhere in the middle. The results are then
shared with the rest of the class.

This leads to the final phase of the activity, which is a whole-group
discussion based on the following questions: How would you feel if you
were a middle school student in a class in which the teacher's primary intelligence was your least intelligence? What impact would this have on
your grade in that class? How would this affect both your present and future attitudes toward school? The students are encouraged to talk about
how they felt when they were in the second group, the one that reflected
their least intelligence.

The next two questions are: "What do we do about all of this?" and
"How can we use what we know about multiple intelligences in our
teaching?" This leads to the next part of the course syllabus, which is a
detailed examination of nontraditional forms of assessment, such as performance-based assessment and portfolio assessment.

COMMENTARY

This activity is enjoyed by all students, and many take the time to mention it on their course information surveys that are completed at the end
of the semester. While the theory of multiple intelligences has relevance
to elementary and secondary schools, it seems to be particularly germane
to middle schools, for this is the time when early adolescents typically
begin to become aware of their own learning styles. In middle schools
throughout the United States, there are students who are experiencing
failure. Perhaps the answer can be detected via an examination of the
theory of multiple intelligences: that there are students whose primary
intelligences are not the same as their teacher's. It is possible that if these

students were given the opportunity to learn using their primary intelligences, the outcome might be radically different. It is certainly a hypothesis that warrants further examination.

REFERENCES

Gardner, H. (1983). *Frames of mind: The theory of multiple intelligences.* New York: Harper & Row Basic Books.

Gardner, H. (1991). *The unschooled mind: How children think and how schools should teach.* New York: Harper & Row Basic Books.

Unmasking Metacognition

MARY C. McMACKIN
Lesley College, Cambridge, MA

STRATEGY/ACTIVITY/ASSIGNMENT

I have used the following activity to help concretize the abstract term *metacognition*, and to focus students' attention on the strategies that mature readers use when constructing meaning from content-area texts.

I begin this activity by having the students brainstorm their definition of "metacognition." I then supply my favorite: "Metacognition occurs when thinkers begin to scrutinize their own thought processes and actively monitor, regulate, and orchestrate these processes in the service of some objective" (Devine, 1987, p. 239).

Second, I explain to the students that the objective for the following origami activity is to help them consciously think about what strategies they use when reading expository texts. I pass out a 3" × 5" index card to each student along with a sheet of paper that contains illustrated directions for making a jumping frog (Temko, 1986). I ask the students to focus on the strategies they use as they follow the directions to make the frog. After several minutes, we discuss the process and the range of strategies used: look at the illustrations, talk to the person beside me, look at the last illustration first to see what the finished frog should look like, read each direction first and then check the picture, reread each step before folding the index card, read the steps out loud, and so forth.

Third, I hand out a list of about twenty generic reading strategies.

These strategies include: generate questions before, during, and after reading; use pictures, graphs, charts; write notes in the margins; and visualize what you are reading. I ask the students to skim the list and check off the strategies they used in the origami activity.

Finally, the entire group tries to add at least three additional comprehension-building strategies to this list. As students make suggestions, their classmates skim the list to make sure these new suggestions weren't already listed.

COMMENTARY

This activity has proven to be beneficial in having students recognize that mature readers apply a wide range of strategies while reading—without always being aware of what they are doing. Yet, many middle school students, especially those with poor study skills, tend to rely on only a few strategies, which may or may not be effective. By going through this paper-folding activity and then discussing it, my students begin to realize the importance of teaching a variety of comprehension strategies to all students.

This metacognitive activity also serves to reinforce many of the concepts discussed in the course. Students who have had experiences with origami, for example, find it easy to create the jumping frog. Thus, the importance of prior knowledge is validated. Many students also discover how reassuring it is to have a "buddy" to talk to while interpreting the directions. We talk about how significant this is, especially at the middle school level, where social components of learning are so important. During the last two steps in this activity, in which the students skim the list of strategies and then add to the list, I try to model that rereading content-area materials for different purposes should be encouraged.

I've found this activity to be fun, easy to prepare, and very effective in unmasking the mystery of *metacognition*, while building awareness of strategies that readers use to construct meaning from texts.

REFERENCES

Devine, T. G. (1987). *Teaching study skills: A guide for teachers.* Newton, MA: Allyn and Bacon.

Temko, F. (1986). *Paper pandas and jumping frogs.* San Francisco, CA: China Books.

Modeling the K-W-L Strategy

LINDA R. MORROW
University of Arkansas, Fayetteville

STRATEGY/ACTIVITY/ASSIGNMENT

Students in my graduate-level "Methods of Middle School Instruction" course are asked to complete the following questionnaire during the first class session:

Name_____   Phone_____
E-mail address_____

1. Describe your teaching experiences in terms of grade level and/or content area. (Include current teaching position.)
2. What college courses and/or staff development sessions have you experienced that focused specifically on middle level philosophy, curriculum, and/or psychology?
3. What are your expectations in terms of the content of this course?
4. What is your motivation for taking this course?
5. What is your most vivid memory of junior high/middle school?

After students have had sufficient time to complete the questionnaire, we sit in a circle and share our experiences and expectations. Following the share time, I use the K-W-L (Ogle, 1986) strategy to activate students' prior knowledge of middle level education and to establish our learning goals. Students are asked to brainstorm what they know (K) and what they want to know (W) about middle level education. These responses are recorded on the board or on butcher paper. I later make an overhead transparency of these responses so that we can revisit them and add what is learned (L) throughout the semester.

COMMENTARY

The combination of the questionnaire and the K-W-L strategy demonstrates the importance of activating prior knowledge before introducing new learning at any level. It also personalizes learning. Early adolescents need to be actively engaged in learning that focuses first on their previous experiences and celebrates individual areas of expertise. Modeling the K-W-L strategy sends the message that active participation is the key to successful learning. Middle level students do not typically use such strategies as asking themselves what they know about a particular topic nor do they pose questions and make a record of new learning without such modeling by classroom teachers. Finally, this activity focuses on recognizing expertise among group members, as prior knowledge is activated and shared in the "What do you know?" stage of the strategy, *and* on inquiry-based learning as questions are posed in the "What do you want to know?" stage.

Practicing teachers report enjoying this activity because the tone of a risk-free, inquiry-based learning environment is established in the initial class meeting. The K-W-L process encourages the sharing of experiences and expectations and enhances a sense of community from the outset. Middle level classrooms should reflect this same environment if early adolescents are expected to flourish as learners.

REFERENCE

Ogle, D. (1986). KWL: A teaching model that develops active reading of expository text. *The Reading Teacher, 39,* 564-570.

Metaphor as a Teaching Tool

CARY LARSON-McKAY
California State University at Bakersfield

Much like the football players who are told by the coach to, "Go out there and win," or "Play good defense," but who are not instructed in the actual mechanics of the game, teachers are told to, "Give these children a good education," but are often sent out to teach without a full repertoire of teaching tools to help them in this endeavor. One such teaching tool that is seldom taught to the preservice teacher is the use of metaphor. Metaphors provide a teaching tool that is both practical and powerful. It fits into almost any classroom setting regardless of how much space is available, number of students in the class, or how much money is allotted for classroom materials. Metaphor as a teaching tool allows for a level of individualized instruction that surpasses most other designs for individualized learning, without the time-consuming need to plan for each student separately. In addition, metaphors can be used with a wide range of developmental levels, from preschool through old age. And, possibly best of all, most teachers are already familiar with the use of metaphor to support communication and learning, thereby minimizing the initial training and learning needed to design a metaphor-rich curriculum. However, to ensure the success of metaphors as a teaching/learning tool, the metaphors used must be clearly focused, understandable to students, and refined sufficiently to illuminate the specific learning goals sought.

STRATEGY/ACTIVITY/ASSIGNMENT

My undergraduate "Development in Middle Childhood" class is structured to make use of metaphors and metaphorical processes as a learning tool. Each section or chapter of the text is examined by the class through selected metaphors. This creates an interesting (in that it is moderately novel) and individualized experience for my students, while at the same time it models the use of metaphor as a teaching tool for the middle school classroom. To create the teaching/learning activities for this class, I preselect specific metaphors for the specific topics covered in our textbook and introduce students to the "metaphorical" approach. Early in the class we discuss the definition of metaphors, where we find them in use, and their potential as a teaching/learning tool. We discuss the potential of metaphors to improve recall, support multiple connections to content, and aid in the transfer of understanding from one domain of knowledge to another. The students are asked to work in small groups to "make sense" of the implied relationships between the content and the metaphor chosen for each topic. The following are examples of some of the metaphors used:

- The metaphor of a river flowing through town is used to explore the topic of increased freedom and attendant increase in responsibility of the young adolescent. I chose this metaphor because the concepts of flow and resistance found in fluid mechanics seems to relate well to this period of change in an adolescent's life.
- Brain development during middle and late childhood is connected to the metaphor of a telephone system. I chose a telephone system because the physical and organizational structures of the connections, use of cables, types of wires and their construction, evolving technology, and communication processes found in a telephone system parallel the physical development of the brain.

- Piaget's concept of concrete operations moving into formal operations is framed against the metaphor of the television news on CNN, where the news event is first briefly reported to the viewing audience, then followed by a more abstract analysis.
- Memory change is a pond of water because of the life cycle of a pond and its physical elements: water, plants, shore, fish, and animal life.
- Academic skill for this age student is a weather storm system because of the presence of chaos and fractal systems.
- Peer relationships are galaxies because of the interdependence and gravitational pulls of the solar system, stars, and planets.

The critical element of using metaphor as a teaching/learning tool is that the predetermined connections made by the instructor to explain and elaborate on the relationships between the specified content and the metaphor are not necessarily the same ones students make. The instructor must appreciate that the specifics of the connections the students make between the content and the given metaphor are not important—as long as the students have organized the material and can explain or defend the connections they make. It is the process of exploration that boosts the teaching power of metaphors. This flexibility of the specific details allows students to use personal knowledge, previous experience, and unique expressions to create a bridge between old knowledge and the new information to be acquired. The students individualize the new information using personal organization patterns to make the required connections for understanding. That is also why this process is so interesting—the students actively personalize their learning.

I ask the students to explain the connections they make by relating them to our textbook and additional readings. They are asked to give examples from their own experience and describe how these examples fit the metaphorical models developed. Whenever possible, the introduction of the metaphor includes actually experiencing aspects of the metaphor. This provides added detail to the relationships explored. We may sit around the pond in the middle of campus, visit the river at the edge of campus, or watch CNN as part of this introductory process. After a first round of small-group discussions and explication, we come together as a class for additional input and sharing, and the students are asked to expand on their models. Each group is also asked to give a variety of explanations and additional examples and to provide supporting data to assure classmates' understanding of the expanded metaphors. The intent of this second go-round is to add detail to the metaphoric connections, make the connections specific, and include as much material about the topic as possible in the relationships implicit within the metaphorical image (justifications and explanations about why certain elements of the topic do not fit are also welcome). Students are also encouraged to develop their own metaphors for the topics as they choose. Many groups develop several metaphors, which they ultimately share with the class.

COMMENTARY

The novelty of using metaphors as a specified learning tool creates a cognitive conflict that enhances interest and motivation. Students make the effort to understand the connections and multiple representations used to increase active learning events. The students spend the first couple of introductory periods, where I introduce the use of metaphor and ask them to explore it, feeling confused and insecure about what they are to do. They keep coming back and asking if this answer is right or if they are on the right track. I am intentionally vague in my answers because I want them to create their own connections and elaborate their own models. I often use an additional metaphor as a reply to describe the complexity of the task. Soon, however, the students are creating their own metaphorical language to communicate with each other and with me (some of it is quite humorous, and it certainly keeps the class entertained).

It is only after a certain comfort level is reached that the students begin to see the possibilities of using metaphors as a teaching tool with children. No matter what a child's experiences, if the child creates the link between the content and the child's own experience, the child "owns" the subject via his or her personal and unique construction of understanding. Younger students, it is reported back to me, actually pick up on the use of metaphors more easily than do the classes of adult students. One preservice student suggested that perhaps, once again, children pick up things quicker than adults do because they do not have so much to unlearn first. The use of metaphor as a teaching/learning tool has the potential to address individual learning style, knowledge level, and cultural heritage because of the personal and individualized construction of learning connections.

Connection-Making: A Visual Model

MARY ANN DAVIES
Northern Arizona University, Flagstaff

STRATEGY/ACTIVITY/ASSIGNMENT

Understanding the developmental transition from concrete to formal operations requires specific examples that illustrate the process. Graduate students in the "Middle School Methods and Materials" course expand their understandings of how to assist students in this cognitive transition by applying a variety of strategies in class. In one activity, "Connection-Making: A Visual Model," they create a graphic organizer that visually depicts cause-effect relationships.

The graphic organizer is called a futures wheel, and it visually represents the potential effects of any event, change, or decision. Its structure encourages identifying immediate consequences as well as indirect links. This graphic organizer helps develop connective reasoning and enables one to "see" the ripple effect of all actions.

DIRECTIONS

Brainstorm various decisions, events, and changes that affect middle level teaching. Divide students into pairs or small groups and give each a different item from the brainstormed list. Direct each pair to construct a futures wheel using the following guidelines:

In the center circle, place the decision, event, or change. Next, in the second-order circles, indicate the consequences that might directly result from the event or decision. For example, the event in the center circle might be the killing of four students and a teacher at a middle school in Jonesboro, Arkansas. For the second-order circles, one asks "What effects might this event have?" Students could identify a wide variety of potential effects, such as stricter gun control, reforms in juvenile law, tighter school security, or refocusing of advisor/advisee programs. In the third-order circles, students list possible effects of the second-level consequences, and so on. As students create the futures wheel, they begin to see the never-ending ripple effects and the interrelationships between consequences.

The final step in the activity involves a discussion of how one might use this activity with middle level students. They identify many possibilities: personal decision-making ("If I experiment with drugs, what consequences could result?"); content-related issues ("How might life be different if the South had won the Civil War?"); and current events ("What effects might result from a decision to raise taxes?").

COMMENTARY

Once students get started on the activity, they want a bigger sheet of paper! They find that given sufficient time, their futures wheel could go on endlessly. In addition, they discover that visually depicting possible effects makes it easier to generate ideas. The power of graphic organizers to translate abstract concepts into understandable ideas becomes readily apparent.

Students do not want to stop the activity. Once engaged in a challenging task that requires thinking, motivation rises. This helps them to realize the fine balancing act required of all middle level teachers: that is, how does one go about challenging students while at the same time providing a supportive climate? The futures wheel does both, as shown in Figure 4.1, below:

Figure 4.1 Futures Wheel

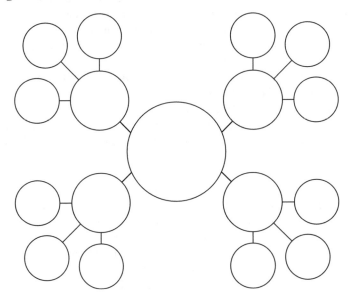

Interactive Lectures

SANDRA L. SCHURR
University of South Florida, Tampa

STRATEGY/ACTIVITY/ASSIGNMENT

Although lectures are overused and abused in most public school and college classrooms, there are constructive strategies that can be used to make them interactive so that they take on the flavor of a lecturette or mini-lecture. It is suggested that students be introduced to each of the following action-oriented lecturettes over a two- or three-week period of time by having the instructor discuss and model each of the formats outlined below as part of the course delivery system. The following seven structures are very effective tools to consider using as part of this process:

1. **The Feedback Lecture:** Students are given a prereading assignment and an outline of the lecture notes prior to the lecture. The teacher lectures for ten minutes and then divides the students into small study groups for twenty minutes. Each study group is given a question to answer, a point to ponder, or a problem to solve related to the content of the lecture itself. The teacher then reconvenes the students for another ten-minute lecture segment and addresses the assigned question/point/problem in the lecture.

2. **The Guided Lecture:** Students are given a list of three to five objectives for the lecture. They are then told to put their pencils down and listen to the lecture for twenty minutes without taking notes. At the end of this time segment, students are given five minutes to write down all the information they can recall. Students then work with a partner, and together they combine their notes to reconstruct the lecture content. The teacher then fills in any gaps through a whole-group recall and sharing session.

3. **The Responsive Lecture:** Once a week, structure the lecture period so that its content reflects only questions the students have generated on a given topic. To prepare for this lecture method, give each student (or small group of students) a 3" × 5" index card and have them write down an important question they have on a current topic or unit of study. Ask the class to order the

questions in terms of general interest. The teacher then proceeds to answer as many questions as time allows.

4. **The Demonstration Lecture:** In this lecture format, the teacher prepares a twenty-minute lecturette that involves an active demonstration, experiment, or hands-on application related to the topic. Students respond by writing a conclusion, summary, or brief explanation of what happened and what they observed.

5. **The Pause Procedure Lecture:** Deliver a twenty-minute lecturette and have students take notes on the content. After five-minute segments, the teacher pauses and gives the student two minutes to share his or her notes with a peer. It is sometimes helpful to give the students an outline that has a series of starter statements on the content that they must complete as the lecture is given.

6. **The Think/Write/Discuss Lecture:** The teacher prepares three questions to ask students throughout the lecture. The first question is a motivational question that is given before the lecture begins. The second question is given during the middle of the lecture and requires the student to write a short response to clarify a point or concept presented in the lecture. The last question is given at the end of the lecture and is a feedback-type question about something learned, something that needs further clarification, or something misunderstood.

7. **The Bingo Lecture:** Prepare a bingo grid and in each cell put a key concept to be discussed during the lecture. As students hear the concept being discussed during the lecture, they cover the appropriate space with a marker. The first person to get the cells filled in either across, down, or on a diagonal shouts "bingo" and wins that round.

After all seven models have been demonstrated in class, encourage students to select a topic for an informal lecture and try to deliver the information using several of the suggested lecture methods just described. This can be done by individuals or by small groups of students to review or teach some of the established course objectives to their peers.

COMMENTARY

It is important that students recognize the lecture as a legitimate technique for instruction if it is well planned, short in length, and interactive in nature. Modeling the interactive lecture formats consistently through-out the course is essential for the instructor to do. Likewise, it is impor-tant to give students several opportunities to "teach" a concept by applying these formats in a nonthreatening environment as part of that same education course.

In short, students of all ages enjoy and benefit from these lecturettes because they (1) limit the teacher's time as "sage on the stage" by divid-ing the content into more manageable chunks of information, (2) provide students ownership in the lecture process through mutual sharing and on-going reflection on lecture content, and (3) cater to a wider range of stu-dent learning styles.

Classroom Experiment in Learning Motor Skill

FAYE AVARD
Grambling State University, Grambling, LA

STRATEGY/ACTIVITY/ASSIGNMENT

What happens when we learn a new complex motor activity? What hap-pens before a well-skilled pattern emerges? High levels of achievement seldom appear suddenly. Learning of this type usually involves a gradual process during which the learner progressively, though not always smoothly, approximates his or her goal.

The problem presented here is to critically examine the course of de-velopment of motor learning as it is exemplified in learning to juggle two tennis balls in one hand. The student first juggles two tennis balls in the preferred hand, performing the 60 trials as described below. After prac-tice time, the learner performs the experiment using the nonpreferred hand. The student should not discuss this experiment with any other classmates. The student should concentrate his or her thoughts on his or her own performance, the learning process, and those activities that he or she is to perform with a partner.

The materials needed for each team are two tennis balls, pencils, and score sheets. Space is required to allow the performer to move about. Each partner will need space to record the trials.

The learner attempts to juggle two tennis balls in the preferred hand for 60 trials. The learner throws one ball up and then the other, alter-nately throwing and catching with the same hand. A trial ends when the learner fails to catch one of the balls. At the end of each trial, a partner records the number of successful catches made. After one person has finished the 60 trials, the total number of balls caught during the exercise is counted and divided by the number of trials (60) to determine *average* score per trial. Subtracting the lowest score (number of balls caught per trial) from the highest score determines the *range*. After two days, with distributed practice time periods of five-minutes duration, three times a day, the learner performs the same exercise using the nonpreferred hand.

This experiment requires the student to perform both as a teacher and as a learner. The student applies the concepts of motor learning (e.g., learning and performance, stages of learning, motivation, whole/part learning, transfer of learning, massed practice versus distributed, knowledge of results, reinforcements, retention, plateaus of learning, and automation). As the teacher, the student acts as the recorder and facilitator of the learning. As the learner, the student receives information from the facilitator and performs the motor activity.

After the students have completed the experiment, they prepare a written report. They need to approach the report from two areas of focus: first as the teacher, then as the student. The following questions and statements are generally presented to provide some guidance in writing the report: Was the skill learned or was it performed? How did you experience the stages of learning? What kinds of motivation did you receive or give? Describe the method of learning as you experienced whole and part learning. Was there any transfer of learning from the preferred hand to the nonpreferred hand? Describe the difference in success or failure as you experienced massed practice versus distributed practice. How did you apply the knowledge of results? What kind of feedback (e.g., preinstruction, concurrent instruction, post-instruction) did you give your partner? As you received reinforcements from your partner, how did you apply these in improving the skill? When did you experience plateaus of learning during the acquisition of the skill? Did the skill appear to be automatic, as if being done without conscious control by you or your partner? How was this automatic phase recognized?

COMMENTARY

These activities can serve as excellent tools in assisting the students in advanced/beginning teaching methods classes to acquire a firsthand understanding of the complicated cognitive and psychomotor tasks involved in acquiring motor skills. By applying the concepts of motor learning using a novel activity such as juggling, the teacher education student experiences similar feelings that any young adolescent or middle level student will experience in acquiring, learning, and performing a new motor skill.

After completing this experiment, students often relate that they have a more positive feeling about teaching motor skills because they now know the frustration and anxiety levels of acquisition while at the same time they have experienced and revived the feelings of satisfaction that come with achievement. They also state that this classroom experiment in motor learning aids them in gaining a better understanding of teaching strategies and learning activities that are known to be effective with middle level students.

CLASSROOM EXPERIMENT IN LEARNING
MOTOR SKILL—SCORE SHEET

Name of Subject _____   Date_____
Preferred Hand _____   Nonpreferred Hand _____

Trial Score	Trial Score	Trial Score	Trial Score
1	16	31	46
2	17	32	47
3	18	33	48
4	19	34	49
5	20	35	50
6	21	36	51
7	22	37	52
8	23	38	53
9	24	39	54
10	25	40	55
11	26	41	56
12	27	42	57
13	28	43	58
14	29	44	59
15	30	45	60

Total Number Caught   =   _____
Average Score   =   _____
Range   =   _____

Book Tables

SAUNDRA BRYN
Arizona State University West, Phoenix

STRATEGY/ACTIVITY/ASSIGNMENT

What is a book table?

A book table is a collection of between fifteen and twenty fiction and nonfiction books chosen for their relationship to an organizing center—that is, a topic, issue, problem, or theme. These organizing centers range from the seemingly ever-popular "Changes or Survival" to "Handicaps" or "The Day the World Changed."

In the undergraduate/graduate course "Middle School Curriculum and Organization," each graduate student constructs and presents to the entire class a book table that is appropriate for young adolescents.

The major objectives are that (1) the graduate students will select high-quality fiction and nonfiction materials that are appropriate for young adolescents and (2) the undergraduate students will expand their knowledge of high-quality fiction and nonfiction materials that are appropriate for young adolescents.

What is the process for completing a book table?

1. Each graduate student selects an organizing center—a theme, topic, problem, or issue—that is appropriate for young adolescents. The organizing center may be appropriate for a single subject area or may encompass several subjects.
2. Students determine the essential questions for their organizing centers. These essential, or guiding, questions should be the "essence of what you believe students should examine and know" (Jacobs, 1997, p. 26) when they are finished with their learning about the topic. Essential questions must be open-ended, conducive to encouraging discussion, and focused on the learning that students should accomplish.
3. Working independently, students gather as many books and related materials as they can find on their organizing centers.
4. To glean the books that are most appropriate for the organizing center, the subject(s) they are targeting, and young adolescents, the students, at a minimum, should "skim read" the books and

consider what activities they could do to enable the students to answer the essential questions. (Option: Students could be required to write out the activities they would use to answer each of the essential questions.)

5. Each student creates a display designed to capture the interest of young adolescents. The display contains the name of the organizing center and the essential questions. The backdrop of the display should be constructed as any effective visual—essential information, letters large enough to be seen from a distance, no spelling errors.

6. Students also develop an annotated bibliography in which they list the organizing center, the essential questions, and the book annotations. Each annotation must include information about how the book relates to the organizing center. Here is an example:

Organizing Center: Choices
Essential Questions: 1. How have choices affected society?
                       2. How have choices affected my life?
                       3. How will the choices made during
                          our lifetimes affect the future?

L'Engle, Madeleine. *A Swiftly Tilting Planet*. New York: Dell Publishing Company, Inc. 1978.

Preceded in the series by *A Wrinkle in Time* and *The Wind in the Door*, this book focuses on the journey through time of Charles Wallace and the unicorn Gaudier as they attempt to prevent the destruction of the world. In the book, the choices that are made in the past affect the present and clearly show the reader "what would have happened if . . . ?"

7. On the day of their presentations, students set up their displays, including the annotated bibliography and copies of the books. (Although they are not required to do so, many students purchase the books for their displays. Others acquire them from their school or public libraries.)

8. When students present their book tables, they tell the class about the organizing center, and why it was selected, introduce four or five of the books that might stimulate the audience's interest, talk about possible activities they could do with the books in various subject areas, and respond to questions from class members. They also distribute their annotated bibliography to members of the class.

9. Students are graded according to the following criteria: appropriateness of the organizing center and essential questions for young adolescents, completeness of annotated bibliography, book table display, and oral presentation.

COMMENTARY

All too often, preservice and practicing teachers of middle level students are not aware of the plethora of high-quality young adult literature that is available. If they are elementary majors, their focus tends to be on children's literature; if they are secondary majors, the focus tends to be on high school "classics." This assignment provides both the investigator (the graduate student) and the rest of the class members with an array of "theme-centered" adolescent literature. As one of the graduate students said in the end-of-course reflections, "I liked the book table because, honestly, I don't know a lot about young adolescent literature. I can tell you about the M & M counting book and other early elementary literature. Now I have some excellent titles to work with. I know the [EED] 494 [undergraduate] students will hate me, but I think they should do it also. I might just be saying that because this is my first book table, and I want more book titles."

An undergraduate student confirmed the book table's value. "I loved the book tables! I am extremely grateful for the wonderful presentations and bibliographies from my [EED] 598 [graduate] classmates. They were well planned and beautifully exhibited—where did they find the time?"

To receive graduate credit for a course, students must complete requirements different from those of the undergraduates. This assignment allows all the students to benefit from the graduate students' work. In addition, since the students in the course work as teams to develop an integrated unit framework that has an organizing center and essential questions, the graduate students are able to extend this learning as they investigate materials to support the unit framework. They can also choose to investigate an entirely different organizing center.

REFERENCE

Jacobs, H. H. (1997). *Mapping the big picture: Integrating the curriculum and assessment, K-12.* Alexandria, VA: Association for Supervision and Curriculum Development.

An Introduction to Reader-Response Theory

SAMUEL TOTTEN
University of Arkansas, Fayetteville

A strong believer in a hands-on, minds-on approach, I always introduce the students in my middle level methods course to reader-response theory. As I explain to them, it is an ideal instructional approach for use in just about all middle level courses. What follows is a discussion of an engaging activity that clearly illustrates the power, value, and beauty of providing students with learning activities that encourage them to bring the full power of their creative and critical abilities to bear on a project.

While the name of the theory sounds rather daunting, the basic idea behind reader-response theory is relatively simple. As John O'Neill (1994) has written in "Rewriting the Book on Literature: Changes Sought in How Literature is Taught, What Students Read":

> Basically, reader response theory differs most radically from previous theories about teaching literature in the degree of emphasis placed on the reader's response to an interpretation of the text . . . In reader response theory, the text's meaning is considered to reside in the "transaction" between the reader and the text, not from the text alone.
>
> . . . In practice, reader response theory considers very carefully how students respond intellectually and emotionally to the text . . . By validating students' responses, teachers can spark a lively discussion from which a careful literary analysis will flow.
>
> . . . Rather than beginning with a discussion of symbolism or metaphor, for example, teachers should allow an exploration of these aspects to develop from students' own observations about the work.
>
> . . . the emphasis on getting students to respond to the literature doesn't mean that any response is as good as another. Students are continuously urged to return to the text to find validation for their views. (pp. 7, 8)

The key, then, is to provide the students with an opportunity to examine literature from their own unique perspective, without imposing either the teacher's or a critic's interpretation on them. It is also a way to avoid having the students attempt to "please the teacher" by coming up with the "single correct answer." As anyone who appreciates the beauty of literature knows, good literature is multilayered; and as a result of that, the meaning inherent in a literary work is also multilayered. Thus, when students are prodded—as they often are in the so-called traditional classroom—to come up with the "correct answer" vis-à-vis the meaning of a poem, story, or novel, the result, more often than not, is a perfunctory response that is bereft of real thinking and engagement by the student, not to mention lacking in true insight into the literary work.

In order to introduce the power of the theory to students, I either place a poem on the overhead, which I read aloud and leave up for the duration of the activity, or I hand out a story and have them read it. Next, I inform the students that they should write the author or poet a letter in which they address virtually *anything* they wish about the literary work. More specifically, the exact directions I give them are: "In your letter, you may write anything you wish about the story (or poem). You may tell the author what you like or dislike about the story/poem, what you don't understand about it, that you simply don't like it, and/or you may ask probing questions about the story/poem or even offer your own interpretation and insights. The point is, you may come at it in any way you wish. It is your perspective—your point of view—that is important. Don't write this for me, the teacher; write it for yourself, in which you compose a letter to the poet about your honest response to the poem."

Once I clarify any questions the students may have about the directions for the assignment, I ask the following: "As a rule, what does every letter begin with?" (The students will generally answer "the date" and "a salutation or greeting"). Then I ask, "And what do letters generally conclude with?" Here the students generally answer "a closing" and "your name."

That completed, I give the students fifteen to twenty minutes to write their letters. Initially, many students moan and groan and complain that they can't think of what to say. I allow the groaning but warn them not to say anything at all about why they feel they don't have anything to say. That, and anything else they wish to comment on, I tell them, should be reflected in their letters. As with any assignment, some students will finish in a matter of minutes, whereas others will still be writing once the fifteen or twenty minutes is up.

At the conclusion of the writing activity, I place the students in groups of three or four and give them the following directions: "Initially, each person should simply read his/her letter while the rest of the group listens. Once everyone has read his/her piece, each person should read his/her letter again. This time, however, after each person reads his/her letter, a discussion should ensue. During the course of the discussion, the other members of the group are free to ask questions and make comments about the other person's letter; and in doing so, one may corroborate certain points by bringing in points from one's own letter or play the devil's advocate by questioning, probing, and so forth. As you discuss the ideas in the various letters, be sure to keep returning to the story/poem in order to substantiate and clarify your ideas. As soon as the discussion of one person's letter wanes, the next person in line should read his or her letter, and the process of discussion starts all over again."

I further explain that in order for the class to conduct a follow-up whole-class discussion, it is necessary for each group to have a recorder who jots down the most pertinent points made during the course of the small-group discussion. That being the case, I ask each group to quickly decide who the recorder is going to be, and I ask for that individual to simply raise his/her hand. Doing so ensures that each group has a recorder. After all of the recorders have been duly noted, I tell the students that during the general discussion the onus will not be on the recorder to carry the discussion for his/her group, but rather it will be the responsibility of the entire group to expound on their collective ideas. Thus, while the recorder will simply relate the key points that have been made in his/her group, any subsequent discussion of the group's points should be a group effort.

As the small groups engage in the aforementioned work, I circulate from group to group, and as a rule I simply listen to the discussion and refrain from making any comments. However, if an individual or an entire group is stuck at a point where they are simply saying "The story (or poem) doesn't make any sense," I offer the following advice and encouragement: "OK, that's a good starting point. Now you need to discuss *why* it doesn't make any sense. What aspects/components of the poem lead you to make that judgment. Start with that and I assure you that your discussion will lead into some very interesting and fruitful areas." Once students broach those aspects/components, I then encourage them to relate these ideas to specific parts of the story or the poem. With some groups it takes more encouragement and prodding than others, but by gently urging them to go with their initial reactions and then examine and wrestle with them, the students inevitably come up with some very interesting insights.

COMMENTARY

Both the written responses and the subsequent discussions are fascinating. While the sophistication of the responses vary from student to student, all responses end up being valuable in the subsequent discussion. That is, all responses prove to be valuable *if* the teacher truly encourages and guides the students to use the ideas, no matter how seemingly inane or off the mark or off the wall they may be, to their fullest.

As a rule, the students almost always perceive this activity and approach as being somewhat magical in that they would have never guessed at the outset of the lesson that either their individual responses or the general discussion would result in such interesting and perspicacious comments.

REFERENCE

O'Neill, J. (June 1994). Rewriting the book on literature: Changes sought in how literature is taught, what students read. *ASCD Curriculum Update*, 1-4, 6-8.

A Story Reenactment Project with Script

KATHERINE A. TRIMARCO
Montclair State University, Upper Montclair, NJ

STRATEGY/ACTIVITY/ASSIGNMENT

Studies of dramatic play and story reconstruction indicate that students develop higher-level thinking skills as they make decisions about characters, plot, and setting when reenacting their stories and developing their characters (Johnson & O'Neill, 1984; McGregor, Tate & Robinson, 1977; Tiedt, 1974). Students also develop social skills as they listen to other students express their ideas. They also learn to compromise with each other in the choices they make as a group.

We know that middle school level students enjoy both the imaginary and the real, making substitutions to stories that vary plots and endings (McCaslin, 1990). After the university students work on this activity, they should reflect on the merits of the activity for their future middle level students.

This activity involves a story reenactment project with the preparation of a script. As members of a group, the students choose a familiar fairy tale or folk tale to revise and develop into a production, making modifications to fit the needs of their group. This project includes a performance of the tale and the development of the revised script into a book. After the performance, the actors engage in a discussion of the elements of the tale with the other groups in the class who comprise the audience. The class should be configured to have a minimum of two groups working simultaneously on story reenactment projects to ensure that all students experience the various learning dimensions of the project.

COMMENTARY

This project enables students working in groups to employ multiple skills and abilities within an exciting framework of rewriting and acting out a familiar fairy tale or folk tale. Harnessing individual and group skills, the students also produce a book using computers, graphics, and artwork to write and illustrate the tale. Performance, discussion, and critique are all aspects of the project.

It appears from the students who worked through this project and evaluated their experiences that they had fun and enjoyed the fact that it was a hands-on and minds-on experience throughout. At the conclusion of the project, the students acknowledged that they learned that process was as important as product. They enjoyed performing as writers, actors, and critics. The students unanimously approved of the activity for their middle level students because it fully engages students in thoughtful and creative work. They also commented on the value of discussing the pedagogical issues related to implementing such a reenactment project. Many of the students expeditiously replicated this activity with middle school students at one of our professional development schools during the semester of their university coursework.

REFERENCES

Johnson, L., & O'Neill, C. (Eds.). (1984*). Collected writings on education and drama.* Evanston, IL: Northwestern University Press.

McCaslin, N. (1990). *Creative drama in the classroom and beyond.* New York: Longman.

McGregor, L., Tate, M., & Robinson, K. (1977*). Learning through drama.* London: Heinemann Educational Books

Tiedt, I. M. (Ed.). (1974). *Drama in your classroom.* Urbana, IL: National Council of Teachers of English.

Philosophy into Practice in Middle Grades Language Arts

HOLLY THORNTON
Augusta State University, Augusta, GA

STRATEGY/ACTIVITY/ASSIGNMENT

Students may enter middle-grades language arts pedagogy classes with limited knowledge of instructional methods and approaches as well as misinformation about alternative approaches. The typical past experiences of the students I teach tend to be grounded in a grammar/text-based approach to teaching English and in a read-and-quiz-for-facts approach to teaching reading. In their experience, reading was often taught separately from, or only loosely tied to, grammar or any form of writing. The political context in which our college of education is situated is a conservative one, where educational talk centers largely on improving standardized test scores and restoring discipline in the classroom. Over the past five years, whole language instruction was introduced in the educational community, with limited professional development and education for the community as a whole. For these and perhaps other reasons, whole language instruction was misinterpreted, greatly misused, and ultimately abandoned. Many students entered my language arts pedagogy class with the notion that whole language was ineffective, chaotic, and deserving of blame for low test scores.

In order to make sense of their own experiences as future middle level teachers and of the political/educational context surrounding the whole language debate in the community, students need to develop a knowledge base related to sound, research-based language arts instruction and the philosophy that undergirds instructional decisions in the classroom. Armed with information, an understanding of various perspectives within the community, and a knowledge base related to best practices and learning, students will be better able to make sound decisions in their own classrooms and school districts in the future.

To enable students to accomplish the latter, they engage in research and data gathering to prepare for a simulated school board meeting in which the topic of whole language versus a back-to-the basics approach to language arts instruction in the middle school is examined. After being assigned roles such as administrators, parents, teachers, board members, and political and advocacy group members, students work in pairs to search the literature, interview individuals, and obtain observational data. These data, which include field notes related to approaches and materials employed in schools and notes from their school-based lab experiences, are used to develop their role and assigned position.

The time for students to engage in research and work together is built into class sessions, as is ongoing conferencing with the professor. Preparation for and participation in the simulation enables students to develop their research skills by collaboratively examining various perspectives related to language arts philosophy and instruction. It also allows them to examine the views and concerns of various constituencies within the educational community. Clear links between philosophy and practice are discovered, and the contrast between implementing practices to meet student needs as learners, and political concerns and issues, are illuminated.

The evaluation of the simulation is based on the following criteria: accurate representation of the assigned perspective and related vested interests/concerns, statements that reflect opinions supported by one's role, accurate references to facts and data gathered, and effective collaboration with one's partner. Prior to the actual simulation, students develop a role stance sheet as a written means of evaluating the process. These sheets must include a brief narrative of the assigned constituent's role, concerns, vested interests, and perspective. The sheets also include a list of related facts, data, and sources of information cited in the simulation, including journal articles, interview responses, and observational data. The role stance sheets (see sample) act as a synthesis of the students' work, which serves multiple purposes. More specifically, the sheet helps the student organize thoughts, plan for the simulation, and document the research process. It also serves as a reference source for the other participants. The professor's task during the debate is to direct comments, facilitate discussion, and generally "run" the board meeting.

COMMENTARY

This activity situates the development of a philosophy of middle level language arts instruction within the broader political context of teaching and learning. Connections between the knowledge base and teacher decision making are discovered, as well as the challenges of putting one's philosophy into practice, no matter how well grounded that philosophy may be.

Students have shared that this experience has helped them to build a knowledge base and the skills necessary to articulate and justify their beliefs related to instruction. It further serves to underscore the *why* behind instructional decisions that they might make as teachers. The simulation also helps them to understand various perspectives and how to deal with people with different viewpoints in a professional manner, with the hope of bridging gaps and building partnerships on common ground. Students also directly see the relevance of and need for educational research, perhaps fostering the proclivity to be a research-based practitioner.

After the simulation, students engage in dialogue related to the activity itself, how this format might be used with middle grade students, its implications as an alternative means of assessment, and the value of active learning for the learner, as opposed to a didactic approach to instruction. The activity itself acts as a model of active/student-centered learning, which they could employ in their future classroom as middle level educators. Practicing what we preach may enable them to do the same in their own classrooms.

Role Stance Sheet Rubric

Synthesize your findings as they relate to both your role's point of view in the simulation and the findings from your research. Include in your research journal articles, interviews and observational data. Make sure your role stance sheet meets the criteria below.

1–4 points

Includes a brief (2-page) narrative:
1. Describes the role's experiences with schools/ language arts, concerns, issues of importance, vested interests   _____
2. Narrative accurately reflects perspective and is well supported by data evidenced   _____
3. Includes synthesis of research found and a list of key "facts" used during simulation   _____
4. Research supports position and is relevant and meaningful to simulation task; includes bibliography of sources (APA format)   _____

Using Shoes as a Tool for Constructing Knowledge

JON E. PEDERSEN

East Carolina University, Greenville, NC

STRATEGY/ACTIVITY/ASSIGNMENT

Shoe Classification

Clearly, one of the most important aspects of my middle level science methods course is to have my students examine the nature of students' learning and the construction of knowledge. It is from this perspective that we, as a community of learners, begin to negotiate and construct our own meaning for the teaching/learning interface. It is paramount that students understand that the nature of learning is a process of building and constructing "knowledge" embedded in their own social-historical context. Basically, students make sense of environs by looking through their own set of "lenses" that shape their interpretations and interactions with the world. Therefore, the following activity, "Shoe Classification," provides one example of how an instructor can assist individuals to make sense of an important science concept.

    Materials: Left or right shoe from each member of your class (*Note:* Do not exceed a maximum of 20–25 students' shoes.)

    Procedures: Instruct students to remove their left shoe and place it on a table or desk where all students can see them. (*Note:* You may want to have the students sit in a circle around a table so the students can all see the shoes.) Tell the students that you have a problem. Indicate that there is a group of shoes, and no one knows to whom they belong. Ask the students to look at the shoes and describe how the group of shoes are similar to or different from one another. Ask them to think about how they might "organize the shoes" in groups based on common characteristics. It is easier to manage the discussion at this point if the students are placed in groups of two or three and each group is given an opportunity to share its ideas about what it sees as critical attributes of the shoes. Students typically begin the categorization process by splitting the shoes into two separate groups, such as tennis shoes and dress shoes. Once students have two groups of shoes, ask them to examine the similarities and differences *within* the smaller groups of shoes. It is easier at this point if just one group of shoes is selected to work with (e.g., work on the "tennis shoe" group first). First, ask the students to consider what makes all of the "tennis shoes" different. Next, ask: "How could we separate this single group of tennis shoes into two different groups based on a single characteristic of the shoes (e.g., number of eyelets, color of sole, type of material the shoe is made of). Continue this process of organizing each group of shoes into smaller and smaller groups based on a common characteristic. The goal is to guide the students in this process so that they have a single shoe that is unique to its group based on a set of characteristics (e.g., a tennis shoe that is white with six eyelets, has a tan sole, and is a Nike). Once a single shoe is left, ask for the first name of the owner of the shoe. As the students develop their categorization scheme, the instructor should draw a tree diagram (see Figure 4.2 on page 124) on the blackboard that represents their thinking about how the shoes are classified. Once this task is completed for tennis shoes, do the same for dress shoes. After classifying all the shoes, ask someone from outside of the class (a teacher, a student, etc.) to see if he or she can find the owner of the shoe by using the classification tree diagram created on the blackboard.

Continue to develop the idea of classification systems by asking the students if there are other classification systems they use on a daily basis (e.g., library, supermarket, video store, etc.). Discuss with them how these entities use classification systems to allow us to seek out information and understand how the information is related (for example, in a video store one would expect to find comedies under the heading of "comedy" or "humor"). Next, ask the students: "What does this have to do with science?" How do scientists use classification systems to help us understand the world around us? Guide them in this discussion and encourage them to give specific examples from their own knowledge of science.

At this point it is important to make the connection to science by using the shoe classification activity as an analogy for the concept of classification and taxonomies. For example, use a simple dichotomous key or classification system to classify a set of leaves. Allow and encourage students to ask questions about why classification systems are arranged the way they are. Finally, give groups of two or three students a large sample of flowers (local florists are more than willing to donate "old" flowers for this activity) and ask them to classify the flowers on the basis of the flowers' individual characteristics. Have them draw a tree diagram delineating how they examined and classified the characteristics of the flowers. Then, examine a dichotomous key for flowers and ask the students to compare what they saw and what scientists see when classifying flowers.

COMMENTARY

Students who have participated in this activity have responded very positively. The excitement that is generated by the initial activity of classifying the shoes is carried over into other aspects of classification in science. The bottom line is that they don't become bored with a somewhat "dry subject," dichotomous keys and classification. Furthermore, students actually begin to enjoy the idea of classification and continue to use these ideas when we discuss other life science and physical science topics. Overall, they have a better understanding of why scientists use classification systems and why it is critical for them to understand the nature of these systems when studying science. One student indicated that shoe classification helped her because she "finally" understood taxonomies and, "[classification systems] organize what we know so we can better study it." This, in and of itself, is a worthwhile accomplishment.

Preservice teachers need to realize that middle level students are at a critical stage of transition in operational thought. Clearly, our goal as middle level teachers is to engage children in the development of their own capacity to think about and understand the world around them. Teaching preservice teachers about how to use analogies or abductive

Figure 4.2 Shoes

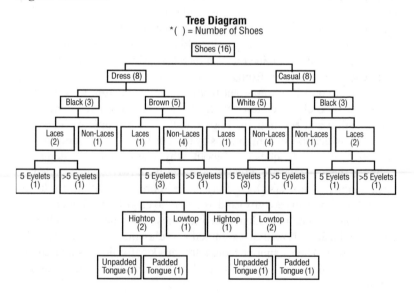

thinking is one way to accomplish this. Abduction is the use of an analogy to apply old ideas in new situations and to invent new concepts and new explanations (Lawson, 1994). These new explanations are constructed by applying a previously acquired pattern from the world of observable objects and events to explain unobservable events. Students in a science classroom can be assisted in their understanding of a scientific concept by having the teacher point out relevant analogies (Lawson, 1994). It would seem, then, that the use of analogies as presented in the "shoe classification" activity, which uses a common everyday item, would assist early adolescents as well as preservice teachers in deepening their understanding of science.

REFERENCE

Lawson, A. E. (1994). Research on the acquisition of science knowledge: Epistemological foundations of cognition, pp. 131-176. In Dorothy Gable (Ed.) *Handbook of research on science teaching and learning*. New York: Macmillan.

Carousel Brainstorming: An Instructional Strategy to Activate Schema, Assess Prior Knowledge, Generate New Ideas, and Focus Instruction

JOHN HELFELDT
Texas A&M University, College Station

STRATEGY/ACTIVITY/ASSIGNMENT

Carousel brainstorming is a small-group strategy that enables an entire classroom of learners to engage in a meaningful, divergent thinking activity within a relatively short period of time. Like all brainstorming activities, it is intended to activate schema, generate a large number of ideas, and provide teachers with an opportunity to assess individual and group understandings or beliefs associated with a specified topic.

This method of brainstorming is called "carousel" because each group or team completes a rotation among strategically placed, open-ended statements or questions posted around the room. It is important to generate and post sufficient topically related statements so that all individuals within each group have ample opportunity to become involved. The process for carousel brainstorming follows.

Brainstorming Ground Rules

To encourage free expression of ideas and to stimulate divergent thinking, the following rules for effective brainstorming must be discussed and understood prior to implementing the procedure.

1. Criticism is prohibited. There is no room for any type of criticism (verbal, nonverbal, tone of voice critical questioning) or value judgments. Fear of criticism undermines trust among participants and inhibits free thinking and sharing of ideas.
2. Freewheeling, far-out thinking is welcomed and valued. The wilder the ideas, the better. Seemingly off-beat, far-out, silly ideas may trigger practical breakthroughs or ideas that might not otherwise emerge.
3. Quantity of ideas is valued. Rapid-paced presentation and off-the-cuff ideas are encouraged. Stimulating, seemingly trivial or obvious ideas frequently stimulates the production of subsequent important ideas or "breakthroughs."
4. "Piggybacking," or combining information, is encouraged. "Hitch-hiking" on the thoughts of others is a way of improving ideas. It should be viewed as teamwork, not as "stealing" ideas.

Getting started

- Divide the class into small groups and give each group or team a *different* colored marker.
- Assign each team to a different easel or chart paper with an open-ended question or statement dealing with various aspects of a topic on middle level education.
- Assign roles (e.g., recorder, facilitator, monitor) to individual team members.
- Allow ample room around each chart and provide enough space between each chart station to allow groups an opportunity to freely discuss and list ideas.

Implementing the procedure

- Establish a time limit (generally 1 to 3 minutes) to generate and list ideas on chart paper.
- After the allotted time, signal the groups (preferably a nonverbal or silent signal such as dimming the lights) to rotate or move clockwise to the next chart.
- Each group *takes their colored marker with them,* but the recorder role should be shifted to another team member at each subsequent chart. Rotating the role of recorder is important because the rapid writing required in response to capturing the quickly paced generation of ideas may preclude the recorder from offering his or her own unique ideas for inclusion on the group list.
- Teams cannot reiterate previously stated ideas but will add new ideas, some of which are stimulated by the previously listed thoughts.
- Continue the rotational "carousel" movement of teams to the remaining charts posted throughout the room. When each team returns to their original chart, the carousel brainstorming has been completed.

Follow-up discussion

- Teacher posts the charts in the front of the room.
- Each group discusses, shares ideas, and explains how they were elicited. Written comments are frequently clarified or explained.
- For each question/statement, the role of speaker or reporter is rotated among team members.
- Final lists become the stimulus for future learning activities or assignments regarding middle level education and early adolescence.

COMMENTARY

Carousel brainstorming can be implemented with equal effectiveness at the undergraduate or graduate course level. One reason that this instructional strategy has such a wide range of applications is because of its lack of dependence on content. The use of broad-based stimulus statements or questions is equally useful for activating the schema and focusing the thinking of middle level educators. Brainstorming initiators, such as: "list the essential attributes and abilities necessary to be a highly effective middle school teacher," or "what are the crucial elements or components of an exemplary middle school?" will elicit numerous responses and comments from novice as well as experienced middle level educators. What might be different is the depth of understanding and specificity of comments that are associated with the ideas generated by individuals with more extensive professional experiences and enhanced schemata associated with middle level education.

Carousel brainstorming is beneficial to course instructors because it provides "snapshots" and insights that aid in assessing the range of beliefs, values, and experiences that exist among the various class members. The instructor may find the brainstormed information useful as scaffolds for future explanations or assignments and springboards to further discussions or class debates.

Students in middle level education courses have characterized carousel brainstorming as a very useful learning activity because it gives these adult learners a firsthand experience with an active thinking-learning strategy. It also encourages learners to consider divergent points of view, stimulates them to think creatively, and empowers them to take ownership and responsibility for new ideas. Students have reported that carousel brainstorming activities helped them to focus their thoughts while considering and exploring ideas for future written assignments associated with their middle level course.

Connecting Geometry to Students' Experiences

DOUGLAS FISHER
San Diego State University, San Diego, CA

LISA DRAKE
San Diego State University, San Diego, CA

STRATEGY/ACTIVITY/ASSIGNMENT

Many preservice teachers, like their middle level counterparts, fear math. For some reason, many people believe that they "can't do math" and that "you never use math in the real world." In an instructional methods course, we encourage students to develop an understanding of and an appreciation for the connections between math and their world. Naturally, several weeks of our course are devoted to math, especially geometry.

During this time, students complete several assignments. In addition to the basic math concepts that are covered, the assignments require students to demonstrate their skills in reading and writing. We make a practice of infusing literacy activities across the curriculum.

The first assignment is a poem (Moretti, 1996) that requires students to demonstrate their understanding of geometric forms. To complete the assignment, students must complete each of the stanzas based on one geometrical form (see Table 4.1). This poem requires them to explore the properties of the form and to understand the form's relation to other forms. In addition, students create visual representations of their poems. These graphics demonstrate the geometric form in use, such as the pentagon. The poems are graded for completeness and consistency with the chosen geometric form. The second assignment is a geometry scavenger hunt. Student groups of four are required to acquire, within legal means, as many of the items on their list as possible. Each item on a team's list is worth five points. Team lists are a random collection of the items listed in Table 4.2. The third assignment involves rewriting a children's story. For this assignment, students are required to find a story that they like and rewrite it for use in a math class. "Alice in Numberland" is provided as an example (House, 1996). The students are graded using the rubric in Table 4.3.

Table 4.1. Stanzas for a Math Poem
1. I am (two special characteristics that your word has)
2. I wonder (something your word would be curious about)
3. I hear (an imaginary sound)
4. I want (an actual desire of your word)
5. I am (repeat first line of poem)
6. I pretend (something your word would pretend to do)
7. I feel (an imaginary feeling of your word)
8. I touch (an imaginary touch of your word)
9. I worry (something that truly bothers your word)
10. I cry (something that makes your word very sad)
11. I am (repeat the first line of the poem)
12. I understand (something your word knows is true)
13. I say (something that your word believes in)
14. I dream (something your word dreams about)
15. I try (something your words makes an effort about)
16. I hope (something your word would actually hope for)
17. I am (repeat the first line of the poem)

Table 4.2. Geometry Scavenger Hunt—

Possible items to include:

- A classified ad for a surveyor or cartographer
- UPC code from three different sizes of the same product
- A letterhead with a geometric logo
- A picture of a quilt that uses congruent triangles
- The number of books in Euclid's *Elements* (and include your source)
- The number of other types of geometry besides Euclidean
- A right circular cone with a diameter of 10 +/− 2 cm, commercially made
- A dodecahedron (an extra point if commercially made)
- A rectangular prism whose volume in cubic inches is greater than the surface area in square inches (include the calculation)
- A square nut
- A pentagonal nut
- A hexagonal nut
- An advertisement for a specific item that shows vertical angles
- A list of geometry words that start with the same letter (pick one letter and create a list of words; only root words count)
- An advertisement from a magazine that uses a conditional statement
- A picture from a magazine that uses concentric circles
- A template
- A template that does *not* contain any of the following: circles, ellipses, squares, triangles, numbers, or letters
- Two different shaped solids with the same volume (show calculations)
- A picture from a magazine drawn in perspective (mark the vanishing point)
- A picture from a magazine of a tessellation or isometry (identify type)
- A student-made platonic solid
- A nonedible torus
- A commercially produced cartoon or comic that involves geometry (tell how)
- A child's toy that can be used to explain a geometric concept (include description)
- A picture that requires 3-D glasses to properly view
- A picture of a traffic sign with the name of the polygon it represents

Table 4.3. Guidelines for Grading Geometry Children's Story (each worth 0-5 points)
1. Story conveyed geometric relationships
2. Story contained geometric vocabulary
3. Story was imaginative, fun to read, and had graphics
4. Story was organized, with appropriate mechanics
5. Story was completed on time and was typed

COMMENTARY

Activities such as the ones delineated here provide connections between math content and a student's background knowledge. Our list is just a small sample of the excellent resources for teachers in math education (e.g., Elliott & Kenney, 1996). Many of these activities have the added benefit of involving reading and writing, skills with which students can use a great deal of practice (Curry, 1996).

Students in our classes had varying degrees of success with the assignments. Many took to the writing and creative aspects of the assignment immediately. Others need encouragement and support to think about math in this way. However, by the third assignment, these future teachers understood the reason for connecting math to other areas of their lives. As one future middle school teacher wrote in her evaluation of the class: "By the third assignment, I was very comfortable with the vocabulary used in our class. These words were no longer foreign to me and I'm a little less afraid of math."

REFERENCES

Curry, J. (1996). The role of reading and writing instruction in mathematics. In D. Lapp, J. Flood, & N. Farnan (Eds.), *Content area reading and learning: Instructional strategies* (2nd ed.) (pp. 227-244). Boston: Allyn and Bacon.

Elliott, P. C., & Kenney, M. J. (1996). *1996 Yearbook: Communication in math, K-12 and beyond.* Reston, VA: National Council of Teachers of Mathematics.

House, P. (1996). Try a little of the write stuff. In P. C. Elliott & M. J. Kenney (Eds.), *1996 Yearbook: Communication in math, K-12 and beyond.* Reston, VA: National Council of Teachers of Mathematics.

Moretti, C. (1996). *Literary creativity with art: A resource teacher project.* La Mesa, CA: Grossmont School District.

Learning to Teach Mathematics to Middle Level Students

TOM R. BENNETT

California State University–San Marcos

STRATEGY/ACTIVITY/ASSIGNMENT

One of the major assignments of the middle level mathematics methods course is for students to participate in the design, construction, and presentation of a "reform-minded" mathematics lesson. In ways that are consistent with the current reform recommendations set forth by the National Council of Teachers of Mathematics (NCTM) in the Standards documents (e.g., *Curriculum and Evaluation Standards for School Mathematics* [NCTM, 1989] and the *Professional Standards for Teaching Mathematics* [NCTM, 1991]), a reform-minded lesson should help students learn mathematics with understanding. For this assignment, students form small groups of two or three individuals and together select a middle level mathematical topic to investigate from a list of topics provided by the instructor (e.g., fractions, algebraic thinking, and geometry). Students are required to: (1) research and identify available resources on their topic that will help them to design and teach their lesson (e.g., teacher support materials, journal articles, manipulatives, sample lesson plans, etc.); (2) define a specific mathematical objective they want their middle level students to learn; (3) design a unique hands-on lesson that will actively engage middle level students in learning the stated objective in ways consistent with the Standards (NCTM, 1989, 1991); and (4) teach their lesson to their classmates as if they were middle level students.

Several weeks before the group presentations begin, each group is required to turn in an annotated list of appropriate resources on their mathematical topic (this is actually a separate assignment; however, it is designed to support this assignment). Then on the day the group is to present their lesson to the class, they turn in one complete lesson plan along with one or two pages from each group member reflecting on what they learned from this assignment, describing their contribution to the group effort, and commenting on whether the workload was evenly shared among the group members.

Each group is provided 30 to 45 minutes to engage their classmates (who assume the role of middle grade students) in their lesson. To make the best use of class time, groups are encouraged to "streamline" the presentation of their lesson by engaging their classmates in only the main components. Each group is asked to begin their presentation by providing some background information on the grade level of the class (the class they are pretending to teach), the objective of the lesson, students' prior mathematical experiences, and some indication of where the class is headed in the unit.

The evaluation of this assignment is based on: (1) the developmental appropriateness of the lesson; (2) whether the lesson adequately teaches the stated objective; (3) how closely the lesson adheres to the recommendations set forth in the Standards (NCTM, 1989, 1991); and (4) whether all members of the group have fully participated and equitably shared the workload.

COMMENTARY

According to students, this assignment helps them understand how to research, design, and teach effective mathematics lessons to middle level students. More specifically, they appreciate the opportunity to participate as learners in mathematics lessons that cover a range of important mathematical topics, the individualized attention each group receives, and the opportunity to discuss as a class the details of each lesson following each presentation. Because all students receive a copy of each lesson plan and bibliography from each group, this assignment provides all students with at least one well-designed lesson plan from each of the major mathematical topics covered in class. It is worth noting that students teach many of these same lessons to middle level students during their student teaching assignment with great success.

Because one of the primary purposes of this assignment is to help students learn what factors teachers should consider when designing an effective mathematics lesson, the instructor should regularly meet with each group to discuss their progress, to provide necessary support, and to further challenge and advance their thinking. Furthermore, it is suggested that instructors regularly caution students to not lose sight of the mathematical ideas they are trying to teach as they attempt to design an engaging mathematical lesson for middle level students. Some students seem to forget about the mathematics as they become more immersed in the context of their activity.

The actual presentation of the lesson is not graded because it is considered to be a time for students to make mistakes and try out new techniques. However, each person in the class, including the instructor, is asked to provide each group with written feedback on the presentation of their lesson. These short write-ups should focus on such issues as: (1) the developmental appropriateness of the lesson; (2) how closely the lesson adheres to the recommendations set forth in the Standards (NCTM, 1989, 1991); (3) the teaching decisions made during the lesson; and (4) the effectiveness of their instructional practices in attaining their stated objective.

REFERENCES

National Council of Teachers of Mathematics. (1989). *Curriculum and evaluation standards for school mathematics*. Reston, VA: Author.

National Council of Teachers of Mathematics. (1991). *Professional standards for teaching mathematics*. Reston, VA: Author.

Engaging Preservice Teachers as Learners of Mathematics

TOM R. BENNETT
California State University–San Marcos

STRATEGY/ACTIVITY/ASSIGNMENT

Early in the term of a middle level mathematics methods course, I engage students as learners in a mathematics activity that addresses an important topic, such as fractions. This lesson typically follows an investigation of the current changes, or "reform," in mathematics education as recommended by the National Council of Teachers of Mathematics (NCTM) in the Standards documents (e.g., *Curriculum and Evaluation Standards for School Mathematics* [NCTM, 1989] and the *Professional Standards for Teaching Mathematics*, [NCTM, 1991]). The purpose of engaging students as learners of mathematics is to provide students an opportunity to experience the effectiveness of reform-minded middle level instructional practices and curriculum (such as teaching and learning with understanding), to challenge students' mathematical understanding, and to create an opportunity to discuss an important middle level mathematical concept. A short description of a fractions lesson on part/whole that I often use with my middle level mathematics methods students will serve to further illustrate this activity.

After dividing the class into groups of four, each group is given an envelope with directions and a tub filled with color tiles, protractors, rulers, scissors, and paper. The envelope contains directions for the project and a realistic problem scenario. The scenario suggests that the group has just purchased some leftover pizzas from a pizza parlor (these are not whole pizzas), and the group members are to evenly share the remaining pizza amongst the four of them and determine the fractional amount each person will receive. Inside each envelope are paper models of the leftover pizzas, which are fractional parts of either all circular or all rectangular pizzas (they are not mixed). The directions ask students to: (1) individually think of a strategy to solve this problem; (2) share his or her strategy with the other group members; (3) decide as a group on a strategy to solve this problem; and (4) solve this problem using the group's strategy. Once the groups have had a chance to solve their problem, the groups share their solutions with the class. Because there are so many ways for the groups to define the "whole" (e.g., all of the pizzas taken together, in terms of one whole pizza, the total number of color tiles to cover one rectangular pizza, using 360° for a circular pizza, and so forth), students quickly come to recognize the necessity of clearly defining the part/whole relationship and the need to consider more than simply students' answers when assessing students' mathematical knowledge.

When teaching the lesson, the instructor should model instructional practices that effective middle level teachers of mathematics might use with adolescents. As illustrated in the pizza problem, instructors might consider incorporating the use of manipulatives, engaging students in collaborative group assignments for at least a portion of the lesson, and fostering a richly supportive and investigative environment. While engaged in the activity, students should be encouraged to think about the lesson from the perspective of both a learner of mathematics and a teacher of mathematics and to take notes on any questions or revelations they may have for later discussion.

After the lesson, the instructor should share with the students some of his or her general thoughts about the lesson, as well as some of the difficult decisions he or she had to make. For example, the instructor might share with the students the thought processes that he or she went through when deciding whether to continue to take class time to follow a particular student's presentation of an incorrect solution strategy. Since teachers must constantly make quick decisions during a lesson that can have a significant impact on the overall success of the lesson, it is important for students to understand factors that might influence a teacher's decision-making process. Students should also be given an opportunity to share their thoughts with the class and to ask questions. Creating a safe and supportive environment in which this kind of dialogue about the teaching of a lesson can occur is important to model for students, especially since they will likely soon be engaged in student teaching, with many people making comments on their teaching.

COMMENTARY

Engaging students as mathematical learners can provide them with the opportunity to: (1) experience reform-minded instructional practices and curriculum in mathematics that are developmentally appropriate for middle level students, (2) learn more about important mathematical concepts, and (3) to make connections between learning theory and how these theories can be incorporated into a mathematics lesson with young adolescents. Since many, if not most, of the students in a mathematics methods course have most likely never experienced the power of mathematics reform, providing students with such opportunities is crucial if we are to expect them to be able to teach in this way.

Because students are engaged as learners of mathematics during a time when they are also learning to be teachers, many have commented that this lesson has helped them to form connections between theory and practice and to think about teaching from the students' perspective. For example, based on their experiences from this activity, students often comment that they now more fully recognize (1) the importance of teachers considering students' thinking when assessing their understanding, (2) the importance of having students talk about and share their mathematical thinking with others, and (3) the potential power of manipulatives. In addition to recognizing the importance of various instructional practices and curricular approaches, students also comment that they were surprised to learn something new about part/whole relationships from this activity.

REFERENCES

National Council of Teachers of Mathematics. (1989). *Curriculum and evaluation standards for school mathematics*. Reston, VA: Author.

National Council of Teachers of Mathematics. (1991). *Professional standards for teaching mathematics*. Reston, VA: Author.

Grouping—Why Not Use Permanent Ability Groups?

DOUGLAS FISHER
San Diego State University, San Diego, CA

STRATEGY/ACTIVITY/ASSIGNMENT

Many preservice teachers experienced ability grouping, or tracking, when they were students in the school system. In fact, when asked, most of our teaching credential candidates easily recall the grouping and tracking strategies used by their teachers. As one student said, "I was in the low reading group starting in first grade, and I stayed there through high school." Concerned that these early experiences may exert a stronger influence on their teaching habits than the research on permanent ability groups or tracking (e.g., Flood, Lapp, Flood, & Nagel, 1992), additional activities and discussions are often required to challenge future middle level educators' beliefs about tracking and permanent ability grouping.

In a student teaching seminar course, an entire session is devoted to the issue of permanent ability groups and tracking. The opening activity is the one that often stimulates the most reflection. Students are handed a drawing (Figure 4.3, on page 138). They are told that the artist who created this drawing was interrupted and was unable to finish. They are then instructed to finish the drawing within five minutes and to turn the paper over if they finish early. The students are also told there are no right or wrong answers. When the five minutes are up, students are told that they will be allowed to score their own paper. Students' papers are worth between 0 and 5 points. They are to give themselves one point for each of the following categories, if germane to their paper:

1. Detail: did they provide lots of detail in the drawing?
2. One picture: did they connect all the shapes into one thematic depiction?
3. Reality: did they draw something real? (no credit for abstract art)
4. 3-D: did they provide a third dimension to the picture versus only 2?
5. Beyond the box: did they draw something outside of the boundary line of the figure?

Figure 4.3

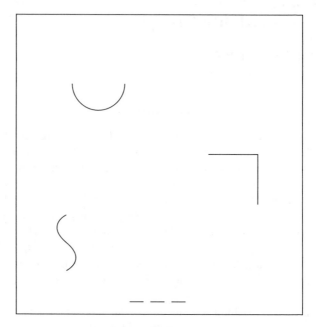

Students calculate their score. Each number is called, and students with that score raise their hands. They are divided into groups based on their scores. Sometimes certain numbers need to be combined to create enough people in a group for the conversation (e.g., there might not be enough people with "0" so the 0's and 1's get together). Then the groups are divided. The zeros (sometimes combined with the ones) are sent outside to wait for further instructions. A "five" can be sent with them to ensure that they stay nearby. The twos, threes, fours, and fives all arrange themselves in groups; it is very effective to place the higher numbers toward the front of the classroom. They are told as a group to discuss grouping strategies used in the schools and that they will present to the whole class. Each group is provided with chart paper and markers to record their conversation. The instructor then walks around the room and quickly gives more specific instructions to the groups. The lower groups are given an article on grouping to summarize, the middle groups are told to make a list on their paper, and the higher groups are told to be very creative and perform their response. (When the activity is over, all the groups get the grouping article. During the simulation, only the low groups have access to this article.) When the instructor talks with the group outside of the class, the students are told to take a quick break and come back within five minutes.

When the groups have finished and are ready to present, each group goes in turn, from highest to lowest. Naturally, students in the lower groups who have summarized the article are surprised by the creativity of the students who scored higher. However, some very good information will be presented by all the groups that can be used throughout the remainder of the session. Students often become frustrated with the grouping strategy and the differential instructions given to the different groups. This is important to debrief during the discussion.

The debriefing of this simulation is very important. Students should be asked to critique the test. Is it valid and reliable? What did the test value? Why was "reality" (and not abstract art) valued? What kinds of information do teachers use to group students? How did they feel in their group? What about the instructions given to different groups? Do teachers ever do this to students? Do our expectations influence student performance? Students in the simulation also need to be told that this assessment is not valid or reliable. It was designed to prove a point; teachers sometimes group students and expect them to perform either very well or very poorly.

COMMENTARY

Students have no difficulty relating this simulation to their experience in the classroom. However, they still have questions about appropriate grouping strategies. The remainder of the four-hour class session is spent on differentiated instruction, flexible grouping, station teaching, and cooperative groups (e.g., Cole, 1995; Tomlinson, 1995). By the end of the session, it is hoped that students understand that grouping patterns can change all the time. There may be a point during the day where teachers may want to meet with a group of students with specific skill needs; however, these groups should not be permanent nor should they be devalued.

As one future teacher said at the close of this class meeting, "I thought the low students did best with students like them; now I understand that it is my responsibility to make sure that all students do well."

REFERENCES

Cole, R. (Ed.). (1995). *Educating everybody's children: Diverse teaching strategies for diverse learners.* Alexandria, VA: Association for Supervision and Curriculum Development.

Flood, J., Lapp, D., Flood, S., & Nagel, G. (1992). Am I allowed to group? Using flexible patterns for effective instruction. *The Reading Teacher, 45,* 608-616.

Tomlinson, C. (1995). *How to differentiate instruction in mixed-ability classrooms.* Alexandria, VA: Association for Supervision and Curriculum Development.

A Strategy for Review

FENTEY BERKELEY SCOTT
Lakeland University, Thunderbay, ON, Canada

STRATEGY/ACTIVITY/ASSIGNMENT

Students in a preservice junior-intermediate course, "Education 4437: Teaching in a Multicultural Setting," are told to imagine they are preparing an interview for a radio broadcast. They must take a problem typical of the grade level. In the exercise delineated, name calling and stereotyping were the problems focused on. In groups of two to four, they formulate three questions about the issue. They are given twenty-five minutes to prepare the questions and the answers. They are then given another fifteen minutes to get the whole interview down to seven minutes. Finally, they have to choose an interviewer and an interviewee and conduct the interview live before the rest of the class.

The other groups function as evaluators and provide feedback on the basis of (1) the effectiveness of the questions for eliciting the relevant information, (2) whether their presentation was made within the time allotted, and (3) the quality of the responses. Two groups then get to present for each review. To make sure that each group gives an honest effort, each group is identified by a number and takes its turn accordingly; the other is randomly selected.

Although this is designed for a class of seventy-five minutes duration, it can easily be adapted for different time frames. For example, a class of fifty minutes might easily do the preparation of questions and the refinement of the interview script on day one and conduct the interviews and feedback on day two.

COMMENTARY

After I had done this once, students asked if we could try it again. We did, but I had them determine what the concept was after they had listened to the interview. The limitation in regard to this variation is that it can degenerate into a guessing game if the instructor is not vigilant.

This assignment was designed primarily to help students develop review skills through a decision-making process. They are forced to make choices about what is important and what are worthwhile questions to ask. The fact that they have to meet a time deadline is an incentive to get directly to the matter at hand, particularly in the second segment of the exercise. In addition to the questions of choice, students also learn to gauge each other's skills and use them to advantage. Listening and evaluation skills are improved as well, since students must listen to form their evaluations and determine what questions they will ask of the performing group.

Student reaction to this exercise was varied. In a discussion of the value of the exercise, some students wanted the time for the first segment reduced; others wanted the time for this same segment extended.

The most frequent reason given for the first position was that when students do their homework, the formulation of questions is easy but then answers have to be framed within the students' understanding of the questions; proponents of the second position felt that the real confirmation of understanding comes in the exchange of ideas and the matter of determining what was really critical and relevant, not just what a student remembered. They indicated that this made the choice in the second segment easier because in the first segment they had to anticipate the kind of information and emphasis needed for "public consumption."

In the end, we all agreed that a split of thirty minutes for the first segment and twenty minutes for the second segment were just about right for us. The remainder of our seventy-five minutes was given over to one interview and the evaluation and feedback.

The feedback provided was also an eye-opener. Students commented not only on whether students met the evaluation criteria we had established, but also on such things as the confidence displayed, the tone of voice and whether the interviewer seemed too aggressive in his or her approach, and whether the interviewees gave the impression that they really knew what they were talking about. Students also thought the process was useful for helping them hone study skills and clarify points for writing essays and papers.

Constructivism/Non-Directive Teaching: Some Thoughts on Developing Independent Learners

REGINA G. CHATEL
Saint Joseph College, West Hartford, CT

STRATEGY/ACTIVITY/ASSIGNMENT

A major premise of my middle level course is that learning comes from within the learner and is not imposed by the teacher. This goes to the heart of all teaching but especially to the middle level philosophy of teaching and learning. In order to help us understand this philosophy, students participate in the design of assignments and the evaluation rubrics. The professor shares two or three samples of assignments and possible evaluation rubrics; however, the class takes on the responsibility of delineating the scope of each assignment.

COMMENTARY

"Why don't you just tell us the guidelines for the assignment and how it will be evaluated and we'll do it! Instead of spending class time arguing over it!"

"Why do we have to discuss everything? You would cover a lot more material if you lectured."

"You give us a lot of theories, but what's the right one?"

A student recently stopped by my office to express the concern that the class is spending a lot of time arguing over the nature of literacy development and how it should be taught to children, negotiating guidelines for assignments, and designing evaluation rubrics that she thought should be done by the professor. The implication being—that is the professor's job! After all, the professor is paid to teach and the students pay to be taught by the professor, not their peers! This discussion gets to the heart of conflict between traditional directive instruction, which is what students expect, and my effort to create a non-directive/constructivist classroom environment.

A constructivist philosophy of education places great demands on the teacher and the learner. It demands that the teacher be a facilitator and an organizer who structures the environment for learning. It demands that the student be a self-motivated, confident, and active learner. The goal of constructivist teaching is to facilitate student learning through the creation of classroom situations that require students to establish personal goals for learning, ask probing questions, gather data, and examine their sources of information. Although guided by the teacher, this newly gained knowledge is much more significant and meaningful to the learner because it is learner controlled. For many students and teachers, this is a threatening innovation in teaching and learning because the teacher gives control of the learning process to the students and the students assume the control and responsibility for learning. So, what are the roles and responsibilities of the teacher in a constructivist classroom?

First, the teacher is a facilitator. Some have used the expression of the "guide on the side" rather than the "sage on the stage." As facilitator, the teacher is accepting of student responses, beliefs, attitudes, and feelings. The teacher may disagree but she also must be supportive, responsive, and sincere in fostering the intellectual development of all students. The teacher "invites" her students to learn!

Second, students are the center of a constructivist classroom. Group discussions, cooperative learning, conferences, interviews, and team work play a major role in the teaching and learning process. Although this does preclude the traditional lecture, which is an example of the sage-on-the-stage approach, the constructivist classroom fosters divergent thinking, independent learning, and self-evaluation. Learning is highly individualized and personalized rather than uniformly alike for all students. Therefore, the teacher must help students articulate the questions that are meaningful to them and will drive their inquiry. With respect to the inquiry process, the teacher helps the students discover ways to conduct inquiries but does not attempt to impose one way to do it. The teacher honors students' ability and desire to learn on their own, from each other, from experts in the field, and from the teacher.

So, what are the roles and responsibilities of the learner in the constructivist classroom? First, the student must be an active learner. An active learner participates in group discussion, works on teams, prepares for class, supports other learners in the classroom, engages in negotiating project guidelines and their evaluation, and participates in self-evaluation. The active learner accepts the teacher's invitation to learn.

Second, the student must assume control of his or her learning. In doing so, the student must ask the question, "What do I want to learn?" rather than assuming the stance of "Just tell me what you want in this assignment and I will do it." Just as it is the teacher's role to develop choices, it is the student's responsibility to make choices. However, if the student has not established a personal purpose and direction for the learning, the concept of choice is meaningless. Choice is then perceived as a lack of clarity or specificity on the part of the teacher.

Let's consider this premise. If we as educators believe that the concepts of prior knowledge, schema, and metacognition are of vital importance in dealing with our children, why are preservice teachers so eager to dismiss these concepts when they are applied to them? If choice, structure, support, and a student-centered classroom are your educational goals when you have your own classroom, why are they met with such resistance in preservice education?

I am constantly grappling with striking that fine balance between satisfying the students' needs for definitive answers and my belief that learning is a constructive process. One student wrote on her course evaluation: "Dr. Chatel was a little difficult to get used to at first because she does not want to give you answers—you are forced to answer things for yourself. I realize now that that allowed me to learn a great deal about the subject and myself. I would take another class with her."

Another student wrote: "I think in hindsight, it was a smooth and organized course. But, during the semester, skipping around the syllabus was a bit unnerving. The Internet portfolio was a little vague in criteria at first and that was frustrating, but again, in hindsight, I think it was beneficial to work it through."

As these students have come to realize, I believe in the constructive nature of learning, which means that it may appear to be messy at times, but it is highly focused and planned. My instructional goal is to help my students understand that knowledge is not just a collection of isolated bits of information delivered by the professor, which can be reduced to definitive chunks of instruction. I am constantly working on striking the balance between a constructive, or non-directive, versus a directive philosophy of teaching and learning.

In summary, the success of our educational experience is premised on communication and an exchange—not a delivery—of ideas. It is contingent upon the student's acceptance of self-reliance and taking personal initiative and the teacher's acceptance of the responsibility to provide structure with choice.

CHAPTER 5

Interdisciplinary Instruction

Matching Middle Level Student Skills and Interests with Learning Activities

WILLIAM E. KLINGELE
The University of Akron, Akron, OH

STRATEGY/ACTIVITY/ASSIGNMENT

This activity is specifically designed to provide a learning experience that links the nature of the middle school student with instructional activities. It is assigned as the transitional activity that occurs at the end of the course unit on middle level student characteristics and the beginning of the unit on the instructional process.

The activity is introduced with the concept that each middle school student has a special skill, which he or she can do better than almost every other student. And each middle school student has a special interest area in which he or she is more interested than almost every other student. Then, in a Will Rogers fashion, the instructor says, "My experience leads me to believe that I never met a middle level student who couldn't do something, perhaps one thing, better than almost every other student, or had an area of interest that was more intense than that of most other students." The resulting discussion always concludes with a great deal of skepticism on the part of teacher education students.

Interdisciplinary teams of middle level education students are then assigned classes of students in specific middle schools and told to test the Will Rogers theory. Through structured interviews and observations of the middle school students and their teachers, the teacher education students attempt to identify a special skill or interest area unique to each student. Examples often include sports-related interests, fashion design, exercise science, food, cars, music, the performing arts, and woodcrafting. This activity, like all other university class field activities performed in partnership schools, are covered under university-school collaboration agreements. These activities are considered field experiences and not research. They do not require, therefore, approval by the university research board or permission by parents. In the schools, they are covered under the same state laws as student teaching.

Based on the identification of skills and interests, teacher education candidates, during their unit of instructional activities, design unique student activities within an interdisciplinary unit of instruction. The student activities must be active-learning tasks. They share and discuss the skills and interests discovered, as well as the instructional activities designed around them. The middle level cooperating teachers are given copies of the student-specific skills and interests, as well as the activities designed for them. These teachers keep a resource bank of skills, interests, and activities that are used in professional development activities involving other teachers of the students on whom the information is based.

COMMENTARY

This lesson is the favorite activity of the middle level methods course for the professor, the teacher education students, and the cooperating teachers. It is the single most productive activity that educates teacher education candidates about the nature of middle school students and developmentally appropriate instructional activities. Something special occurs when prospective teachers sit down and talk to middle level students about their interests and skills. Teacher candidates are transformed from disbelievers to believers of middle level students. Beginning field experiences often tend to result in skepticism on the part of teacher candidates. This experience, however, results in a communication that fosters understanding and a sense of realization of why middle level students act as they do. Teacher candidates' attitudes become more positive concerning their potential to address middle level students' needs now that they understand them, like them, and feel they can reach and teach them. Typical comments have been, "Now I understand them," and "Now I really like them."

The information gleaned about their middle level students has had similar results on their teachers. Cooperating teachers have developed a much better understanding of their students, an improved attitude towards middle level teaching, and significantly improved instructional approaches geared toward the unique skills, talents, and special interests of their students. The ultimate results are middle level students with improved positive self-concepts who are given opportunities to enrich their skills, talents, and special interests, which lead to overall personal, social, and academic achievement.

An important aspect of the lesson appears to be the generation and accumulation of resources, the lists of skills and interests, and the resulting interdisciplinary units and instructional activities. Both cooperating teachers and teacher candidates have responded favorably to the resources that result from this activity. The cost for copying these materials for teacher candidates and cooperating teachers can be covered through a course fee.

Introductory Activity on Interdisciplinary Units

SAMUEL TOTTEN
University of Arkansas, Fayetteville

STRATEGY/ACTIVITY/ASSIGNMENT

The main goal of the following introductory activity on interdisciplinary units, which I use in both my undergraduate and graduate middle level principles and methods courses, is to illuminate the interdisciplinary nature of the major issues confronting society. By keeping this exercise in mind as the students plan their interdisciplinary unit, it prods them to dig below the surface as they attempt to ascertain the interdisciplinary nature of a topic. In doing so, it helps them to avoid a perfunctory situation where the unit is merely skimming the surface vis-à-vis a topic or the issue's interdisciplinary nature.

The instructor selects four or five recent articles from major newspapers and magazines that generally feature fairly in-depth pieces on important topics or issues. Some of the journals and magazines used are: *The Bulletin of Atomic Scientists, The Christian Science Monitor, The Chronicle of Higher Education, Holocaust and Genocide Studies, The Los Angeles Times, Newsweek, The New York Times, Science, Time Magazine, U.S. News and World Report,* and *The Washington Post.* Reports from major organizations—Amnesty International, the Sierra Club, the United States Holocaust Memorial Museum, the Nuclear Control Institute, Friends of the Earth, Klan Watch in Montgomery, Alabama—are also used. Copies of the same articles are provided for each student in the class. For the sake of expediency, relatively short (2 to 3 pages) but infor-

mative articles are used. The topics of the articles have been rather eclectic: the banning of certain articles and/or color clothing in schools in various cities and towns across the United States, the U.S. Holocaust
Memorial Museum's definition of the "Holocaust," tobacco bans across
the United States, the advertising and marketing of U.S. tobacco-
produced products in Third World countries, horizontal nuclear prolifer-
ation (or the spread of nuclear weapons across the globe), the destruction
of the rain forests and its many ramifications, the increased incidence of
slavery in various parts of the world, the use of corporal punishment in
schools, and the question "Is it incumbent on professional athletes to be
role models for today's youth?"

Each student reads each article and simply lists all of the disciplines
(e.g., psychology, biology, philosophy, literature, genetics, physics, basic
mathematics, biology, and sociology) that bear, in one way or another, on
the topic they are reading. Each time they jot down a discipline, they
have to write a short note as to exactly how the discipline bears on the
subject. For example, if the students are examining the issue of the definition of the Holocaust, someone might write down "religion" and after
that he or she might simply jot the note: "the Nazis were influenced by
the long history of traditional Christian antisemitism."

Once the initial part of the activity is completed, students are placed
in groups of threes or fours. In their groups, they share their ideas, discuss them, and develop a single list of disciplines for each article on
which there is a group consensus. Again, each group must note the discipline and provide a succinct explanation as to how the discipline directly
relates to the topic.

Once the group has reached a consensus, it is provided with a large
sheet of butcher paper and a magic marker on which they write, in large
letters, their insights. Each member of the group signs his or her name on
the front of the sheet and hangs the sheet of butcher paper on the wall.
Then, still in their small groups, each group moves from one piece of
butcher paper to another in order to ascertain what the other students
listed. Each group is encouraged to write, in pencil, on any of the sheets,
questions it has about a particular point. These questions will subsequently be addressed in a general class discussion. Each group is also
asked to select the one sheet that is both most comprehensive and most
accurate and to write down the name of the individuals in that group on a
slip of paper. It should be pointed out that it is not enough for a list to
simply be the most comprehensive; accuracy is also a must.

A general discussion ensues that addresses a host of issues, including, but not limited to, the following: the various disciplines that bear on the topic or issue at hand, the way in which the topics are intertwined and influence one another in order to create the issue, any disciplines that might have been overlooked, any disagreements over whether certain disciplines truly bear on the topic at hand or not, the way in which the individuals and groups figured out which disciplines were germane to the topic, and so forth.

The coup de grace is when I posit this question: "What if we removed the influence of a certain discipline from the overall equation of the issue? Would it really make any difference?" This final question often generates a fascinating—and sometimes heated—discussion which forces all of us to probe even deeper into the interdisciplinary aspect of the issue or topic.

Finally, I share my own delineation of the topics. I usually place my observations on an overhead, and we compare and contrast them with the students' insights and discuss the accuracy and/or inaccuracy of my insights.

In the hour-and-a-half session, this activity can be conducted a minimum of two or three times, thus accomplishing the examination of two or three articles. To thoroughly prep students to critically examine the interdisciplinary nature of issues, it is essential to conduct this activity at least twice.

COMMENTARY

This activity provides students with an opportunity to wrestle with the complexity of an issue as well as to discern just how many disciplines are at play in a single issue.

The beauty and power of the activity becomes evident during the students' work in class on the development of their own interdisciplinary units. When working in groups of three or four to plan their units, it is not unusual to hear a member of a group say, "Remember that initial activity and how . . . ." In that regard, the introductory activity not only serves as an exemplar of sorts, but also as a strong reminder of the complexity of issues and how various disciplines interact in a multiplicity of ways in the development of a single issue.

Long-Range Planning

TONI SILLS-BRIEGEL
Southwest Missouri State University, Springfield

STRATEGY/ACTIVITY/ASSIGNMENT

Planning for instruction normally involves long-range planning, unit planning, weekly planning, and daily lesson planning. The key to good planning at every level is long-range planning. Long-range planning is essential to middle level teachers in that it allows teams to coordinate plans for interdisciplinary instruction. Preservice teachers are normally concerned with how to utilize a curriculum guide or course resources to develop a coherent program of instruction. They want to know "when to do what." Developing a long-range plan provides them with a sense of the flow of activities over a semester or a school year. Teacher teams use the long-range plans to identify opportunities for a variety of interdisciplinary learning experiences and to create further opportunities as teachers work together to flex and rearrange their plans.

Long-range plans are relatively easy to learn to design using the following procedure. Using a transparency with a semester's worth of school days (Monday through Friday) typed on it, the professor models long-range planning. The first step is to cross out all holidays and non-teaching days (assemblies, teacher workdays, etc.) Students are amazed at how many interruptions occur in a typical school semester. The professor blocks out the first week of school for introductory activities; three or four days at the end of each quarter for testing; and discusses game days, assemblies, and other normal, but unexpected interruptions in the school day. In addition to planning, this activity illustrates the importance of instructional time and the need for flexibility. The professor emphasizes that units of instruction must be designed so that the most important points will be taught first and less important points are covered as time permits.

The professor then quickly marks in units of instruction based on a specific subject area. (I use language arts since that was my subject area specialty when I was a middle level teacher.) Using this one-page overview of a semester's instruction, the professor selects a unit, outlines it, then selects a week from the unit, outlines it, then finally chooses just one day and creates a one-page lesson plan. Students see the entire process of planning from long-range plan to daily lesson plan. Each of the four types of planning is about a page long.

The next step is to place students in pairs or in groups of three according to their discipline. Students usually know their discipline fairly well, but are uncertain about how much material constitutes a unit and when that unit should be taught and how long it should last. Working in pairs allows student to discuss both their content field and the planning process. Using a long-range planning calendar page provided by the professor, students work to create a long-range plan suitable for their subject area.

The creation of a long-range plan is the first step in designing interdisciplinary units that fulfill the state and national requirements for a content area. Once students have created their long-range plans, they are placed in interdisciplinary teams to coordinate their plans and search for places where their plans can be modified to support other disciplines and to open up opportunities for true interdisciplinary instruction.

The calendar handout can be used as a nonblock plan using traditional 50-minute periods, or it may be divided into an ABABC block schedule. Other block variations require slightly different designs for long-range plans.

COMMENTARY

Students are appalled by how little uninterrupted instructional time is available to them. We usually have to interrupt class for a few minutes to discuss the needs of education versus the desires of the community. Students quickly understand the need for long-range planning, accepting the analogy that putting such a plan together is much like completing a complex puzzle. Working together to analyze their content areas for suitable units causes many of them to identify weaknesses or even gaps in their subject knowledge base. Comments from reflective journals cite this activity as one of the few that has given them a concrete example of long-range planning, "I have been overwhelmed thinking about the first few days of school. Where to start, what to teach. This has made it all make sense to me."

Long-Range Planning Calendar

A Monday	B Tuesday	A Wednesday	B Thursday	C Friday
Aug 27	28	29	30	31
Sep 3	4	5	6	7
10	11	12	13	14
17	18	19	20	21
24	25	26	27	28
Oct 1	2	3	4	5
8	9	10	11	12
15	16	17	18	19
22	23	24	25	26
29	30	31	**Nov 1**	2
5	6	7	8	9
12	13	14	15	16
19	20	21	22	23
26	27	28	29	30
Dec 3	4	5	6	7
10	11	12	13	14
17	18	19	20	21

Holidays and interruptions to normal routine:
Memorial Day, 9/3
9 week exams, Oct. 24-26, Dec. 18-20
Holiday program, 12/21
Assembly programs (2 hours), 8/29, 9/27, 10/17, 11/15, 12/5
Teacher workdays (1/2 day), 9/24, 10/22, 12/3
Other possible interruptions: Halloween, fire/tornado/earthquake drills, called assemblies

Modeling Interdisciplinary/ Learner-Centered Instruction

CHARLES T. WYNN
Wesleyan College, Macon, GA

STRATEGY/ACTIVITY/ASSIGNMENT

It is extremely important that middle level preservice teachers experience interdisciplinary/learner-centered instruction as learners and as future teachers. To facilitate this experience, instructors in the senior methods block (language arts, science, and social studies) at Wesleyan College model quality interdisciplinary instruction. The modeling process involves the implementation of a variety of instructional methods within an interdisciplinary/thematic structure with both preservice teachers and middle level students. To this end, the middle grades methods block instructors developed a unit entitled "Maka Island." The unit is designed for middle level students to inductively develop an understanding of imperialism and to practice decision-making skills as they answer the question posed in a fictional scenario: Should the United States, in 1895, take or control Maka Island? The complete Maka unit, including lesson plans, material, and assessment can be accessed free of charge at http://168.17.224.250/finley/eduhome.html.

In preparation for this decision-making activity, each lesson guides students in gathering and using historical, geopolitical, cultural, and scientific (island formation, geologic stability, and natural resources) information to support or reject a proposal of U.S. expansion. The purpose of implementing this middle grades unit at the beginning of the methods block is to help preservice teachers gain a conceptual understanding of interdisciplinary and learner-centered instruction.

The unit is team-taught by the instructors during the first nine sessions (each one of which is approximately one hour in length) of the methods block. Upon completion of the unit, preservice students participate in a debriefing session that allows for critical examination of unit activities from dual perspectives—the learner's and the preservice teacher's. Preservice students use insights gained through unit activities to recognize and identify how disciplines overlapped and were integrated within a theme or topic. Students also identify to what extent knowledge gained from the unit was more meaningful and connected when taught through integrated, learner-centered instruction. The Maka unit also serves as a model of lesson-plan development, including format, scope, sequence, and so forth.

A second, equally important part of this strategy is the modeling of effective interdisciplinary/learner-centered instruction with middle level students. After the preservice teachers have completed the unit as learners, they have the opportunity to compare and contrast their experience by viewing a video of the methods-course instructors teaching Maka to fifth graders at a local public school. Instructors and students then discuss specific questions or concerns regarding the implementation of the unit with fifth graders (i.e., sequencing and structure of lessons, rationale and developmental appropriateness of content/methods/strategies, student performance and response to each lesson and method, student behavior, and classroom management strategies). Methods students also are asked to point out specific differences or similarities between the fifth graders' experience with Maka and their own. The Maka experience then moves back to the fifth-grade classroom, where methods students and cooperating teachers observe the methods-course instructors teach the Maka unit to a new group of fifth graders at the same public school. Preservice teachers, cooperating teachers, and methods-course instructors participate in a debriefing session at the end of the day regarding the Maka Island experience from a teacher's and learner's perspective.

COMMENTARY

The rationale for the Maka Island activity at the outset of the methods block is threefold. First, students should have the opportunity to gain a clear conceptual understanding of interdisciplinary and learner-centered instruction through experience. With the understandable anxiety and skepticism that students often bring to the preservice experience, it places the burden of proof on the instructors. Common questions such as "What do you mean by interdisciplinary/integrated/thematic?" and "Will this work?" and "Can you really do these kinds of things with middle level students?" will be answered through experiencing and observing actual instruction. This not only sets a tone that bridges the gap between theory and practice, but it shows in a powerful way that instructors can indeed practice what they preach. The modeling process is a powerful and needed practice that can make all participants in the methods block a community of learners and teachers. Second, initially providing an exemplary model that will serve to facilitate unit/lesson-plan development also eases anxiety and stress among preservice teachers. From the very beginning of the methods-block experience, the modeling process provides an organizational structure from which students can build. Third, it is hoped that the Maka Island experience will increase the probability that preservice teachers will develop and use interdisciplinary/learner-centered units when they become teachers.

Thematic Integrated Units

MELANIE W. GREENE
Appalachian State University, Boone, NC

STRATEGY/ACTIVITY/ASSIGNMENT

One of the major assignments for middle level preservice teachers is to design a thematic integrated unit that is developmentally appropriate for the young adolescent learner. Students are required to work as members of interdisciplinary teams and to work jointly with their content-area methods professors as plans are designed. Themes should emerge from the intersection of the early adolescents' personal and social concerns and should incorporate content from the core curriculum as well as from exploratory courses. The theme should include novel ideas not traditionally found in textbooks, yet resources should be available to support the interactive activities incorporated into the unit. In addition, the theme should be motivating and enjoyable for the learners. Popular themes include transitions, conflict resolution, justice, caring, and the power of the media.

A comprehensive rubric is presented that details the specific requirements for the integrated thematic unit. The rubric contains items such as an overview of the unit, curriculum connections, exploratory elements, key concepts, essential questions, launching event, instructional activities, service learning component, time frame, culminating event, assessment instruments, and a bibliography. Each element is evaluated according to the following levels: outstanding, commendable, needs improvement. Explanatory comments are also provided for each aspect of the rubric.

Student interdisciplinary teams are required to present these units in written and oral form to their faculty team and peers as the culminating experience for the course. Multimedia must be incorporated into the presentation. In addition, outstanding units are presented to a forum of middle level educators who serve as their cooperating teachers in ensuing internships in the public schools. Each year, teams are selected to present these units at the state middle school conference.

COMMENTARY

When preservice teachers enter the middle-grades program, they are accustomed to completing assignments on an individual basis and have had limited experience working collaboratively. This assignment affords students the opportunity to experience planning as a member of an interdisciplinary team and to organize core curriculum subjects and exploratory courses around themes that are developmentally responsive to the needs of the young adolescent. While the teams are collaborating on this assignment, they have the opportunity to experience the teaming concept and to engage in the stages of team development including forming, storming, norming, and performing. Team leaders emerge, and mock program improvement council meetings are held with the faculty team to solidify plans and to discuss concerns and issues that evolve during the completion of the assignment.

Students are further challenged to become contributors to their profession. They have this opportunity as they present their units to audiences, which include teachers from the local school district and across the state. Unit overviews later become an artifact for their professional portfolios that are prepared in the course.

Developing an Interdisciplinary Curriculum Unit

STEVEN A. GREENGROSS
Southern Connecticut State University, New Haven

STRATEGY/ACTIVITY/ASSIGNMENT

In my course, "Interdisciplinary Teaching in the Middle Grades," there is an assignment that enables graduate students to experience the development of an interdisciplinary curriculum unit. By definition, an interdisciplinary unit is thematic; in other words, English, mathematics, science, and social studies are all taught with a common theme. Traditionally, each of these academic subjects has been taught separately and its content has been unrelated to any of the other three disciplines. The major drawback to this approach is that many early adolescents have a difficult time seeing relevance to their lives. "Why do we have to learn this stuff" is a typical early adolescent reaction. By utilizing a thematic approach, there is a continuing relationship among the four disciplines. For example, if the theme is the Olympics, the content in English, mathematics, science, and social studies is always the Olympics. Because students are able to see this connection, each subject becomes more relevant.

The specific task for the students in the course is to develop a ten-day interdisciplinary unit. The students work in teams of four: One student represents an English teacher, one a math teacher, one a science teacher, and one a social studies teacher. Although the theme for the unit is left to the team's discretion, the entire unit and every lesson plan must be skills-based, and there must be a unit plan and daily lesson plans for each subject. *Skills-based* means that the unit must stress the development of skills as opposed to just the memorization of content. Thus, for example, a social studies unit would use the Civil War as a way to teach cause-and-effect relationships in addition to requiring students to learn factual information.

In order to simulate a real school environment, the students are given certain parameters and conditions. There is a 180-minute consecutive block of academic time each day. Only those instructional methods (such as cooperative learning) that work best with early adolescents may be employed. Flexible scheduling must be used, which means that while each subject does not have to be taught every day, each subject must receive a total of 450 minutes of instruction in the unit. Finally, integrated lessons that combine two or more academic subjects within the same lesson are encouraged. Each lesson plan must include, as appropriate, specific adaptations for attention deficit hyperactivity disorder (ADHD) students, learning disabled (LD) students, and gifted students.

Although grade level is optional (5 through 8), in each hypothetical team there are 100 students (52 boys and 48 girls): 25 (15 girls, 10 boys) are working above grade level; 50 (25 girls, 25 boys) are working on grade level; 25 (8 girls, 17 boys) are working below grade level. Included in these 100 students are 12 special needs students. Five of these students are ADHD and are on grade level, and none receive any direct special education services. The other seven students are all LD. Four are below grade level; three are on grade level; all have reading decoding and comprehension difficulties as well as written-expression difficulties. Each LD student's IEP calls for special education services in English. There are also three gifted students (one girl and two boys) in the above-grade-level group. An inclusion model is followed, and all special needs students are in all regular education classes all day. The four LD students who are below grade level are in the same English class, and a special needs teacher is in that class each day. There is also a special needs instructional aide who is assigned to the team for the entire academic day.

COMMENTARY

For many students in the course, this assignment represents a paradigm shift from one-subject, content-based teaching to instruction that is multi-subject and skills-based. Time is provided in class for students to work together in groups and for whole-class discussions about the assignment itself. Because the students self-select their groups at random, some groups come together more quickly and easily than others. In addition, the majority of students typically have not had many opportunities to experience group process. Since both possibilities simulate potential teaming difficulties in an actual middle school, they become positive learning experiences.

The professor's main role during this activity is to facilitate learning. Thus, another benefit of this experience is that it simulates a group learning experience in a middle school. The students in the class have the opportunity to experience working in a group, and they are also able to see the professor model the role of a middle school teacher in group learning.

On the last day of the semester, each group gives a brief oral presentation that highlights the major points of its interdisciplinary unit. The students are also able to obtain copies of the other units through the university duplicating services.

The students in the class are all either teaching or in a fifth-year masters/certification program. Those who are teaching in middle schools are encouraged to use what they have learned from this experience to try to develop an interdisciplinary unit of instruction in their own schools. The students who will be applying for teaching jobs are encouraged to include the unit in their portfolios as an example of what they can already do. The reaction of students to these suggestions has been highly positive.

It is always a pleasure from an instructor's perspective to watch the changes that take place in the students during the creation of this unit. A sense of well-being replaces initial discomfort with the group process, and a "this is fun, kids would really like this" attitude replaces initial skepticism with this type of skills-based, interdisciplinary curriculum.

Finally, in spite of all the research to the contrary, too many middle schools are still mired in departmentalized, content-based curriculum. An effective way to work toward changing this is by teaching graduate students how to develop interdisciplinary curriculum and empowering them to become agents of change in their respective schools.

Interdisciplinary Instruction in Practice

CHARLENE JOHNSON
University of Arkansas, Fayetteville

STRATEGY/ACTIVITY/ASSIGNMENT

A major assignment in my undergraduate middle level principles course is the development of an interdisciplinary lesson or unit. Preservice teachers work in groups of four or five, with different disciplines being represented, in order to develop a team lesson plan. The plan includes objective(s), introductory set, procedure/activities, and evaluation procedures. For special education students, the plans must incorporate the modifications they would include to meet students' needs. An oral presentation of the team's final product is also required. The evaluation of the lesson plan is based on: (1) the grade appropriateness of the objectives, (2) the developmental appropriateness of the activities, (3) integration of the subjects, and (4) the synchronization of the objectives, activities, and evaluation within each lesson.

Based on the number of preservice teachers in the course and the differences among their majors, the assignment varies from semester to semester in scope and comprehensiveness. The requirements that remain consistent are the need to: (1) focus on at least two different subjects within the unit, (2) decide on a common theme for the lesson or unit, and (3) develop at least two lessons based on the theme and show how the two (or more) subjects are interwoven within the theme.

Additions to this assignment have included requiring information on the school (demographics, size, grade configuration, region, resources) and the community to be served by the plan. Preservice teachers have also been required to provide a layout of the middle level school building to be served by this interdisciplinary unit. This additional information encourages the preservice teachers to reflect on their student population and the relevance of their theme, activities, and evaluation within the unit.

COMMENTARY

When the assignment is first given, it is one of the least liked or understood assignments. Preservice teachers are accustomed to writing lessons for their discipline but are uncertain and uneasy on how to relate to different disciplines. As we progress through the semester, preservice teachers are given class time to work in their groups/pairs (exemplifying common planning time). During this time, preservice teachers can ask questions, decide on themes, and begin the process of developing the lessons with my direct guidance. Once the themes are decided on and the preservice teachers make connections among their different ideas, the resistance diminishes and preservice teachers become engaged in the process. Although it is recognized that the lessons, buildings, and schools/classes are hypothetical, the experience is designed to familiarize preservice teachers with the process of making connections among different disciplines/subjects and the importance of understanding the student population and their community for effective instruction.

Students have often commented that this is one of the most challenging but useful experiences of the class for their professional development. The culmination of the experience—the oral presentations—often receive rave reviews for their educational and practical use. As they listen to their peers' lessons, they glean ideas for other units and/or activities they may use with their students.

It is recommended that preservice teachers keep their lesson for possible use during their intern year and/or their professional portfolio to show to potential employers, especially those seeking positions in schools serving the middle grades. The interdisciplinary unit demonstrates that the preservice teacher is already familiar with this practice and has worked on one. One student wrote to inform me that he had used the unit he had developed in class and that potential employers were impressed with his knowledge and skills in this area.

Integrated Curriculum Reflected Through Practice

PATRICIA M. LAMPHERE
Oklahoma State University, Stillwater

KATHRYN S. REINKE
Oklahoma State University, Stillwater

STRATEGY/ACTIVITY/ASSIGNMENT

An activity that provides a foundation for preservice teachers to experience teaching in an integrated environment is the development and implementation of an integrated thematic unit. The preservice teachers enrolled in the four academic content areas (mathematics, social studies, science, and language/literacy methods courses) are assigned to instructional teams. The goal is to develop a five-lesson thematic unit that can be taught in the middle school.

The university instructors arranged for the teachers at the local middle schools to have the preservice teachers present the units to the middle school classes. The preservice teachers, with their teams, plan and then present the individual lessons in the assigned classes. For example, the mathematics lessons are presented in the mathematics classes by the preservice teachers who are seeking their endorsement in middle school mathematics. As many as four preservice teachers representing each content area are included on the team so that each team member is responsible for preparing and presenting several lessons from the unit. The topics for the units are selected with the guidance of the middle school teachers so that the objectives mesh with the existing curriculum. However, the preservice teachers have full responsibility for selecting content, designing instructional activities, and implementing assessment techniques.

The preservice teachers develop a theoretical framework for the use of integrated thematic units in middle school curriculum. Background information includes a discussion of how middle school students learn and the social, psychological, emotional, and physiological factors that influence such learning. Preservice teachers must research their content areas, draw practical ideas for integrating the curriculum from articles, and design alternative approaches to assessment in order to evaluate student learning. The following outline highlights the components that must be included in each unit:

    I. Table of contents
   II. Goals and rationale for the unit
  III. Lesson plans must: comprise a unit of five lessons and include both an introductory and culminating activity; contain specific lessons for each content area; reflect a balance of integration among the subject areas; and address academic and cultural diversity issues
  IV. Letter to parents about the unit
   V. Teaching schedule for the unit and a one-day, minute-by-minute schedule
  VI. Resource/materials list
 VII. Two lesson plans adapted to meet the needs of students with special cognitive or physical needs or other special needs
VIII. Description of assessment instruments and expectations of learner outcomes
  IX. Student evaluation of the unit

Preservice teachers developed all the lessons, designed assessment instruments, and taught the unit. Once the unit was presented, the preservice teachers reflected on the success of the planning and delivery of the lessons, the results of the assessment (what the students actually learned), and the evaluations completed by the middle school teachers and students.

COMMENTARY

When middle school methods courses are taught through an integrated approach, preservice candidates benefit from not only having firsthand experience with an integrated curriculum but also from witnessing the collaboration that can exist among content specialists. In programs where preservice candidates receive an endorsement rather than certification, middle school methods courses are taught in isolation and are taken by both elementary and secondary preservice candidates. When this occurs, the chance that preservice candidates take more than one of the specialized methods courses is rare. Instructors must make special arrangements in order to collaborate and demonstrate for their students how successful integration of the curriculum can be. When organizing schedules, care should be taken to schedule middle school methods courses in such a way that their times overlap, thereby providing students opportunities to work together. Choice of text materials that reinforce the ideas of integration should also support this endeavor.

In their evaluations of the course, many of the preservice teachers reflected that they learned more by completing this assignment than they did from any other activity. Through this one experience, they constructed their own knowledge about integration of the curriculum, gained invaluable experience as contributing members of a collaborative instructional team, and practiced what they had learned about students, teaching, and assessment. Admittedly, most preservice teachers reported that it was the hardest, most demanding assignment they had completed during the semester. However, according to the preservice teachers, it was also the most beneficial. By providing preservice teachers with opportunities to be in the middle level classroom presenting lessons they have developed, we have established a precedent they will carry into their student-teaching experience. The experience will also contribute to their desire to integrate the curriculum across the content areas in the middle level setting in which they teach.

Interdisciplinary Instruction: Where Do We Start?

CAROLINE BELLER
University of Arkansas, Fayetteville

STRATEGY/ACTIVITY/ASSIGNMENT

The activity described herein was originally used with in-service teachers enrolled in a thematic science course at a state university. Some of the teachers were seeking additional degrees or certification, and others were enrolled to develop an understanding of integrated/thematic science (merging the concepts of life, earth, and physical science through the use of thematic units). The activity was then adapted for use as an interdisciplinary experience to be used with middle level teacher teams. Each team attending the course consisted of one teacher from each of the four main academic areas. These teachers functioned as an interdisciplinary team at the same school. Ideally, such staff development should take place over a period of several months in order for the teachers to practice each component with their students and then participate in a follow-up session of reflection, discussion, analysis, and further team-planning.

On the first day of in-service or on a Saturday, the teachers should assemble for a field trip. The field trip should be at least one-half day in length and preferably one full day. This trip could be to a zoo, an aquarium, a botanical garden, a state or local park, etc. As the teachers tour the trip location, each person should be asked to write out as many ideas as possible concerning themes and topics related to their subject area.

After the field trip is completed, the interdisciplinary teams should work together for the remainder of the course. Each team should list any common themes and topics that emanated from the field trip. The next step is for each team to select one of the common topics and plan one day for the whole team to use that topic as the focus of their lesson for the specified day. At the next session, each teacher should be prepared to discuss student reactions to studying the same topic in all of their classes and to share any suggestions for possible changes in the future. The team of teachers should also plan their next interdisciplinary topic and create/plan a week's worth of activities related to the topic. Another round of reflection, discussion, analysis, and planning should follow the week's activities. The team of teachers is now ready to plan a complete thematic unit that can last as long as they feel is necessary.

COMMENTARY

Learners construct knowledge based on new information and how it relates to prior experiences. Individuals from different backgrounds need to experience common activities before they can discuss ideas concerning student learning. That is the purpose of the field trip—to provide the participants with a common experience.

In an attempt to avoid overwhelming the teachers with lengthy, complex assignments, a divergent approach is used. In this approach the teachers progress from the simple, one-common-topic activity to the complex development of an interdisciplinary unit. Short assignments are given to provide teachers with a feeling of success. Once the short, simple assignments are mastered, additional levels of complexity are added to the assignments until teachers are able to develop a complete interdisciplinary unit for their students.

Assessment of the staff development program focused on the teacher reflections and student comments. At first the teachers felt confused about planning their lessons and activities around a common topic.

They were afraid that the individual subject curriculum requirements would not be met. With careful planning and implementation of the lessons and activities, the teachers were able to resolve their concerns. The main factor that convinced the teachers that interdisciplinary teaching could be successful was the reactions of their students. They found that students were more interested in all of the subjects and were eager to share their ideas and opinions. A student who may have been solely interested in science in the past would only talk science to the science teacher. After the implementation of interdisciplinary instruction, this same student was able to discuss ideas with all of his or her teachers, because all of the teachers had knowledge of the topic. On the basis of favorable student reactions, the teachers found themselves accepting the learning potential of interdisciplinary instruction.

SUGGESTED RESOURCES

Armstrong, D. G., Henson, K. T., & Savage, T. V. (1993). *Teaching today: An introduction to education*. Upper Saddle River, NJ: Prentice-Hall, Inc.

Jacobs, H. H. (1989). *Interdisciplinary curriculum: Design and implementation*. Washington, D.C.: Association of Supervision Curriculum and Development.

Meinbach, A. M., Rothlein, L., & Fredericks, A. D. (1995). *The complete guide to thematic units: Creating the integrated curriculum*. Norwood, MA: Christopher-Gordon Publishers, Inc.

Exploring the Science of Music: Interdisciplinary Instruction

KAREN B. FREDERICKSON
Queen's University, Kingston, Ontario, Canada

STRATEGY/ACTIVITY/ASSIGNMENT

This lesson is designed to help teacher candidates think about alternative methods for presenting one of the most common topics selected by general music teachers: the instruments of the orchestra. This topic usually focuses on visual and aural identification of the instruments, frequently ignoring the role of culture. The role of culture in the study of music and musical instruments should be a primary focus in middle school music education, as nothing is "culture-free" (Brady, 1989, p. 20).

This lesson also introduces one of the most common topics selected by general science teachers: the physics of sound. The method employs an integrated approach, with activities grounded in both science and music, and may be used by music teachers, science teachers, and classroom teachers; either individually or as part of a team. It facilitates concept formation and perceptual skills and supports the exploration of the role of culture in the creation of music.

The activities in the unit are designed to help middle school students construct concepts about the physics of sound, and encourage exploration of the musical potential of the physical properties for each conceptual category, resulting in a classification system. The classification system embraces all instruments of the world, thus providing a framework for scientific principles, and encourages exploration of musical instruments that extends beyond the boundaries of any specific culture. The categories are (1) aerophones, instruments that create sound using air; (2) chordophones, instruments that use stretched strings on a resonator to create sound; (3) idiophones, instruments that produce sound from vibrating objects; (4) membranophones, instruments that have stretched membranes over resonators to produce sound; and (5) electrophones, instruments that depend on electrical energy for some or all of their sound production.

LESSON 1

The students are divided into four groups and assigned to one of four science activity stations. They are to follow the directions and answer all questions.

1. Solid sound
   This station explores how sound passes through solid materials. The station includes a wire coat hanger attached to a pencil (with eraser) with a string.
   Directions:
   (a) Tie the string to the hook of the wire hanger and tie the other end of the string to the pencil at the end opposite to the eraser.
   (b) Place the eraser end of the pencil in your ear. Now hit the hanger with a solid object and listen.
   (c) Describe in your own words how the vibrations from the coat hanger reached your ear.

(d) Why didn't you hear the vibrations from the coat hanger through the air?

(e) Hang other objects from the string and compare the sounds you hear.

2. Solid amplifier

This station explores how sounds can be amplified by transferring the vibrations to a solid object.

Directions:

(a) Pluck a comb while holding it in the air.

(b) Place the end of the comb on a desk and pluck it again.

(c) What happens to the pitch of the sounds as you pluck different sized teeth of the comb? Which sounds are higher? Lower? Why?

(d) What happens to the sound of the comb when it is plucked while touching the desk? Why?

(e) What are some other ways that sound may be amplified? Can you try some of them?

3. Milk carton guitar

This station explores the variety of pitches that can be created by stretching elastic bands over an amplifier.

Directions:

(a) Using the milk carton provided, stretch different lengths and widths of elastic bands across the opening.

(b) Pluck each elastic band and listen to the pitch created.

(c) Describe the pitch created by each elastic band.

(d) Which elastic band produces the highest pitch? Which produces the lowest pitch? Why?

4. Pipe music

This station explores the vibrations of solid objects of varying lengths.

Directions:

(a) Take the tubing provided and suspend the varying lengths from a stand using string. Be sure the tubes are tied at the center.

(b) Hit the tubes with a hard object and listen.

(c) Stop the vibrations by holding the tubes at either end.

(d) Suspend and strike the tubes at various places along their lengths and listen.

(e) Strike the tubes with various materials such as pencils, cork, mallets, or metal tubes.

(f) Does the sound change when the tube is struck at different places? Describe.

(g) Why can you stop the vibrations by holding the tube at various places?

(h) Why does the tube produce different sounds depending on where the tube is suspended?

(i) Do different materials such as copper produce different sounds? Why?

(j) Why does the sound change when the tube is struck with different materials?

(k) Why do the tubes of different lengths produce different pitches?

(Frederickson & Smith, in progress, pp. 10, 32, 42)

After approximately ten minutes, the groups rotate so that all class members have the opportunity to try each activity. At the end of the class session (or the next class session, if there is insufficient time), a time for reflection takes place and the scientific principles of sound are discussed and related to conventional musical instruments.

ASSIGNMENT

In a group of not more than four students, each student must locate three objects that produce interesting sounds, relating them to scientific principles of sound, and create a musical composition. Each group presents its composition during the next class session. During each group's performance, the remainder of the class reflects on (1) the composition, (2) the scientific principles illustrated by the instruments, and (3) the musical knowledge displayed.

COMMENTARY

After this lesson, students are to reflect on the implications of presenting the study of musical instruments in this way. The use of this classification system advocates an exploration of instruments of any culture, not just instruments comprising the Western orchestra. If the curriculum stipulates that the study of orchestral instruments be included, the teacher should ensure that the students examine how the ensemble originated, how it has developed and changed, and how it might be reconceived in the future. An introductory unit on the physics of sound can facilitate this exploration.

The approach to composition included in this lesson allows teachers to discover what students already know about music. Students have already constructed concepts about the music they hear every day, and this should be the foundation for learning and teaching. Changing music education from a subject-centered approach to a student-centered approach should result in more meaningful learning for students.

The teacher candidates respond very positively to these lessons. They frequently remark on the "practical, hands-on approach" to the class. The lessons foster creativity and sharpen listening skills. Many of the students repeat these lessons during their teaching practica and report very positive responses from middle school students and classroom teachers. They are heartened by the enthusiasm of middle school students to explore musical instruments in this way. The students become excited at the prospect of teaching middle school students.

LESSON 2

While the professor reads a description of the creation of snow crystals, the students draw their own representation of the description on a piece of paper. The class members share their drawings, and the professor reads the description again. The students move to a large space in the classroom and, either alone or in a group, use movement and sounds to illustrate the description of the creation of snow or the movement of a snowflake. The class members share their inventions. After returning to their seats, the professor shows a book of pictures of snowflakes (Bentley, 1962). The class learns how to make their own snowflakes out of paper and uses them to illustrate a poem (their own creation or a poem from another source), which will be used to create a song.

ASSIGNMENT

The students are to select other science concepts and devise creative activities that will support the exploration of those concepts. They may work alone or in a group.

COMMENTARY

After exploring some examples of integrating creative music making with science concepts, the student projects are often quite imaginative. The students are encouraged to reflect on the relationship between music and other subjects and the meaning of holistic education, which should include the arts. Many students use these activities in their teaching practica and report very positive responses from middle school students and cooperating teachers.

REFERENCES

Bentley, W. A. (1962). *Snow crystals*. New York: Dover.

Brady, M. (1989). *What's worth teaching?* Albany, NY: State University of New York Press.

Frederickson, K., & Smith, M. (under review). *Sound connections: Integrating science and music*.

An Interdisciplinary Off-Campus Residential Experience (OCRE)

DAVID W. FRIESEN
University of Regina, Regina, SK, Canada

STRATEGY/ACTIVITY/ASSIGNMENT

In the third year of their four-year program, middle level teacher education students attend a three-day interdisciplinary off-campus residential experience (OCRE) at a retreat center an hour away from the university. Located along the chain of lakes that follow the valley in which the retreat center is located, is a prairie town, a village, an Indian community, and summer cottage subdivisions. The middle-years section, composed of thirty students, is joined by sections of early childhood, French immersion, and aboriginal student teachers for this two-and-a-half day event. Prior to leaving campus, students are organized into five across-grade, heterogeneous "site groups" of about thirty individuals, each selecting a specific site in the valley to study, such as the town, the village, the First Nation community, the valley as a social and natural environment, or the center itself, which used to be a tuberculosis sanatorium. Before going out to the valley, each site group subdivides into five or six subgroups. Each of these subgroups gathers resources on a specific aspect of their site, such as history, culture, recreation, spirituality and religion, economics, natural and social environment, the arts, and so on. The instructors ensure that all aspects of each site are explored.

On the first day off campus, each subgroup explores its assigned site to determine resources needed to create interdisciplinary experiences for middle level pupils. For example, a subgroup focusing on the history of a specific site might use the local museum, conduct interviews with local residents, and visit cemeteries to collect information. On the morning of the second day each subgroup assembles its resources and designs an experiential activity to contribute to their site group's interdisciplinary unit. Later in the day, the subgroups at each site engage each other in the activities they have designed. Reflective sessions on the third day provide a forum to discuss the value of the activities developed and to share experiences across site groups. The middle level preservice students meet as a section to share what they have learned from other students in their site groups—especially those students from other cultures. Following the off-campus experience, the students assemble a document containing the units the site groups have constructed. Some of the middle level teacher education students also give a presentation on the OCRE experience at a teachers' conference held later in the year.

University faculty who teach in the various curriculum areas act as a resource to the different site groups. Their role is to help the students frame questions and strategies to explore the various sites, to construct activities appropriate for the various developmental levels of children, and to guide the reflective process.

COMMENTARY

OCRE is designed to expand students' notions of teaching and learning beyond the classroom walls by engaging them in interdisciplinary and experiential learning activities in an off-campus setting. It enables students to assess the learning possibilities of out-of-classroom sites, link these to the curriculum, and plan appropriate experiential and interdisciplinary learning activities for middle level pupils. In developing an awareness of possibilities for learning outside the school, students learn to adapt to new environments, take responsibility for their own learning, and work with new people.

Other than the sixteen-week school practicum in their final year of the program, students rate this experience as the most meaningful in the middle level program. It has a profound effect on their development as teachers. One of the students captured the sentiments of many of the students in his post-OCRE journal entry: "In the Qu'appelle valley there is a world unique and beautiful yet so close. It was like being in a library with hundreds of resources, wandering down a corridor you had not noticed before and at the end of this hall finding yourself in a wing of the library completely new to you that is filled with thousands of books. My experiences at OCRE are the kind of experiences I would want to recreate for my students."

Another student reflected on the value of this experience for middle level group dynamics: "The struggle to feel comfortable and find a place within the dynamics of my group raised some very important challenges for me as a teacher. How am I going to provide learning experiences for my students in which they discover who they are as individuals, and develop their role within society? What I did learn from my experience at OCRE was how the remarkable outdoor environment can be used to develop group skills."

Attitude changes are also attributed to OCRE by the students. The following reflected the impact the experience had on the middle level section: "I was pretty sure I wouldn't be staying in the province after graduating. I was positive that I would not be teaching in a small rural town. Now I think that I might be able to do it and have a great time."

As a result of the most recent OCRE experience, the middle level section changed the well-known "I love (heart symbol) N.Y. life" to "I love (heart symbol) M.Y. life," in which the line to change N to M was written in freehand graffiti style. They put the symbol on a large flag that now adorns the middle level university classroom. It serves as a reminder of their experiences at OCRE and the unique teacher identity they are developing.

Surfing the Web: Using the Internet to Locate Interdisciplinary Units

SANDEE SCHAMBER
Black Hills State University, Spearfish, SD

STRATEGY/ACTIVITY/ASSIGNMENT

This assignment is part of an undergraduate course on the principles and practices of teaching in the middle school. This assignment demonstrates to students that they need not "reinvent the wheel" every time they prepare to teach a unit. Instead of creating interdisciplinary units on their own, students are directed toward the Internet, where they are to locate two interdisciplinary units. This assignment is begun in class as a class activity; but instead of meeting in the regular classroom to perform this activity, the class meets in the computer lab. This provides students with limited computer skills the opportunity to begin the assignment with the assistance of their instructor and their more technologically able peers. Once the units are located, they are printed out and evaluated.

The evaluation is accomplished by following an evaluation rubric that is provided to the student at the beginning of the course (see below). The evaluation rubric includes criteria related to student objectives, the big questions or the unifying themes, the level of integration, content-area objectives, learning process objectives, the accuracy and depth of the content, lesson plans or activities, grade level, assessment procedures, and grading criteria. Students are encouraged to *select units from two different sites* in order to increase their awareness of the variation of the quality and usefulness of educational materials available on the Internet. Selecting two units also affords students the opportunity of comparing and contrasting the units.

COMMENTARY

This assignment provides students with the opportunity to learn about technology as they learn about middle level interdisciplinary units. During the course of their searches, students learn how to navigate the Web, discover how different search terms result in different findings, and learn about search engines. Most importantly, students learn that not all interdisciplinary units are created equal. Comments such as, "This sounded really great, but when I got to the site it was nothing!" or "This isn't at all what I expected!" or "Wow, I never knew there was so much on the Internet. I never knew there were lessons out here!" or "I found so many great units at this site, can I print out more than two?" echo across the computer lab on an ongoing basis. Such comments provide a valuable platform for class discussions relative to the quality and usefulness of information secured from the Internet. It is through these discussions that the utter necessity of an evaluation process comes to the fore.

A valuable aside to this activity is the collegiality evidenced in completing this assignment. The use of technology is intimidating for some students and exciting for others; while one student comforts a classmate who sits at the computer keyboard in tears, another student mentors a peer in sending the two interdisciplinary units to a home computer via e-mail. This assignment not only actively engages students in a learning activity, but it also creates bonds of friendship between classmates. In the end, students have not only learned about interdisciplinary units and technology, but more importantly, they have learned about helping one another.

Interdisciplinary Unit Evaluation

30 Points

Content . . .

The Objectives / Goals . . . (1)

    4 Are clearly and behaviorally stated, and are appropriate to the middle level.

    2 Are clearly stated and are appropriate to the middle level, but not all are behaviorally stated.

    1 Are not clearly stated and/or not appropriate to the middle level.

The Unifying Theme Reflects a(n) . . . (2)

    4 Interdisciplinary approach and is stated as an essential question.

    2 Interdisciplinary approach

    1 Multidisciplinary approach.

Content Areas . . . (3)

    2 Number 5 or more.

    1 Number 2-4.

Content Concepts/Skills Taught in the Unit . . . (4)

    4 Are listed according to content areas and include higher order/ critical thinking skills.

    2 Are listed according to content areas.

    1 Are listed.

The Information in Each Content Area . . . (5)

5 Is accurate and of appropriate breadth and depth for the stated grade level.

3 Is accurate and of questionable breadth and depth for the stated grade level.

2 Is accurate, but lacks breadth and depth for the stated grade level.

1 Is inaccurate and lacks breadth and depth for the stated grade level.

Activities / Lessons . . . (6)

4 Are described and can be implemented from the provided information.

2 Are described, but are incomplete.

1 Are listed.

Logistics for Implementation . . .

Grade Level . . . (7)

1 Is stated and is within the parameters of the middle school.

The Time Frame . . . (8)

2 Includes overall length of the IDU and specific time frames within the day.

1 Includes overall length of the IDU.

Assessment/Student Product . . . (9)

The unit includes information which . . .

4 Describes the elements of the final assessment activity and grading criteria.

2 Describes the elements of the final assessment activity.

1 States what the final assessment activity will be.

CHAPTER 6

Technology

MIDDLE-L Listserv

LINDA R. MORROW
University of Arkansas, Fayetteville

STRATEGY/ACTIVITY/ASSIGNMENT

Students in my preservice and graduate-level middle level methods classes are required to subscribe to MIDDLE-L listserv (LISTSERV@ POSTOFFICE.CSO.UIUC.EDU) and use it as a resource to follow a specific issue being discussed and/or to initiate a discussion on the listserv by positing questions about middle level philosophy and practice. Printouts to document listserv use are collected weekly, and students receive participation points for each set of printouts. All printouts are kept in the student's portfolio as a means of documenting uses of technology. Information from the listserv is shared in class on a regular basis by the instructor and students. Students are required to use MIDDLE-L as a resource for their research on some aspect/component of middle level education or for writing their interdisciplinary unit of study.

COMMENTARY

Listservs constitute an excellent source vis-à-vis current issues, research, and practice. Discussions hot off the listserv provide practical, real-world connections to issues being discussed in class. Students are delighted with the immediate responses they receive from questions posted on the listserv and with the plethora of information received daily. My goal in using the listserv in these ways is to model uses of technology that provide easily accessible support systems for middle level practitioners.

It is also worth noting that I expect students to communicate with me via e-mail. In fact, I ask for e-mail addresses at our first class meeting.

As these uses of technology become routine means of investigation and communication for students, they are more likely to incorporate such strategies in their classrooms.

Integrating the Internet in the Middle Level Classroom

THOMAS A. TEETER
University of Arkansas, Little Rock

STRATEGY/ACTIVITY/ASSIGNMENT

A recurring theme throughout my middle school methods course is the integration of Internet resources into the middle level classroom. Students are required to locate Internet resources in five categories: (1) early adolescent development, (2) parent/school partnerships, (3) exemplary middle level programs, (4) primary sources for teachers, and (5) lesson planning. Students then evaluate these resources for technical merit (ease of navigation, design, interactivity) and appropriateness for the classroom (authority, timeliness, curricular fit, etc.)

Within each category, students select sites to review from a list provided by the professor. In the lesson-planning category, for example, students may choose one or more sites from the following selection:

- Apple Computer Lesson Plan Library
- ARTSEDGE Subject Area Resources
- AskERIC: Lesson Plans
- The Awesome Library: Lesson Plans
- Blue Web'n
- Busy Teachers' Web Site
- Collaborative Lesson Archive
- Education World Lesson Plans Lesson
- Global Schoolhouse
- The Mining Company: Lesson Plans
- Newton's Apple
- Taylor Road Middle School Lesson Plans
- TeacherServe
- Teacher Talk Lesson Plans

- Teacher's Edition Online LESSON IDEAS
- Teacher's Tips
- Teachers.Net Lesson Exchange
- Teachers Helping Teachers
- Works4Me Tips Archive

Students review and evaluate each site. First, students complete a technical assessment of the site, which is based on the following criteria or attributes:

Navigation: How easy was it to find the site? Does the page download efficiently? Could you easily move around the Web site? Does the page have a "site map" that describes the content of the site? Is the most important information easily located?

Design: What is the overall visual impression of the site? Is the text easy to read? Are colors used effectively? Do the graphics help clarify the content? Do the graphics, sounds, or video make a contribution to the site?

Interactive: Can users ask questions or give comments? Does the site allow users to interact with other people (e-mail, bulletin boards)? Are there quality links to other helpful sites?

Overall Technical Evaluation: Is the overall experience of the site positive or negative? Did you want to continue exploring?

Students then complete a second evaluation of the site's substance and appropriateness for the classroom. This evaluation focuses on the following criteria:

Purpose: What goals are the authors and developers trying to accomplish? What is the scope of the site? Is the site's role and scope made clear to users? Are there costs for using the site?

Target audience: Is the sight designed for young people? Adults? Both? What subjects or topics are treated?

Authority: Are the developers qualified experts in the content area?

Content: Is the information valid and reliable? Is the content objective? How often is site content updated? How well is the content organized? Is the content interesting? What is the breadth and depth of content provided? Scholarly? Popular press?

Timeliness: Is the information up-to-date and of current interest?

Curricular Fit: Is the content appropriate for the curriculum? Does the site encourage students to extend their thinking and learning?

COMMENTARY

This activity is consistently a class favorite. While many students lack experience searching for and evaluating Internet sources, most are interested in learning these computer skills. Through this project, students gain the knowledge, attitude, and skill to become effective managers of classroom resources available on the Internet. Four project outcomes seem to be especially valuable: (1) the ability to locate middle level teaching materials, (2) skill in reviewing and evaluating Web sites, (3) development of classroom activities that utilize Internet resources, and (4) experience sharing teaching materials with other teachers across the country.

At the conclusion of the course, students' site evaluations are combined into a *Best of the Web—Middle School* booklet for each participant.

A Technology-Enhanced Learning Environment

DOUGLAS FISHER
San Diego State University, San Diego, CA

CAREN SAX
San Diego State University, San Diego, CA

STRATEGY/ACTIVITY/ASSIGNMENT

College students from yesteryear would hardly know some of our "smart" classrooms today. Imagine the class of 1985 visiting their alma mater today. Now, they would find high-tech computer labs used by students from all majors. They would also find instructors assigning work that requires students to access the World Wide Web, not only for research, but for interaction with experts in their content area. Imagine their surprise when the professor refers to "virtual" office hours that are held in a chat room and via electronic mail! Meet some members of our seminar class for middle level student teachers and learn more about their interactions and assignments.

The student teaching seminar is a common way to help students integrate theory and practice. During seminar time, student teachers are encouraged to discuss the successes and challenges they experience in the classroom. In our middle level student teaching seminar, we encourage students to reflect on their practices in a variety of modes, including, but not limited to, journals and class discussions. Recently, we incorporated electronic discussions and Web-based assignments into the seminar.

Jaime's new priorities

Jaime rushes home after a long day at work. His student teaching schedule has been busy lately with parent conferences. Driving home, he listens to a cassette tape assigned in class about school reform and thinks about how this author's theory fits with ideas in the course textbook. Jaime is rushing home this Friday evening for two reasons. First, he has promised his study group that he would attach his section of the research paper to an e-mail tonight. Second, he has a date.

At home, Jaime logs onto his computer to get his e-mail. Fifteen new messages! Before he reads them, he decides to post a message to his classmates. The tape he was listening to sparked an idea that he wants to share with the group. Jaime writes in his e-mail:

> Hello everyone . . . . Jaime here. I was listening to this week's cassette tape and was thinking that individuals *are* essential in the change process. I know that several of you "systems thinkers" disagree with me, but particularly as we think about middle school in which everyone struggles with identity issues, the role of the individual is essential. I know that individuals can't do it all, but we have to talk more about this before I'm ready to give it up. Remember Jaclyn Kostner's book, *Virtual Leadership*; every person in Camelot had to share the vision or they would be building a pile of rocks! Anyway, I have to do some homework, then get ready for a date :-) For those of you in my group, I'll attach my section of the paper so you can look it over. Talk to you all soon!

Jaime then sends a second message addressed only to his group and attaches his section of the group paper. Checking his "to do" list, Jaime finds that he is keeping up with class responsibilities. Being a virtual student requires a great deal of self-motivation; it's easy to fall behind when messages accumulate daily and visits with the professor occur less frequently. Jaime still has a few more messages to read. The first e-mail is from Kaila. She is working on a class paper on school change related to diversity issues. Jaime remembers a presentation he attended a few semesters ago and decides to respond. He hits the reply button and types:

Hey, Kaila. Jaime here. Last semester I attended a seminar and heard about several schools thinking about diversity in new ways. You may want to check out the following: *Anti-Defamation League, Race & Human Relations* in our district office, and *A World of Difference*. I know that sounds like a strange group, but they all presented at the symposium I went to. If you're interested, let me know and I'm sure I can find some names. LATER. Oh yeah, BTW, do you know if we are having a F2F this week?

Jaime enjoys using the abbreviated phrases that are becoming standard language for e-mail discussions. From BTW (by the way) to F2F (face-to-face) to the simple graphics that people use to clarify that a joke's been made :) or to express sadness or disappointment : (, a new language is clearly developing. Not only is Jaime always eager to learn the latest about teaching and learning, but he knows that this new language is also becoming commonplace for his middle school students, particularly those who already seem to know more about computers than many of their teachers.

The next e-mail is from Bevin, a computer "techie." He is asking for additional information about specific schools and how they're using technology to change the look of instruction. Jaime doesn't know any details, but notices that other classmates respond with a wealth of information. One message refers to a number of videoconferencing projects that use "CUSee Me!" technology to connect schools with universities and businesses. Several middle schools received funding through the Technology Innovation Challenge and developed their own Web site to demonstrate the integration of technology throughout the curriculum (e.g., Global SchoolNet Foundation, http://www.gsn.org/). Creative lessons are also available, including the Triton project, based on thematic units about the ocean (e.g., http://edtech.sandinet/triton/); Earth Day, offering environmental activities (e.g., http://earthday.wilderness.org/); and MayaQuest: Mysteries of the Rainforest, a site where students and teachers accompany explorers on archeological trips through Mexico and Central America (e.g., http://www.classroom.com/mayaquest/default.html). How handy to click on the URL (universal resource locator) that's linked directly to the Web site!

Following that message is one from Justin. Jaime remembers from the introductory class activity that Justin has some type of disability. He thinks that Justin uses a wheelchair and operates a computer with voice-activated software. Justin's e-mail includes a list of Web sites that Kaila can use in her quest for information about diversity. Jaime transfers the message to a folder that he created on his hard drive for later use. He writes to the group:

> Hey Justin . . . thanks for the list of sites. OUTSTANDING. I know I'll be able to use it when I take the cross-cultural class next semester! More soon :-)

Jaime has just enough time to send a note to the professor requesting a change from the Tuesday night teleconference to Thursday, as he planned a F2F with his study group for the final draft of their paper. He also informs his professor that he would "show up" for office hours in the chat room to make sure it was okay. Then Jaime was off for his date!

Assignments

The assignments in our class required access to the World Wide Web. We asked students to work in pairs, matching students who were computer-literate with "newbies," offering a less intimidating introduction to the Web. The first assignment was to complete a "WebQuest" in search of specific resources, printing the first page as a sample. Jaime and his partner, Kaila, started with the Yahoo, Lycos, and Excite search engines to investigate how school reform is approached in different states. They entered key words and phrases in each search engine and, after much trial and error, developed an understanding of how the computer interprets this information. As they completed the required list of ten sites, they also discovered that even the most popular search engines cover only a small percentage of available information. As a result, they learned to expand each search by using a variety of keywords for each topic.

The next assignment was to create a "Webliography." Aside from being a clever word for a new format, the assignment gave students the opportunity to describe and critique the Web sites that they found in their WebQuests. Jaime and Kaila listed the URL of each of their ten sites, and wrote a brief description of the site's content. They reported on the following features: (1) ease of navigation through site; (2) appropriateness to subject area; (3) links to related sites; and (4) use of graphics, pictures, sounds, or alternative formats. Each pair of students submitted their Webliography to us by attaching it as a file. After we reviewed the assignments, the files were then linked from the class home page for all students to access.

COMMENTARY

More and more students in middle school are proving to be effective "guides on the side" not only to their peers, but also to many of their teachers. As student teachers create Web sites and videoconferencing sessions, they build self-confidence, increase their collaboration skills, and identify strengths and abilities to include on their first resume. Student teachers must learn these skills in their preservice education if they are going to take their students to the next level of technology integration. Student teachers tell us that the only way they've become comfortable using the Internet for learning is by just doing it!

One student reported: "Surfing the Web for my Webliography assignment forced me to get in there, get a little lost, and then find all sorts of sites that I never would have considered. Linking to everyone else's searches is such a great resource—I've already used a couple of URLs from the list that will be a goldmine for teaching middle school!"

Another student teacher commented: "I can't believe how friendly everyone was on line! The students who are typically quiet in our on-campus class were much more 'vocal' on line. Having time to think about and edit responses instead of just blurting them out made for much more thoughtful and balanced discussions. I'll remember that when I have students who may demonstrate their knowledge better in writing than in person."

How Different *Are* Middle-Grades Kids?

ADELE B. SANDERS
University of Northern Colorado, Greeley

STRATEGY/ACTIVITY/ASSIGNMENT

This is a discovery lesson that takes students well beyond their city limits.

Materials: Several e-mail addresses for middle-grades teachers from various parts of the world. (I contacted NMSA, AERA and regional Middle Level Educators conference attendees to acquire possible participants. I also scouted addresses and teachers on the Middle-L listserv.)

Procedure:

1. After choosing locations that represent the kind of diversity one is looking for ("four corners" of the continent/world, rural/inner city,

small/large schools, etc.), contact the participants to explain what the college students are to do—interview, via e-mail, their students with nonintrusive and safe questions. I used the teachers' e-mail addresses and sent out either a reminder or a first-time "plea" (because I had chosen the teachers from a listserv and was making my request known for the first time). I explained that there would be about eight to ten questions and that none of them would be intrusive, that is, asking students questions that would lead them to mention other teachers' or classmates' names or to divulge highly personal information. I even gave the teachers a few questions my students had used to interview local students as examples of the nature of the questions they could expect. The questions will come, with the instructor's guidance perhaps, from the college students who are preparing to become middle-grades teachers.

2. After some preliminary reading about characteristics of young adolescents or reflection on their own attitudes or concerns as former "middlers," have the college students brainstorm the questions they want answered from a pool of 10- to 15-year-olds. I usually write out all their questions in class and then we select (via a vote) the ones that have majority interest. So as not to overwhelm our participants, I limit the total number of questions to be asked to about eight and leave no more than two "runner-up" questions for the college students to ask, should they choose to do so.

3. I put the selected questions out on e-mail to all teacher participants. They have used various methods to have their students' responses forwarded to us: (a) each student sent his or her responses directly to us via e-mail, (b) two or three students worked together sitting at one computer, and one student input the answers of the others, and (c) one class period—or a part thereof—was devoted to the teacher describing what we were doing, reading the questions, collecting the answers from the middle level students as they called them out (one teacher reported that this resulted in some interesting discussions), and then e-mailing the responses later from school or home.

4. The college students, in teams of three, select one of the schools to "work with." When answers come in from "their" students, the group decides if any need to be followed up for clarity or elaboration, and who will send their follow-up question(s). When all responses are satisfactorily assembled, each group looks for trends or patterns—or outliers—across their students' responses. They come to class with their ideas and there is an exchange across all groups about the middle school students' responses.

COMMENTARY

The freshman-level teacher preparation course in which this activity takes place is called "Exploring Teaching, with an Emphasis in the Middle Grades." What exciting discussions we have had with the whole class sharing as the college students' expectations or personal experiences are shot down or raised high! What I remember most about one class, besides the high level of interest most college students showed toward the responses they shared, was how, before that class ended, one future teacher piped up, "You know, those authors are right," referring to Kellough and Kellough (1996). What that student and the others discovered is that the authors were really describing *typical* living and breathing 10- to 15-year-olds. The ways in which real children were describing themselves, their preferences, needs, and attitudes towards friends and school, were the same as the "professionals'" descriptions. That was a boost to my credibility and to the college students' acceptance of professional knowledge.

Another discovery for them was that it didn't really matter where the middlers went to school, their responses were incredibly similar. Whether the students were in Honolulu (HI), Groton (CT), Sierra Vista (AZ), or Pueblo (CO), they wanted loyal friends and caring teachers; they learned best with hands-on experiences and demonstrations; and they liked school because they got to be with their friends.

Among some of our previous questions were: What characteristics do you look for in a friend? What makes a "good" student? What do you want from a teacher? What is your "ideal" teacher like? How do you learn best? Do you like school? Why or why not?

Note: Because a university-linked laboratory school is across the parking lot from us, the college students have been able to ask the same questions of groups of 6th, 7th, and 8th graders in order to compare the responses of local kids with the responses of the "e-mail kids." While no new information came from that group of 12 students, their responses reinforced the conclusions drawn from the e-mail kids' responses.

REFERENCE

Kellough, R. D., & Kellough, N. G. (1996). *Middle level teaching, 2nd edition.* Englewood Cliffs, NJ: Prentice Hall, Inc.

Electronic Pen Pals or E-Pals

DENISE JOHNSON

University of Central Arkansas, Conway

STRATEGY/ACTIVITY/ASSIGNMENT

At the beginning of the semester, each preservice teacher is given an e-mail account through the university and then assigned a middle level student as his or her electronic pen pal, or e-pal. There are many middle level classroom teachers willing to have their students communicate with a university class. A call for participation can be sent to a listserv or through a Web site (see note at the end of this article) for international, national, regional, or local e-pals. It is essential for the classroom teacher and university instructor to agree on the topics of conversation that will take place between the middle level students and preservice teachers over the course of the semester. It is equally important to decide how often messages will be sent (i.e., weekly, biweekly).

Prior to sending the first e-mail message, the preservice teachers should be given the opportunity to go to the university computer lab as a class and participate in a training session on how to use e-mail. At this time, the preservice teachers can then practice typing their e-pal's e-mail address and send their first introductory message. Typically, the e-mail address for the middle level students will be the teacher's e-mail address with the student's name typed in place of the subject. Thereafter, all messages can be sent outside of class time. Topics of discussion can revolve around a book, a project, a report, or a subject in which the students (both university and middle level) are involved.

The preservice teachers are required to bring printouts of the students' letters to class periodically to share with their classmates. Copies of the preservice teacher and e-pal's messages are then submitted to the instructor. Since this part of the project changes the nature of the messages from individual communication to a public forum, it is critical for the middle school teacher to inform his or her students of the possibility that the entire university class may discuss their messages. If a middle level student does not wish for his or her message to be shared with the entire university class, then that wish must be honored.

As a culminating activity at the end of the semester, the students can meet their e-pals either physically, if the school is local, or through a video exchange. They can also trade pictures.

It should be noted that this is not a graded assignment. All students are expected to participate, and the instructor can opt to give participation points. Furthermore, the instructor will need to check with the institution's internal research review board to determine whether the project will need clearance before conducting this project in the classroom. It will also be necessary to provide a detailed description of the project in the course syllabus.

COMMENTARY

There are many benefits of incorporating e-mail into middle level methods courses. Preservice teachers are provided with hands-on experience as to the effectiveness of technology in the classroom. This is accomplished through their own experiences as well as observing the reactions of the middle level students. The preservice teachers actually participate in a project they can easily implement in their own classroom once they enter the teaching field. In addition, e-pals can serve as another "field experience" for preservice teachers. Preservice teachers and the instructor can discuss the thinking processes of middle level students and why they responded in certain ways; plan, discuss, and assess the effectiveness of the communication between the preservice and middle level students; discuss and assess the developmental level of certain writing samples; and brainstorm other ways e-mail could be incorporated into the classroom. The combination of real-life application and effective instructional practice will increase the likelihood that preservice teachers will incorporate the use of technology into their own classrooms.

I have conducted this project in my methods courses each semester for several years. I have never assigned points for participation in the project. I begin the semester discussing the project and expressing my expectations. I explain to the preservice teachers that by participating in this project they have a responsibility to continue communication throughout the semester with their assigned e-pal. Through continued communication with the middle level classroom teacher, I remain aware of those students who may not be maintaining communication with their e-pal.

Initial reaction to the project by the preservice teachers is usually somewhat hesitant. Many think it is going be "busy" work. Others are apprehensive because they do not remember how to use e-mail, while others are simply computer "phobic." However, any initial hesitancy on the part of the preservice teachers to participate in the project always disappears. As one student stated, "It's such a rewarding experience and I would suggest and encourage all teachers to get on the system and use it with their students."

As the semester progresses, both the preservice teachers and the middle level students come to know each other very well and become very close. One preservice teacher stated, "Over the course of the semester, we've told these students about our lives, we've given them descriptions, we have talked about what it is that we do and we have become real to them. We are real people even though it is through electronics." Throughout the semester we regularly talk about the messages they are receiving and the projects in which they are involved with their e-pals. The benefits to the middle level students include individualized instruction, content connections, authentic reasons to write, and use of technology.

It is essential that the middle level teacher inform his or her students that they are contributing to the education of the preservice teachers through their e-mail messages. It was obvious that one group of students understood this concept when they were asked, "Why do you want to be e-pals with college students?" The e-pals simply responded, "We are helping them to be good teachers."

Note: A comprehensive list of Web sites dedicated to matching students or teachers can be found at: http://www.keypals.com/p/wwwsites.html.

Electronic Mentors

DENISE JOHNSON
University of Central Arkansas, Conway

STRATEGY/ACTIVITY/ASSIGNMENT

A major goal of any methods course is for preservice teachers to gain a thorough understanding of different teaching philosophies, including the advantages and disadvantages of each as well as the way in which teachers' philosophical stances influence their choice of instructional strategies. It is one thing to read about the theory behind different philosophies in a textbook and a very different thing to actually observe the approach a teacher uses to teach as a result of his or her personal philosophy. One way to provide an avenue for the preservice teachers to gain a greater understanding of different philosophies is through collaboration with practicing teachers across the country via electronic dialoguing.

At the beginning of the semester, each preservice teacher should be given an e-mail account through the university and then assigned a practicing middle level teacher mentor. There are many middle level classroom teachers who use technology as a resource for professional development by participating in listserv discussions and searching educational Web sites. These teachers welcome the opportunity to share their knowledge and expertise with preservice teachers. It is essential, of course, for the university instructor to establish clear guidelines for topic(s) of discussion and time frames for both the preservice teachers and mentors.

Prior to sending the first e-mail message, the preservice teachers should be given the opportunity to go to the university computer lab as a class and participate in a training session on how to use e-mail. At this time, the preservice teachers can send their first introductory message to their mentor. Thereafter, all messages can be sent outside of class time. The introductory message should include personal information the preservice teachers want to share with their mentor as well as a brief statement of their teaching philosophy at this time. This is a good way to begin communication about teaching philosophies that can develop over the course of the semester. As mentor teachers share their teaching philosophies and describe how their philosophy affects classroom activities, the preservice teacher should be encouraged to ask questions. Many times the mentor teachers provide the preservice teachers with resources such as Web site addresses, book and journal publication information, sample letters to parents, teaching units, certification information, etc., that result from such discussions.

The preservice teachers are required to bring printouts of their mentor's messages to class periodically and share them with the instructor and each other. This is an excellent opportunity to discuss the different teaching philosophies gleaned from the electronic discussions and how these philosophies affect classroom practices and student learning. This assignment is not graded, but participation is expected. The instructor can opt to give participation points for this assignment.

COMMENTARY

The benefits of incorporating electronic mentors into middle level methods courses are many, for both the preservice teachers and their mentors.

First, students are able to see telecommunications as a multifaceted resource. Second, students are given an avenue to collaborate with middle level educators in a nonthreatening environment. Third, they are given the opportunity to experience the power of technology as a tool for communicating, problem solving, brainstorming, and finding information. Fourth, students are involved in a different type of field experience. Fifth, students are provided with a broader set of experiences than are available during their field placements by extending the "face-to-face" collaboration through electronic dialoguing. Finally, students are able to collaborate with experienced, technology-using teachers. The mentors are able to share their experiences as classroom teachers as well as encourage students to view technology as a tool to promote professional development. Mentor teachers gain the satisfaction of being able to share knowledge accumulated through extensive professional practice. Questions from the preservice teachers provide opportunities for the mentor teachers to reexamine their own classroom practices and the effects of accepted instructional techniques on the teaching/learning process. The unique aspect of this assignment is that it capitalizes on the classroom teacher as teacher educator and gives them the opportunity to expand the teaching role while remaining a classroom teacher.

I have conducted the mentor project in junior-level methods courses each semester for several years. Overall, the students are very impressed with their mentor e-pals and became very close to them. The mentor e-pals take their roles very seriously and spend hours responding to the students' questions. The preservice students find the information and insights their mentors provide over the course of the semester very valuable. During class, I provide many opportunities for the preservice teachers to discuss the messages they receive, which is an excellent way to gain insight into the differing philosophies teachers hold across the United States.

Note: A comprehensive list of web sites dedicated to matching students or teachers can be found at: http://www.keypals.com/p/wwwsites.html

Smart Teachers, Smart Students: Applying Educational Technology in the Middle School Classroom

MARGARET E. ALBERTSON
Azusa Pacific University, Azusa, CA

NANCY BRASHEAR
Azusa Pacific University, Azusa, CA

STRATEGY/ACTIVITY/ASSIGNMENT

There are smart houses, smart classrooms, and even smart toasters. Likewise, there are smart students and smart teachers. Smart "things" rely on automated and highly sophisticated machinery. Smart people creatively use automated machinery in highly sophisticated ways—therein lies the difference. Humans manipulate the logic that governs the machine. By teaching this logic to their students, middle level educators can encourage them to be "smart" users of technology.

Using a cyber scavenger hunt is an especially fun and effective strategy that teaches computer logic. This is a timed activity that requires grouped participants to search the World Wide Web (WWW) for specified information (which is predetermined by the instructor). Teams receive one point for each correct universal resource locator (URL or Web address) that they find.

Higher education students can complete the exercise in portions of two class sessions. The first session is "minds-on" searching. The second session is "hands-on" searching. Computers are needed for the hands-on activity. On college campuses, instructors can reserve space in student computer labs, classrooms with Internet access, or the library. Similarly, middle school teachers may use the school computer lab, the library, or their classroom. Middle school teachers who have daily class sessions need only one computer with a Web browser.

Teams of four or five participants should be formed at the beginning of the minds-on session. Give each team the same retrieval list of ten specific pieces of information, e.g., Bill Gate's e-mail address, the publication date of *Gone With the Wind*, a list of top-ten hit songs, or the name of the best-selling book in Japan. Now have students strategically plan their search. Four steps should guide their strategies:

1. *Do a broad search.* Use a broader descriptor to search the subject. This will help you to see if indeed the general information for which you are searching is present on the Web.

2. *Enclose a series of words within quotation marks.* Decide which words belong in a sequence. Enclose the phrase within quotation marks. The search engine will only select information that has those words together in the same sequence. For example, "Gone with the Wind" would produce the literary title. If quotation marks are not used, the search might render *gone, with, the,* or *wind.* The results are appreciably different.

3. *Use a logic command (AND, OR, NOT).* To combine pieces of information, the word AND could be used. Note the word AND is written in capital letters. Many search engines ignore logic commands if they are written in lower case letters. The logic command OR gives a word or its alternative. The word NOT excludes information. For example, one could enter "Gone with the Wind" AND publication AND date OR year NOT movie. This would produce only those items containing the title and the words "publication" or "date." Any entries with the word "movie" would be excluded. This could prove problematic if the publication date of the book and movie were written on one entry. It would not be included in the results. Careful planning is needed to refine the search.

4. *Use an advanced search.* Many search engines offer an advanced search option. This tool will prioritize the list. If one wants to know specifically about the publication date of *Gone with the Wind*, enter publication AND date OR year in the ranking order text box. The resulting items are ranked by percentage of matching words. This is helpful if a large number of items result from the search.

To encourage efficient searching strategies, students are timed during the hands-on session. They use the written search strategies from the previous session. If the requested information is retrieved, they record the URL. When the predetermined time is reached, students stop their search and discuss their results.

COMMENTARY

The question that we answer most frequently is, "How can I get fewer than 30,000 hits each time I search the Web?" This Web-searching strategy usually refines searches to less than 50 hits. This is more manageable for the middle school student.

A word of caution is advisable to middle school teachers. The Internet contains inappropriate material for middle school students. Yet, information retrieval is and continues to be a much needed skill for students. One strategy may be to use filters that disallow specified content from being displayed. Another strategy would be to download many home page screens from the Web. Because the information is now stored internally in the computer, students can search off-line. In other words, students would only have access to the screens that the instructor has previewed.

The Electronic Resume Project: A Multimedia Portfolio

DAVID W. FRIESEN
University of Regina, Regina, SK, Canada

STRATEGY/ACTIVITY/ASSIGNMENT

It is often difficult to find class projects for middle level preservice teachers that meet the needs and interests of the students, the assessment needs of the professor, and yet is transferable to the school classroom. The electronic resume project appears to do all of these.

Students are always interested in information and activities they think may give them an edge with the job search. With this in mind, I designed the electronic portfolio project as one of the centerpieces of my middle-years Professional Studies course, which all middle-years preservice students take in year three of their four-year undergraduate program. Early in the semester, the students attend a workshop on HyperStudio, a multimedia program that can integrate text, sound, and video. They then design a personal resume to include elements of their experiences and capabilities as middle-years teachers. This exercise involves gathering video clips and photos of their teaching; interviews with their cooperating teacher; a statement of their educational philosophy, particularly as it relates to diversity in the classroom, providing evidence of their capability with cooperative and experiential learning; and evidence of their ability to plan interdisciplinary units related to important middle-years themes (the other centerpiece of the course). Finally, they assemble the electronic resume from the portfolio evidence collected.

After completing their teaching internship in the first semester of year four, the preservice teachers return to campus for their last semester. Although neither required for graduation nor part of their final courses, students are encouraged by the middle-years faculty advisor to design a personal Web page that will include the resume developed in their earlier Professional Studies course. Instructional technology support to develop the Web page is provided by the program. The electronic connection gives them a wider audience in their job search activities.

COMMENTARY

Perhaps the most exciting aspect of this project is that it motivates the students so well. The job search is a real-life problem for them, and this project is seen as a practical solution. Students do not see this as a simulation because the product is immediately useful to the job search. Because the course evaluation is on a pass/fail basis, the evaluation of the project consists of feedback to improve the resume for the job search. This project also provides the students with the skills and knowledge to design a multimedia activity for their interdisciplinary unit.

Preservice teachers are increasingly becoming aware of the need for computer-literate teachers at the middle-years level. They hear this from teachers and administrators in the schools, and they see it in the advertisements for new teachers. The project provides the multimedia experience needed to incorporate experiential activities into their classrooms that engage their pupils in the use of multimedia. In other words, the project raises their technological capabilities in the use of multimedia, as well as their pedagogical awareness of instructional technology.

Finally, the project provides the professor with an excellent vehicle to monitor reflection and professional growth. The key course themes in which the project takes place are: planning interdisciplinary units; employing a range of instructional strategies, with a focus on experiential and cooperative learning; using classroom management suited to early adolescents; and addressing diversity in the classroom through multiple intelligence and learning styles. After years of reading and responding to student journals, I am convinced that this kind of project provides better evidence of their capabilities than anything else because it goes beyond the use of educational language to include evidence of performance and professional growth. The development of the resume keeps the students focused on the elements of the course, not as abstract entities, but as practices that a future employer wants to know about.

Students are enthusiastic about this project and enjoy designing and assembling the resume. However, it is crucial that they have some background experiences with computers so they can more easily learn to use HyperStudio or a similar program. Fortunately, all of my students had already learned to use e-mail and the Internet in the first two years of the program. Several had taken an optional computer class and had been exposed to the software used in this project. On a different note, because of the experience gained in this project, the students now include planning for the use of multimedia in their multidisciplinary units.

Teaching Instructional Methods Using Hypermedia

DAVID DEVRAJ KUMAR
Florida Atlantic University, Davie

STRATEGY/ACTIVITY/ASSIGNMENT

How technologies, such as hypermedia, can be used in the instruction of prospective middle level teachers may be borrowed from a National Science Foundation–funded elementary teacher preparation project, *Improving Science Education: A Collaborative Approach to the Preparation of Elementary School Teachers,* at Vanderbilt University (Barron, Joesten, Goldman, Hofwolt, Bibring, Holladay, & Sherwood, 1993). The project has developed a set of video-based lesson examples, *Approaches to Teaching Science,* as a supplement to elementary science methods course assignments for students at Peabody College of Education at Vanderbilt University. The project videos highlight a set of classroom teaching episodes of science teachers using different instructional techniques, useful for inservice and preservice teachers. According to Goldman and Barron (1990), "showing video contrasts that focus on what the experienced teacher does and what the beginning teacher is likely to have trouble doing is one way of helping preservice teachers understand both effective techniques and the consequences of not communicating clear expectations or not predicting potential trouble spots" (p. 25).

The objective of the *Approaches to Teaching Science* video is to reduce the gap between science content and methodology in preservice teacher education. A component of the *Approaches to Teaching Science* is the hypermedia system, which involves a 30-minute video that provides real-world examples of effective and ineffective science instructional strategies. Through a programmed HyperCard (TM) stack on a computer, students can gain random access to view various segments of classroom practices on the video. The system deals with three major categories of science learning: types of discovery learning, instructional contrasts, and models of instruction (Hofwolt, 1993). The following discussion highlights types of discovery learning and instructional contrasts, as these categories involve more interaction with the video than models of instruction.

APPLICATION

Types of discovery learning: In this category, a text describing three types of discovery learning in science (such as guided discovery, modified discovery, and free discovery) in a HyperCard stack is linked to selected video segments of three classroom teachers actually teaching using the discovery method. For example, the preservice teacher can explore modified discovery (where the teacher often initiates the discovery lesson and the students carry out the investigation and arrive at solutions) by closely watching the video segments describing the general pattern of modified discovery learning. This includes: problem identification, background and lesson set up, student activity, and drawing conclusions. The preservice teacher is also challenged with additional assignments in the hypermedia system. These assignments require further review and analysis of selected segments of the video to answer assigned questions. Such questions may include: "What was the problem for students to investigate?" "Who was the source of the problem?" and "Do you think the teacher provided a step-by-step approach to solve the problem or did the teacher just provide some general cautions?" (Barron et al., 1993, p. 45)

Instructional contrasts: In this category, the interactive video provides opportunities for comparing and analyzing effective and ineffective teaching practices in terms of lesson introduction (e.g., communication of objectives, set induction), lesson design, degree of concreteness, active involvement, use of appropriate examples, use of scientifically correct explanations, use of questioning techniques such as questioning for understanding, and use of questioning for critical thinking, etc. By browsing the field "Introducing," for example, the preservice students can access lesson introduction strategies of effective and ineffective teachers. In the event that the preservice teacher needs a quick review of lesson introduction techniques, such as set induction or communication of objectives, links to a stack of HyperCard are available to provide background information on the topic.

Models of instruction: Through HyperCard stacks, this category presents four models of learning in science: rote learning, reception learning, discovery learning, and meaningful learning. Students can click on each learning type to find out more about that particular type.

COMMENTARY

The *Approaches to Teaching Science* video was used in the methods course "Principles and Methods: Elementary and Middle School Science" at Florida Atlantic University, Davie campus. This course is required for certification in elementary and middle grades, and the class-size limit is 30 students. The course revolves around hands-on, minds-on approaches to teaching and learning science. The activities using the video involved viewing contrasting classroom teaching episodes, analyzing discovery learning, analyzing teaching episodes using observation instruments, and comparing instructional strategies between effective and ineffective classroom teaching practices.

Students seemed to appreciate the *Approaches to Teaching Science* video-based instruction of methodology. They were able to apply what was learned in the videos, especially the scientific process, in a follow-up discovery lesson-planning assignment that was part of the course requirements. The video also allowed students the opportunity to see concrete examples of effective instructional strategies. After completing the course, one of the preservice teachers wrote in her evaluation that the experience with the videos was important for two reasons. First, she was able to identify with many of the drawbacks of traditional instructional strategies in science in her own space and time. Second, she was able to view, analyze, and understand what discovery learning is and realize why it is better than "teaching by telling." In a study involving preservice students at Vanderbilt University, Barron and his coauthors (1993) found that the science instructional strategies learned during the hypermedia-based methods course appeared to have a lasting effect on students' conceptual understanding, and the students were able to apply the strategies during student teaching.

As students develop, the concrete learning experiences they gain at the elementary level are vital for making a smooth transition into the abstract level at the secondary school as they pass through the middle grades. In this context, it is critical that middle level teachers are given an opportunity to improve their understanding of effective instructional strategies by engaging in analysis of classroom practices. The hypermedia application described here provides an opportunity for meaningful learning practices for preservice teachers.

REFERENCES

Barron, L. C., Joesten, M. D., Goldman, E. S., Hofwolt, C. A., Bibring, J. B., Holladay, W. G., & Sherwood, R. D. (1993). *Improving science education: A collaborative approach to the preparation of elementary school teachers.* A final report to the National Science Foundation under grant number TPE-8950310. Nashville, TN: Vanderbilt University.

Goldman, E. S., & Barron, L. C. (1990). Using hypermedia to improve the preparation of elementary teachers. *Journal of Teacher Education, 41*(3), 21-31.

Hofwolt, C. A. (January, 1993). *Using hypermedia to develop effective elementary science teachers.* A paper presented at the annual meeting of the Association for the Education of Teachers in Science, Charleston, SC.

The Computer in the Classroom

STEVEN A. GREENGROSS
Southern Connecticut State University, New Haven

STRATEGY/ACTIVITY/ASSIGNMENT

To say that the age of the computer is upon us is a gross oversimplification; to think that the computer is fully used as an instructional tool in middle schools is a huge misconception. In far too many classrooms, the computer is either underused or misused as an instructional tool, or both. Used correctly, computer software and the Internet both have the potential to enhance teaching and to present learning to early adolescents in a totally different way. Thus, it is essential that middle level teachers learn how to utilize the computer as an essential, integrated instructional tool.

In my Technology in Middle Grades Education course, the primary focus is the integration of the computer as a primary instructional tool in language arts, mathematics, science, and social studies classes. The class is open to graduates and undergraduates and includes students who are already teachers as well as those who are in certification programs to become teachers.

The degree of computer literacy among the students typically covers the entire range, from novice to experienced. However, the extent to which a student who is already a teacher utilizes the computer in his or her middle school classroom is usually limited to enrichment as opposed to a curriculum-based format. Thus, all students, regardless of their teaching experience, begin the course at roughly the same point.

For this reason, the major student activity is to prepare and teach simulated lessons in which the computer is the major focal point of the lesson. Each student chooses from either language arts, mathematics, science, or social studies and prepares three separate lessons of 30 to 40 minutes in length. Each student chooses the grade level for the lesson, and his or her colleagues in the course are the middle school students who would be in that hypothetical class. It is emphasized that this is a simulation and not a role-playing activity. Each student must submit a formal lesson plan for each lesson, and the computer must be the primary instructional tool that will be used to meet the objectives of that lesson.

The first two lessons must be designed to take place in a classroom in which there are three computers. The first lesson must be a whole-group activity in which a software program is used in conjunction with an LCD monitor and an overhead projector. This activity has the added benefit of giving those students in the class who are not comfortable with a computer the experience of operating one. The second lesson must utilize a small-group format in which the students are grouped in pairs and work with a software program at the computer. There must be a learning activity that must be completed before going to the computer, an activity to be done at the computer, and a follow-up activity that is to be completed after the students correctly complete the activity at the computer. Thus, the students in the class are able to see that the correct use of the computer as an instructional tool involves integrating the computer into the lesson.

The third lesson utilizes the Internet as the major focus of the lesson. The student must plan a lesson in which the students in the simulated middle level class utilize the Internet independently. The lesson must include all of the following: instructions to get on the Internet; the type of information to search for; the correct method to download the information once it is found; and ways to effectively use the information. This lesson has the added benefit of giving students who are not Internet users the experience of going "on line."

COMMENTARY

The belief that underlies this activity is that one learns to teach by teaching and that any activity in which a student actually teaches helps that student grow professionally. Each student is expected to give written feedback for each lesson that is presented and to critique his or her own lesson as well. This feedback is not taken into consideration in grading (that is the sole responsibility of the professor), but it is meant to help the student grow.

The goal of this course is that each student will be more comfortable using the computer as a primary instructional tool at the conclusion of the semester than he or she was at the beginning. The degree to which this happens depends, to some extent, on how computer literate the student was at the beginning of the course. While every student shows growth toward meeting this goal, the less computer literate a student is when the course begins, the more progress he or she typically makes.

The feedback from the students in this course has generally been very positive. The students are asked to complete a course evaluation at the end of the semester, and, with rare exceptions, the quality of the course is rated as either very high or high. Even students who are already utilizing the computer in the middle level classroom comment that the course has shown them new and better ways of doing so. A number of the students, both preservice and inservice teachers, have reported that they have used the lessons they developed in this course in their middle school classrooms and are pleased with the positive impact on student learning.

CHAPTER 7

Assessment

Mind-Mapping What We Know About Middle Level Education: A Pre- and Post-Assessment Activity

SAMUEL TOTTEN

University of Arkansas, Fayetteville

STRATEGY/ACTIVITY/ASSIGNMENT

At the outset of both my basic undergraduate and graduate courses on middle level education, the students develop a mind-map/cluster/web around the target term "middle level education." It is important to note that this is done prior to discussing anything about the course, including the course syllabus, for it is imperative that the students solely use their own knowledge in developing the mind-map.

In order to inform students how to develop an in-depth and comprehensive mind-map, I model how to develop such a mind-map on the blackboard. The model mind-map is always on a topic other than middle level education (e.g., genocide, the value of gardening, etc.). When developing the mind-map, I model that which constitutes a simplistic map versus one that is comprehensive and illustrates sophisticated connections. Initially, the mind-map is comprised of the target word and four to six single bubbles (ideas) that radiate out from the target word can be drawn. I comment on the fact that what is illustrated with these four to six bubbles is a rudimentary knowledge of a topic and nothing more. Then I add related topics and subtopics radiating off each of the bubbles, and do the same with each additional bubble. Once the board is filled with bubbles, I use a broken line to make connections between ostensibly disparate, but related, bubbles.

Next, students are asked to individually pull out a clean 8 1/2" by 11" piece of paper or are given a large sheet of butcher paper and told to place the phrase "middle level education" in the center of the paper and circle it. Then they are asked to be as comprehensive and accurate as possible in developing their mind-map. To ease their anxiety, they are assured that the task will not be graded.

The class is given fifteen to twenty minutes to complete the mind-map. Upon completion of their mind-maps and using their individual map as a guide, the students should develop a working definition of "middle level education." Finally, they are asked to sign their map.

I collect the maps and read them as I would any preassessment assignment. The information in the mind-maps and the definitions provide me with a sense as to each student's knowledge base, including the accuracy and sophistication of the latter.

At the conclusion of the course, the students are required to complete another mind-map/cluster/web (without referring to the initial one) around the target phrase "middle level education." The students are given exactly the same directions but provided more time to complete this mind-map (about 30 minutes). Once the mind-maps are completed, each student develops a definition of "middle level education," using his or her map as a guide.

Next, the original mind-maps completed at the outset of the course are returned to their owners. Students are asked to compare and contrast their original mind-map with their most recent mind-map. Then, in one to three paragraphs, they are to delineate the key differences found in the two maps. They are required to comment on how the latter mind-map is indicative of their progress in gaining a deeper understanding of middle level education.

Next, the students are divided into groups of four or five students. Their task is to take the most recent individual maps they have developed and discuss and debate the accuracy, sophistication, and comprehensiveness of the individual maps. Following the discussion, which often lasts from fifteen to thirty minutes, they are asked to collectively develop a single map that conveys their best thought. It is imperative to inform them that their job is not simply to transpose each of the individual maps onto a single map—as that would be a waste of time and bereft of the real thought—but to develop the strongest, most comprehensive, and most accurate map possible. The groups are given between an hour and an hour and a half to complete this assignment. Upon completion of the map and using their map as a reference, each group develops a single definition of "middle level education" based on their map. The latter need not include all of the ideas on the map, but should be as comprehensive as possible. Once all the groups have completed their maps and definitions, each group presents and explains its concept map and definition and then entertains questions from the larger group in regard to the accuracy and sophistication of their map.

COMMENTARY

By using the mind-map on the first day of class the instructor can gain a clear sense as to what the students know and don't know about middle level education, including the sophistication of their ideas as well as any misconceptions they may have. By using the same activity at the end of the course, it provides the professor and the students with a clear sense of the growth that the students have made in coming to understand middle level education, particularly as to how the latter attempts to meet the unique characteristics and needs of young adolescents.

Upon completion of the post-assessment map, most students are amazed by how much they've learned as well as the depth of their new understanding regarding middle level education. Many claim that they plan to use mind-maps in their own classrooms as both pre- and post-assessment instruments.

What We Know and Don't Know About the Middle Level: A Pre-Assessment Exercise

SAMUEL TOTTEN
University of Arkansas, Fayetteville

STRATEGY/ACTIVITY/ASSIGNMENT

On the first day of each class meeting in both my preservice and graduate introductory middle level courses I give the students a pre-assessment quiz on middle level education. (Generally, it is given during the last half hour of the class session, following the discussion of the class syllabus.) The quiz includes questions about key concepts such as: the unique needs of early adolescents; middle level philosophy and how it differs from those that drive the elementary and/or junior high levels; small communities of learning; major middle level components such as advisor/advisee, interdisciplinary teaming, exploratory curriculum, flexible scheduling; and other major issues/concerns that will be addressed in the course such as community service and service learning, multiple intelligences, and so forth. (See the appendix for sample questions.)

The quiz is generally fairly lengthy (about thirty to fifty questions) and comprised of both closed and open-ended questions. On average, it takes students about twenty to thirty minutes to complete the quiz.

There are several reasons for conducting such a pre-assessment. First, it provides the instructor with a fairly good indication of the students' knowledge base vis-à-vis middle level education, thus providing him or her with a foundation on which to build the course. Second, it provides the instructor with a sense as to any misconceptions students may have about various facets of middle level education. This, in turn, signals what needs to be addressed in class to ensure that students leave with a clear and correct understanding of key concepts. Third, it provides students with a solid sense as to what they know or don't know about middle level education and the task in front of them in this course. Fourth, students discover what the course will cover, and they glean this in a more powerful manner than by simply reading the course syllabus. Fifth, it provides students with the means to compare and contrast their initial knowledge at the outset of the course with their newfound knowledge at the conclusion of the course. In regard to the latter, it is worth noting that many of the questions that appear on the original pre-assessment are included on the final examination.

The pre-assessment is corrected in class and, generally, each question and answer leads to a short discussion of key concepts, components, and issues. Each student is required to make a copy of his or her completed pre-assessment quiz. He or she retains a copy and turns one in in the next class session to the instructor.

COMMENTARY

It is not uncommon for many students—particularly those who did not matriculate at a middle school and/or never visited one during earlier field experiences—to leave a large portion of the items on the pre-assessment blank. Others, even those who attended a middle school or visited one or more during earlier field experiences, may be somewhat familiar with a term or concept but not to the point of being unable to correctly answer a question. Be that as it may, those who generally do the best on the pre-assessment are those preservice students who attended a middle level school and those graduate students who either are or have been teachers in a middle level setting.

At the outset of the course many of the students are nervous about taking such a lengthy and detailed pre-assessment, especially one in which they leave so many questions blank or offer wild guesses. This is true even though prior to giving the pre-assessment the instructor states that the quiz is just that, a pre-assessment quiz, and if everyone knew every single answer or even a majority of the answers, then there would be little to no point in taking such a course.

APPENDIX

Middle Level Education Questionnaire

1. An **early adolescent** is generally between the ages of
   a. ____ 5–8   b. ____10–14   c. ____8–14   d. ____11–16

2. The term **"middle level"** refers to
   a. ____ only middle schools
   b. ____ grades 6–8
   c. ____ schools that incorporate the middle grades philosophy
   d. ____ middle schools and junior highs

3. **Interdisciplinary teaming** refers to:
   a. ____ team teaching
   b. ____ a situation in which teachers from various disciplines share the same students, same schedule, and the same area of the building as well as work together on curriculum coordination
   c. ____ planning and teaching interdisciplinary units

4. **Advisor/advisee** is best described as:
   a. ____ counseling sessions for students with problems
   b. ____ probing into the students' home life
   c. ____ study hall
   d. ____ an affective program that includes peer relations, self-awareness, group cooperation, self-esteem, and goal setting

5. **Block/flexible scheduling** at the middle level is:
   a. ____ a seven-period day divided into blocks
   b. ____ a situation in which a team of teachers coordinates a daily schedule that is interchangeable
   c. ____ a schedule designed to be the same every day of the week

6. An **exploratory program** is
   a. ____ comprised of traditional electives
   b. ____ always a graded class
   c. ____ a program designed to offer a multitude of special interest mini-courses that are not traditionally academic in nature
   d. ____ basically a semester-long class

7. What is the ultimate goal of the ideal middle level program?

8. Name three basic differences between an exemplary middle level program and a traditional junior high?

9. Two key purposes of incorporating flexible scheduling into a middle program are:

10. Name three unique characteristics of early adolescents.

Student Responses/Exit Slips

LINDA R. MORROW
University of Arkansas, Fayetteville

STRATEGY/ACTIVITY/ASSIGNMENT

Following middle level methods class sessions, university students are routinely asked to respond to prompts such as "I learned . . . ," "I enjoyed . . . ," "I wonder . . . ," or "I wish . . ." as exit slips. The purpose of the exit slips is to give students an opportunity to clarify their learning, to ask questions, and to connect new information with previous learning and public school classroom experiences. These nonthreatening written responses are used by the instructor to plan subsequent class discussions. In addition, pre- and inservice teachers are also asked to respond to the following questions at midterm and at the end of the semester.

Midterm

1. What changes would you suggest to enhance your learning experiences in this class? Consider routines, modes of presentations, and interactions.
    Or

2. What are your suggestions for changes and/or improvements in content and/or routines and expectations in our class for the remainder of the semester?

End of Semester

1. What have you learned about middle level education? (Consider the rationale for middle schools, stages of development during

early adolescence, individual differences, appropriate curriculum/ planning, interdisciplinary teams, advisory groups, and grouping practices.)

2. Identify the ideas or strategies that you learned in this course that you think will have the most useful applications for your (future) classroom and explain why this is so.

3. What are your burning questions about middle level education? What do you still want to know?

4. What changes and/or improvements would you suggest to enhance the learning experiences in this class? Routines? Assignments? Expectations? Modes of presentations and interactions?

5. Which learning experiences worked best for you?
Why do you think that is so?

6. Which learning experiences were least effective for you?
Why do you think that was the case?

This not only models for them the point that a critical aspect of student-centered teaching is to frequently ask for student responses to learning experiences, but it also keeps the instructor's finger on the pulse of individual student learning.

COMMENTARY

As an instructor, these responses are invaluable to me as I plan subsequent class sessions and revise plans for future courses. The key to success and credibility is addressing the responses in subsequent class sessions and implementing appropriate changes for the remainder of the semester.

The questions posited at midterm have resulted in university students asking for changes in class routines such as: beginning class sessions focused on that day's reading material, then addressing issues from the previous session's exit slips. They also requested that the instructor utilize a wide range of instructional strategies that are ideal in meeting diverse learning styles.

End of semester comments ranged from "Middle level is unique, unique, unique" to "Stages of adolescent development [are] like colors in the rainbow, constantly changing hues." One preservice teacher responded with: "It [middle level education] is not as bad as I thought it would be. It sounds like something I would like to try." Questions still unanswered were characterized by the following: "When will middle level education be the norm, and when will middle level be a major at this institution?"; "Are all communities going to move toward this type of organization of middle schools? How can we get communities to change?"; and "I still wonder about how to change the curriculum."

Suggested changes in classroom routines and assignments included the following: "I would discuss the response cards at the beginning of class"; "I think I would get into the team unit writing sooner"; and "I got more out of our discussions and articles than reading the textbook. It is very dry and very repetitive."

Students noted that effective learning experiences for them included: modeling cooperative learning and interdisciplinary teaming, the inclusion of guest speakers, the midterm exam (narrative description of an exemplary middle school), group discussions, response cards, hands-on projects, and field experiences in the middle schools.

Among the least effective learning strategies listed were: listserv assignments, written responses to reading assignments, and cooperative learning groups where all members did not contribute equally.

From these responses, it is quite clear that some teaching/learning strategies were successful whereas changes are in order for other strategies used in this class. In addition, through such questions and requests for feedback, an example is demonstrated in regard to the value of such student participation in any classroom at any level.

Assessment Simulation

JONATHAN A. PLUCKER
Indiana University, Bloomington

STRATEGY/ACTIVITY/ASSIGNMENT

After specific assessment topics are discussed, students working in groups participate in various simulations (i.e., groups attempt Scenario A after discussing the construction of traditional assessments, Scenario B after discussing alternative assessments, and Scenario C after a discussion of attitude measurement). The activities can be discussed at the end of the class period, or, if necessary, at the beginning of the following class period.

SCENARIO A

Your group is responsible for assessing the effectiveness of a bicycle safety program for fifth graders. The program was developed and implemented because several fifth graders were recently hit by cars as they rode their bikes to and from school. The program is almost completed, and the superintendent is curious about whether the fifth graders learned anything about bicycle safety during the program. He or she would like a traditional pencil-and-paper test of bicycle safety knowledge.

You protest because you know that the most effective measure will be a performance assessment (i.e., comparing bike-auto interaction before and after the program). You further protest that the most important evaluation would occur over the course of several months, long after the program has finished. Alas, the superintendent is from the "old school" and politely ignores your protestations.

Your task

- Design eleven traditional items: two multiple-choice items, two true-false items, two sentence-completion items, two short-answer items, one matching item (with at least 5 possible responses and three stems), and two essay items.
- When necessary, provide scoring guidelines.
- Upon completion of the eleven items, exchange your test with another group. Critique their test on the basis of the guidelines we discussed in class. At the end of class, we will get back together and share our results.

Suggestions

- Write out what you consider to be the objectives of a bicycle safety course. If time permits, we will do this in class.
- Construct a "table of specifications" to aid in test construction.

SCENARIO B

Flashback

Your group is responsible for assessing the effectiveness of a bicycle safety program for fifth graders. The program was used because several fifth graders were recently hit by cars as they rode their bikes to and from school. At the superintendent's request, you designed a traditional, pencil-and-paper assessment of bike safety knowledge.

Back to the present

The students took the test and exhibited a high degree of bike safety knowledge. However, in the past two weeks, several more students have bounced off of cars while riding their bikes. While none have been seriously injured, the superintendent is still alarmed, as are parents and community members. The superintendent proposes to the town council that cars be banned from town roads at the beginning and end of each school day, but the council politely rejects that suggestion.

Your superintendent approaches your group and requests that you design a performance-based assessment (PBA) of bike safety skills. Since you are not a bitter person, you choose not to remind the superintendent that you had suggested a PBA in the first place.

Your task (Part I)

Design a PBA that can be used to assess the effectiveness of the bicycle safety course.

Suggestions

- Discuss what the objectives of a bicycle safety course ought to be.
- Construct a "table of specifications" to aid in assessment construction.
- Decide who will assess the students (e.g., each child's teacher, the same group of outside raters)
- Design a set of tasks according to your table of specifications.
- Create an assessment rubric that assigns values to specific performance levels.

Your task (Part II)

Create a system for communicating the results of your assessment process (both the written and performance-based assessments) to:

1. the students
2. the principal
3. the school board
4. a reporter

SCENARIO C

Synopsis

1. Kids on bikes are getting hit by cars.
2. Your school implements a bike safety course.
3. The principal asks you to design a traditional test to evaluate the effectiveness of the course.
4. You do so, but the results of the test are moot since kids keep getting hit by cars.
5. The principal asks you to design a performance-based assessment.
6. You do so, but the principal decides that the PBA is too expensive.
7. The principal asks you to design a technique with which the school can measure the attitudes of students toward the course and bike safety.

Your task

Design a technique for measuring student attitudes toward bike safety.

Suggestions

- Define the attitudes you would like to assess.
- Create a list of associated positive and negative feelings.
- Create a list of behaviors associated with those feelings.
- Decide what type of instrument you want to construct.
- Pick a type of scale (if applicable).

COMMENTARY

Instructors are strongly encouraged to work with the entire class to create the objectives of the bicycle safety program before everyone begins. This "common ground" prevents misinterpretation, and any lack of understanding about bicycle safety can be addressed before the exercise begins. In one recent iteration of this activity, the class created three groups of objectives, with roughly five specific objectives in each category: rules of the road (e.g., proper arm signals, yielding to pedestrians), bicycle maintenance (e.g., oiling a bike chain), and safety (e.g., wearing a helmet).

After students complete each scenario, groups should present their assessment strategies to the rest of the class. The instructor should interject when an assessment strategy appears to be misused, although personal experience suggests that the students will provide ample praise and criticism during the presentations. A fun twist on this exercise is to have groups exchange their measurement strategies so that they may critique each other. Quite often, two groups will make the same exact suggestions about one another's work (e.g., "Your multiple-choice responses each use a different verb tense." "So do yours!"), reinforcing the importance of having colleagues proofread tests, assessment protocols, and rubrics.

Scenario C is most effective if students have already been exposed to the unique social needs of early adolescents. In fact, the content in the examples was chosen because bicycle safety was a hot issue in many area towns. Any content that can be efficiently summarized into fifteen to twenty general objectives is suitable for this activity; content that reinforces recommended middle level curriculum practices or important aspects of adolescent development would also be useful.

This range illustrates the tough decisions that need to be made when making assessment decisions. If less time is available for the activity (e.g., one class period), the instructor could assign each simulation to a different group (and have the class agree on only five to ten objectives). Since each group will exchange their work with the others, students will still need to apply a majority of the assessment topics in the course of the exercise.

The simulations were originally designed to be used after the class discusses the design of specific types of assessments. Given the level of assessment knowledge that students need to apply in order to complete each scenario successfully, using the simulations to introduce each assessment type would probably lead to a great deal of student frustration.

Authentic Assessment

SANDRA L. SCHURR
University of South Florida, Tampa

STRATEGY/ACTIVITY/ASSIGNMENT

Introduce students to the concept of authentic assessment by providing them with a brief description of what it is and how it differs from more traditional types of assessment. An outline of this descriptive passage or lecturette is provided below.

Authentic assessment is a type of student evaluation that attempts to make the testing process more realistic and relevant. Specifically, it involves assessing student achievement or performance in situations that closely match the standards and challenges of the world outside the classroom. There are three major forms of authentic assessment: (1) *product assessment* requires a concrete result as evidence that some skill has been applied or some concept has been learned. These products can range from the making of videotapes or audiotapes and exhibits to the writing of scripts, manuals, and reports; (2) *portfolio assessment* is based on a meaningful collection of student work that exhibits the student's overall efforts, progress, and achievement in one or more subject areas. Portfolio contents can range from paper-and-pencil tests or worksheets to creative writing pieces and drawings or graphs; (3) *performance assessment* is based more on the processes the student goes through than on the final product or outcome. It relies on the professional judgment of assessors who observe the student performing a predetermined task. Performances can range from oral reports or speeches to scientific demonstrations and poetry readings.

Some basic characteristics of authentic assessment that are important to keep in mind are:

- They are public rather than private and involve an audience of some kind in addition to the teacher.
- They are not restricted by rigid time constraints.
- They offer questions or tasks that are already familiar to students or that students have been apprised of well in advance of the assessment occasion.
- They require some degree of collaboration.
- They involve the student's own research or application of knowledge.
- They are scored by a multifaceted system.
- They include self-assessment.
- They identify strengths as well as weaknesses.
- They allow for individual learning styles, aptitudes, and interests.
- They minimize needless and unfair comparisons.

Next, it is suggested that the instructor use the following questions and tasks as springboards for a small- or large-group discussion on the concept of authentic assessment:

1. How do you think one should be tested, evaluated, and graded in a classroom setting?
2. What things have you learned in your college courses this semester and what evidence do you have that such learning took place?
3. How would you define the word "authentic" as it relates to assessment?
4. Are you better at producing products or giving performances to document your growth in a particular area? Explain.
5. Choose a course you are presently taking and list five things that you would want to include in your portfolio from that course to convince a prospective employer or professor that you have achieved something important.

Finally, as a follow-up to the discussion, instruct students to complete one or more of the following tasks:

1. Explain what is different about authentic assessment measures when compared with more traditional assessment measures. Outline an oral presentation and be prepared to give it for a group of peers or parents.
2. Design an information bulletin for the public that clearly explains the characteristics of authentic assessment. Give specific examples of tasks associated with each type of authentic assessment strategy for a class of your choice.
3. Develop a portfolio of artifacts that show the unique characteristics, achievements, and opportunities representative of a subject area, discipline, or course that you have completed.

COMMENTARY

Students relish the opportunity to dialogue with their teachers, instructors, or peers on the purpose of assessment, the forms of assessment, and the expected outcomes of assessment in the schooling process. The whole idea of making measurement tools and techniques more authentic and student-centered is both intriguing and challenging to them. This activity, with some modification, of course, can also be used with both parents and middle level students as a springboard for bridging the transition from more traditional types of measurement to more authentic measures.

Types of Tests That Teach and Tantalize

SANDRA L. SCHURR

University of South Florida, Tampa

STRATEGY/ACTIVITY/ASSIGNMENT

Many students have had little exposure to nontraditional methods of testing but are fairly comfortable with multiple choice, matching, short answer, and/or essay types of assessment tasks. It is suggested that during the semester of any given course, the instructor should develop a legitimate test that follows each of the suggested formats outlined below. These tests (or quizzes) should be graded and should provide additional methods of feedback to students on how well they are doing in the course. Varying the design of classroom testing instruments can be motivating to students because it offers students more options, encourages more open-ended responses, and permits more creative ways to demonstrate student competence in a given subject area.

One good way to introduce students to alternative testing measures is to have them reflect on past and present testing practices by answering these questions either individually or in small-group sessions:

1. How do you prepare to study for a test?
2. What type of test question is best for you on a quiz or exam? Why?
3. When is a test not a fair measure of what you know or can do?
4. Can you describe an ideal testing format for you and the way you learn?
5. What makes a test worth taking for you?

After you have administered the alternative testing formats described below, these same questions can be used again to compare a student's reaction and performance on traditional versus nontraditional testing formats.

Design a Bloom Test

Create a test around Bloom's Taxonomy, which contains only six questions or tasks—one for each level of knowledge, comprehension, application, analysis, synthesis, and evaluation. Assign ten points for the knowledge and comprehension level tasks. Assign fifteen points for the application and analysis level tasks. Assign twenty-five points for the synthesis and evaluation level tasks. You now have a test whose six questions total 100 points.

Try another variation of this type of Bloom test. Develop a bank of five or six questions at each level of Bloom's Taxonomy using the same point value system. Allow students to self-select their own questions, instructing them to choose questions whose total point value is 100.

Design a Fact-Finding Test

Prepare a set of information cards on a topic to be studied in class, making certain that you have a different card for each student. The information cards should contain a relevant paragraph or two on an important concept or issue associated with the topic under study. You may want to create duplicate cards for concepts that are especially important and/or difficult. Each student receives an information card to read and study for five to ten minutes. Once the students understand their assigned concept, they stand and circulate, pausing just long enough to share their information informally with one another. The cards may be used for reference only; students cannot read directly from the card. During this interaction, each student both teaches and learns new information. After approximately thirty minutes, students sit and respond in writing to the following five summary statements. These are then collected by the teacher for review and grading.

Directions to student: Now that you have interacted with your peers for thirty minutes to discuss our topic of study for the day, take a few minutes and complete these starter statements based on the activity:

- The information from my card that I taught to others was . . .
- Three new things I learned about the topic from talking to other students are . . .
- Something I learned from talking to one of my peers that I already knew was . . .
- Something I learned from talking to one of my peers that I would like to know more about is . . .
- To me, the most interesting thing about the information on my card is . . .

Design a Hands-On Test

To develop this test, one must identify nine key terms or concepts related to a specific topic. Each student is then given nine 3" × 5" file cards on which he or she writes out these terms or concepts, putting only one idea on each card. The student then randomly places the cards down on the desk or table with three cards across and three cards down (much like a tic-tac-toe grid). The student then writes a statement for each horizontal row (three statements), for each vertical row (three statements), and for each diagonal row (two statements). The statements should show how the three terms or concepts are related. The terms in the statement can appear in any order, can be used only once, and can be embellished by additional words that are necessary to convey the interrelationship of the ideas with one another.

Design a Reasons/Cause-and-Effect Test

This testing format requires the student to explore a variety of causes and effects on situations that are related to one another in some way and that are part of an overall theme or subject. For example, some sample cause-and-effect questions that might be asked in an English classroom are:

- Give two reasons why it is important to learn the parts of speech.
- Give three reasons why students make spelling errors in their writing.
- Give two reasons why students should get in the habit of using dialogue in their stories and quotations in their reports.
- Give four reasons to limit or support the use of word processing in the English classroom.
- Give six reasons why the act of writing is both an art and a science.

COMMENTARY

Students appreciate variety in the assessment process as much as they do during the instructional process. In fact, it makes much greater sense from an educational viewpoint to structure testing formats that are more compatible with delivery systems of information and that reward diverse responses from the learners. It brings us one step closer to a system that values a setting where instruction drives the assessment process rather than an assessment process that tends to dominate instruction.

Multiple-Choice Exams
as Assessment and Learning

CHARLENE JOHNSON
University of Arkansas, Fayetteville

STRATEGY/ACTIVITY/ASSIGNMENT

Designing exams for use in the undergraduate course on middle level principles and practices is always a challenge because, despite the fact the students often prefer it, regurgitating previously learned material is not the most effective method of ascertaining what students have really learned. Yet, in modeling the belief that there should be a variety of assessment strategies used to ensure that all students' strengths are tapped, one cannot deny that multiple-choice tests are the preferred evaluation tool for some students. With this in mind, multiple-choice tests are given in my course but the format and questions as well as the process differ from the more traditional exam experience.

In preparation for the exam, preservice teachers are advised that there are few, if any, questions that ask them to recall a concept, name, place, or time as they may have previously experienced with multiple-choice exams. Rather, the questions are analogies, true/false statements that require an explanation or rationale for their choice, and other types of questions that ask about a concept's relationship to another concept. Questions are usually structured so that thought and analysis are needed to determine the most appropriate response.

After a multiple-choice exam has been given individually, the class members get a chance to raise their individual grades by some percentage, for example, 20 percent, by completing the exam again via a group effort. The instructor assigns preservice teachers to groups of three to five prior to the class period in which the group exam will be completed. The groups are structured to include some preservice teachers who excelled on the exam, some who did average, and others who did poorly on the exam. Without knowledge of how they fared on their individual exams, each group is given a blank copy of the exam to complete within the class period. Books, notes, and any other resources may be used. Once the exams are completed (sometimes a time has to be set for completion), the class corrects it and addresses the questions, including which answer is correct and why. This can be done at the end of the class session or during the next session. Either way, preservice teachers as a class discuss the correct answers to the questions and their rationales.

All group exams are submitted to the instructor at the end of the class session. The group grade is calculated and the percentage increase is decided (e.g., 100 percent = 20 percent of the total points, 90 percent = 18 percent of the total points, etc.). Each group member's individual grade is increased according to these percentages.

The instructor may be present or not during the process. That said, I find that it is beneficial and enlightening to hear the concomitant discussion regarding the questions and possible answers. If the instructor is present, he or she only clarifies and/or asks probing questions that may lead the group to the correct answer. He or she is not to provide answers to the questions for the group. A customary response to questions is, "Have you asked the other group members?" This forces the group to depend on each other for the "correct" answer and be responsible for the answers. If the instructor is not present, the urge to provide answers is removed.

COMMENTARY

By working on the exam a second time in a group of their peers, preservice teachers gain a deeper knowledge of the subject. As they discuss and debate the answers with their classmates, they construct meaning for themselves. Whereas when the teacher gives an answer, it is generally taken without question or deliberation, with classmates, preservice teachers are more likely to debate and question answers.

This activity intensifies the learning process and exemplifies the power of peers in the learning process. Many times preservice teachers just want to get their individual exams and correct the answers, but that is not the intent of the activity. It is pointed out that for middle level learners this is mostly the case also. The focus, however, should be on ascertaining why an answer is more appropriate or correct, as well as on how to find or figure out the "correct" answer. For middle level learners, this is also true.

The possibility of increasing their grade by as much as 20 percent motivates most of the preservice teachers, and they get quite involved in this exercise. Discussions can become intense when there is negotiation and collaboration taking place. Preservice teachers often remark that this experience taught them a lot about themselves as group members and educators. Some leaders emerge in the process. Others remarked that they discovered that they were more direct and focused than they realized when there were different ideas and styles of learning integral to their assessment or grade.

There is a possibility that different members of the group may overshadow others, and some may feel left out or not included in the process. Thus, one of the "rules" is that all group members must be involved in the process and all voices heard if the scores are to be increased on the exam. Compliance with this mandate varies and is hard to monitor, especially when the instructor is not present. Some students have remarked in their journals that their voices were not heard during this process, and I am still wrestling with this issue.

Students report that this is one of the most positive and educational experiences of the class. Although we have addressed the material assessed on the exam, students report that this experience helps clarify misunderstandings and/or solidify understandings based on the discussions with their group members. Hearing others' thoughts on the questions and the answers helps students to better understand the material as well as what was being asked. They learn about themselves as educators, group members, and learners. In addition, they discover a method of assessment for use with their students. Several students have commented that they believe that this process would serve their students in much the same way as it helped them.

Narrative Essay Exams

LINDA R. MORROW
University of Arkansas, Fayetteville

STRATEGY/ACTIVITY/ASSIGNMENT

In both the undergraduate and graduate levels of my middle level methods classes, I use narrative essays as a means of assessing learning for midterm and final exams. Rather than giving a more traditional exam, I challenge the imagination of my students and encourage the integration of content knowledge (Stotsky, 1984) by asking them to share what they have learned in a writing mode (narrative) very familiar to them.

Because we are by nature storytellers, it only makes sense to allow students the chance to do something at which they are already good

(Nicholini, 1994). When using the narrative mode, the writer has control over the event because it is familiar, thus creating a less intimidating situation.

Generally, both children and adults find it much easier to remember and use material presented in a story format versus a categorized list (Bretherton, 1984; Egan, 1986). In addition, if we believe that writing parallels thinking and that it should be used as a tool for learning, then we should be providing students opportunities to use this tool in a mode that is familiar to them as they struggle with new information.

For learners at all levels, writing can be used as a tool to make learning personal and as a means of consolidating learning. In addition, since narrative is, according to Bruner (1988), a primary form of cognition and a way of making meaning out of experience, I use this mode of writing to give students the freedom to write in a comfortable form, thereby enabling them to concentrate on the content of their learning about middle level philosophy and practice. Thus, I use one of the following scenarios for midterm or final exams:

(1) You are applying for a job in an *exemplary* middle school. Imagine that the roof of the building has been removed and that you are hovering over the building in a hot air balloon. What do you expect to see going on in the building? Discuss the implementation of various middle level components through descriptions of physical structures and the activities of such individuals as students, teachers, administrators, parents, and support staff. [Note to reader: I leave the directions open ended to allow students the opportunity to demonstrate their knowledge of middle level philosophy and practice rather than give them an outline to follow.]

(2) You are a member of an evaluation team from the National Middle School Association. During a site visit to Beane Middle School in Middletown, USA, it is your job to assess this school on the basis of the *components* or *essential elements* of an *exemplary* middle school. What components will you expect to find and why are they necessary to meet the unique needs for this population of 10- to 14-year-old students?

COMMENTARY

I have used these scenarios for both in-class and take-home exams. Using narrative mode gives students control over the testing event and creates a less intimidating situation. Offering these scenarios results in much more interesting, lively writing as students integrate content knowledge into narrative form. True to the opinions of the experts in writing and thinking, students report actually enjoying this assignment because they can tell a great story while integrating their knowledge of middle level philosophy and practice. The exams are certainly interesting reading for me because each one is unique, yet focused on specific content.

REFERENCES

Bretherton, I. (1984). *Symbolic play*. New York: Academic Press.

Bruner, J. (1988). Research currents: Life as narrative. *Language Arts, 65*, 574-88.

Egan, K. (1986). *Teaching as storytelling: An alternative approach to teaching and curriculum in the elementary school*. Chicago: University of Chicago Press.

Nicolini, M. (1994). Stories can save us: A defense of narrative writing. *English Journal, 83*(2), 56-61.

Stotsky, S. (1984). Imagination, writing, and the integration of knowledge in the middle grades. *Journal of Teaching Writing, 3*(2), 157-190.

An Exam by Any Other Name

CHARLENE JOHNSON

University of Arkansas, Fayetteville

STRATEGY/ACTIVITY/ASSIGNMENT

In my undergraduate and graduate course on middle level education, two exams are given during the semester. The first (the midterm) exam focuses on those areas covered/addressed during the first part of the course: middle level philosophy and its foundation, and early adolescent development (physical, emotional, social, and intellectual). The final exam is comprehensive and emphasizes the synthesis of the concepts covered in the course, i.e., middle level philosophy, unique characteristics and needs of early adolescents, instructional concerns, unique attributes of the middle level curriculum, unique middle level components such as advisor/advisee and exploratory, and parent and community involvement.

The format of both exams includes case studies and class presentations. For the midterm, a case study of a misguided faculty's attempt to implement the middle level philosophy based on its outmoded, distorted views of early adolescents is used. The faculty's understanding is skewed due to the fact that they simply latched on to the latest fashion ("band-wagon effect") without understanding the concepts. Preservice teachers are required to develop a written presentation for this misguided faculty based on the following:

1. A historical profile of middle level programs and how they have come to be what they are today. Include the philosophical beliefs, their beginnings in this country, how the concept of the "middle school" has evolved over time, where the middle level movement is today, and what is forecast for it in the twenty-first century.

2. A description of a middle level program and how it differs from a traditional junior high school. Differentiate early adolescence as a developmental period and how this understanding is incorporated or reflected in middle level program. Be as comprehensive as possible in discussing the various dimensions, how they interrelate, and their individual differences based on different factors and variables.

3. Formulate a rationale for middle schools in terms of the future of students as well as the nation. Include the major players, their roles in the development and implementation of a middle school, and how the different groups interact or relate in this endeavor.

[Number two is required of all preservice teachers; they choose one of the other two to also address.]

One semester, in lieu of a written final exam, the preservice teachers opted to present a dramatization of their ideas on middle level schools. They asserted that such an approach was the most beneficial way to relate their ideas. After some discussion and compromising, it was decided that a dramatization would serve as their final exam, with the understanding that the grade received would be the same for all members of the class (small class of ten students). Together, we developed the criteria for the evaluation of their presentation. The emphasis was on demonstrating what they knew about middle level programs. Specifically, they were to address curriculum and instruction (i.e. practices advocated and supported by research as the most effective for this age); and key components of middle level programs (i.e., advisor/advisee, interdisciplinary teaming, and exploratory), and how these concepts related to the development of early adolescents.

An evaluation sheet pertaining to responsibility, collaboration, cooperation, and contribution to the class's final exam product and process was developed. Each class member completed an evaluation on each of the others in the class. These evaluations were anonymously submitted to the instructor, and they only affected the final grade of the preservice teacher if the scores were not at least satisfactory (scale: excellent, above average, satisfactory, fair, and poor) from the majority of the class. This was to ensure some individual accountability and responsibility to the group effort.

COMMENTARY

The exams are an excellent source of feedback regarding the preservice teachers' understanding of various concepts. After reading the midterm exam case studies for one class, the misconceptions and misunderstandings concerning the different topics addressed were very apparent. The majority of the class had somehow misinterpreted the different dimensions of development unique to this age group and their implications for middle level programs. Therefore, we spent another class session reviewing early adolescent development and why and how their answers were inaccurate or incomplete. Some of the responses to the exam questions were restated on a paper for the class to review as a group. The groups were to explain why the statements were inaccurate in scope or interpretation. They seemed to have a better understanding of the concepts after working with their classmates and discussing the ideas and constructs in depth.

For the dramatization, several students remarked they preferred this method because of their comfort in expressing themselves orally. Discussions concerning middle level learners and their preferences and reactions to this method of assessment resulted in a valuable learning experience in regard to student preferences and alternative modes of assessments.

Designing and Using Alternative Assessment in Mathematics

DAVID K. PUGALEE
The University of North Carolina at Charlotte

STRATEGY/ACTIVITY/ASSIGNMENT

As school assessment practices undergo changes, students preparing to teach young adolescents should have occasions to deal with some of the issues related to these new approaches. The following activity provides students in a middle level mathematics methods course with an opportunity to explore assessment issues and develop a rubric to use in assessing their own mathematical problem-solving activities. Although this activity takes place in mathematics methods, instructors will find that,with some modifications, this activity is adaptable to any subject area.

The first step in this process involves students becoming familiar with standards in mathematics via the *Curriculum and Evaluation Standards for School Mathematics* (NCTM, 1989). Through discussion and critical analysis, the students are able to articulate those competencies that are being emphasized and how these changes affect assessment. The importance of problem solving, reasoning, and communication in mathematics is underscored, and students become aware of the central role of these skills in learning and teaching mathematics. Students come to realize that a process approach to mathematics demands assessment practices that enable "the teacher to understand the students' perceptions of mathematical ideas and processes and their ability to function in a mathematical context" (NCTM, 1989, p. 192).

Next, students review several rubrics that could be used to assess performance in mathematical problem solving. These rubrics come from various sources, including various state assessment documents, NCTM publications, and other texts. They focus on the mathematical processes emphasized and how these processes are measured. These first two steps, which are undertaken in two class sessions, assist the students in identifying some common beliefs related to teaching and assessing mathematical problem solving.

Students are now ready to develop their rubric. Students are asked to develop a rubric that reflects (1) an emphasis on the process of doing mathematics, (2) a workable scale that delineates various levels of performance, and (3) performance criteria for each level of the scale. The amount of time necessary to complete this step varies from class to class. Normally, we spend most of a class session collecting ideas and discussing any discrepancies. The instructor takes this information and consolidates it into a written document. The first fifteen to twenty minutes of the next two class periods are used to distribute the document, gather feedback, and make revisions. After this development phase, one rubric emerges that students, in general, support.

Throughout the course, the rubric is applied through peer evaluations to math problems assigned as homework. The assignment requires students to provide detailed steps of the mathematics used to arrive at a solution and to provide a narrative explaining and justifying the mathematical reasoning used in the problem. Although it recognizes the importance of correct answers, the rubric underscores the importance of being able to justify and explain the mathematical processes necessary to arrive at an answer. These problems are important in reviewing key mathematical concepts germane to the middle level math class. One example is to find the largest volume for a box that can be built from a 9" × 12" piece of cardboard by cutting squares of equal sizes from the sides and folding the sides up. The methods students are asked to solve the problem showing all of their mathematical work and to provide a written explanation of their reasoning as they go through the process. Student papers are collected at the beginning of the following class and redistributed for anonymous peer review. After discussing the problem, students rate the paper based on the accuracy of the answer and the ability to justify and explain the mathematics as specified in the rubric that they developed. Papers are returned and become part of the student's notebook, which is used as part of the final assessment.

COMMENTARY

This exercise works well with both undergraduate and graduate math methods students. The final rubrics that are developed vary from class to class; however, they contain similar components that emphasize problem-solving processes. Below is a representative sample of one of the rubrics designed by students. It captures the complexity of the assessment process and demonstrates the level of involvement of the students in the design.

Mathematics	**Reasoning**	**Communication**
0 → no effort	0 → no explanations	0 → no effort
1 → incorrect process	1 → inaccurate explanations	1 → unclear explanations
2 → minor errors	2 → incomplete explanations	2 → clear explanations
3 → correct answer	3 → accurate explanations	

Students commented that they appreciated the holistic nature of this assessment process and that they believed they could have benefited from such practices if they had been used in their mathematics classes when they were in school. Such comments reflect an appreciation for the emphasis on the process of mathematics and how assessment practices, such as the use of rubrics, provide a more thorough means of assessing mathematical understanding. Through this exercise, students were faced with the complexity of the assessment process from the viewpoints of both a student and a teacher. As such, they were presented with an opportunity to question assumptions and practices regarding assessment as they considered alternative methods and means of measuring student performance. Confronting preexisting beliefs about mathematics and assessment is vital if these future middle school mathematics teachers are to (1) reflect on their ideas about teaching and learning and (2) implement new approaches as deemed necessary to improve the learning of their students.

REFERENCE

National Council of Teachers of Mathematics (1989). *Curriculum and evaluation standards for school mathematics.* Reston, VA: Author.

Assessment: Using an Interview as the Final Exam in a Middle School Mathematics Methods Course

PATRICIA M. LAMPHERE
Oklahoma State University, Stillwater

KATHRYN S. REINKE
Oklahoma State University, Stillwater

STRATEGY/ACTIVITY/ASSIGNMENT

The final examination we use in a middle school mathematics methods course is an individual interview conducted between the preservice teacher and the instructor. The interviews last approximately thirty minutes and take place during the week of the regularly scheduled final examinations. Preservice teachers prepare for the interview in much the same way they would prepare for a traditional exam. Questions for the interview are drawn from course content, readings, class discussions, field experience assignments, course assignments, and student-teaching placement interviews. Students receive a copy of a set of questions prepared by the field placement office to help them prepare for the student-teaching placement interview. Candidates for student teaching must complete a successful interview with their perspective building administrators in order to be assigned to that school. Requirements for the final also include "professional attire" and the completion of a written essay reflecting that preservice teacher's philosophy for teaching middle level mathematics. The essay is handed in twenty-four hours prior to the scheduled interview session.

The interviewer posits a series of questions that reflect the goals of the course. However, the interviewer remains flexible and encourages the preservice teachers to provide additional information, augment their responses, or to give a more in-depth response. After the interview session, the responses to the questions are assessed using a scoring rubric (see below), and a grade is assigned for the interview. In addition to the interview and to determine whether students can analyze strengths of classroom instruction, a short video of a teaching vignette is used. The preservice teachers are asked to discuss the appropriateness of the instructional practices and mathematical content demonstrated in the lesson clip.

Scoring Rubric

8 points
Response was clear and well thought out. Interviewee gave examples, extended response without prompts, and indicated a thorough understanding of ideas and concepts.

5–7 points
Response was concise. Interviewee supported ideas, indicated some understanding of ideas, but needed prompts to extend concepts.

2–4 points
Response was limited. Interviewee gave no supporting evidence, and prompts did not help interviewee extend information. He/she seemed unsure of ideas and important concepts.

0 points
No response. Interviewee could not articulate ideas.

Interview Examination Questions

1. What guides your philosophy of teaching mathematics in the middle grades? Explain what your principal will be able to discern about your philosophy by observing your classroom and your teaching.
2. What teaching methods/strategies do you think will be the most effective in your classroom for teaching middle school mathematics? Explain.
3. There are several new curriculum guidelines for the improvement of mathematics instruction. Which do you feel are the most important and the most beneficial? Explain.
4. Describe your view of assessment, the important considerations, and the "assessment plan" you expect to implement in your classroom.
5. How is the teaching of mathematics in the middle school the same as teaching mathematics in the high school? How should it be different?
6. Aside from basic computational skills, what do you think is the most important mathematics knowledge a student should take from your class?
7. What is the role of manipulatives in the middle school mathematics curriculum? What is the role of technology? What is the role of problem solving?

8. Briefly describe how you will conduct your daily mathematics class.
9. Where do you see yourself as a professional educator in the next five years? In the next ten years?
10. For what one thing would you most like to be remembered as a middle school mathematics teacher?

COMMENTARY

Using an interview as a final exam is a unique way for the instructor to model for the preservice teachers how the format of an assessment can reflect the goals, objectives, and breadth of topics specific to a middle school mathematics methods course. The interview provides an opportunity for the preservice teachers to demonstrate how they integrate their knowledge of the various concepts presented in class. The act of communicating helps the preservice teachers clarify their thinking and engage in internalizing their understanding of what comprises effective mathematics teaching. Interviewing is seen by the instructor as a process of understanding what preservice teachers are thinking through a discussion of ideas that promotes learning and assists them in examining their own thinking.

As previously stated, the interviews take place during finals week. When there are more than twenty students in the class, the time commitment on the part of the instructor is at its peak. When considering whether to implement an individual interview as a final exam, the instructor must weigh the time it takes to develop a traditional exam, the time the preservice teachers spend taking the test, and the number of hours the instructor spends in grading the responses against the time the instructor will be involved conducting the interviews. Although very time intensive, the value and benefit to the preservice students of using this technique usually outweigh the drawbacks.

Conducting Student Interviews in Mathematics

TOM R. BENNETT
California State University, San Marcos

STRATEGY/ACTIVITY/ASSIGNMENT

One of the major assignments in my mathematics methods course is for preservice teachers to conduct a series of four mathematics interviews with middle level students. The purpose of this assignment is to provide preservice teachers with an opportunity to consider how middle level students think about specific mathematical concepts and how this information might be used to affect the instructional decisions and practices. This assignment can help preservice teachers improve their use of inquiry for assessment purposes while also giving them an opportunity to learn how to interact and relate to students in the middle grades.

Working in pairs, preservice teachers first design a series of developmentally appropriate mathematical problems that include realistic word problems and traditional computation problems that are related to an important middle level mathematical topic (e.g., adding fractions). In addition to investigating students' procedural ability to correctly solve the various problems, preservice teachers are told to focus their assessment on whether students have an understanding of the mathematical concepts being represented in their strategy. Therefore, particular attention is given to identifying problem-solving tasks that will provide preservice teachers the opportunity to assess whether a link exists between students' procedural and conceptual knowledge. Next, the preservice teachers share the problems created with each other and then, as a class, determine which problem(s) they might want to include as part of their interview. Once completed, each pair of preservice teachers will have a few unique mathematical problems as well as the problem(s) the class has agreed to include on all interviews.

Because our middle level program is taught on-site at a local middle school, we have immediate access to middle level students and, therefore, we do the first interview together as a class. For this first interview, I make arrangements with one of the school's mathematics teachers to borrow a number of willing student participants and secure parent and school permission as needed. Each preservice teacher pair is seated at a different lunch table. Individual students are instructed to sit with one of the teacher pairs for the interview. Although the preservice teachers usually do not know the student they interview, this lack of familiarity forces the preservice teachers to work harder on their questioning techniques because students often respond with short answers that shed limited insight into their thinking.

Prior to conducting the interview, the preservice teachers should anticipate what kinds of responses and questions middle level students might have vis-à-vis each problem in order to better understand their student's mathematical thinking. In order to accommodate a range of potential strategies, preservice teachers will want to have paper, pencil, and a variety of manipulatives available for student use.

After making the necessary introductions, the preservice teachers should inform the student that they will be posing a series of mathematical problems for them to solve and that after the student explains how he or she solved the problem, they will be asking follow-up questions to better understand the student's thought process. After the student has explained his or her strategy, preservice teachers should try to follow the student's explanation by asking probing questions that will reveal the latter's depth of mathematical understanding and procedural knowledge. Because it is not uncommon for students to be able to solve mathematical problems with little understanding of the mathematical concepts, the preservice teachers must ascertain whether their student truly understands the concepts or is merely coming up with an answer, correct though it may be.

Once the interview is complete, the preservice teacher pair should debrief, discussing what they learned about the student's mathematical understanding and the kinds of mathematical experiences they might suggest for this student based on the results of the interview. Then, on the day that that particular mathematical concept is scheduled to be discussed in the mathematics methods course, each preservice teacher submits a short written reflection that: (1) identifies what he or she learned about the student's mathematical understanding, and (2) discusses instructional recommendations, given the results of the interview. Prior to turning in their written reports, the preservice teachers share highlights of their interview as part of a whole-class discussion, including the results to the problem(s) they all had in common. These written reports are evaluated on the basis of the depth and completeness of answers.

COMMENTARY

For the first interview, the instructor might want to make arrangements for the class to visit a local middle school together if the class is not already located at a school site. Conducting the first interview together seems to not only decrease preservice teachers' anxiety about this assignment but also provides the class with an opportunity to discuss their results immediately after their interview while it is still fresh in their minds and they are still emotionally charged. I have found that the discussion that follows the interviews on this day is typically exciting and upbeat, especially as the preservice teachers begin to recognize the value of investigating students' mathematical thinking. Furthermore, my preservice teachers have enjoyed sharing the questioning strategies that they found to be the most successful when assessing students' mathematical thinking.

After the first interview, preservice teachers select student volunteers on their own for the subsequent interviews. After consulting with the classroom teacher, preservice teachers should be careful to select an appropriate student to interview (e.g., a student who is willing to participate and has parental and school approval if necessary). It is also important that preservice teachers gain experience interviewing a wide range of middle level students (e.g., students who differ in mathematical ability, English proficiency, gender). For best results, it is recommended that preservice teachers conduct at least three or four interviews over the term, with each interview focused on a different important mathematical topic (e.g., fractions, algebraic thinking, and so forth).

Because many preservice teachers are inclined to *teach* the student who does not understand how to solve particular mathematical problems, preservice teachers often need to be reminded that their goal is *not* to teach the student mathematics but, rather, to investigate the student's mathematical thinking. Some of the most common comments preservice teachers have made about this assignment is that it has helped them to better understand the connection between assessment and instructional planning and to clearly recognize the importance of investigating students' thinking.

Writing for Publication

EDWARD N. BRAZEE
University of Maine, Orono

STRATEGY/ACTIVITY/ASSIGNMENT

An assignment I use in each of my three middle level courses (Curriculum and Organization, Teaching in the Middle School, and Seminar in

Middle Level Education) grew out of the writing of graduate students/practicing teachers who comprise these classes. In responding to student assignments (e.g., weekly letters, classroom try-outs of instructional strategies, student or teacher shadow studies, and inquiries), I found myself suggesting to more and more students that they use that piece of writing as the basis for an article and submit it for publication. Incorporating a "writing for publication" component into all middle level graduate classes became a natural outgrowth of their writings and my suggestions. While the purpose was simply to have students' work used for something other than a graduate school assignment, other benefits have occurred as well.

In entry-level courses, the "writing for publication" requirement begins at a basic level. Students are encouraged to select one piece of writing from class assignments, revise it, and submit it for publication. For example, some students write letters to parents explaining developmental growth issues and their implications; others may use impassioned and informed pieces on various topics such as ability grouping, integrative curriculum, and athletics as opinion pieces for local newspapers or in-school (or in-district) newsletters. Still others summarize shadow study data for colleagues by preparing a written analysis of a particularly challenging student. In these instances, writing for publication means that their writing is used meaningfully in some way for an audience outside the graduate class.

The publishable piece assignment, for a later and more advanced course, is more sophisticated. In this course, students are required to write a manuscript to be submitted to a state, national, or international journal. Students conduct a major inquiry on some aspect of middle level education, and the inquiry often becomes the topic of their publishable piece. In other cases, students write a more reflective piece about a student, some aspect of their teaching, or even a more global interpretation on teaching and learning.

In all courses, the requirement is to prepare and submit a piece of writing for publication. Students are cautioned that while actually publishing their written work is the ultimate goal, neither they nor the instructor has any control over whether it will be accepted for publication.

COMMENTARY

Thanks in part to the "opportunities" provided by the writing for publication requirement, students have published articles in *Middle School Jour-*

nal, *Principal*, *New England League of Middle Schools Journal*, *Mainely Middle*, *Middle Link*, and *Instructor*, as well as dozens of local newspapers, school and district newsletters, letters to parents, and more. Some students are initially uneasy about this challenge, especially if they have not written for publication before, but this is always a wonderful opportunity for them to compare their "writing reluctance" with that of their own middle level students.

Because they know about this assignment from the beginning of the semester, students are ever vigilant for journals, newsletters, and the rich variety of publications available to them as possible sources for their writing. When searching the literature for an article to abstract for other assignments, students also pay attention to the publication's audience, tone, general style of writing, and requirements for publishing. We also discuss all aspects of writing and devote class time to critiques of drafts as students prepare their written pieces.

Several side benefits accrue from this assignment. For many, this is the first time they have considered preparing their writing for other adults to read. If approached properly, this is a developmentally responsive opportunity for these adults, and it allows them to be reflective about their middle level students as well. Adult students' attention to their writing and the pain it takes to make it "right" enhances their understanding of the learning processes that their students face every day.

This assignment is also a professional development opportunity. Many students have gone on to other writing, presentations at conferences, and involvement in professional associations because once they have experienced a professional activity such as writing for publication, they appreciate the intellectual stimulation that such involvement brings. In addition, writing for publication fulfills an obligation that all educators have to give back to their profession.

Over the years, some of the best articles have been written by the students most reluctant to tackle this assignment. While few are ecstatic about the writing for publication "opportunity" at the outset, once their articles have been written and submitted, many students thank me for "making them write." They admit that without this gentle nudge, they would not have written for publication.

Inspiring Student Achievement by Radicalizing Assessment

PETER HALLINAN

Central Queensland University, Rockhampton, Queensland, Australia

STRATEGY/ACTIVITY/ASSIGNMENT

By way of introduction, I coordinate teaching subjects for undergraduate teacher education students in the area of elementary and middle school education with a specialization in the inclusion of students with special needs in regular classes. A particular final year unit, "Learners with Special Needs," serves as the vehicle for this. This particular subject is taught in an innovative manner, with the entire course being devoted to (1) guest lectures from school guidance counselors and specialist support teachers and (2) practical work in a wide variety of educational placements, ranging from preschool, elementary, middle, and high school to community settings such as technical colleges and correctional centers. Herein, I comment on how one student's initiative radicalized my approach to the assessment of teacher education students, the majority of whom were preparing to teach in middle level settings. Basically, I want to share one of those turning points in history that shape forever one's future work as a researcher and teacher.

It was almost eight years ago to the day when final-year student Jenny Smith (a pseudonym) knocked on my office door. She brought an assignment for her final teaching practice unit with her and showed it to me very tentatively because "I thought you might be interested." From my perspective, what she had done was not just interesting, but riveting. She'd conducted a simple survey among the middle school children she taught, asking them how they would feel if a child with a physical disability was to become part of their class. Now there have been reams written in the literature on integration (or "inclusion," to use the current buzzword) ever since PL94-142 was passed into law over twenty years ago, especially from the point of view of teachers, administrators, and, to a lesser extent, parents; but very little has been written about what children themselves think of the inclusion philosophy. Yet this was just what this student had done. I told her I thought it was brilliant and deserved a far wider audience than one or even two lecturers, and I suggested she submit it to a journal for publication. I will never forget her answer, which haunts me to this day: "I'm only a student . . . who'd care what I had to say?"

I did handstands of disbelief. After telling her that I cared, for starters, for the reasons I've just outlined, I worked hard on boosting her self-esteem, concluding by asking her what she had to lose. Looking unconvinced and muttering about student workloads, she left. That was it until early in the following year, when I got a phone call from Jenny, now a teacher out in Queensland's back country. "Guess what? I took your advice and my article's been accepted by *Classroom*!" And so it came to pass that (to the best of my knowledge), Jenny became the first undergraduate education student in the history of this institution to become published in a professional journal.

I then thought, "If Jenny can do this, why can't any student?" Thought Number Two quickly followed: "It's a lot of work—how can I persuade students it's worth the effort?" followed by Blinding Flash Number Three, "What a total waste of time most assignments are! To be written hurriedly for the eyes of one person, who reads them equally hurriedly before scribbling a few comments and the all-important grade on them. How far removed from the realities of life is this? Where is the training for transfer to real life?" Such thoughts are echoed by Taylor (1994) in a call for us to enable students to become coauthors of their own learning.

Coupled with a dislike of "grading to the curve" for all kinds of good educational and psychological reasons, Jenny's initiative gave me the beginnings of the approach that followed. I've reflected deeply on just what a grade means. Does it *really* only indicate that the student has achieved within the top x percent of his or her group. What does *that* mean? I referred to a recent document within our own university that pointed out considerable differences between faculties—education was one of the good guys, in that this faculty was the only one that both gave broad assessment principles and spelled out student assessment criteria in highly specific detail, providing students with such information at the beginning of the semester (Flexible Learning Advisory Group, 1997).

Contrary to the facile and superficial normative comparisons achieved by the curve, I've come to the conclusion that the deeper meaning of a high grade (A or A+, call it what you will) is that it is a mark of professional maturity and educational leadership—and also, it is hoped, an indicator of an embryonic educational researcher. Here is work that is worth being shared with educators in general, not just for one professor's eyes as just another assignment.

A student who achieves a grade of A or A+, in my opinion, is one who is prepared to share ideas that reflect incisively and critically on experience, and in so doing meet certain criteria. Such criteria include accuracy and relevance to the topic in question, in this case the school setting. This writing also includes originality and depth of insight in addressing the question at issue. Jenny has a lot to answer for! Students are asked to state a contracted grade aim in writing at beginning of semester, ranging from high distinction (A+), distinction (A), credit (B), or pass (C). Students are free to renegotiate these aims throughout semester, also in writing. In practice, some students negotiate a downward grade, as they see time to achieve a high grade begin to slip away from them, but most students still achieve higher grades than would be possible under a norm-referenced system (Hallinan & Danaher, 1994).

To date, in terms of publication, we have had thirty-eight articles published in a wide variety of both scholarly and professional journals. I believe this undergraduate record of writing excellence in teacher education would be unmatched, or even uninitiated, by any other Australian university. An alternative to publication, subsequently suggested by the students themselves, was to deposit a piece of work in the university library worthy of reading by future students, as judged independently both by myself and the faculty's liaison university librarian. The students drove this process, suggesting such further assignment possibilities as teaching plans, children's games, resource kits, and tactile books. We now hold seventy-three such pieces of work in the curriculum materials section of our university library. The technical details of assessment were spelled out in the unit outline.

Equally exciting was the sheer joy of students who see themselves recorded as "authors" for their units of work (known in Queensland as Current Curriculum Program, or CCP) in the university library catalogue, once these have been accessed and placed on library shelves, or when they come into my office waving letters of acceptance from a journal editor (cf. Taylor, 1994).

COMMENTARY

Independent evaluation of this approach was made through my colleague, Patrick Danaher, who surveyed a small sample of elementary and middle school teacher education students in some depth about their experiences in this subject (Hallinan & Danaher, 1994). We were particularly interested in what led students to stick with or to alter their grade aims and how they felt about such decisions.

In terms of maintaining and achieving the original grade aim, students commented:

> "[This was] the first time I had a criterion-referenced subject, [and] I felt really motivated to go. I thought, 'Oh, well, I've got a chance, if I do all the criteria that's been supplied I can achieve a[n] HD [high distinction], initially, and a D [distinction].' Not like I'm just going to get slotted in with the rest of them, why put in all that extra effort, you know . . . It is really motivating."
>
> " . . . to prove to myself that I could get a distinction . . . kept me going, that's why I stuck to my grade."
>
> " . . . knowing what you're going to get gives you more of a will to do it."
>
> "If I fulfill . . . [those] criteria, then I will get that mark."
>
> "It was up to me, not comparing me against everyone else."
>
> "It was for me. It was something I had to deal with for myself."
>
> "I think it's a very good motivation technique . . . [for middle school] students."
>
> "I've actually proved to myself and to other people that I can get that mark, and it's just through a lot of work and dedication that I could get it."

In terms of preferring this style of assessment to other more conventional ones:

> "Well, we had people conducting orchestras and all those sorts of things and here I am, I came in with no music background and I learnt . . . how to play the guitar, which I think was a great achievement for me . . . [but] I only got passes in the subject, which I was really disappointed with."

In terms of deciding to renegotiate the contracted grade downwards:

> "I think it [attaining lower grades than those contracted for] depends on how you look at it . . . I just look at it like I ran out of time. I did everything possible to finish it, but the time factor just came into it. So I claim something out of my control really. If I claim something that I was in control of, then my self-esteem will go down, won't it, and I won't feel so good about it."
>
> "That's fair enough that there's other people that'll be doing better than you, but that's just the way life is. You can't always be the best . . . I'm quite happy being myself."

The results of this survey are public information (Hallinan & Dana-her, 1994) and, together with unit assessments from later student cohorts, were sufficiently encouraging for me to continue using this approach.

A final thought is that it is, or should be, our responsibility to model the role of inspirational teacher to our future middle school educators. While I believe the approach has been successful for the students as part of their preparation as teachers, perhaps the ultimate test will be whether they in turn can inspire children in the middle school grades towards higher levels of achievement. Such higher achievement comes at a critical time in their young lives, leading, hopefully, in the longer term, to greater success in the senior schooling years and beyond. I welcome further comment on the implications of this approach from readers.

REFERENCES

Flexible Learning Advisory Group. (1997). Issues concerning alternative pedagogies: Assessment of students' work at CQU. An unpublished discussion paper produced by the Flexible Learning Advisory Group on invitation of the Education Committee of Academic Board. Rockhampton, Qld: Central Queensland University.

Hallinan, P. & Danaher, P. (1994). The effect of contracted grades on self-efficacy and motivation in teacher education courses. *Educational Research, 36* (1), 75-82.

Taylor, P. G. (1994). Reflections on students' conceptions of learning and perceptions of learning environments. Unpublished paper presented at the Annual Conference of the Australian Association for Research in Education (AARE), University of Newcastle 27 November–1 December, 1994.

CHAPTER 8

Multicultural Perspectives

Voice, Schema, and Multiculturalism at the Middle Level

CHARLENE JOHNSON
University of Arkansas, Fayetteville

STRATEGY/ACTIVITY/ASSIGNMENT

Multicultural perspectives and issues are interwoven into the fabric of my undergraduate and graduate middle level principles course via various activities. The importance of culture and language for effective, relevant classroom practices is consistently emphasized. How culture affects perceptions, realities, and interactions is thoroughly examined. In addition, the point is made that "loving" everybody is not a sufficient or major goal of designing and implementing culturally relevant pedagogy (instructional practices and materials that recognize and incorporate different cultural perspectives). Although this point is made on a regular basis, my preservice teachers, who are overwhelmingly middle- to upper-class and of European descent, insist that they can design effective, relevant, and culturally sound pedagogical practices for use in a class of widely diverse students with little or no knowledge of their cultures, beliefs, and/or rituals. This activity was designed to increase understanding of how culture affects perceptions, communication, and interaction among individuals and its implications for schema.

I enlisted the help of two African American adolescents to develop a list of common terms and statements used by them and their peers. Some of the statements were: "Just chillen"—just relaxing or cooling out; "ole dusty brother trying to talk to me"—old man trying to "hit" or make advances to me; "bumping them sounds"—playing music loudly; and "man came in, his grill all messed up"—teeth were bad. As they dictated and interpreted, I conveyed the statements to a sheet of paper to give to the class. Interpretations were not provided on the list.

In class, the list was given to the preservice teachers, and they were directed to determine the meanings of each. They could collaborate with each other if they chose. After a suitable amount of time (fifteen to twenty minutes) we resumed as a class and reviewed the list. The correct meanings were given after the preservice teachers offered their interpretations of them.

Following the interpretations, we discussed how they addressed or approached the terms and how their schema was used to make meaning of the statements. In addition, we discussed how different aspects of an individual's make-up interact when trying to interpret the statements. For example, one of the statements is, "toe [tore] up from the flo up" [ugly from head to foot]. Several of the preservice teachers suggested that this referred to something being on the floor that was ripped. Having never been exposed to a similar phrase before, they constructed meaning based on their experiences and use of the language. I shared that, although I was older and not familiar with the phrase itself before the adolescents offered it, as an African American I inferred it had something to do with being ugly ("toe up") because the phrase is common among African Americans, regardless of age.

It is important that such discussions also address the implications of language usage for early adolescents in finding their place in the world (identity development) and social development. An additional point for the preservice teachers is to understand that until one understands how differently individuals see the world and make sense of it, it is difficult to "love" and educate adequately.

COMMENTARY

This strategy is most memorable for preservice teachers. Some have remarked about its significance a year or two after the experience. The activity and interactions are extremely intense as the students try to interpret the statements. As we discuss how they tried to bring meaning to the statements, the importance of schema is underscored. Students experience firsthand how language has different meanings and implications for learning.

It is important that this exercise/strategy is not trivialized as being one of those interesting, "fun" exercises that has little, if any, meaning for those involved. It is imperative to include follow-up discussions that emphasize schema, development (social, emotional, and intellectual), identity development, and culture's influence on perceptions. These discussions must be facilitated so that preservice teachers recognize their personal cultural make-up and its impact on schema and perceptions and how that might influence their interactions with students in the classrooms.

African American is only one of many cultures and dialects/languages that may be used for this exercise. Others are equally viable as well to assist preservice teachers in understanding the impact of these variables on schema and perspectives and their implications for educational practices with early adolescents. When developing the list or collection of statements, it is wise to utilize the expertise of early adolescents from the local area. Another idea is to invite the developers of the list to visit the class and observe and comment on the preservice teachers' struggle to make meaning of the words. The terms and ideas change often so it is important to stay in contact with early adolescents to ensure that the list remains current and "accurate."

Cultural Queries: Exploring Gender and Multicultural Issues

M. GAIL JONES
University of North Carolina at Chapel Hill

STRATEGY/ACTIVITY/ASSIGNMENT

This activity is an excellent way to get students to think about their own stereotypes and preconceptions about gender and culture. Each question should be printed on an index card and either hung from a string or taped to a student's back. Questions can easily be used several times with more than one student. (For examples of questions and answers, see the accompanying list entitled "Cultural Queries.")

The directions for this activity are as follows:

A question related to gender or culture has been placed on your back. You should walk around and ask five different people to give an answer to your question. You will not know what the question is, only the answer that they give. Each answer should be given as a percentage. Record your answers and when you have five responses, sit down and average your responses. Once you have your average response you may look at your own question.

The instructor can then read each question aloud and ask all those who had that question to share their averaged response. Students are often surprised to see how far their average is from the actual answer. The differences in the averaged response and the actual response can suggest areas where students hold stereotypes about certain groups of people.

COMMENTARY

This activity can serve as an engaging way to introduce gender and multicultural issues. The format of the activity involves student-student dialogue, mathematics skills, and physical movement. The process involves using a group's average response rather than an individual's response, which can be an effective strategy for getting reticent students to share and participate in the discussion. Generally, students are very surprised to see how far off their beliefs about gender and multicultural issues are from reality. The averaged responses effectively highlight the stereotypes that many of us hold about minority populations.

Cultural Queries

1. In 1986 four times as many males as females took AP physics exams. What was the ratio of male to female exam takers in 1993?
   Answer: Three times more males than females took the AP physics exam.
   Source: Schmittroth, S. (Ed.) (1995). *Statistical record of women worldwide*. NY: Gale Research Inc.

2. In 1972 only 1.3% of high school senior girls indicated they wanted to be a manager. What was the percentage in 1992?
Answer: 5.4%
Source: Schmittroth, S. (Ed.) (1995). *Statistical record of women worldwide*. NY: Gale Research Inc.

3. In 1995 white males who held a bachelor's degree made $35,839. What was the median salary for black males?
Answer: $30,000.
Source: National Center for Education Statistics. (1997). *The condition of education 1997*. US Department of Education, NCES 97-388.

4. 3.8% of Native American students took calculus in 1994. What was the percent for Hispanic students?
Answer: 6%.
Source: National Center for Education Statistics (1997). *The condition of education 1997*. US Department of Education, NCES 97-388.

5. What is the ratio of white high school dropouts to black high school dropouts?
Answer: 4.5 to 6.4
Source: National Center for Education Statistics. (1997). *The condition of education 1997*. US Department of Education, NCES 97-388.

6. What percentage of children ages 5 to 17 speak a language other than English in the home?
Answer: 13.1%
Source: National Center for Education Statistics. (1997). *The condition of education 1997*. US Department of Education, NCES 97-388.

7. What percent of students in special education classes are black?
Answer: 18.4 percent.
Source: Reddy, M. (Ed.) (1995). *Statistical record of Hispanic Americans*. NY: Gale Research Inc.

8. Mathematics has been called the critical filter that can block access to careers in science and technology. In 1982, 57% of black students took Algebra 1. What percent took Algebra 1 in 1990?
Answer: 78%
Source: Reddy, M. (Ed.) (1995). *Statistical record of Hispanic Americans*. NY: Gale Research Inc.

9. Among 8th-grade students, 49% of white students reported having used a telescope at home and at school. What percent of black students reported use of telescopes?
Answer: 36%
Source: Reddy, M. (Ed.) (1995). *Statistical record of Hispanic Americans*. NY: Gale Research Inc.

10. When asked "Do you like science?" only 72% of 8th-grade males said yes. What percent of females said yes?
Answer: 64%
Source: Reddy, M. (Ed.) (1995). *Statistical record of Hispanic Americans*. NY: Gale Research Inc.

11. 43% of whites report having a computer in the home. What percent of blacks report having a home computer?
Answer: 16.1%
Source: Reddy, M. (Ed.) (1995). *Statistical record of Hispanic Americans*. NY: Gale Research Inc.

12. In 1972 only 9% of women aspired to attend graduate or professional school compared to 16% of males. What was the percent for women in 1992?
Answer: 35% (an increase of 257%)
Source: Schmittroth, S. (Ed.) (1995). *Statistical record of women worldwide*. NY: Gale Research Inc.

13. When adolescents were asked "Who do you think of as the special adults in your own life, who are the adults who really care about you?" what percent of students said fathers? What percent of students said mothers?
Answer: 79%, fathers; 93%, mothers
Source: Chadwick, B., & Heaton, T. (Eds.) (1996). *Statistical handbook on adolescents in America*. Phoenix, AZ: Oryx Press.

Adolescent Profiles:
Characteristics of Early Adolescents

M. GAIL JONES
University of North Carolina at Chapel Hill

STRATEGY/ACTIVITY/ASSIGNMENT

In this activity students are involved in exploring their understandings of middle school students. Through a series of questions, students predict and then examine statistics related to young adolescents' culture and characteristics both in and out of school. For teacher education students, the activity helps them narrow the gap between their lives and the lives of their future students by highlighting the statistics that define their cultural habits.

Each question related to adolescents should be printed on an index card and either hung from a string or taped to a student's back (see the accompanying list of questions and answers that follow). Questions can easily be used several times with more than one student.

The directions for this activity are as follows:

> A question related to some aspect of early adolescence has been placed on your back. You should walk around and ask five different people to give an answer to your question. All of the questions are answered with a numerical response. You will not know what the question is, only the numerical answer that they give. Record your answers and when you have five responses sit down and average your responses. Once you have your average response you may look at your own question.

The instructor can then read each question aloud and ask all those who had that question to share their averaged response. Students are often surprised to see how far their average is from the actual answer. The differences in the averaged response and the actual response can suggest areas where students hold either correct or incorrect notions of young adolescents.

COMMENTARY

This activity helps students see how their own teenage years may have differed from early adolescents today by emphasizing current statistics about adolescent behaviors. The format of the activity involves student-student dialogue, mathematics skills, and physical movement. The process involves using a group's average response rather than an individual's response, which can be an effective strategy for getting reticent students to share and participate in the discussion.

Early Adolescent Profiles

1. Adolescents were asked, "What adults do you look up to and admire, and maybe would like to be like when you're an adult?" What percent of students said teacher or coach?
   Answer: teacher or coach, 15%; mother, 39%; father, 35%
   Source: Chadwick, B., & Heaton, T. (Eds.) (1996). *Statistical handbook on adolescents in America*. Phoenix, AZ: Oryx Press.

2. When teens were asked about topics they had discussed with their parents, 95% said they had discussed school work. What was the percent that had discussed sex with their parents?
   Answer: 58%
   Source: Chadwick, B., & Heaton, T. (Eds.) (1996). *Statistical handbook on adolescents in America*. Phoenix, AZ: Oryx Press.

3. What percent of adolescents would like to discuss drugs with their parents more often?
   Answer: 49%
   Source: Chadwick, B., & Heaton, T. (Eds.) (1996). *Statistical handbook on adolescents in America*. Phoenix, AZ: Oryx Press.

4. What percent of 12- to 14-year-old students consider themselves to be "brand loyal" when shopping?
   Answer: 47.4%
   Source: Schmittroth, S. (Ed.) (1994). *Statistical record of children,* New York: Gale Research Inc.

5. What is the average amount of money spent by 12-year-olds in a week?
   Answer: $11; for 13-year-olds it increases to $15 per week.
   Source: Schmittroth, S. (Ed.) (1994). *Statistical record of children.* New York: Gale Research Inc.

6. Middle school students report that the number one item they buy with either their own money or their parents' is clothing. What percent of students indicated that they are likely to buy candy when they have money?

Answer: 41%. The top five items purchased are: clothes, 47%; cassettes/CDs, 42%; candy, 41%; fast food, 33%; and movies, 28%.

Source: Schmittroth, S. (Ed.) (1994). *Statistical record of children.* New York: Gale Research Inc.

7. What percent of middle school students work extra chores, babysit, or have jobs such as a paper route to earn money?

Answer: 62%.

Source: Schmittroth, S. (Ed.) (1994). *Statistical record of children.* New York: Gale Research Inc.

8. The percent of 8th-grade boys who indicated that they had used tranquilizers last year was 1.6%. What was the percentage indicated by 8th-grade girls?

Answer: 2.3%

Source: Schmittroth, S. (Ed.) (1994). *Statistical record of children.* New York: Gale Research Inc.

9. Among 8th-grade students who plan to attend college, 0.4% indicated that they had used heroin last year. What was the percentage for noncollege-bound students?

Answer: 2.7%

Source: Schmittroth, S. (Ed.) (1994). *Statistical record of children.* New York: Gale Research Inc.

10. What percent of 8th-grade students report having had five or more drinks in a row over the last two weeks?

Answer: 13.4%. Four percent of these students indicated having had five or more drinks in a row three or more times in the last two weeks.

Source: Schmittroth, S. (Ed.) (1994). *Statistical record of children.* New York: Gale Research Inc.

11. What percent of 8th graders believe it would be easy to get crack if they wanted some?
    Answer: 17.6%. For marijuana it was 29.7% and for steroids it was 15.1%.
    Source: Schmittroth, S. (Ed.) (1994). *Statistical record of children*. New York: Gale Research Inc.

12. Four percent of 8th-grade students reported that they had consumed alcohol at school during the day. What percent indicated that they had used alcohol at a school dance, game, or other event?
    Answer: 11%. For marijuana it was 3% during the day and 4% at school-related events.
    Source: Schmittroth, S. (Ed.) (1995). *Statistical record of women worldwide*. New York: Gale Research Inc.

13. What percent of middle school students report that their school has members of fighting gangs?
    Answer: 38%
    Source: Schmittroth, S. (Ed.) (1994). *Statistical record of children*. New York: Gale Research Inc.

14. Out of every 1,000 children, how many are reported each year to protective services for abuse or neglect?
    Answer: 45 each year (2,936,000 in the United States).
    Source: Schmittroth, S. (Ed.) (1994). *Statistical record of children*. New York: Gale Research Inc.

15. What proportion of public school lunches served within the United States are provided to students for free or at reduced prices?
    Answer: 47%
    Source: Schmittroth, S. (Ed.) (1994). *Statistical record of children*. New York: Gale Research Inc.

Gender Issues

LINDA R. MORROW
University of Arkansas, Fayetteville

STRATEGY/ACTIVITY/ASSIGNMENT

One means of bringing the issue of affirming diversity to a conscious level is to ask preservice teachers and graduate students to complete the SIQ-R (Sexist Intelligence Quotient Revised) test (Cassidy et al., 1994). The purpose of this instrument is to measure awareness of gender issues and their influence on literacy instruction. The key accompanying the instrument provides research information regarding gender issues in literacy education and offers suggestions for initiating changes in teacher behavior regarding such issues.

This 25-item instrument can be completed and self-scored within a 30-minute time frame. The resulting class discussion is a lively exchange of experiences of being victims, both male and female, of sex-role stereotyping and/or gender bias, and of a heightened awareness of needed changes in student-teacher interactions in the classroom. For example, a male preservice teacher related his struggles with the expectations in elementary school that he should be successful in playing baseball even though his interests were in other extracurricular activities. Female students often report having experienced lower expectations of them in math, science, and athletics. This learning strategy brings the topic of gender issues to a very personal level as research is connected to individual experiences.

COMMENTARY

Preservice teachers and graduate students often leave this class session with the resolve to change teaching strategies and to be aware of more inclusive student-teacher interactions. In one graduate-level class, the instructor offered the class the option of documenting the number of her interactions with male and female students during a class session. The results were that there were more instructor interactions with male students than with females. This led to further discussions of all the circumstances that defined the context of this class and how classroom teachers can keep these issues at a conscious level. In addition, the graduate student, a former elementary school principal, who tallied the classroom observations, chose gender issues as his middle level research project.

REFERENCE

Cassidy, J., Smith, N., Winkeljohann, R., Ball, R., & Blouch (1994). The SIQ-R test: Assessing knowledge of gender issues in literacy education. *Journal of Reading, 38*(2), 104–108.

E-mail Exchange Between College and Middle School Students

DILYS SCHOORMAN
Florida Atlantic University, Boca Raton

STRATEGY/ACTIVITY/ASSIGNMENT

Description

This activity is designed as a project in an undergraduate course in multicultural education. The e-mail correspondence takes place between students in a college course and those of an English teacher at a selected middle school. The school selected for this activity is in an economically depressed community that serves a predominantly migrant population.

Purpose

This project is designed to be mutually beneficial to all participants. For the undergraduates in a course designed to broaden students' culture-based perspectives and to engage in critical thinking about issues of equity, this is an opportunity to interact with students whose life experiences are vastly different from their own. To achieve this goal, students are provided guiding questions to be answered and criteria to be met throughout the project. These questions are centered around the university students' biases and preconceived notions about their penpals' schooling and lifestyles; information about their penpals' interests and disinterests in schooling; and their perceived "readiness" for teaching their penpals. All letters were to be reviewed by the writers for spelling and grammatical correctness, appropriateness of content and language, tone (e.g., friendly, rushed), responses to their penpals' inquiries, and the opportunity to engage the penpal in further appropriate inquiry.

For the middle level students, this project was originally designed as part of their literacy curriculum and grew to incorporate interests in other content areas. The opportunity to correspond with penpals whom the students had not seen represented both the academic as well as social dimensions of this project. Students had to build a relationship based solely on their writing.

Procedures

Students in both institutions are paired up by the instructors. The students write to each other once each week for the entire semester via the e-mail account of their respective instructors. Letters are distributed in class in both institutions. The middle schoolers are allowed time in class to compose and revise their letters. The undergraduates write outside of class hours. Incoming and outgoing letters are reviewed by the college instructor each week and relevant issues (e.g., asking appropriate questions, paying attention to spelling or correct letter writing protocol, use of age-appropriate language) are addressed through weekly feedback e-mailed to all undergraduate participants. Class discussions around topics such as equity; negative teacher expectations; and ethnic, class, and gender bias are usually related to the children involved in the project. At the end of the semester, the undergraduates present a written project report that details what they learned (about themselves, their partners, schooling in general, and the implications for teaching) during this activity. Each student is given an opportunity to discuss the highlights of his or her report in class.

COMMENTARY

Bridging the Cultural and Experiential Gap

Many preservice teachers (predominantly middle-class Euro-American females) have had limited contact with persons of diverse cultures (Segall & Wilson, 1998; Sleeter & Grant, 1999). Such limited experience often leads to misconceptions and stereotypes about students who are of different cultures. This project facilitates an interpersonal relationship across cultures. What typically begins as a relationship framed in the context of difference inevitably ends up in the discovery of commonalties. Ultimately, the child is seen as "special"; someone who deserves every opportunity to succeed in school.

Advantages and Disadvantages of E-mail

The fact that the project is e-mail-based makes the physical proximity of the two cooperating institutions a nonissue. The college instructor can select schools that are typically underserviced (e.g., lack of university-school partnership efforts) in the community or populations that are of particular significance to class discussions. The ability to selectively target a school is especially useful in contexts where the college community is homogeneous or exclusive.

One of the potential disadvantages is that many schools do not have computer facilities to support such a project. This can be overcome if a member of the school community is willing to type in the handwritten notes of the children and e-mail them to the college via a private e-mail account. If the school is in relative proximity, a member of the community who attends the college (as a student or employee) can personally deliver the handwritten notes of the children.

Possible Adaptations

Many teachers have found it more useful for students to handwrite their letters first. The project could be extended to include the participation of computer/media personnel in the school to assist students with the electronic aspect of the project. The correspondence could be designed to include the specific discussion of topics addressed on other content areas such as science, social studies, or reading. One of the features of the current implementation of this project is a field trip to the university made by the middle schoolers. Plans are underway to arrange a reciprocal visit by the undergraduates.

Learning Outcomes

For many, this was a useful way of making the somewhat "theoretical" and "abstract" discussions more relevant and personalized. The sending and receiving of letters created a sense of excitement for all students involved in the project. The effort to please their college correspondents made the middle schoolers (for many of whom English was not their first language) more particular about spelling and grammar and writing a "proper" response. The undergraduates worried about what they could do to "draw out" their students in their writing and actively sought advice from peers and the instructor about appropriate responses.

Among the unexpected outcomes of this project was the fact that many of the undergraduates ended up playing the role of personal mentor to their middle school correspondent. The students raised issues of academic problems, career choices, or social dilemmas and were guided through their deliberations by "someone who was always there to listen." At the end of the project, many middle school students noted that the correspondence had made them interested in going to college. In most cases, they would be the first in their family to do so.

REFERENCES

Segall, W. E., & Wilson, A. V. (1998). *Introduction to education: Teaching in a diverse society.* Upper Saddle River, NJ: Merrill Publishing Co.

Sleeter, C. E., & Grant, C. A. (1999). *Making choices for multicultural education: Five approaches to race, class and gender. (3rd ed.).* Upper Saddle River, NJ: Merrill Publishing Co.

Barriers to Interpersonal Communications for Students Who Are Deaf or Hard of Hearing and Learning to Resolve These Barriers Through Assistive Devices and Related Communication Accommodations

ED R. WILLIAMS
University of Arkansas, Little Rock

STRATEGY/ACTIVITY/ASSIGNMENT

Middle level education should thrive on the diversity that students bring to the classroom. Interactions with students who are deaf or hard of hearing make up part of this diversity. Loss of hearing is the most common chronic disability in the United States, with about one in ten people experiencing some type of hearing loss. Types of hearing loss range from difficulty in hearing soft or low-volume sounds to the inability to hear spoken words or other loud sounds.

An essential ingredient to middle level education is the integration of students into the family and community. This inclusion can be successful when students with disabilities are considered to be a part of the diversity that makes middle level education so unique. The suggested strategy is to expose students who hear to a sampling of communication barriers that students who are deaf or hard of hearing are likely to encounter in everyday situations. The learning objectives are to: (a) directly experience a barrier to interpersonal communication; (b) become familiar with the language and modes of communication used by deaf or hard of hearing students; and (c) learn about the assistive devices and related communication accommodations available to help resolve or minimize these communication barriers.

This classroom activity is enhanced when people who are deaf or hard of hearing are included and when devices and accommodations are demonstrated and used (e.g., Telephone Typewriter (TTY)/Telecommunications Device for the Deaf (TDD), alerting devices, hearing aids, FM loop systems, computers, and interpreters). Recruit students, teachers, or adults in the community who are deaf or hard of hearing to participate in the class. People who are deaf or hard of hearing can be used as actors in the activity, and instructors can teach your class sign language. In addition, they can demonstrate how to use devices and other accommodations and show the students how using them can resolve communication barriers.

The activity is to engage in selected everyday interactions experienced by an individual and his or her family (e.g., buying a ticket to a movie, asking for directions, conversation at the local "hangout," buying groceries, and conversing with a schoolteacher). The rules applied in this strategy are: (1) no talking; (2) all communication must be carried out in the form of either natural gestures (e.g., charades), speechreading, sign language, or finger spelling; and, (3) during each interaction only one of the above listed communication styles may be used. Speechreading is the more appropriate term for lipreading. Sign language could be the whole continuum of signing from American Sign Language (ASL), Pidgin Sign English (PSE), to Signing Exact English (SEE). Finger spelling is using the sign language alphabet to spell out words. As each student completes the interaction, a communications "cop" will award points for completing the activity as well as give out tickets for violating the rules.

Again, only one communication style per scenario is allowed. For example, in one scenario, buying groceries, only sign language is allowed. For the next scenario, asking for directions, only gestures are allowed. The communications cop should subtract points for students who talk or use other forms of communication. For example, when buying groceries, if they used gestures, in addition to sign language, points should be subtracted.

Additional resources to help one become familiar with sign language might be the school library or a sign language interpreter who works for the school or school system. As part of this learning objective, it is hoped that the learning of a few signs from a textbook or from the school interpreter will encourage students to learn sign language from a sign language program. The objective of this initial activity is for students to experience communication barriers and to begin to become familiar with language and different modes of communication.

Involve the students in discussing typical interactions they experience. Pick four or five interactions and assign a form of communications to each interaction (e.g., gesturing to buy tickets, speechreading to carry on a conversation at the local hangout, sign language to buy groceries, finger spelling to talk to the teacher). During each activity, the student interacts with another individual, preferably someone with expertise in the assigned communication style, and attempts to complete the activity.

Learning objectives include not only experiencing the barriers to interpersonal communication but learning about the communication styles and accommodations available to help overcome or minimize these barriers. As a result, the activity should be divided into two sections: one in which the above rules (e.g., using only one communications style) are applied and the other in which the students use devices or accommodations to resolve communication barriers. An example of using a device would be a student buying groceries from someone who is deaf or hard or hearing. What devices can that student use (e.g., a note pad or hand-held computer)? Another example of an accommodation would be providing a sign language interpreter. In this section, educating the students about devices and other accommodations to address barriers and how to use the devices is important.

The Vocational Rehabilitation Services office in one's state is an excellent resource for information on the devices, and it can identify or contact adults in the community who are deaf or hard of hearing. Some states have service providers or rehabilitation counselors that specialize in providing services to individuals who are deaf or hard of hearing. In addition, many communities have organizations of people who are deaf, schools for students who are deaf, or community-based service centers that are also good resources to use.

An additional resource is Barbara Ray Holcomb, an instructor at the National Technical Institute for the Deaf (NTID), who developed the workshop *It's a Deaf, Deaf World* and other situational activities. Training materials can be requested from Barbara at 1-716-475-6271 (TDD only) or voice message at 1-716-475-6497. Also, mail can be sent to her at Rochester Institute of Technology/NTID, 52 Lomb Memorial Drive, Rochester, New York 14623-5604. Other resources are the Research and Training Center for Persons who are Deaf or Hard of Hearing, 4601 W. Markham, Little Rock, Arkansas, 72205, 501-686-9691, and the Cornell brochures on the Americans with Disabilities Act (ADA). The web address for the center in Little Rock is http://www.uark.edu/depts/rehabres, and the Cornell address is http://www.ilr.cornell.edu/ped/ada/.

COMMENTARY

Students who have participated in this activity have gained considerable knowledge about various barriers to interpersonal communications experienced by people who are deaf or hard of hearing. Students learn that when using the proper assistive devices the barriers to communication can be overcome. This type of positive direct exposure is one method for teaching middle level preservice teachers methods or strategies for problem solving.

It is important that students experience barriers to communication and measures to address them. In activities where only the barriers were experienced, students have expressed frustration, and they leave the activity with the opinion that they are not deaf, so why worry about it? For this type of activity to be successful, participants need to be in direct contact with individuals who are deaf or hard of hearing and be made aware of the various devices that individuals who are deaf or hard of hearing can use to resolve communication barriers.

Book Clubs That Encourage Students to Examine Their Cultural Assumptions

JAMES FLOOD
San Diego State University, San Diego, CA

DIANE LAPP
San Diego State University, San Diego, CA

DOUGLAS FISHER
San Diego State University, San Diego, CA

STRATEGY/ACTIVITY/ASSIGNMENT

Students arrive in our classes with a number of assumptions about people. Often these assumptions are stereotypes born of inadequate information. Providing students the opportunity to discuss individual differences, especially based on literature selections, provides them with new insights about people who are different from themselves. Although it has been said before, literature does allow us to experience worlds and ways that we may never know ourselves. Discussing literature allows us to challenge one another as well as our own values, beliefs, and behaviors.

In our instructional methods courses, we require students to read a variety of works of contemporary fiction that provide a natural opening for discussion and examination of the multicultural world in which we live. Seated in a large circle, students read, write, speak, and listen based on a process that is established during the first week of school (see Table 8.1). As a class, we agree on several general guidelines for operating our book club (see Table 8.2).

Selecting the specific pieces of literature is very important. Because our goal is to expand student understanding of cultures other than their own, we purposely select literature that is representative of the range of human experience found in our world. For example, we read about Salvador (Cisneros, 1991), a boy who takes care of his siblings. We also read about Rebecca (Anderson, 1992), a young woman with Down syndrome whose family is faced with a difficult decision. A longer class discussion on *In the Year of the Boar and Jackie Robinson* (Lord, 1991) provides students the opportunity to think about the use of this type of literature in their classrooms with their middle school students.

COMMENTARY

Managing time in a methods class to discuss literature, especially using a structured process, has produced a number of interesting results. First, students learn the literature discussion or book club process (Roser & Martinez, 1995) and gain enough practice to implement it in their classrooms. Second, stereotypes and myths are debunked, and our students gain an appreciation for the lived experiences of their middle school students. Third, these future teachers are exposed to a number of books that could be used in their classrooms. As one of our students wrote in her journal: "I thought I was very open-minded. However, while reading Salvador, I realized that I had more pity than anything else for many students. I'm glad I had the opportunity to talk through my attitude with members of my class in a nonthreatening way. I have a very different understanding of the world now and feel much more prepared for the multicultural world in which I live and work."

Another student wrote in his journal: "Literature takes a person places that he may not be able to experience firsthand. Our book club allowed me to explore differing perspectives freely without pressure to conform to some 'correct' viewpoint. I plan to use book clubs in my class because they made me concerned about missing class, not because I thought it would affect my grade, but because I would miss out on a great interaction about something I cared about. I hope I can do the same for my students."

Table 8.1. Guidelines for Moderators (teachers or students)
1. Have students write a journal response to the text being read (2–4 minutes; individually)
2. Share responses with a partner (2–4 minutes; pairs)
3. Lead discussion with the group (1–15 minutes; group)
   - Begin by asking students to share thoughts based on their reading/writing and discussion of text with their partner
   - Have content-specific questions ready to focus the discussion if it strays too far afield or becomes bogged down on a point that seems to be unresolvable
4. Post-discussion writing (4 minutes; individually)
5. Share responses with a partner (4 minutes; pairs)
6. Return to discussion with whole group (10 minutes)
   - Invite responses based on the previous writing
7. Write a journal entry (2–4 minutes; individually)
   - Ask students to write about their response to the text as a result of reading, writing, and discussing with their peers

Table 8.2. Classroom Guidelines for Literature Discussion
- Be prepared to discuss your thoughts about the text by completing your reading and writing prior to the literature discussion
- Be courteous by listening to everyone's comments
- Be sensitive to people's feelings as you make contributions to the discussion
- Wait until the speaker is finished speaking before beginning your comments
- Make your comments positive and constructive
- Feel free to question and agree/disagree by clearly and calmly stating your opinion
- Assume responsibility for your own growth

REFERENCES

Anderson, R. (1992). *The bus people*. New York: Holt.

Cisneros, S. (1991). *Woman hollering creek and other stories*. New York: Vintage.

Lord, B. (1984). *In the year of the Boar and Jackie Robinson*. New York: Harper & Row.

Roser, N., & Martinez, M. (Eds.). (1995). *Book talk and beyond: Children and teachers respond to literature*. Newark, DE: IRA.

Society's Eye: Viewing Others Through Music, Gender, and Ethnicity

MARGARET E. ALBERTSON
Azusa Pacific University, Azusa, CA

SHARON TOOMEY CLARK
Claremont Graduate University, Claremont, CA

STRATEGY/ACTIVITY/ASSIGNMENT

To restate a familiar cliché, "society is in the eye of the beholder." It is through a personal lens that individuals view others. Beliefs about gender, ethnicity, or language filter this view. Examining these beliefs through music offers an alternative to preconceived notions. By noting embedded beliefs or values in music of different times, places, and traditions, middle level students can challenge their assumptions. This teaching strategy gives middle level educators an opportunity to expand the worldview of their students.

For centuries, musicians have borrowed themes, or, for that matter, entire existing compositions, from predecessors or contemporaries. New lyrics may be added—often in a different language. Changed rhythms accommodate newer dance steps. New instrumentation often reflects technological advances. For example, themes from Beethoven's Fifth Symphony, written in the nineteenth century, were incorporated by the Beatles in "Roll Over Beethoven" in the twentieth century. Later in the twentieth century, both compositions evolved into the musical score for the movie about a rather large St. Bernard called *Beethoven*. A more poignant example is Elton John's and Bernie Taupin's rewrite of "Candle in the Wind," which was heard by a world audience during the funeral of Diana, Princess Wales, on September 6, 1997.

This activity takes five class sessions to complete:

Session 1. Middle level educators form musical analysis groups (MAG) based on a common societal concern—e.g., poverty, sexism, racism, war. Each group then designs three critical questions to apply to the chosen concern. For example, if poverty were chosen, three critical questions might be: (1) Does the end justify the means? (2) Who is responsible for helping the poor? or (3) Can you be both poor and happy? These questions then become a lens through which to examine the musical works. This lens is refined through small-group discussion as members seek to answer the relevant questions they have formed.

Session 2. Class members select an evolved musical composition. The selection should be examined in its original form as well as its evolved form(s). Students note differences and similarities between the pieces. A Venn diagram is a useful tool for this session.

Session 3. During this class period, students bring examples of other cultural artifacts that are related to their personal experience as well as to the focus in session two. Again, they examine each through the lens developed in session one. As more questions arise, students may refine their critiquing lens.

Session 4. During this class session, students prepare an issue collage. A 3" × 5" box is drawn on chart paper. Students label the columns: (a) original song (title), (b) evolved song (title), and (c) related art (title of one of the cultural artifacts explored in session 3). The rows are labeled by the issues that the students identify as most central to the social concern.

Session 5. To conclude the activity, each group shares the music and the issue collage. They lead the other class members in a discussion of the central themes. At the very end of the session, students individually write a growth reflection that considers: (a) exploring multiple ways of representing cultural beliefs; (b) understanding social injustice issues of diverse populations; (c) providing avenues of expression through art genres; and (d) engaging students in personal learning growth.

COMMENTARY

Many students, especially those who have never experienced social injustice, have difficulty with this assignment. Often, they do not see why the assignment is important or relevant to their lives. This attitude usually changes by the third session because students are asked to bring personally selected artifacts to class. By connecting these artifacts to the individual stories of classmates' experiences, issues of social justice become more intimately understood. After the culminating activity, most students feel they have gained initial insights into complex issues.

Promoting Multiculturalism in Middle Level Education

HAROLD L. SORKNES

Northern State University, Aberdeen, SD

STRATEGY/ACTIVITY/ASSIGNMENT

All of us grew up within a culture surrounded by many beliefs and behaviors that we accepted without question. As young children we probably associated with persons from the same culture and tended to consider our way of thinking and behaving to be the "right" one. Stereotypical thinking may have begun, and we may have become prejudiced against those who thought and acted differently. If minds are opened to new ideas, teachers, students, and parents will revise stereotyped thinking as they learn to accept differences and to realize that "different" does not mean "deficient" or "wrong." According to Tiedt and Tiedt (1995), "Learning to get along with the people of diverse backgrounds, needs and expectations who make up the American multiculture requires commitment . . . Teachers have a significant role to play in guiding children to recognize and respect diversity as they interact with other young people in and out of school" (p.1). Tiedt and Tiedt (1995) also note that research has suggested that next to parents, teachers are the most significant people in the lives of their children and, therefore, play a significant role in the formation of children's attitudes. Teachers have the job of building learning experiences into the educational process that will encourage positive attitudes about racial, ethnic, and cultural differences.

In my middle level methods class, I introduce the concept of multiculturalism and its relevance for middle level students. Social and emotional growth are important aspects of middle level education. Middle level students are searching for identity, and they are sensitive about themselves. Helping students achieve pride in their own heritage, as well as developing a respect for others, is important in a middle level school. I also believe that middle level students who are guided into reading and discussing significant books about the experiences of others in the world will have the opportunity to grow and to become more globally aware citizens and more caring individuals.

In my middle level course, I have my preservice and practicing teachers develop lessons that integrate various subjects as well as a multicultural perspective. This provides an opportunity for preservice teachers to work in teams and to develop an integrated unit. I divide the class of preservice teachers into teams of approximately four or five teachers. I make sure that each team is made up of members whose backgrounds include social studies, language arts, science, and math. Members representing other subject areas such as physical education, music, art, and so forth are distributed among all the teams. The team's assignment is to think of a unit topic that would integrate each of the subject areas. The teams then develop a unit with individual lessons in the various subject areas. Team members are instructed to integrate a multicultural aspect into at least one of the lessons involved in their subject area within the unit. That said, they are encouraged to include a multicultural aspect into as many lessons as possible within the unit. It is imperative that the multicultural aspect be germane to the lesson. For instance, within a unit on the 1950s, social studies teachers could include Native American relocation programs and termination policies as they affected various tribes in the United States.

During class, I place each of the team members at a particular "station" in the classroom and divide the remaining class members into groups so that each "station" has a group with which to start. The "stations" are simply locations within the classroom, or adjacent classroom space, where each "teacher" can present his or her lesson. The teacher at each station then does a microteaching lesson involving his or her subject area related to the overall topic. Because of time limitations, each lesson is limited to approximately ten minutes. Although it is not possible to teach a full lesson, class members get an opportunity to take part in at least one activity that would be part of the particular lesson. The groups are rotated among the stations so that each group has an opportunity to visit each station. Each teacher also has the opportunity to "teach" his or her lesson more than once. This has been very effective, and the preservice teachers appreciate the opportunity to teach a lesson more than once.

COMMENTARY

On course evaluations, this activity has been rated by preservice teachers as one of the most beneficial aspects of the course. The preservice teachers indicated that they not only practiced integrating various subjects, but they also learned more about and developed a more positive attitude toward Native American culture. Although Native American culture was used as the primary topic in this case, the ideas involved could be extended to other cultures as well. The preservice teachers indicated that they felt more comfortable about incorporating multicultural materials after this class activity. The activity provided them with many ideas for incorporating multicultural information as well as actual experiences utilizing multicultural materials in the development of lessons.

Some of the comments on evaluations indicated their positive response to this class activity. "Today our group gave our lesson presentation . . . . I really enjoyed this part of the class because of all the interesting things people chose to do . . . . I thought this part of the class was the most beneficial for teachers or future teachers." Another entry stated, "The group presentations have been very valuable and I hope to incorporate some of the techniques . . . when I become a teacher." A third entry referred to the experience of working in a group. "I liked working within a group; it is very important for us to learn to teach together." Finally, this entry seemed to indicate to me that I had accomplished what I had intended when I developed this assignment: "The lesson presentations have been a real success! What a great experience for both presenters and the students. It is due to these that I have received a lot of neat and creative ideas as well as new material to use in my classroom."

REFERENCE

Tiedt, I. Y., and Tiedt, P. (1995). *Multicultural teaching: A handbook of activities, information, and resources.* Needham, MA: Allyn & Bacon.

CHAPTER 9

Physical Movement

Connecting Early Adolescent Physical Needs to Instruction

LINDA PAYNE YOUNG

Asbury College, Wilmore, KY

STRATEGY/ACTIVITY/ASSIGNMENT

Middle school teachers need not only to *know* what physical changes are taking place in the early adolescents that they see each day in the classroom; they also need to *understand* how these physical changes should impact instructional design. Restless energy from rapid muscle growth coupled with natural aggressive activity from physiological changes does not usually create passive students. In addition, the awkwardness resulting from disproportionate growth and the fact that most early adolescents are very self-conscious of the physical changes make some classroom situations a nightmare for students.

The objective of this activity/assignment is to aid students in learning to design instruction that accommodates the physical needs of the early adolescent. After the class has become acquainted with the physical changes that are part of the middle school years, the students spend a class period in a middle school. Although one block-class period is usually sufficient to meet the needs of this assignment, additional sessions add more data for the students to use. Students in the class may also compile all the data gathered to obtain a "picture" of the entire class.

Using the "observation instrument," students record the physical activity of five students assigned to them. The assignment is part of the course practicum and is not officially a research project; therefore, it is considered a clinical field experience and the students in the teacher preparation program will adhere to the contractual agreement between the educational program and the school district. Selected teachers in the middle school have agreed to allow education students to observe in their classroom during the semester. Education students are assigned to a teacher in their discipline and are instructed not to breach confidentiality. Names are not to be used or any identifiable notes made.

In class following the observation, the education students discuss the physical activity of the early adolescents and what can be done during instruction to accommodate the need for movement exhibited by many of the middle schoolers. The assignment is to design a lesson that takes into consideration the need for movement and activity. A criterion for meeting the physical needs of the early adolescent is added to the standard grading criteria used to evaluate the lesson plan.

Observation Instrument

Record of Adolescent Physical Activity

Length of Observation: _____

Instructions: During the class period, mark the observed predominant behavior of each student during 5 minute intervals. Tally the number of occurrences.

Activity	Student 1	Student 2	Student 3	Student 4	Student 5
Sleeping, daydreaming					
Sitting quietly, listening					
Sitting quietly, working					
Fidgeting, restless movement					
Disturbing others unintentionally					
Out of seat					

Activity	Student 1	Student 2	Student 3	Student 4	Student 5
Annoying others intentionally					
Aggressive behavior: hitting, pushing, kicking, taking objects					

COMMENTARY

Using this assignment early in the course creates awareness throughout the semester of the need to accommodate physical needs. Students always enjoy the opportunity to be in a middle school classroom, but the focused observation helps them to really "see" what they often overlook concerning movement. Discussion usually reveals that students have become more understanding of "normal" behaviors that were often labeled "misbehavior" in the past.

Incorporating Movement into the Classroom Via "Academic Games"

SAMUEL TOTTEN
University of Arkansas, Fayetteville

STRATEGY/ACTIVITY/ASSIGNMENT

A valuable way to model a method of incorporating movement into the middle level classroom as well as an enjoyable and effective means to assess how well students have completed the previous night's homework or have mastered key concepts is to develop a game that is hands-and-legs-on. The following game was developed for the latter purposes when I was teaching a middle level methods and principles course.

To conduct the game I do the following: first, I divide the class into two teams. Second, I explain that one student from each opposing team should come up to the board at a time. Third, once both are at the board, I read aloud a question (which is prepared prior to class by the professor and/or the students). The point of the contest is to see which student is able to come up with the correct answer first.

In order to facilitate and expedite the playing of the game, the questions are arranged so that answers are in a true/false, short-answer, or multiple-choice format. If a student doesn't know the answer he or she can call on the team for help, and another member of his or her team must come up to the board (and running is fine) and write out the answer. Team members can only come up after the person at the board has asked for help, and they are not allowed to call out the answer. If the answer is called out, then the other team automatically gets the point. The person who gets the correct answer first gets the point for his or her team.

Following this activity a discussion can ensue about concepts, issues, facts, and ideas that are either not clear to students or those for which students may wish more detail.

COMMENTARY

This simple activity models one way to incorporate physical activity into a middle level classroom and still concentrate on academic concerns.

On a different level, this activity also serves as an enjoyable and thought-provoking anticipatory set to a discussion on the physical make-up and needs of young adolescents. It is remarkable how much university students enjoy this format. They laugh, groan, and ache to run up and help a stymied partner, and they cheer when their team gets a point. They quickly come to appreciate that with a little planning, some set rules of dos and don'ts, a review of a chapter or a set of concepts can be fun and instructive. They also learn that there are legitimate ways to get middle level students out of their seats during an academic exercise.

It should be noted that prior to or following this exercise, a heavy emphasis is placed on an examination of the physical needs of early adolescents (including the need to stretch and move their often aching and quickly growing bodies) and how that need directly relates to their cognitive, social, and emotional needs.

Living Haiku: Scenes of Sound in Motion

NAN McDONALD
San Diego State University, San Diego, CA

DOUGLAS FISHER
San Diego State University, San Diego, CA

STRATEGY/ACTIVITY/ASSIGNMENT

In our preservice teacher preparation course, "Teaching in the Content Areas," we encourage students to think about teaching through a variety of modalities. We are especially interested in methods that allow students to use a variety of literacy processes, including reading, writing, speaking, listening, and viewing. We develop lessons that these future teachers can use with their middle school students, such as teaching poetry. One form of poetry is the Japanese art of Haiku writing (Navasky, 1993). Haiku poems consist of three unrhymed lines of text, with a total of 17 syllables. The following lesson was originally developed in a music education class and then adapted for use in a middle level teacher training program. It is one that incorporates movement into the classroom, thus also meeting the physical needs of young adolescents.

Haiku, if written masterfully, moves. The form offers us spaces for our own thoughts and designs. One senses its setting, a season, a moment in which delicate outlines of action and reflection are offered to the reader. Classic Haiku reflects the simplicity and beauty of line found in the painting and the music of the great Japanese masters.

Setting the Scene with Movement: Slow-tempo Koto (Japanese zither) and Shakuhachi (flute) music is playing softly in the background (see sources). We begin by having the students silently mirror the ultra-slow, very connected movements of the teacher. Now, we tell them, silently, find a partner, alternating who leads the movement. The follower must mirror the actions exactly, even if the leader chooses to take the movement to the floor level, or "move the ideas across the room." Insist that the movement be connected and slow, as if under water. The teacher may give quiet cues, i.e., "Move in a low space" or "Move with your partner across the floor space" or "Now change to the other leader," signaling the students with a windchime or other quiet sound.

Keep the music playing. Show pictures of classic Japanese watercolors, watercolors with poetry characters, flower arrangements, Zen gardens, and so forth. Talk about the simplicity and beauty of the designs. Explain how many Japanese poets were also artists and musicians.

The Poetry: (Keep the music on). Quietly tell the students that you have decided to create "scenes" for Haiku. Next the teacher models a selected Haiku, for instance,

> *A flash of lightning . . .*
> > *the sound of dew*
> > > *dripping down the bamboo*

The teacher models the Haiku in three distinct ways:

1. Speaking only: Use highly expressive/dramatic speech that varies the tempo (speed) and dynamics (softs and louds) according to the feeling and meaning of the words.
2. Dramatic speech with movement: Repeat the Haiku, but this time add simple movements to the mood of the expressive speech. For instance, "flash!" might be a jagged double-arm movement that "freezes" in space. The "dew" could be a spiraling movement descending to the floor as if drops were actually winding their way down a bamboo.
3. Movement only: Think the words, even mouth them if necessary, while performing the Haiku "movements" without sound. Have students try the movement sequence with you once. Discuss how the poetry comes alive with movement.

Assign groups made up of four students. Give each student a copy of several Haiku poems and then give the following directions:

Read several Haiku aloud with your group before you decide on one. Each group will select their Haiku. Create a Haiku "scene" with expressive speech, movement and speech, and then movement alone. (List instructions on the board.) When you have practiced your three ways of performing your Haiku and feel you are ready, come to me and I'll give you paper and art supplies to draw a scene or backdrop for your Haiku. We will be performing our Haiku for each other in about 25 minutes.

Finally, gather the actors/movers/artists together. Let them know that each group will unroll their "scenery" and perform their poetry in the three ways (speaking only, dramatic speaking with movement, and movement only). End the performance with all the Haiku groups performing their "movement only" sequence all at the same time. Use recorded music throughout and fade at the very end. Have the students write and/or illustrate journal reflections about their experiences within "Living Haiku."

COMMENTARY

During the class discussion that followed this "Living Haiku" lesson, students shared ideas about using this format with their students. As one said, "The three-step process for performing the Haiku required that we use inner speech as advocated by Vygotsky." Another student added, "We could use the movement warm-up and three-step process with all kinds of text. I think I will always remember that Haiku because our group had to say it over and over again to memorize it." Another quickly added, "Yeah, and how often do we get our students to read a text more than once! I know it is advocated in our text book [Lapp & Flood, 1992], but it is hard to do." Someone else commented, "I really liked the movement warm-up. There was no right answer. I was really making eye contact with my partner, using hand-eye coordination, and following a leader."

The student journals and illustrations were as positive and contained even more evidence of the learning that occurred through movement. As one student wrote: "I really appreciate the fact that the Haiku activity was not talent-based. We were all expected to participate and each of us got in there and did something to contribute to the group. We had choreographers, illustrators, memory-aide teachers, and directors. Along the way, we learned a lot about Japan, poetry, our interaction styles, and literacy." This student had drawn a picture of a computer and written the following Haiku as the final entry of her journal.

> *Out of memory.*
> *We wish to hold the whole sky,*
> *But we never will.*

REFERENCES

Lapp, D., & Flood, J. (1992*). Teaching reading to every child* (3rd Ed.). New York: Macmillan/McGraw Hill.

Navasky, B. (1993). *Festival in my heart: Poems by Japanese children.* New York: Harry N. Abrams.

Rielly, E. J. (1988). Reading and writing Haiku in the classroom. *Children's Literature Association Quarterly, 13*(3), 111-114.

Silver-Burdett and Ginn. (1995). *The music connection: K-8 music series.* Englewood Cliffs, NJ: Author.

Stewart, H. (1969). *A chime of windbells: A year of Japanese Haiku in English verse.* Rutland, VT: Tuttle.

The Metropolitan Museum of Art. (1985). *Talking to the sun: An illustrated anthology of poems for young people.* New York: Author.

Yasuda, K., & Fletcher, J. G. (1976). *A pepper-pod: A Haiku sampler.* Rutland, VT: Tuttle.

Young Imaginations. (1994). *Being in motion: Multicultural music and movement activities to enhance awareness and cognitive skills.* San Rafael, CA: Author. (Book, CD, and video available from Young Imaginations, 54 Terra Linda Drive, San Rafael, CA 94903. CD features authentic Japanese instrumental music.)

Silent Movie: Representing Knowledge Through Signals and Movement

MARGARET E. ALBERTSON
Azusa Pacific University, Azusa, CA

SHARON TOOMEY CLARK
Claremont Graduate University, Claremont, CA

STRATEGY/ACTIVITY/ASSIGNMENT

Middle level educators often ignore the vast amount of nonverbal knowledge that is available to diverse populations of their students. An especially effective teaching strategy for teachers of multilingual classrooms is to have students produce a silent movie. This strategy is equally effective for all students because language does not mediate the activity. In this lesson, students aren't prevented from participating by their limited English vocabulary; students don't have to overcome their fear of public speaking; and students develop a sense of community through shared interaction.

Middle level education students simulate this activity during one class meeting. They form groups of four to six students through random assignment using index cards. Each card contains one of three written movie role descriptions. In the first role, a teacher tries to convey a concept or procedure to a small group of students. In the second role, a student cannot understand the concept that is being taught. In the third role, a pair or a group of students is able to grasp exceptionally well the concept that is being taught.

Once the actors understand their roles, they begin brainstorming a list of scenarios they want to silently illustrate. They then plan how to nonverbally demonstrate their plots within three to four minutes. Next, they choose music from a selection made available by the instructor. The group practices their skit with the music. When satisfied, they videotape their production.

Before adjourning, the class views and orally critiques the films. Final reflection considers: (a) exploring multiple ways of representing knowledge; (b) meeting the needs of diverse learning populations; (c) integrating curriculum; (d) providing avenues of expression for language minority students, and (e) engaging all students in creative expression.

COMMENTARY

Many students, especially those who do not have experience in an arts discipline, feel more comfortable as spectator rather than as participant. This is largely because of the perfect performances seen through different broadcast media. The pressure of performing in front of peers should also be considered.

Using pre-acting exercises can greatly increase their level of comfort. Activities might include saying the alphabet using different intonations to a partner or acting out some charades. Structure and guided practice throughout the activities provide further support.

One middle level educator used the lesson in her bilingual classroom. She then showed the movie at her school's open house. Later, her principal commented how impressed he was with her creative implementation of curriculum.

Pair-Em-Up!
An Activity for Mathematics Preservice Educators

LAURA BRADER-ARAJE
University of North Carolina at Chapel Hill

STRATEGY/ACTIVITY/ASSIGNMENT

One way to facilitate movement in a middle school mathematics class-room is to implement what I call "Pair-Em-Up." This activity provides an opportunity for students to not only move about the classroom area, but to become partners with someone through a process of chance.

In order to conduct this activity, the teacher must prepare an index card for each student ahead of time. These cards will be given out to students either as they first enter the classroom or during the class period for a change of pace. Students will have either a *math sentence* on their card, say, −2<=X<=4, or Y=7, or a *line graph* displaying the solution to a math sentence on a horizontal axis. Students are to talk with each other and mill about the room in order to locate their partners—partners are those students whose math statement and line graph solution correspond. In the end, students can check to see if their pair-ups are correct by identifying any paired students whose cards do not correspond. If there is one pair that does not match, then, of course, there is at least another that needs repairing! ("Repairing" is a pun that a middle school student of mine pointed out a few years ago.)

This activity takes very little time, and the cards can be used more than once with the same group of students if so desired (I recommend lamination). Sets of cards can get progressively difficult or different, as new mathematical concepts concerning solutions to math statements and variations on graphing are introduced.

COMMENTARY

Pair-Em-Up! is an activity that is quick and easy to prepare, takes few materials, can be used more than once, aids in assessing students' mathematical knowledge, presents an opportunity for students to move about the classroom, and creates partnerships for that period. As students get the hang of the activity, they too can create their own Pair-Em-Up! game to share with the class. And of course, Pair-Em-Up! card themes are not limited to just linear inequalities (as outlined above).

As co-instructor of a special topics mathematics course where content is taught in conjunction with the modeling of various pedagogical practices and skills, I have found that this activity is useful not only to model an educational strategy that facilitates movement in the classroom, but to promote interaction and content awareness among the undergraduate students who take the class. Both time-efficient and fun, this activity has been a well-received invitation to further involvement in middle school mathematics. Mathematics can be a stressful experience for many young adolescents, and providing opportunities to interact with each other and the mathematics simultaneously can help foster a mathematics culture that values the student as well as the content.

CHAPTER 10

Classroom Management

Behavior Management from Classroom to Detention Center

TONI SILLS-BRIEGEL
Southwest Missouri State University, Springfield

STRATEGY/ACTIVITY/ASSIGNMENT

To assist middle level preservice teachers in understanding the range of early adolescent behavior with which they will be dealing in their classrooms, the following sequence of field experiences has proven to be an eye-opening experience. Students enrolled in "Classroom Management for Middle Level Teachers" have completed introductory middle level courses and have an understanding of the needs of early adolescents. Still feeling insecure about their classroom management and discipline skills, students enroll in this course to acquire specific techniques and to observe different elements of a school system's total management system in action. During seminar sessions, students are introduced to a series of management models, including Dreikurs, Glasser, Canter, Curwin/Mindler, and Nelsen/Lott/Glen (Charles, 1999). The following field experiences are designed to reinforce seminar information and generate reflective discussion.

Field Experience 1: Teachers
and Building Administrators

Arrangements are made by the course instructor for the class to interview either the principal or vice-principal of an area middle school. Preservice teachers and the administrator discuss the behavior management plan for the entire school. Samples of documentation used by the school to record student behaviors are provided, and their use is explained during the meeting. The administrator explains his or her responsibilities in the management system and answers specific questions.

After the whole-group interview, students, either individually or in pairs, are assigned to specific classes to observe management techniques of teachers. Teacher volunteers have been previously solicited by the administrator. The college students are quickly matched on the day of the observation according to subject or grade-level interests. Students are not allowed to take notes during the observation, but are required to jot down as much as they can remember after leaving the school. This requirement was made by the instructor after an unfortunate incident in which a student's classroom notes were too blunt and the teacher read the notes over the student's shoulder. In addition, some teachers become nervous when visitors are noticed to be writing continuously. The no-notes-in-class policy does seem to lead to a more relaxed observation experience for many. Student observers stay with their assigned teacher during the entire time available for observation, usually one-and-a-half to two hours. This usually allows students to observe a teacher ending and beginning a class and working with two different groups of middle level students. A brief but formally written paper (two to four pages) reflecting on the entire experience is due by the next seminar class, at which time individual experiences are shared. College students are carefully instructed to protect the privacy of both the teachers and the middle level students observed.

Field Experience 2: Counselor and
Middle Level Student Interviews

This whole-group experience also takes place in a middle school, but this time the interviewee is the school counselor. If the class is small or if the office is large, the site for the class's interview is the counselor's office itself. This allows the counselor to explain the design of the office and to point out where and how student records are kept. The counselor explains his or her place in the behavior management system of the school. The counselor presents his or her services as providing positive support for students with problems and explains how students access counselor services. He or she also discusses the types of problems students may have that teachers should not be expected to deal with in the classroom.

A common question asked by preservice teachers concerns the procedure for reporting child abuse. Another request is a desire to see a student's cumulative file. Although the counselor is not allowed to show actual files, he or she may generically describe the contents of a file, thus protecting the identity of students. Preservice teachers are generally impressed by the amount of documentation kept on each child.

As time and class size permit, college students are paired with individual middle level students to share experiences. College students talk about what it's like to be in college, and middle level students share their opinions of school rules and personal preferences for treatment both in the classroom and the school at large.

Again, preservice teachers do not take notes onsite, but record impressions as soon as possible after the event. Reflective papers are shared at the next seminar.

Field Experience 3: Alternative School Tour

Students who are unable to succeed in conventional classroom settings are increasingly being referred to alternative schools that are maintained by the district. Such schools typically provide low teacher-student ratios, less structured instruction, individualized or small-group projects, and teachers who have an affinity for working with the "at-risk" student.

Preservice teachers immediately sense differences when entering one of the area alternative schools. The majority of students are boys. The general atmosphere is much more informal than that of a traditional middle school. Attitudes of both teachers and students vary from traditional classes.

The administrator or head teacher conducts a tour through the school, explaining policies and listing common student behaviors that brought about their assignment to the school. College students are also paired with alternative school students to share information. College students are usually surprised at how open most students are to share their problems and their often detailed descriptions and explanations for their aberrant behavior. Again, preservice teachers do not take notes. Reflective papers are shared at the next seminar.

Field Experience 4: Juvenile Detention Center

The final field experience is a visit to the area juvenile detention center. Until this visit actually occurs, most of my students do not realize that this is a real prison. It has bars. It has cells. It has big, burly guards who handcuff young people who refuse to obey the rules. The center also has a school with a certified teacher. The lounge contains Ping-Pong tables, television, an adjacent basketball court, and opportunities to engage in numerous other activities. Young inmates earn points for appropriate behavior, which may be traded for social time, television time, or other rewarding activities. The juvenile detention center is the end of the line for students with behavior problems that endanger others or whose behaviors break the laws of the community.

The tour guide, usually one of the guards, walks the college students through double-locked steel doors, and identifies himself and visitors at various checkpoints. He tells about keeping suicide watches on children and describes breaking up fights. Young prisoners who break rules are returned to bare cells. College students ask about behaviors that cause children to be detained here. Crimes range from rape to grand theft to arson to murder.

Our tours are scheduled to take place while student inmates are attending school, since visitors to the center are not allowed to see the prisoners. Paper is placed over the windows of the schoolroom to further protect the privacy of the children. No interviews may take place here.

Student reflective essays on this experience generally express sorrow.

COMMENTARY

This series of field experiences is intended to develop in my middle school majors an understanding of the complete system of behavior management established by the community and state. I emphasize that the first step to keeping young people out of the detention facility is to have each teacher learn to manage his or her own classes well. Prevention is the most important element of any classroom management system. Some preservice teachers express concern that they won't be able to "handle" the really tough management problems that they are sure they will face. It is necessary to ask them to think about how many thousands of students attend school in the local school system and to notice how very few children were actually housed in the detention center. Most are encouraged to know that a complete system exists. They begin to understand their place in it. The point is made repeatedly during every field experience that teachers need not handle every problem alone.

REFERENCE

Charles, C. M. (1999). *Building classroom discipline, 6th edition*. New York: Longman.

Writing Cases

LAURA VAN ZANDT ALLEN
Trinity University, San Antonio, TX

STRATEGY/ACTIVITY/ASSIGNMENT

Research on the developmental stages of becoming a teacher indicates the centrality of classroom management issues once the initial focus on idealism subsides (Kagan, 1992). Thus, much of the student-teaching/internship experience at our institution revolves around management dilemmas, especially in the realm of student discipline. Helping preservice teachers embrace the means of understanding these stages and moving through them successfully is the challenge teacher educators face. Having preservice teachers construct their own classroom management cases based on personal experiences allows them to simultaneously examine their worst fears while providing a safe distance between self and the actual situation being studied. The use of the story grants the student author control and perspective, which allows for an objective analysis and evaluation of the situation. Following is the assignment I use with graduate interns in a five-year MAT program who are teaching at a middle level professional development school. The course, "The Middle School," is nested within a six-hour secondary block entitled "Pedagogics."

Groundwork

1. Before students can write meaningful cases, they must have read, studied, and debriefed a number of cases beforehand (from five to ten). Some of these should address management issues.

2. Since students must have a personal experience on which to draw, the case writing must be assigned after a number of weeks in the field, not near the beginning of the semester.*
3. Students must have studied classroom management theories. In this class, base groups were assigned one theory from Charles' (1999) *Building Classroom Discipline*, which addresses the theories of Glasser, Kounin, Canter, and others. During case debriefings, each group is ultimately responsible for addressing the case from their theorists' perspective (i.e., what would Curwin and Mendler do in this situation?).
4. An atmosphere of mutual respect and support must be developed within the class so that students feel safe in sharing personal "failures."
5. Students must be taught how to write cases.

*If field experiences are not available, have students interview middle level teachers about a management episode that took place in their classrooms that presented a dilemma.

Teaching Case Writing

While a number of excellent sources exist for examining the process of case writing, one of the most useful is Hansen's (1997) "Writing Cases for Teaching: Observations of a Practitioner." The article takes the reader through the process of case development step by step while providing examples and specific do's and don't's. In addition, Shulman's (1996) four attributes of a case taken from "Just in Case: Reflections on Learning from Experience" in *The Case of Education: Contemporary Approaches for Using Case Methods* provide a framework from which to begin:

Four attributes of a case

1. *Intention:* The existence of a formal or tacit plan, itinerary, or purpose.
2. *Chance:* The plan is interrupted by a surprise, by a "glitch," by the unexpected.
3. *Judgment:* In the face of uncertainty and surprise, the actor must exercise judgment, because no simple answer is available.
4. *Reflection:* Examining the consequences of action taken in light of judgment and learning in a way that produces the basis for a new plan or intention (pp. 207-208).

Writing the Case

The three-week assignment includes both individual and group work:

Week one *(individually)*
1. Reread the Hansen article on writing cases.
2. Select a classroom management incident from your own recent teaching experience that includes the four attributes of a case.
3. Write a three- to five-page draft (typed, double-spaced) of this incident and give your case an appropriate name. Disguise your case to protect your own and others' confidence (use pseudonyms for names of people, classes, schools, etc.). Use third-person narrative rather than first person.

Week two *(in base groups)*
4. Each group member distributes copies of his or her case to the group and to the instructor and then gives a brief oral summary of the case to group members.
5. The group chooses one case.
6. The groups function as a sounding board to help extend, refine, edit, and finalize the case.
7. Three to five study questions are written for the case that address the key issues (underline the key issues in each question).
8. Write a one-page teaching note (to the instructor) that highlights the key issues that need to be brought out during the discussion and provide possible resolutions (not singular) for the case.

Week three
9. Final cases are due. The groups should provide copies for the instructor and each class member.
10. For the following class meeting, groups begin presenting their cases to the class by facilitating a 20-minute discussion that includes possible solutions and fielding questions from the class.

COMMENTARY

Having students write their own cases based on their experiences with classroom management issues has been one of the most powerful tools I have found for inducing metacognitive thought. It provides a structure for reflecting on and examining the day-to-day classroom actions and responses both with self and with others. At first, students groaned about having to write a case; however, once base groups began to share their cases with one another, the enthusiasm grew. Afterwards, students felt it the most meaningful "assignment" of the semester, rivaling only the day-to-day experience in schools. Although cases can focus on any topic (i.e., instructional strategies, collaboration, etc.), dealing with management issues speaks to students about the concerns and fears presently confronting them in their journey toward becoming teachers. This relevancy, combined with the cognitive processes involved in the assignment, makes great strides in moving students from a survival mentality to a learner-centered focus on curriculum and instruction in the classroom.

REFERENCES

Charles, C. M. (1999). *Building classroom discipline*. New York: Longman.

Hansen, A. J. (1997). Writing cases for teaching: Observations of a practitioner. *Phi Delta Kappan, 78*(5), 398-403.

Kagan, D. M. (1992). Professional growth among preservice and beginning teachers. *Review of Educational Research, 62*(2), 129-169.

Shulman, L. (1996). Just in case: Reflections on learning from experience. In Colbert, J. A., Desberg, P. & Trimble, K. D. (Eds.) *The case of education: Contemporary approaches for using case methods*. Boston: Allyn and Bacon.

Create a Classroom Plan

MAUREEN REILLY LORIMER

California State University, San Marcos

STRATEGY/ACTIVITY/ASSIGNMENT

Any preservice teacher embarking on the journey to become a middle level educator must be fully aware of the unique and varied needs of early adolescents. This requires that teacher preparation courses focus student attention on the foundations of middle school philosophy and early adolescent development. Once students are fully conversant with this theoretical base, they can apply this information to all aspects of teaching.

A major component of the "Learning and Instruction in Middle Schools" course is the establishment of a positive and developmentally responsive learning environment. Through various readings, class discussions, school-site observations, and modeling—in this case, the development of a positive learning environment for preservice teacher instruction—students gain an understanding of its significance for effective teaching and learning. One way to solidify these concepts and apply them in a practical manner is to create a classroom plan. Preservice teachers use background knowledge and understanding, based on course readings and school observations, to develop their "dream" classroom. The project requirements are to:

- Draw a map of the physical environment, including the furniture arrangement, location of specific centers, bulletin boards, and other necessary items.
- Develop a list of classroom procedures, delineating the daily operations of your classroom (e.g., moving about the room, distribution of materials, speaking in class, assignment headings).
- Develop a classroom management plan, describing expectations (i.e., rules and consequences) and implementation of this plan. Please specify your intentions for positive reinforcement of this model. Will you offer tokens, praise, or other rewards for students who follow the classroom rules? Describe how student input will be utilized. Will students provide input for determining class expectations? Will this be done at the beginning, middle, or end of this process? Will this input occur in a whole-class, small-group, or individual setting?
- Write a letter of introduction to parents/guardians that describes your philosophy and expectations, classroom procedures, and other pertinent information. Advise parents/guardians of the supplies students are expected to bring to class. You will want to encourage parent participation.
- Develop a list of "sponge" activities that can be used at the beginning of class, as an attention getter, an anticipatory set, or for emergency time-fillers.
- Develop a list of "signals" (devices for gaining student attention).
- Include a rationale for the content of each section. Each rationale should explain your thinking and relate directly to middle level philosophy and include young adolescent development research.

Evaluation is based on a rubric developed by the students and the instructor. Criteria include: the comprehensiveness of the rationale included for each section, details provided for specific ideas, completion of all requirements, and quality of presentation (e.g., organization and appearance).

COMMENTARY

This assignment allows students to create their "dream" classroom where money and other extraneous factors are not considered. Students become excited about this assignment because they can visualize the type of learning environment they would like to have. As they begin to review the criteria and requirements, they believe that this project is fairly straightforward. Once the actual working and planning begin, in-depth thinking and attention to critical details take over. The students soon realize that each decision in their design must be thoughtfully and carefully considered. The rationale portions for each section test their ability to justify their own thinking/choices with middle level theory and adolescent development research.

Many graduates have shared their thoughts about this assignment. Although this design is hypothetical, they said that "it was a useful reference tool." Former students, now employed as teachers, have told me that during the preparation for the new school year they referred to this project for assistance and ideas. They conveyed that their "visionary plan" provided a basis for designing a developmentally responsive learning environment.

Ultimately, this create-a-classroom-plan activity connects the underpinnings of middle level philosophy with practical application in a meaningful way.

Team Classroom Management Plans

TONI SILLS-BRIEGEL
Southwest Missouri State University, Springfield

STRATEGY/ACTIVITY/ASSIGNMENT

Creation of an interdisciplinary team classroom management plan is a function of teaming that should take place well before the first day of school. Teachers should discuss and resolve their differences, if any exist, in order to develop a sound and fair plan as well as to present a united front to both students and parents. Typical areas of discussion covered during planning include:

1. Identification of roles and rules for team members
2. Equitable division of team responsibilities
3. Homework policies
4. Team rules
5. Positive and negative consequences
6. Positive recognition systems
7. Specific classroom management systems
8. Implementation of selected management system
9. Parental contacts and parent/team conferences
10. Documentation policies to record student behaviors (Charles, 1999; Canter & Canter, 1995)

Preservice teachers in a middle school methods class are required to create both a team and a personal classroom management plan. The point is made through discussion that while a team plan coordinates the activities of the group, teachers still have individual teaching styles and different management needs when working alone in their own classrooms. Thus, the team should coordinate as many rules and procedures as possible, but must leave room for each teacher to adapt student behaviors to meet his or her own teaching requirements.

Students are placed in interdisciplinary teams of four to approximate as closely as possible their future teaching environment. Teams meet several times throughout the semester, and the college professor provides them with sufficient information to begin to make informed decisions about their needs as teachers and the instructional needs of their future students. Teams of students begin to establish rapport similar to actual teacher teams as they share information about their likes and dislikes and perceived needs as instructors.

Each student interdisciplinary team is charged with the task of creating a written team plan suitable for mailing home to parents. The team plan is given a group grade. Each student writes an essay evaluating his or her own team plan, reflecting on the experience of working collaboratively to create the group document. Students discuss compromises made and perceived strengths and weaknesses of the plan. The team plan and reflective essays are turned in at the same time. That day is set aside for class discussion. Teaming issues and specific management points are examined.

COMMENTARY

Students become very involved in the project. They quickly realize that getting four people with often conflicting philosophies to agree is going to be more of a challenge than anticipated. A few teams seem to magically coalesce. At this point, I step in and have them try to determine reasons for their compatibility, for such is the "stuff" of which successful teams are often made. Other groups of students are not so lucky. Most have at least one student who finds compromise difficult. Sometimes the other members give in, and sometimes they convince their "holdout" to move toward their viewpoint.

The reflective essay requires students to analyze their involvement and roles in the creation of the team plan. The discussion generated as a result of this intensive self-evaluation is an excellent way to bring a middle level classroom management course to closure.

REFERENCES

Canter, L., & Canter, M. (1995). *Behavior management in the middle school classroom: A teacher's guide to meeting the special challenges of early adolescents.* Santa Monica, CA: Lee Canter & Associates.

Charles, C. M. (1999). *Building classroom discipline, 6th edition.* New York: Addison Wesley Longman, Inc.

Glasser: Choices and Responsibility

TONI SILLS-BRIEGEL
Southwest Missouri State University, Springfield

STRATEGY/ACTIVITY/ASSIGNMENT

One of the most powerful models of classroom management and discipline that I present in my middle level methods class is one designed by William Glasser. Glasser (Charles, 1999) developed a short series of steps that teachers can use to guide students in making wise choices about their behavior. Glasser found that if a student could not be reinvolved in the lesson in 20 seconds or less, that student should be removed from class (to another teacher's room, the principal's office, or other supervised area) and counseled individually. As soon as possible, but only when both student and teacher are able to converse in a calm manner, the teacher asks the following questions:

1. *What did you do?*

   The student must state the action he or she committed that caused the private conference to be held with the teacher. The teacher must have witnessed the action.

2. *Did it help you learn? Did it help me teach? Did it help your classmates learn?*

   The student admits that this behavior was not helpful. This is a powerful step. The process does not work if this step is omitted. If the student is reluctant to admit that his or her action was inappropriate, the teacher should continue to ask variations of this question gently until the young person agrees that the actions were counterproductive.

3. *What needs to happen to help you stop doing this? Make a plan.*

   The student is required to create his or her own plan to modify behavior before readmittance to class. In the majority of cases, the plan can be designed immediately, and the student can be allowed to rejoin the lesson. In rare cases, the student may require more time to think. The teacher may offer assistance, but the student must make his or her own choices. The plan created by the student must have the approval of the teacher. Plans vary greatly from student to student. No set format exists for a plan. Each child considers his or her own behavior and creates a unique plan for improvement. The only restriction is the willingness of the teacher to support the plan. For example, a teacher should not approve a plan in which the child requests corporal punishment. Both teacher and pupil must agree to the plan. After the conference, the student returns to class to implement the plan with the support of the teacher (Charles, 1992).

The problem with teaching this system to preservice teachers is they are skeptical of its effectiveness. It's just too simple, they argue. However, students in the class who are also parents often try it with their own children and return the next day shaking their heads in disbelief over its effectiveness.

I have found that modeling the Glasser procedure convinces other students. After introducing the system to the class, I ask students to think of a scenario involving a discipline problem. A volunteer is invited to play the part of the student while I model the actions of the teacher. Preservice teachers normally think of easy situations, and it is simple to work with them. The challenge comes during summer school classes when experienced teachers often enroll in management classes. Their examples, based on real children and real situations, create a realistic and challenging platform for modeling the procedure.

After this initial role-playing demonstration, I pass out slips of paper describing common situations teachers may face in the classroom. Students work in pairs to role-play Glasser's method. Each preservice teacher participates in two role-playing situations, one as the "student" and one as the "teacher." I walk around observing ongoing scenarios, nudging some "teachers" into better word choices as they paraphrase the Glasser questions, encouraging "students" to try to model real middle level student behaviors as closely as possible, and answering questions as they arise in the course of the activity. The entire lesson can be completed in a two-hour block class.

COMMENTARY

Students quickly find out that the procedure is more complicated than it appears. "Teachers" are often stopped cold by unexpected "student" responses. They need support in learning to paraphrase the basic questions. "Students" can't believe that they are actually creating their own plans to improve their behavior. Classes enjoy the activity, and the practice helps lock the procedure into their personal repertoire of management skills.

Students are reminded that the procedure requires the teacher to be an empathetic and supportive listener who refuses to make decisions for the child. This is difficult to do if one or both parties are upset. It is also difficult for some adults to believe that an early adolescent is capable of creating his or her own behavior management plan. The use of modeling moves preservice and experienced teachers toward acceptance of teacher/student interactions based on respect and trust.

The Glasser technique is a particularly valuable strategy to use with early adolescents. Middle level students are just learning to think for themselves and make responsible choices. Correctly administered, Glasser's questions often lead to treating the source of a discipline problem rather than controlling the symptoms of the problem. Preservice teachers learn a technique that assists early adolescents in accepting responsibility for their own behavior.

Common Classroom Situations to Be Used in Role-Playing Scenarios

1. A student throws a paper wad at the teacher while the teacher is writing on the chalkboard. The teacher catches the student in the act when quickly turning to face the class.
2. A student fails to turn in homework over the course of several days.
3. Two boys keep yelling across the room at each other. Deal with each one separately.
4. The student has been caught writing sexually explicit comments on his or her desk.
5. A student refuses to work in a group with other students.
6. A student refuses to do an assignment that no one else in the class seems to mind working on.
7. Two students have been warned to stop passing notes to each other, but the behavior persists.
8. One student heckles other students as they try to participate in class activities. He or she makes fun of wrong answers, calling other students stupid, and so forth.
9. One student continually gets up out of his or her seat and walks (wanders) around the room as instruction is taking place.
10. One student comes to class without his or her materials on a regular basis.
11. One student "borrows" other students materials without permission, then often "forgets" to return them.
12. One student does consistently sloppy work even though you know that he or she can do much better.
13. One student sits very quietly in class every day and has never caused a behavior problem of any kind. He or she, however, does no work of any kind—even when materials are provided.
14. One student is tardy to class almost every day.
15. One student has developed a series of annoying personal habits: making thumping noises on his head and with his mouth, drumming on his books or desk, scooting his desk back and forth, making grinding little sounds, and bumping into people in front and in back of him.

REFERENCES

Charles, C. M. (1992*). Building classroom discipline: From models to practice*, *5th edition*. New York: Longman.
Charles, C. M. (1999). *Building classroom discipline: From models to practice*, *6th edition*. New York: Longman.

Classroom Management: Planning, Managing, and Reflecting

J. GORDON EISEMAN
Augusta State University, Augusta, GA

PURPOSE

For years the field of classroom management has been shortchanged, if not completely ignored, in middle-grades teacher preparation. In the content areas, we illustrate through our teaching the way to break the unproductive methods of the past. We model planning, teaching, assessing, and reflection in content pedagogy. We practice what we preach. We teach our students that children construct their own knowledge. We tell them to have their students engage in inquiry-based problem solving with real-world situations. Do we teach classroom management in this way?

Classroom management has been left out of the reform movements in teacher education. To a large extent, we are still giving students theories and practices separated from practical experiences in our classrooms. There is little or no chance to plan for, put into practice, and reflect on classroom management. We expect students to construct for themselves a personal model of classroom management with no active experiences to draw on. The purpose of the following strategy is to give middle level preservice teachers experiences in handling management situations. The activity is conducted in a preservice education course called "Classroom Management and Family Involvement."

STRATEGY/ACTIVITY/ASSIGNMENT

Preservice teachers need the same background information and activities for this activity that they need in any content-area pedagogy course. There is a need to learn about and discuss a variety of theories and models for classroom management; read and reflect on classroom management scenarios; and plan for preventive, supportive, and corrective classroom management. With the proper background students are ready to participate in microteaching.

Students come to class prepared to teach a lesson they have prepared in advance. When it is one's turn to teach, the student briefly explains the lesson he or she will teach, draws a management problem out of a hat (without looking at it), and leaves the room. When the student is out of hearing range, the class reads the problem and discusses who will participate in the situation. The microteacher returns and proceeds to teach his or her lesson. At some point during the lesson, the management problem occurs. The microteacher must handle the situation and resume teaching. After the instructor ends the lesson, the class discusses what happened, what management techniques were used, and what else could have been done to solve the situation. The microteacher must reflect on the situation outside of class and report his or her findings in written form.

COMMENTARY

This activity allows students the opportunity to engage in practices that we put forth as important parts of teaching. Planning for management, management in action, and reflection all come together in a constructivist activity that puts into practice ideas and methods normally only talked about.

Students' views of the assignment change. Initially, students dread this assignment. Even though the students fear managing student behavior, most have never considered planning for or handling management problems in a practice situation. The students are nervous about teaching their peers. However, they are not shy about "acting out" as part of the management problem. After the experience most students want to participate again.

The best commentary on the effectiveness of the strategy comes from former students. Rarely a week goes by that a former member of this class does not share an experience he or she has had in the "real world" related to this activity. Time after time students tell about finding themselves in a tense management situation and knowing how to handle the problem because of this assignment. They are bursting with excitement when they find they can handle the problems they feared and give the credit to participating in the management microteaching. The students express much gratitude at this attempt to practice what we preach.

Role-Playing Classroom Management Problems and Solutions

SAMUEL TOTTEN

University of Arkansas, Fayetteville

STRATEGY/ACTIVITY/ASSIGNMENT

Classroom management always seems to be a major concern of a vast majority of my middle level preservice students, and I believe it behooves teacher educators to address this issue in as solid and comprehensive a fashion as possible. Too often it is a subject or an issue that is treated in a perfunctory manner in teacher education programs and that is because it is such a tough issue to satisfactorily address.

Not totally satisfied with anything I had done in the way of teaching classroom management, I finally decided to combine role playing, reflection, and an examination of research germane to a given classroom management problem. When conducted correctly—that is, with experiences based on real-life examples and with an attempt to play a role as if it were actually taking place—role playing can reach students in ways that textbook examples, films, and discussions generally do not.

That said, I place on index cards a dozen different types of classroom management problems based on my actual experiences and/or observations as a teacher in various 7–12 programs in Australia, California, Israel, New Jersey, Washington, D.C., and as a principal in a K–8 school in California. Among the problems highlighted are: excessive talking, use of profanity, refusal to work, putting down other students, confrontational behavior toward the teacher, fighting in class, teacher putdowns of a student, a teacher yelling at a student or students, a teacher shoving a student, a teacher kicking students out of class over any and every infraction no matter how inconsequential, a teacher personally disregarding school rules such as "no chewing gum" in class, teacher inconsistency in addressing a specific infraction, and a student threatening to "get a teacher" or a teacher's car after school.

At the outset of class, an overhead transparency is displayed that succinctly delineates each classroom management problem. The students are asked to select the problem he or she wishes to role-play. Once they have decided on the problem they wish to focus on, they are asked to pick up a card explaining the problem in more detail. Not only is the problem delineated on the card, but so are suggestions as to how they (the students) might want to approach the role playing, e.g., the type of behavior they may wish to display.

The students are then given several minutes to consider how they wish to role play the part. When time is up, the instructor explains that during the role play, the rest of the class should do the following: (a) carefully observe the words, facial expressions, body language, and actions of the student involved in the classroom management problem, the "teacher," and the rest of the students; (b) note in writing how they felt about what was taking place, including how they felt toward each of the participants (student and teacher); and (c) jot down information in regard to what they perceived the classroom management problem to be; the factor or incident that precipitated the problem; details and impressions as to how the teacher handled the situation, and whether the method was effective; if and how the initial situation could have been avoided; how the problem possibly could have been handled differently and, perhaps, more effectively; whether the teacher did anything to exacerbate the problem, and if so, what; and, finally, what one could learn from this situation as one looks ahead to managing his or her classroom.

Once the role playing of a particular classroom management problem is concluded, a debriefing session follows based on the issues the students addressed in their notes. The length of the various role-playing scenarios varies from a couple of minutes to ten minutes. Contingent on the length of the class session, either one three-hour class session or two one-and-a-half hour class sessions are devoted to classroom management issues.

Either during or following the debriefing, the instructor should bring in solid classroom management research that addresses the type of situation that was role played. The research should be in a form that can be easily and quickly digested by the students. Ultimately, the research should illuminate what should be done to avoid or diffuse classroom management problems effectively. The full citation for any and all research addressed/discussed should be included on the handouts students receive, and the students should be encouraged to obtain the full article, essay, or report in order to bolster his or her efforts to solidify his or her future classroom management efforts. Ample discussion should be held on the research as well as the student-generated questions and concerns that arise from the discussion.

COMMENTARY

Over the years I have tried a number of different approaches to addressing the issue of classroom disruptions, classroom management, and discipline, and until I came up with the above plan, I always felt that I had
come up short. This approach is research-based, predicated on reflective,
practical, and hands-on/minds-on practice. It is also one that induces
powerful discussions, if not debate, and leaves the students thinking and
weighing critical issues long after they have left the class session.

Since it involves role playing, it is always engaging. Because the
role-playing exercises are based on actual incidents I experienced while
a teacher of various subjects and as a principal in settings across the
globe, there is an authenticity that shines through and engages the attention of the students.

The mix of role playing, the analysis of the roles of the teacher and
the students involved in the role playing, and the subsequent discussion
of the research moves this from a "fun and games" activity or a dry pedagogical exercise to a dynamic activity that brings to bear the best of the
cognitive and affective domains. Most students find the class sessions on
classroom management to be interesting, thought-provoking, and helpful. Many comment that they need more experiences like this in their
teacher preparation program.

Classroom Management:
The Gambling Analogy

CHRISTOPHER BELCHER
Central Missouri State University, Warrensburg

STRATEGY/ACTIVITY/ASSIGNMENT

It is a difficult task to have preservice educators truly understand the psychology behind middle level students who become disruptive or exhibit
off-task behavior in the classroom. The following exercise allows the
preservice educator to gain insights into a middle level student's mind in
regard to disruptive behavior. The instructions are as follows:

1. Take a deck of playing cards and shuffle them in front of the
   class.

2. Walk around the room and ask a student if he or she would be willing to (hypothetically) give one dollar for a chance to draw an ace of spades from the deck, knowing that if successful he or she would receive a payoff of $52. Therefore, the preservice educator has a 1 in 52 chance of winning. Have the preservice educator take a card.

   Note: Some preservice educators may say that they would not take the chance. This still plays well when processing this activity. Simply reply, "OK, this person is not willing to take the chance." This person represents the segment of students who rarely disrupt in the classroom.

3. Go to the next student and say, "You have just witnessed your colleague taking a chance to win $52, and he or she lost out. Are you willing to take a chance?"

4. Repeat instruction 3 several times.

5. At the end of the demonstration, show the class that there really is an ace of spades in the deck. (They always want to know.) If a student should happen to draw the ace of spades, it should be acknowledged that in any gamble a person may win. The winning serves as a reinforcer and increases the likelihood that he or she will gamble again.

6. Have the preservice educators form pairs. Then give the pairs 15 minutes to discuss the activity and develop a written statement on how this is related to classroom management. Randomly choose one from each pair to stand and read the statement to the class. The instructor does not provide input at this time. It is appropriate to ask a probing or guiding question to those sharing.

7. At the end of the 15 minutes, inform the class that ineffectively managed classrooms often have teachers who respond to disruptions in an inconsistent manner, or who ignore or are unaware of multiple disruptions. Therefore, if a student disrupts and does not receive any consequence he or she has won the poker game because the teacher has folded. The more the student wins, the more willing she or he is to gamble in the future. By folding (not providing a consequence) the teacher has reinforced the negative behavior. When teachers ignore a disruption, by their own inactivity they simply declare open season for disrupting and, as long as disruptions are free, they continue to occur and reinforce themselves (Jones, 1987).

8. Have pairs combine to form groups of four. The new group will now have 15 minutes to compare their statements and discuss

how the gambling analogy fits with classroom management. At the end of the 15 minutes, a preservice educator is randomly selected from each group to share his or her revised statement and to offer commentary regarding their group's discussion.

The instructor needs to take the information shared by the students and discuss the gambling analogy. Critical issues to be covered are:

1. If a middle level student disrupts or is off-task and does not receive a consequence (as simple as teacher attention), he or she has just been empowered to take the chance again. Therefore, not addressing the behavior results in the increased likelihood that it will recur. "Students are gamblers. They are good gamblers and they know the odds. They will gamble as long as they can get away with it. It is the rare student who messes up by going just a little too far and getting called on it. Most students most of the time are far too shrewd to get the teacher's attention when they don't want it" (Jones, 1987, p. 36).

2. If the middle level student disrupts or is off-task and does not respond to the teacher's first intervention (usually eye contact and body squared toward the student), this is the equivalent of the student "upping the ante" to see if the teacher is bluffing. Therefore, the teacher has to increase the intervention (usually moving closer to the student).

3. This model of "upping the ante" until someone folds is the critical element in understanding discipline. Each time the student is allowed to disrupt without a consequence, the student becomes more empowered to take the gamble again. Each time the teacher addresses the situation successfully and causes the student to get back on task, the student becomes more likely not to gamble in the future. *It is important to note that addressing the situation need not be a large-scale intervention. In many cases, the teacher may simply make deliberate and effective eye contact with the disruptor until the disruptor gets back on-task.* This entire process may take less than 20 seconds. However, if the student doesn't get back on-task then the teacher must "up the ante" by moving closer, prompting the student, or eventually using a verbal intervention.

4. The teacher wins the game when the student gets back on-task or aborts the disruptive behavior. A skilled teacher can get this to occur with little verbal intervention.

5. The following are examples of when the teacher folds and loses the game: (a) when the teacher uses sarcasm to get the student back on-task; (b) when the teacher threatens the student immediately with punishment; (c) when the teacher does not respond to an off-task behavior; and (d) when the teacher argues with the student about whether he or she was disruptive or off-task.

COMMENTARY

This activity allows for a natural introduction to how teachers use non-verbal behaviors to manage their classes. It also provides a framework for discussing the hierarchy of intervention as the student "ups the ante."

This activity creates a very effective and humorous anticipatory set for in-depth analysis of behavior management. After the activity, student discussion is very energetic and specific. The students are able to connect discipline scenarios and problem-solving with the gambling analogy for the remainder of the unit. In many cases, during essay testing or reflective journaling, the students use language and examples from this analogy to support a position or observation.

REFERENCE

Jones, F. (1987). *Positive classroom discipline.* New York: McGraw-Hill.

CHAPTER 11

Interdisciplinary Teaming

Modeling Reflection and Interdisciplinary Teaming in Middle-Grades Methods Courses

TONI BELLON
North Georgia College and State University, Dahlonega, GA

JONELLE POOL
Gettysburg College, Gettysburg, PA

Written in memory of Dr. William Impey and his contributions to our team.

STRATEGY/ACTIVITY/ASSIGNMENT

Providing experiences that assist preservice teachers in developing inter-disciplinary teaming skills is a challenge for teacher educators. Recognizing that teacher training institutions can restructure preservice programs to more closely reflect middle-grades reform efforts and to transform teacher training practices to include reflection on authentic field experiences, we redesigned the existing methods and materials undergraduate classes in the middle-grades program of a southeastern university.

In the old middle-grades program design, students spent their first two years taking a variety of core courses. When they entered the teacher education program, they enrolled in classes related to pedagogical knowledge in all four content areas (science, math, social studies, and language arts). Two quarters prior to student teaching, preservice teachers were required to enroll in four separate and unique content-specific courses, analogous to methods and materials courses offered at other colleges and universities. We reconfigured the methods block so that middle-grades preservice teachers take two content-speciality methods courses rather than four, each class corresponding with the students' chosen major and minor. Professors for these methods courses taught them in an interdisciplinary team format.

Redesign of Our Program

Traditionally, the goal of the methods courses was to tie educational theory to teaching practices in schools. We extended this connection by modeling reflection on practice and an interdisciplinary approach. Prior to offering the collaborative courses, we identified elements of the middle school philosophy that could be incorporated into the college setting. Interdisciplinary planning, flexible and block scheduling, and multiple grouping patterns with a variety of teaching methods became our seminar focus.

Using block and flexible scheduling, we arranged the four content specialities so that they overlapped. All students enrolled in the four methods and materials courses had their schedules blocked out for the first half of every day. This gave us the opportunity to hold large-group seminars for extended periods of time or to focus on small-group concerns as needed. The first five weeks of the quarter consisted of biweekly, large-group interdisciplinary seminars designed to address common pedagogical and classroom issues (e.g., learning styles, assessment, and technology). In addition, students attended two biweekly small-group meetings that paralleled major and minor concentration areas. We designed early sessions to encourage student reflection in connecting topics from the interdisciplinary seminars to specific content concerns through discussion and journaling. During the second half of the quarter, we mixed classroom instruction with a five-week, half-day field experience. Knowing that practicing the skill of reflection was important in relating theory to practice, we scheduled reflective seminars at the college for our students to share their field experience journals.

Teaming by Professors

Each of the four professors involved taught a content-area specialization from mathematics, social studies, science, or language arts and worked together to jointly teach various concepts.

Teaming by Students

Professors responsible for each content-area speciality guided the students in an overview of related curriculum issues (e.g., national standards, state curriculum, and curriculum integration) before we assigned our students to interdisciplinary teams in which each of the four content specialities was represented. A few teams reflected only three areas, and some included reading as a fifth content specialty.

Student teams used concept mapping to identify possible interdisciplinary connections. From these, units of study and individual lessons were created. Each team presented a portion of their unit during a videotaped microteaching presentation followed by both individual and class analysis and reflection.

Team Teaching During the Field Placement

Students were placed in the middle schools in intact teams for their field experience. Student teams were assigned to cooperating teachers who were also members of interdisciplinary teams at the school sites. The composition of each student team mirrored the content-area specialities of the field-based cooperating teachers.

COMMENTARY

By the end of the quarter, professors had modeled teaming while students both practiced and extended the concept in their classroom field experiences, supported by middle school teachers. By authentically conceptualizing our students' teaching roles, we scaffolded their learning of actual interdisciplinary team instruction. Supporting student efforts to become better skilled team members included such strategies as cueing students to upcoming transitions or response modes, task analysis, planning, and modeling. Gradually, as students began to demonstrate more skill, cooperating teachers and college supervisors were able to withdraw support mechanisms in order to allow the teams of students to teach an interdisciplinary unit at the school site.

Positive Aspects of Teaming

Creating a multidisciplinary team approach for these courses culminated in many positive results. As professors, we experienced greater empathy for middle school teams as we practiced compromise and improved our consensus-building skills. Working together also provided an opportunity for higher levels of communication among the content-area specialists as well as more collaborative programming.

Students were aware that the interdisciplinary design of the university classes was a pilot program, and they provided us with regular and honest feedback. The classroom climate became more supportive and energized. Teaming prompted us to begin a dialogue with middle level classroom teachers about the realities of preparing preservice teachers in implementing middle school philosophy and practice.

Challenges Associated with Team Teaching

1. *Faculty:* Traditional views of faculty load have not addressed the issues of the time needed to support collaborative planning and the difficulty of overcoming the historic isolation of the college professor. Physical space for our seminars was inadequate for facilitating team-oriented, student-centered active learning. Although shared leadership is necessary and desirable, we felt that a designated team leader may have helped lessen confusion experienced by both professors and students, particularly in the area of shared assignments and grading. Similar communication styles and the need for like-mindedness of team members proved important as well. We found that all team members must be involved in decision making and be willing to compromise and take risks.

2. *Students*: Some students described teaming as a great experience; a few found it difficult to collaborate across disciplines. In follow-up evaluations prior to student teaching, students reported feeling "prepared" for a full-time student teaching experience. A pattern emerged documenting a positive view of teaming, and a number of students reported that their experience with interdisciplinary team teaching helped them secure middle school employment.

Interdisciplinary Teaming: A Simulation of Interdisciplinary Team Organization

MELANIE W. GREENE
Appalachian State University, Boone, NC

STRATEGY/ACTIVITY/ASSIGNMENT

Interdisciplinary team organization is an essential element in an effective middle level program. Therefore, it is imperative that preservice teachers gain a comprehensive understanding of this key feature during their university teacher education program. Through a simulation activity, students can gain a deeper understanding of this middle school concept. To begin this activity, students complete various surveys to determine personality types, academic concentration areas, expertise in technology, and background experiences. Results from these surveys are used by the professor to establish diverse teams, with two to four members per team.

Once interdisciplinary teams are formed, the entire class is expected to create a mock middle school, to determine its geographic location and name, and to assume grade-level assignments. The class must then create a school philosophy that is aligned with middle level beliefs. Then, each team selects a name to give it a sense of identity, designs a motto, selects colors, determines a theme, creates a cheer to set it apart from other teams, and schedules special events such as intramural sports, field trips, and advisory activities. Other assignments include planning events to recognize the achievement of individual students and teams, organizing orientation sessions for parents and students, and researching opportunities for the group to engage in service learning projects. Following these initial tasks and activities, the teams must identify classroom management strategies and plans for developing an integrated thematic unit.

Team organization is integrated into these assignments. Each team is expected to select a team leader as well as a recorder to keep detailed minutes of the meetings. Other roles may include a timekeeper, an encourager, and a facilitator, depending on the size of the team. Teams are required to meet three times each week outside of class to complete these assignments. A summary of team meetings is forwarded to the professor on a routine basis.

COMMENTARY

Team development requires training and experience. Preservice teachers who have an opportunity to complete the aforementioned assignments gain a working knowledge of the organization and advantages of working as a member of an interdisciplinary team. Preservice teachers thus become empowered when they work together to plan a quality educational experience for young adolescents. Likewise, as preservice teachers begin their internships and student teaching, each one has a clearer understanding of the teaming process. They have experienced the challenges and rewards of teaming and understand its purpose in an effective middle school.

Teaming Simulation Activities

NORMA J. BAILEY
Central Michigan University, Mt. Pleasant

STRATEGY/ACTIVITY/ASSIGNMENT

Throughout the semester of our introductory middle level education course, in which students learn about the needs and characteristics of young adolescents and the various aspects of middle level education, students participate as faculty members of a hypothetical middle school, with each student serving as a member of an interdisciplinary grade-level team. In this semester-long simulation, the students engage in a number of teaming activities similar to those they will most likely participate in as a faculty member in a middle school. Although each activity by itself is interesting and valuable, it is the composite of all of them that makes the simulation work in terms of the students getting a more realistic understanding of the teaming process.

On the first day of class, students complete a student information sheet, which elicits the following: level of certification; content majors/minors; qualifications/strengths/experiences in content areas; grade level most interested in teaching; and perceived strengths and weaknesses as a team member. Then, on the basis of the information they provide, the students are placed by the instructor on a teaching team, and they collectively determine the name of their hypothetical middle school.

During the next several weeks, some class time is reserved for the teams to engage in planned get-acquainted activities, as well as professional team conversations about the various aspects of the course content. At this time, they specifically discuss the needs and characteristics of young adolescents. In addition, each team chooses its own team name, slogan, and logo, with the understanding that, ideally, their students should be involved in making these decisions. Subsequently, each team is referred to by its team name.

Their first major project as a team is their "midterm," which is a performance assessment of their knowledge of the needs and characteristics of young adolescents and their capacity to articulate this in lay language to the parents of their students.

Each team of preservice teachers is a sixth-grade team (for purposes of this exercise only) and each is to prepare an orientation for the parents of their students. This orientation includes sharing with the parents what the team wants them to know about key changes their children will be going through in the next few years, suggestions to assist parents in dealing with these changes, and information as to how they as teachers will be dealing with their students in their classrooms and on their team. As with "real" teaming, there is no required format nor "right" way to accomplish this task. In the following class period, each team briefly presents its orientation format to their "teaching colleagues" (the other class members), and the process is debriefed in both written (a written reflective paper by each student in response to the team performance assessment) and oral form (reflective discussion during the class period).

Flexible organizational structures and the teaming process are presented in the ensuing weeks with all their aspects and variations (rationales, schedules, team roles, uses of common team planning, flexing the schedule, regrouping students, benefits, and so forth). Other than occasional professional team conversations about course content topics, there are no other significant team projects until near the end of the semester. For their final major project, each team simulates a meeting whose purpose is to prepare for the new school year (e.g., it is assumed that this takes place sometime in the late spring of a school year or at the end of the summer). Based on the knowledge gained in this course, each team must develop its team goals and guidelines for the year; develop a daily (or weekly) schedule for the team, given the school's master schedule; provide a "thumbnail sketch" (in several paragraphs) of the exploration program the team would devise to supplement the unified arts program (physical education, art, shop, home economics, and music); describe (in several paragraphs) the year-long program they would devise to meet the affective educational needs of their students, including a typical schedule and the kinds of activities that might be planned; and provide a "thumbnail sketch" (in several paragraphs) of the team activities for the year to promote and maintain the involvement of the families and the community in the lives of their children. The teams are given two full class periods to work on their projects, and, on the third day, each team gives a 10-minute presentation of its project, highlighting any aspects that the team members wish. Again, the process is debriefed in both written and oral form.

As the final team activity for the semester, each team generates a set of questions that might realistically be asked of a candidate for a middle level teaching position. These are to be based on the aspects of middle level education learned during the semester. These questions are then synthesized by the instructor into one set of questions to be used for the "final exam," a performance assessment. The final assessment is a mock job interview in which each student is "interviewed" by one of the teams of teachers (as if they were team members interviewing candidates for a position on their team) and the instructor (as the principal of the school). (The interview teams are the established teams, and the interviewee is from another team.) This process requires that the students not only have knowledge about the various aspects of middle level education they have studied, but also be able to clearly articulate their beliefs about middle level education in a reasonably "authentic" situation. The final grade for this activity is decided by the "principal" (the instructor), guided by input provided by the "team of interviewing teachers" (the students).

COMMENTARY

One of the most important aspects of having students engage in simulated teaming activities is to give them the opportunity, both formally and informally and in both written and oral form, to reflect on and process the teaming experiences themselves. The instructor needs to be available while teams are working together to answer, or not answer ("Now how are we supposed to do this?"), questions. He or she needs to share occasionally with the students how "real" teams have responded in various situations. Students also need to write occasionally their reactions (10-minute "fast-writes") to the teaming situations—their likes, dislikes, frustrations, concerns, and/or surprises—and get some feedback from the instructor.

Simulated teaming activities are very effective in an introductory middle level education course, especially if they are interwoven throughout the course with content presentations, guest speakers from middle level teams to answer students' questions, and other field experiences. Students indicate that they really get a "feel" of what it is like to be a member of a middle school team, get a better sense of their strengths and weaknesses as a team member, learn about the kinds of things they are actually going to do as a team, and gain a sense of what it means to be a team colleague and an educational professional discussing real concerns.

Mock Team Plan

SANDEE SCHAMBER
Black Hills State University, Spearfish, SD

STRATEGY/ACTIVITY/ASSIGNMENT

In this activity students are divided into middle school teaching teams of three to five members. An attempt is made to create true core teams based on the four content areas, but this is not always possible. Each team is then given an envelope, each of which includes different information that has been gleaned from middle school teachers in the field. Within each envelope is a task that needs to be completed and an "interruption." Tasks include any activity that a middle school team might need to accomplish during a planning period, including, but not limited to: deciding on a plan of action regarding a discipline issue, scheduling a guest speaker, finalizing an upcoming interdisciplinary unit, meeting with a student, planning a field trip, writing midterm reports, and similar team activities. Interruptions constitute scenarios that commonly disturb the team planning period, such as a late or absent team member, an uncooperative team member, an unscheduled visit by a parent or fellow faculty member, a student emergency, and other unexpected events.

The role each student will play in the mock team plan scenario is outlined on an index card that the student selects from the packet. Some index cards contain only the task, whereas others contain both the task and the interruption. Consequently, at least at the onset, not all team members are aware of the impending disruption. After about a 20-minute simulation of a team planning period during which each team attempts to accomplish its assigned task despite the interruption, each team reports to the class regarding the interplay of their task and their interruption. In the debriefing discussions that conclude this activity, students share their frustrations in not being able to complete their assigned task and their attempts, some successful and some not so successful, to resolve their interruption in order to complete the task at hand.

COMMENTARY

This activity gives students a unique glimpse into team life. Both the benefits and the storm and stress of team planning become evident in this class activity. This activity also becomes a springboard for discussions on how teams should be formed, how team planning periods should be conducted, and the issue of professionalism among team members. When this activity is conducted by guest teachers who are members of a real middle school team, students are given an even better glimpse into middle school teaming as these teachers meet with each team and offer their own expertise relative to both accomplishing the tasks and managing the interruptions. When guest teachers choose to bring their own tasks and interruptions for use in this activity, students are brought even closer to the everyday realities of teaming.

The reactions of the students to this activity typically center around a new-found realization of the complexities of the team planning period and the challenges of teaming. The latter seems to be especially true in reference to those scenarios involving an absent or uncooperative team member. When middle school guest teachers conduct this activity, students express enjoyment in hearing directly from teachers who are in the field. As one class member stated, "The fact that a real team told real stories about their classes and students lent credibility to the exercise."

Using Scenarios to Teach Preservice Middle Level Teachers about Interdisciplinary Teaming and Instruction

ALYCE HUNTER
Wagner College, Staten Island, NY

STRATEGY/ACTIVITY/ASSIGNMENT

The use of realistic scenarios requires preservice middle level teachers to apply their knowledge to situations that they might encounter when they enter the "real" world. (See below for examples of possible scenarios.) Teachers of potential middle level educators can set up these scenarios in a variety of ways: (1) Class members can critique the scenario and then share and discuss their responses as an entire group. (2) Alternatively, the instructor can distribute a scenario to small groups of students. Students could record their reactions and then each group could share them with the entire class. (3) Another alternative is the inner circle/outer circle discussion method. Two circles of chairs should be formed, one inside the other. The inner circle is given the scenario, and the outer circle listens to the role playing. Then the outer circle critiques the inner circle's reactions, and both groups proceed to reach conclusions about middle level issues. The chief benefit of this method is that students are challenged to apply their knowledge and evaluate their own responses as well as their peers' responses. (4) The students themselves can come up with additional scenarios and problems as they student-teach or observe other middle level teachers. (5) A further extension of this activity would be to require each preservice learner to develop a middle level scenario and to use this scenario with his or her peers.

Sample scenarios that specifically relate to interdisciplinary teaming and instruction are:

1. One of your teammates has decided that she would like the entire team to be involved in creating and implementing an interdisciplinary unit on the rain forest. You don't think this is a good idea because it doesn't fit into your curriculum. When you go to your next team meeting to discuss this unit, what do you do?
2. Every other team member thinks it would be a great idea to show your eighth-grade team the movie *Gandhi* during all five class periods on the day before Thanksgiving vacation. Your team-

mates feel that this film relates to the curriculum, and it's a great way to entertain the students on the day before a vacation. You have your doubts about this movie's appeal to eighth graders, besides which you had planned to complete your unit on geometry by testing your classes on this day. What do you say to your teammates?

3. You didn't get to select the other people you work with on your interdisciplinary team. One of them you particularly dislike because you feel she is constantly whining and is a negative person who should have retired years ago. Yet, you must meet with her every day during team planning time, share students with her, and arrange parent conferences with her. You have kept your cool until January, but she is really getting on your nerves as she whines about her terrible students and everything else in the world. What do you do?

4. One of your teacher team members is a nice person and a competent teacher. Yet this team member irritates you because he is not a team player. He always shows up late for meetings. When you think about it, you realize he never participates in the decision-making process, and instead he simply goes along with everyone else. Should you keep your mouth shut and just do your job? Should you confront the individual? Should you go to the administration to voice your concerns? Should you enlist other team members to talk to this individual? What do you really want the teacher to do?

5. You have a team conference with parents about a certain student. The student is achieving in your class and is behaving well. However, in all the other team classes the child is a terror. When you conference with the parents, do you state your findings or do you concur with your teaching peers so that you present a united front?

COMMENTARY

Just as the scenarios can be presented to students in a variety of ways, students can respond to the use of scenarios and these particular scenarios in different ways. Some preservice teachers delight in the chance to consider and discuss problems and concerns they might experience as they work with other adults to provide interdisciplinary instruction for students. Others worry that they do not have sufficient teaching experience to comment on such issues as interdisciplinary teaming and instruction.

Learners like the support and modeling provided by a large-group discussion of and reaction to each scenario. For example, the first scenario on the rain forest prompts individual learners to think about their own curriculum. Debates often ensue as the whole class gets involved in discussing and defending their particular curricular area and the respective content. It is most interesting for an instructor to watch as a prospective middle level language arts teacher, perhaps for the first time, is challenged by his or her peers to defend what he or she teaches and to listen to what others consider important in their own subject areas. As each preservice teacher is challenged to respond to a scenario as a member of a group, he or she gains the confidence to consider in greater depth the complexities of interdisciplinary teaming and teaching. Ultimately, the instructor of these teachers can require personal responses from students or require students to create new scenarios. Generally, individuals will provide richer responses because of their prior group interactions.

An Analysis and Evaluation of Teaming

TONI SILLS-BRIEGEL
Southwest Missouri State University, Springfield

STRATEGY/ACTIVITY/ASSIGNMENT

After discussion of a selection of literature concerning interdisciplinary teaming, the preservice middle level methods class is broken into groups composed of four students, each from a different discipline, to generate a list of at least twenty requirements for effective teaming. Then, using whole-group discussion, the class combines their list into one comprehensive list. This list is further analyzed, and items are organized into three to five general categories. For example, students might come up with "organizational skills or needs," "affective needs of team members," "curriculum concerns," and "classroom management and discipline." Once categories have been identified, students return to their groups of four. The professor randomly assigns one of these newly created categories to each group. Students then work together to create a plan of action to accomplish the following:

1. Develop a research-based rationale for the items in the category and expand the category as necessary. Each student is required to turn in a one-page review of findings along with copies of two recent research-based articles.
2. Develop a rubric suitable for use by middle level team members or administrators for evaluating the effectiveness of interdisciplinary teams in the given category.
3. Identify possible barriers to implementation of the category by a middle level team. Include at least one possible solution to each identified barrier.
4. Prepare a brief 10- to 20-minute presentation in which the group presents their findings and rubric to the class. Copies of each group's rubric are to be distributed to the entire class.

This activity typically takes two class periods. Each class is a two-hour block class that meets once a week. During the first class period, students work together in groups to brainstorm their lists and organize categories for effective teaming strategies and requirements. Members decide on a plan of action to meet directives 1 through 4 before the second class meets. During the second class period, students move immediately into their teams to review their research, refine their rubric, and polish their presentation plan. The last hour of class is devoted to team presentations. Depending on the number of students in class and the amount of discussion generated, presentations may be completed in a third class meeting.

After all presentations have been completed, students briefly meet as a group one last time to refine their rubrics based on whole-class discussion. Each team turns in a clean copy of their rubric to the professor so that copies of rubrics may be provided to all students.

COMMENTARY

This activity involves students in a rigorous analysis of the various aspects of middle level teaming while requiring them to work within a team. They explore the research basis for teaming, then they create an evaluation instrument that will assist them in identifying the strengths and weaknesses of their future teaming experiences. Creation of the rubric itself generates an enormous amount of discussion. Each group creates its own rubric, which results in a variety of formats. This is positive because it affords students multiple examples for future use.

As students generate their own lists of requirements for effective teaming and as they create their own categories to explore, results may vary slightly from semester to semester. Usually, however, after perusing the research base, students settle on reasonably common elements, such as "The team follows a planned agenda at team meetings," "The team develops a common plan of action for dealing with behavioral concerns," and "The team develops interdisciplinary instructional units or lessons."

A Close-Up View of Teaming

SAMUEL TOTTEN
University of Arkansas, Fayetteville

STRATEGY/ACTIVITY/ASSIGNMENT

Even with numerous reading assignments and ample discussion about interdisciplinary teaming, many preservice teachers misunderstand how teaming works and/or the benefits that accrue from this method for teachers as well as students. Thus, an assignment in my "Middle Level Methods and Principles" course is for groups of students to form teams to interview teachers on interdisciplinary teams in local middle level programs. Ultimately, this provides them with a more in-depth and "close-up" understanding of teaming.

The directions for the assignment are as follows:

1. Form a group for the purpose of interviewing a group of teachers who are members of the same interdisciplinary team. You may work in pairs or in groups of threes or fours. It is mandatory that each member of the team you select to work with be interviewed. Thus, if there are two members in your student group and you select a team with four teachers, both members must interview two teachers. Likewise, if there are four members in your student group and a team has five teachers (one each in English, math, science, social studies, and a resource teacher, for example) then one member of the team will have to interview two teachers. Finally, if your group is composed of four students, then you must interview a team with no less than four members.

2. Each member of the student group is to interview (at least) one member of the interdisciplinary team.

3. Prior to contacting a site administrator to seek permission to interview a team, devise a set of questions that each member of the group will ask each member of the interdisciplinary team. At a minimum, the questions posited to the members of the team should address the following issues: how long the teacher has been involved in interdisciplinary teaming; whether the teacher initially looked forward to being on a team, and why; how the teacher currently feels about being on a team; what the teacher perceives as the greatest benefits about being on the team—for the individual teacher, teachers in general, the students; the drawbacks and/or difficulties about being on a team; how the team develops an esprit de corps among the students; whether the team has a common planning time and all that that entails; whether the team has a team leader, including how the leader is selected and what the leader does in that role; what the team does in the way of shared planning and implementation vis-a-vis classroom management, parent interviews, curricular and instructional programs, and other concerns; whether the teacher would go back to either a self-contained classroom or departmentalization if he or she had an opportunity to do so, and why. Please add other key questions that you and your team members are curious about. Your list of questions will be examined to assess your own input and industriousness.

4. Contact a site administrator in order to seek permission to conduct the interviews.

5. Individual members of the student group should contact the members(s) of the team he or she plans to interview in order to make an appointment for the interview.

6. Conduct the interview.

7. Type the interview.

8. Each interview must be accompanied by a commentary regarding the most important insights and information gleaned from the interview.

9. A concluding statement (two to four pages, double-spaced, typed) must be written by all the group members in which they discuss/delineate the following: (a) The similarities in responses among the different members of the team; (b) The differences in responses among the different members of the team; (c) The

general sense gained regarding the value (or lack thereof) that the teachers you collectively interviewed place on interdisciplinary teaming, and why; and (d) Any additional comments the group wishes to add about any aspect of what you learned about teaming and/or the nature of this assignment.

COMMENTARY

By hearing firsthand stories, this assignment assists students in gaining a solid understanding of what teaming is, how it works, teachers' insights and feelings about it, and why it's generally referred to as "the heart of middle level education."

Among the comments made by students about this assignment are: "Meeting and interviewing the individual teacher and then reading and analyzing the rest of my group's interviews provided me with valuable insights into the pros and cons of teaming"; "The assignment was fun in that we worked as a 'team' to investigate teaming"; "The teachers were great! They love teaming and instill a love in you for it."

Note: This assignment can be adapted to explore any aspect of middle level education, including, but not limited to, the following: advisor/advisee, exploratory programs, block and/or flexible scheduling, community service or service learning, and full-service middle level programs.

CHAPTER 12

Scheduling

Block-Scheduling Exercise

TONI SILLS-BRIEGEL
Southwest Missouri State University, Springfield

STRATEGY/ACTIVITY/ASSIGNMENT

Prior to this activity, students in an introductory middle level methods class have discussed block scheduling versus traditional scheduling and have analyzed a typical block schedule. In their book, *Middle School Teaching: A Guide to Methods and Resources*, Kellough and Kellough (1996) offer examples of typical block schedules and exercises useful in assisting students to analyze and develop an initial understanding of scheduling formats.

Once students are able to interpret schedules that have been designed by others, the next step is to have them develop a simple schedule on their own. Using two versions of the alternating-day model, students are divided into cooperative groups to analyze a given model, create a two-week schedule using the model, and prepare a brief presentation concerning their experience for the entire class.

Definitions

"ABAB" Alternating-Day Model: Classes meet every other day. Over a two-week (10-school-day) period of time, each block class will meet five times.

"ABcABc" Alternating-Day Model: "A" classes meet every Monday and Wednesday. "B" classes meet every Tuesday and Thursday. On Friday, "C" day, the schedule is shortened so all classes can meet for brief periods of time before the weekend. Over a two-week (10-school-day) period of time, each block class meets for four full 90-minute blocks and for two briefer periods of time.

Required Assumptions for the Activity

1. 100 students (25 students per core class) assigned to core team
2. Basic four-teacher core team (social studies, language arts, mathematics, and science)
3. Exploratories (1 per teacher)
4. Electives (at least 4, but may be more)
5. Advisory (1 per teacher)
6. Lunch, 30 minutes
7. Only core classes must meet for the full 90-minutes. Other classes may be of different lengths and may meet from one to five days a week.

Each school day consists of (minimum):

1. Four 90-minute blocks
2. A 30-minute lunch period
3. A 20-minute advisory

Each student must be enrolled in:

1. All four core classes
2. Two electives
3. Physical education/health
4. One exploratory
5. One advisory
6. Lunch

Directions

Each teacher must do the following:

1. Teach a core class four times
2. Teach one elective
3. Teach an exploratory

4. Have a team conference period (common planning time)
5. Have a personal conference period (need not be in common with other team members)
6. Work with one advisory class

To complete the exercise, each college group must do the following:

1. Assign one person to use overhead markers and a transparency to record the completed schedule.
2. Assign one person to list problems and insights as they are discovered.
3. Select electives. (Additional electives to be taught by teachers outside the core team may be created.)
4. Use a wheel design to decide on exploratory classes for their team.
5. Block out a time schedule for the school day.
   (a) When does the school day begin and end?
   (b) What time of day would the group like to schedule advisory and why?
   (c) Don't forget lunch and transition time between classes.
6. Complete a two-week schedule using the requirements listed above.
7. Using their completed transparency, each group shares their results with the rest of the class and leads a discussion of their ideas.

A few minutes before the end of class, students are asked to provide a written reflection of this experience.

Suggested steps for beginning the activity:

1. Decide on the time schedule for the school days.

Then schedule:

2. Advisory classes and lunch
3. Common team planning time
4. Core classes (must be common team time)
5. Exploratory wheel (must be common team time)
6. Electives (variable)
7. Physical education/health (variable)

COMMENTARY

Preservice teachers have a difficult time with this activity. They are so accustomed to traditional six- or seven-period days that it presents a real problem for them to break out of that mind set and creatively schedule their two-week block. The list of suggested steps for beginning the activity has proven helpful, giving students a concrete starting point.

Through this activity, preservice teachers develop an appreciation for the difficulties of creating the middle school schedule. Consensus varies each semester as to which version, ABAB or ABcABc, is the most effective or efficient block design. Most, however, lean toward the ABcABc form. The common argument for steering away from the simple ABAB format is the length of time between classes over the weekend. Generally, excellent discussions are generated in regard to when advisory class should be scheduled and how long it should be. Students debate over when school should begin in the morning and end in the afternoon and how many minutes students require to move from class to class. Some students want bells to be rung to signal the start and end of classes, and some do not. A common error is to schedule team and personal conferences on the same day, leaving no break for the second day.

Students often comment on the complexity of this assignment. Many compare it to solving puzzles and seem to enjoy the challenge. Written reflections are almost unanimous in evaluating the activity as a worthwhile experience.

REFERENCE

Kellough, R. D., & Kellough, N. G. (1996). *Middle school teaching: A guide to methods and resources, 2nd edition.* Englewood Cliffs, NJ: Prentice-Hall, pp. 157–164.

SUGGESTED RESOURCES

Canady, R. L., & Rettig, M. D. (1996*). Teaching in the block: Strategies for engaging active learners.* Larchmont, NY: Eye on Education, Inc.

Fogarty, R., Ed. (1996*). Block scheduling: A collection of articles.* Palatine, IL: IRI/Skylight Training and Publishing, Inc.

Schurr, S. L., Thomason, J., & Thompson, M. (1996). *Teaching at the middle level: A professional's handbook.* Lexington, MA: D. C. Heath.

CHAPTER 13

Advisor/Advisee

Introducing a Need for Advisory Classes

TONI SILLS-BRIEGEL
Southwest Missouri State University, Springfield

STRATEGY/ACTIVITY/ASSIGNMENT

Well into the semester of an introductory middle level course, after students have acquired a basic understanding of the characteristics and unique needs of early adolescents and have explored curriculum and most of the components of middle level education, I begin introducing my students to advisories using the following strategy.

Without telling students the specific topic for the day, I ask them to take two or three minutes and write down a list of things early adolescents need in order to be successful in school. Then students are placed in pairs or in groups of three to share and expand their lists. A third step involves having one student from each group go to the chalkboard and write his or her group's list. When students are seated, I invite them to consolidate responses from all lists into one single list. Elements of this list are then identified as cognitive or affective. Invariably, most—sometimes all—items are affective. Students list such items as: parent-child relationships, good study skills, friends, friendly teachers, personal goals, good attitudes, and any number of support systems offered by the community.

The point can easily be made from this activity that there is a great need for advisory classes in the middle school. The things that most people think contribute to successful educational experiences are seldom taught in conventional core classes. If not there, then where? Carefully designed advisory classes are the answer middle level educators have created to solve this inconsistency. At this point, preservice teachers are ready to begin serious consideration of the advisory component in middle level education.

COMMENTARY

"I had no idea" is a common response. Classroom teachers returning to acquire middle level certification and who may have had negative experiences with poorly administered advisory programs in the past are particularly impressed with this strategy. "I guess I'm going to have to try it again. I knew it was important, but I really didn't understand just how important it was," one student told me after class one semester. At the end of this activity students throughout every class can be seen nodding and quickly writing notes. It is a small step to move to generating ideas for advisory lessons using the chalkboard list as a base. For example, after categorizing items on the chalkboard into broad "themes," students may be teamed to create sample lessons to share with the class.

Becoming Comfortable with Advisory

ALISON BROOKE BUNTE
University of Wisconsin–Platteville

STRATEGY/ACTIVITY/ASSIGNMENT

A common problem in the development of an advisory program in the middle school is the incomplete development of topics and activities. On a different note, Trubowitz (1994) reports that teachers have major concerns in regard to the proper way to implement advisor/advisee programs. As a result of the above, it is necessary to help preservice middle level teachers become comfortable with the concept of advisory so that they will not resist the idea in their future careers as middle level educators.

The second middle level block at UW-Platteville is made up of two different courses that are team taught in a single block. The courses are

"Teaching the Transescent" and "Advising, Interacting, and Communicating." There is a heavy emphasis in the second block on the first recommendation in *Turning Points* (Carnegie Council on Adolescent Development,1989), creating small communities for learning. This is where students learn about advisory program rationale and design. Topics such as group dynamics, how to lead a group discussion, and others are included. One of the most useful activities, however, is the modeling of effective advisory activities by the professors and by the students themselves.

For the first few weeks of the semester, the instructors plan and conduct an advisory activity at the end of each class period. Students not only participate in the activity each week, but have a chance to discuss and reflect upon the activity. A written outline of the activity is provided for the students to place in their portfolio. During the fourth week of the semester, the students begin planning and implementing the advisory activities each week. Activities may be selected from commercially prepared materials or they may be original. Students must follow the criteria outlined by the professors (see appendix), which include an objective for the activity, a description of the activity, and a rationale for how the activity meets the unique physical, intellectual, emotional, social, or moral developmental needs of the young adolescent. The activities last about fifteen to twenty minutes and are followed by a discussion led by the students responsible for the advisory. Again, a copy of the advisory activity is provided for each person in the class. The format for the handout follows. At the end of the semester students have participated in fifteen or more advisory activities and have a notebook that describes each activity.

COMMENTARY

The advisory activity is one of the most enjoyable parts of the class. Students and instructors get to know one another well. There is much laughter and humor, and the class always ends on a positive note. The strength of the activity is in the actual application of advisory activities. Their notebooks contain a number of activities that can be conducted in their own classes. Students leave the class with a belief in the practice of advisory, a belief in the application of advisory activities, and a comfort level that is so important in their careers as middle level teachers.

REFERENCES

Carnegie Council on Adolescent Development. (1989). *Turning points: Preparing American youth for the 21st Century.* New York: Author.

Cole, C. G. (1992) *Nurturing a teacher advisory program.* Columbus, OH: National Middle School Association.

Trubowitz, S. (1994). The quest for the good advisor-advisee program. *Middle Ground.* Winter.

APPENDIX:
Middle Level Block Two: Criteria for Advisory Activity

Description: Students will be assigned to groups of three or four. Each group will be responsible for the development and delivery of one *advisory activity* involving the whole class. This assignment consists of two parts, a handout and a presentation. *(Value: 10 points)*

The Handout: Each group will be responsible for providing each member of the class and the instructors with a copy of the advisory activity. The handout should include the following sections: *(Value: 5 points)*

1. Title of the activity
2. A list of the group members
3. Objective: What is the intended outcome of the learning activity?
4. Skill area: Does this advisory involve the physical, intellectual, emotional, social, or moral development of the young adolescent?
5. Time requirement
6. Group size that is best for the activity
7. Materials needed
8. Procedure: The advisory activity should be broken down into steps that could be easily followed by someone unfamiliar with the activity.
9. How will the learning outcome be evaluated? Caution, the evaluation must reflect the objective.
10. The source of the activity. Use APA to cite your source.

The Presentation: All presentations will be judged on the following *(Value: 5 points)*

1. Displays essential middle level teacher qualities: enthusiasm, conviction, organization, and knowledge of the topic.

2. Models good team skills with other team members—equitable distribution of responsibilities, shared teaching, and so forth.
3. Involves the entire class in *active learning.*
4. Responds appropriately and thoroughly to student questions.
5. Approximate length is 15 to 20 minutes.
6. Explains *rationale* as well as the *relationship* of the activity to middle level curriculum, instruction, and philosophy.
7. All materials, visuals, and manipulatives are well prepared.

Defining and Designing Middle Level Advisory Programs

LAURA VAN ZANDT ALLEN
Trinity University, San Antonio, TX

STRATEGY/ACTIVITY/ASSIGNMENT

I find that preservice teachers have difficulty with the concept of advisory programs for one of two reasons. First, although many have first-hand knowledge of advisory programs as a middle level student, a lot of the programs were in the initial stages of development and implementation and were often chaotic and disorganized, causing students to view them negatively. Second, many students view schooling as an academic endeavor, with affective objectives tacked on as a bonus rather than a valued aspect of the middle level curriculum. While preservice teachers readily acknowledge the need to focus on social, emotional, and psychological development, they have difficulty allotting time to such activities during the traditional school day.

To counter these perspectives, I use a four-part inductive lesson with graduate interns in a five-year teacher education program. The course, "The Middle School," is nested within a six-hour secondary block entitled "Pedagogics."

Step 1: Introduction

To begin, I ask students how many of them have ever attended or worked at a summer camp or retreat. Invariably, most or all of the class has and this helps initiate a discussion regarding such experiences in our lives (i.e., importance, organization, activities, effects, etc.). The primary goal here is for students to begin to associate affective curricula with positive experiences as well as to become aware that aspects of society are devoted to this end.

In pairs, students each share one or two activities/experiences in camp settings that were personally meaningful to them. The pair then chooses one and writes a short description of the activity/experience, determines the objectives targeted, and assesses how well these were carried out. Pairs then share these with the whole class.

Afterwards, students read an article (R. J. Sternberg's "IQ Counts, But What Really Counts Is Successful Intelligence") that reinforces research confirming that intelligence alone is insufficient for achieving "success" in society today. This is discussed formally in the following class, with students providing examples from their own lives that reflect the need for both sets of skills.

Step 2: Defining the Advisory Program

Next, the term *advisory* is introduced generally rather than specifically as a vehicle middle level educators use to meet a number of students' affective needs. Stress is also placed on the multiple modes of organization and implementation found from school to school (i.e., multigrade groups of 10 to 12 students meeting daily versus same-age groups of 25 organized into service organizations that meet twice a week; teachers only serving as advisors versus whole-school adult involvement; a study-skills-based curriculum versus minicourse offerings such as etiquette and dance taught on a rotating basis) .

In the same pairs, students conduct an open-ended telephone survey of local middle schools to help answer the question, "What is advisory?" Each pair is given the name and number of one school and one contact teacher. (*Note:* These are prearranged by the instructor and do not include the professional development school [PDS]. It is helpful to give students teachers' home numbers if teachers give their consent.) As a result, 10 to 15 area middle schools are represented, given a class size of 20 to 30 students.

Survey Questions

1. Do you have an advisory program? If so, how is the program referred to (i.e., advisor/advisee, homeroom, etc.)?

2. Do you have a schoolwide statement of goals and objectives for the overall program? If yes, what are they? If no, would you describe your understanding of the goals and objectives for advisory on your campus?
3. How long has the program been in place?
4. When does it occur within the daily schedule (length/days/time)?
5. Is it organized by grade level or by multigrade levels?
6. What is the average size of each advisory group?
7. Who leads these groups?
8. What type of preparation have teachers had for teaching advisory?
9. How were parents informed about the program? What has been their reaction?
10. Describe the advisory curriculum.
11. Is the curriculum standardized across grade levels or is it developed individually by teachers and/or teams?
12. What types of activities/units have been most successful? Why?
13. What types of activities/units have been least successful? Why?
14. What types of units would you like to see developed for advisory programs?
15. What impact has your advisory program had on students at your school?
16. On a scale from 1 (low) to 10 (high), how successful has the advisory program been at your school? (*Note:* Success may be defined using student affective outcomes, such as an increase in student responsibility observed through completed homework assignments or improved attendance, as well as traditional academic outcomes, such as improved grades or higher standardized test scores.)

The next class is a debriefing session. A chart is drawn on the board with categories that parallel survey questions (i.e., name, purpose, organization, curriculum, etc.), which is filled in as each pair reports findings. Thus, as a class, students create their own definition of advisory similar to the who, what, where, why, and how of journalism. (*Note:* Including a large map of the city and using Post-it notes to mark school and district locations helps students become familiar with the locations of schools implementing middle level practices in the area.) The next reading (George and Bushnell's "The Teacher as Advisor") provides students with a foundational background of the advisory concept to supplement what was discussed in class. This also provides examples of teachers' favorite topics and lessons taught in advisory programs in preparation for designing the unit.

Step 3: Designing a Unit

After I share sample advisory units with the class and cover problem areas such as writing and assessing affective as opposed to cognitive objectives, each pair designs and writes a one-week advisory unit (five-days, 45-minute periods). Students are encouraged to consider developing units based on some of the ideas teachers noted in the "would like to have" category from the survey results. Units must include a rationale, objectives, activities, and assessment(s) and must be written in lesson-plan format.

Step 4: Editing and Sharing

Pairs bring two copies of their unit to class, one for the instructor and one for the editing group, which consists of four class members (each editing group critiques two units). One class period is devoted to the peer-editing of units. Each pair makes final revisions on the basis of group and instructor suggestions. The units are then bound into a book and distributed to all class members and teachers who participated in the survey. (*Note:* Some students have actually helped teach their unit in the schools surveyed.)

COMMENTARY

Students enjoy this assignment because it allows them to be active learners, it allows them to "feel like a real teacher" by designing their own curriculum, and it provides them with an actual product. It also instills positive views of affective instruction by allowing a glimpse into schools where such practices are working well. One student rhetorically asked, "Can we get jobs where we only teach advisory?" A final by-product is the collaboration between the university and the local schools that are not PDS sites. Too often these schools feel left out as a result of the PDS model, and this give-and-take activity acknowledges the importance of all area schools in the preparation of outstanding middle level teachers.

REFERENCES

George, P., Lawrence, G., & Bushnell, D. (1998). *Handbook for middle school teaching*. New York: Longman.

Sternberg, R. J. (1996). IQ counts, but what really counts is successful intelligence. *NASSP Bulletin, 80*(583), 18-23.

Promoting Advisor/Advisee in the Middle School

SANDEE SCHAMBER
Black Hills State University, Spearfish, SD

STRATEGY/ACTIVITY/ASSIGNMENT

This assignment is part of an undergraduate course that focuses on responding to the characteristics and needs of the young adolescent learner using developmentally appropriate schoolwide and classroom practices. One of the salient characteristics of developmentally responsive middle level programs is the inclusion of an advisor/advisee program. This assignment provides students with the opportunity to become advocates for the implementation of such a program.

For this assignment, the preservice students create a facsimile of a letter to a school board in which they request permission to implement an advisor/advisee program in their middle school. The letter begins with a rationale statement that relates the developmental needs and characteristics of young adolescents to the goals and objectives of the advisor/advisee program. The rationale statement demonstrates how the proposed program is necessary in facilitating the growth and development of the *total* young adolescent. This section typically notes that the emotional and social developmental concerns of young adolescents need to be addressed directly, in a formal and organized program, and not merely incidentally in the course of academic core and encore classes. The letter addresses the issues of logistics: When will the program begin? Who will coordinate the program? How will this program be scheduled into the school day? Who will serve as advisors? How will advisors be prepared for their new role? How will students be assigned to advisors? What activities will be included?

Upon its completion, the letter is evaluated by the instructor using a grading rubric (see below), which has been distributed to students along with the course syllabus. This syllabus serves as an assist to students in completing the assignment and as an assist to the instructor in grading the assignment.

COMMENTARY

Advisor/advisee programs are often difficult to implement because their true nature and purpose are often misunderstood by both administrators and teachers alike. This assignment provides students with the opportunity to not only explain such programs, but also to formulate a rationale that uses theory to validate the necessity of such programs in meeting the social and emotional needs of young adolescents. This activity guides students in explaining these programs, which should have the same credibility as those that meet the intellectual needs of young adolescents.

The advantages of this assignment are twofold. First, this assignment provides students with the opportunity to link theory and practice; second, this activity exposes students to the protocol that is often necessary in implementing any new program in a school district. Initially, students are intimidated by this assignment because the advisor/advisee program is so different from any other program they have studied. However, once they begin the assignment and spend some time with it, they invariably become quite excited and proclaim: "This wasn't as hard as I thought it would be. As a matter of fact, it was fun! I can't wait to do advisor/advisee!" Students also react with surprise to the necessity of having to write such a proposal to a school board. Repeatedly, over the semesters, students have commented that they had no idea that new programs had to be approved by the school board. Frequently heard is the comment, "I thought I could do whatever I wanted to do in my classroom!"

Rubric for Advisor/Advisee Letter

(45 points)

Explanation of the program

- The program is described in detail and includes a complete listing of monthly themes and tentative activities by grade level. (15)
- The program is described in detail and includes a complete listing of monthly themes and tentative activities. (10)

- The program is described in detail and includes a partial listing of monthly themes and tentative activities. (5)
- The program is described in very general terms. (2)

Rationale for the implementation of the program

- The rationale is stated in specific terms and is based on the unique developmental needs of young adolescents. (15)
- The rationale is stated in specific terms and mentions the unique developmental needs of young adolescents. (7)
- The rationale is stated in very general terms. (2)

Format: The letter

- Is completely free of grammatical errors and informal language. (5)

flows in a clear and logical manner . . .

- Consistently. (5)
- Inconsistently. (1)

Follows appropriate business letter format . . .

- Consistently. (5)
- Inconsistently. (1)

Connecting to Students Through Books

ADELE B. SANDERS
University of Northern Colorado, Greeley

STRATEGY/ACTIVITY/ASSIGNMENT

Advisor/advisee programs are struggling in many schools. Even though conventional wisdom promotes exploring young adolescents' interests, ideas, and questions about their world, "few teachers have been prepared to be advisors, and many . . . are uneasy about having to invent ways to make the program work" (Stevenson, 1997, p. 315). Not trying, however, should not be an option. "Kids in the middle grades need special help in their struggle to grow. If we fail to provide help . . . , they may grow up never fully realizing all [that they can be and do in the world]" (Doda quoted in George, Lawrence, and Bushnell, 1998, p. 300).

To help preservice and graduate students in a teacher education program experience how natural it can be to begin discussions on topics close to the heart and sensitive to the mind, I give them a two-part assignment: (1) read a novel in which the young adolescent characters are faced with a troubling "life issue" and (2) develop a lesson, lessons, or brief unit based on that issue. One premise of this assignment is that middle-grades students will be more likely to participate in these kinds of important discussions when a book's characters are at the center of the discussion—not themselves, their friends, or relatives. In addition, the college students are more at ease because their lesson(s) focus on ficti-tious characters and events.

This assignment/activity is called the "Life-Issues Lesson" because the college students are asked to choose and read an early-adolescent or "young adult" novel in which the characters grapple with some of life's real, yet difficult, issues (e.g., parental divorce, rejection, abuse, gang membership, friendship, etc.). Several book titles and reference re-sources are provided to students to help them make their selections, which are based on their interest in and ability to discuss *that* issue. This part of the assignment is intended to help the future teachers learn how "fictitious" life-issue situations arise and how they are handled by ficti-tious characters, as a way to explore part two of the assignment, the les-son(s), as well as to give the students something to refer back to (if they so choose).

Once the life-issues novel is read, the student develops a lesson or brief unit to be implemented during the time designated as advisor/advisee time (which is also known by many other names) in their school. Of course, not all schools have such a time during the day, but most schools do have homerooms, base rooms, or some other start-of-day pe-riod in which students are together for something other than a core con-tent focus. An important decision point is now at hand: Will the book's story be read over the course of several days, all together in the middle-grades classroom, and discussed as they go? Will the teacher read se-lected pages of "critical" importance (one that highlights the issue)? Or will he or she relate a pivotal scene or hard-hitting development to open a life-issues discussion that invites students' sharing of opinions, experi-ences, or knowledge? As with any teaching goal, the purpose and time needed to achieve it will be determined by the duration (one lesson or a series of lessons).

As mentioned earlier, the opportunity to use the book, its characters, and its events as the vehicle through which to explore important issues is typically safer for teachers and students than just saying, "Let's talk about _____." Ideas and feelings can rush to the surface as the lesson unfolds and as students feel comfortable giving advice or commenting on the book's characters' motives and actions. The teacher can play the devil's advocate and push students to think critically, answering "why" and "how" questions that might not work as well or as safely had the discussion stemmed explicitly from the students' own experiences.

Some college students are not in the field or in a field-based program during this course, so the lesson or unit is taught to college peers in a manner representative of how the lesson would be taught in the middle-grades classroom. Props (one college student made a map with the important places and events labeled on cards push-pinned to the map's surface), questions, and in-class activities that would be appropriate to the lesson's implementation are also used with peers.

COMMENTARY

Regardless of the student's content/teaching area, being required to read a young-adolescent novel is often a first-time adult experience. Reading the novel with a focus on the problem in the story and the ways in which the characters deal with each other and the problem stimulates the student's own thinking and reactions. Designing a lesson or unit that targets middle-graders' interactions and reactions requires the college student to consider the focus and sequence of the lesson/unit, their ultimate goal or objectives in pursuing the issue in the way selected, and the questioning strategies needed for focusing on a potentially sensitive topic for their middle graders.

I have had college students conduct their lesson(s) with classmates and with middle level students in the actual classroom. In debriefing the experiences of reading, planning, and designing the lessons(s), I learned that many of the college students had not read early-adolescent novels since they were middle graders themselves. For some students, their eyes were newly opened to the ways in which authors approached certain issues and how they allowed characters to deal with them. All the college students who participated in this activity stated that they felt they would be much more comfortable using this approach than they would addressing the same topics more directly with their students.

Some examples of the books my students have used in the past are *Can You Sue Your Parents for Malpractice?* by Paula Danziger (focus =

self-actualization, autonomy); *Hello, My Name is Scrambled Eggs* by Jamie Gilson (focus = friendship); and *The Rumour of Otters* by Deborah Savage (focus = safety, choices, responsibility). Another student did a unit on gangs and gang membership (possibly from *The Outsiders* by S. E. Hinton). She cut out a variety of newspaper articles with headlines about gang shootings, youth curfews, and new youth laws. The discussion that followed revealed both the fear and knowledge her classroom students had.

REFERENCES

George, P., Lawrence, P., & Bushnell, D. (1998). *Handbook for middle school teaching, 2nd ed.* New York: Addison Wesley Longman, Inc.

Stevenson, C. (1997). *Teaching ten to fourteen year olds, 2nd ed.* New York: Addison Wesley Longman, Inc.

Bringing Advisor/Advisee to the University Classroom

SAMUEL TOTTEN
University of Arkansas, Fayetteville

STRATEGY/ACTIVITY/ASSIGNMENT

Since most students in both my undergraduate and graduate middle level principles and methods courses have little or no experience with advisor/advisee (a/a) programs, I find it useful to provide them with a full session of hands-on a/a experiences. In order to do so, I invite one or two middle level teachers who are noted for being strong advocates of a/a to my class in order to (a) provide a general overview of the purpose of advisor/advisee, (b) speak about the topics they address in their advisory programs, and (c) take the university students through three or four different and powerful a/a activities that they use with their middle level students.

Prior to the arrival of the guest speakers, my students read at least one essay or chapter on advisory programs. Each student is also required to develop a minimum of three questions about advisory that he or she wishes to have answered by our guests. The students are required to type the questions and bring a copy for each of the presenters, the professor, and one for themselves. On the day of the presentation, the guest(s) are provided with the questions and, generally, they answer these at the end of the session.

Over the past five years the activities that the middle level teachers have engaged my students in have been extremely eclectic. Three of the most engaging and thought-provoking activities will be succinctly described herein. (*Note:* The author has created the names for each of these activities, realizing that the middle level teachers who presented the activities may refer to them by a different name. It is also important to note that the following activities were probably not originally created by the guest speakers. It is more likely that they were introduced to them in in-service sessions or presentations they attended at annual state or national middle level education conferences.)

- **Who Am I?** This is a simple activity in which each student is required to write down three statements about himself or herself, two that are true and one that is false. Once everyone has written the statements, each student is asked to read his or her statements. Following the reading of the statements, the rest of the class members vote on which statements are true and which are false. This process is repeated until everyone has had an opportunity to share his or her statements. This is a highly enjoyable activity that results in many surprises and much laughter.

  The activity can be used for several different purposes, such as: (1) an introductory activity to help the students get to know one another at the outset of the academic year; (2) an activity that focuses on the diverse backgrounds and experiences of each class member; or (3) an introduction to a session on honesty, and what that means to the individual, to his or her friends, and/or to a group.

- **The Pat on the Back.** Each student is asked to write his or her name at the top of a piece of blank paper. All students are then asked to have the person sitting next to them attach the paper with tape to the back of their shirt or blouse. Next, everyone in the room is to get up with a pen in hand and write a *positive comment* on the back of each person's sheet. The comment can relate to virtually anything about the person being written about, e.g., his or her personality, characteristics appreciated in the person, or something he or she has said or done in class. Once everyone has written something on each sheet, everyone takes the sheet off and reads the comments. A discussion follows as to how each student felt throughout the activity and on reading the comments on one's sheet. This is an excellent introduction to issues of positive self-esteem, positive interactions with others, finding the positive(s) in people, treating *all* others with kindness, and acknowledging that everyone has positive characteristics.

- **The No Talking, Paper Edifice Activity:** In this activity, groups composed of four students are given a bundle of newspapers and a roll of masking tape, along with the following directions: Without talking and within fifteen minutes, using as much or as little newspaper as you wish, three of you must construct an edifice with a roof that must stand on its own and hold all of the participants in your group. You may not use anything in the construction of your edifice other than the paper and the tape. Throughout the activity, the fourth person is to take notes on the processes the group used to communicate and build the edifice. These notes will be used during a general class debriefing session. This individual is also not allowed to speak during the activity.

  Once each group has completed its edifice, members should get the attention of the instructor (in this case, the visiting middle level educator), and the entire team must fully enter the edifice. The instructor will ascertain whether the edifice is solely constructed with newspapers and tape, has a roof, stands on its own, and that it holds all of the participants of the group.

  Once the activity has been completed, the class reconvenes to discuss (a) the experience itself, (b) the point of the experience, and (c) why this is an ideal activity for use in an advisory class.

  This is an excellent activity for engaging students in a discussion of team work, following directions, creativity, and barriers to communication.

COMMENTARY

Most of the students over the past five years have commented that this is one of their favorite class sessions. They note that it is fun, hands-on, and thought-provoking. They particularly like the fact that they are able to interact with teachers from "the trenches" who can answer their (the students') questions about the purpose, development, and implementation of advisory programs. They also get specific answers to their questions about the reactions of young adolescents to such programs. Finally, they are more appreciative of the type of activities that top-notch advisory programs include, and they see the value in hands-on/minds-on activities that generate rich discussion.

Advisor/Advisee Activities That Assist Students in Exploring and Sharing Who They Are

SAMUEL TOTTEN
University of Arkansas, Fayetteville

STRATEGY/ACTIVITY/ASSIGNMENT

In the introduction to advisor/advisee programs in my "Middle Level Principles and Methods" course, I use a variety of warm-up activities to emphasize that the focus is on affective issues as they relate to both individual students and their place in groups, including families, schools, and the larger community. Herein I shall share three of the activities I have used in the past. As a rule, I only use one or two of these per class session, but never all three of them.

- **Name Exercise:** The instructor writes his/her name vertically on the blackboard.

    S
    A
    M

    Then, he or she uses each letter to form a word or phrase that provides an insight into who he or she is:

    Serious
    Analytical
    Matter of fact

Students should be informed that the result can be serious, like the one above, or funny, or a combination of the two. Or, it can describe interests and talents. It can also take some latitude with the form:

> **S**chool-bound (e.g., rarely left school from kindergarten to becoming a professor)
>
> **A**mnesty International member
>
> **M**addeningly anal retentive

A student may use both his or her first and last name or simply his or her first name. Once everyone is finished, the student tells the class his or her name and then relates the words he or she has formed from the name. This simple introduction prods one to think about one's perception of self and/or one's most prominent characteristics. It also provides others with a little insight into oneself.

- **Bio-Poem:** A more sophisticated variation on the name exercise: This unrhymed "poem" provides a student with the opportunity to dig a little deeper into him- or herself. The following pattern should be given to the students to follow:

    Line 1   Your first name only

    Line 2   Four traits that describe you

    Line 3   Sibling of . . . (or son/daughter of . . .)

    Line 4   Lover of . . . (three activities, sports, or hobbies, or a combination)

    Line 5   Who feels . . . (3 items)

    Line 6   Who needs . . . (3 items)

    Line 7   Who gives . . . (3 items)

    Line 8   Who fears . . . (3 items)

    Line 9   Who would like to see . . . (3 items)

    Line 10 Resident of (your town; street/road name)

    Line 11 Your last name only

- **The Calling Card:** Students are informed that they are going to create a "business card" on 8 1/2" × 11" paper that delineates key aspects about themselves. While modeling the process, the instructor states the following: in the middle of the paper, each person needs to write his or her name and, under that, any nicknames she or he has. In the upper right-hand corner, each should note three areas in which he or she has an expertise. In the lower right-hand corner, each should note a favorite song, favorite novel, and favorite movie; in the upper left-hand corner, each should note three words that aptly describes himself or herself; and in the bottom left corner, each should note his or her greatest success or dream.

Driven	Holocaust Education
Serious	Aspects of Genocide
	in the 20th Century
Conscientious	Existentialism

Samuel Totten
Sharkey
Tiger
Tiburoncito

Write a highly	*Zorba the Greek*
acclaimed novel	*The Brothers Karamazov*
	Amarcord

COMMENTARY

These activities, and others like them, are engaging and revealing for students. They reveal, at least to a certain extent, how one thinks about oneself and what one is willing to reveal to others. For others, it provides some insights into a person they may not know and/or new insights into a person they may think they know fairly well. As far as the advisor/advisee classroom is concerned, these introductory activities can assist students in becoming acquainted with one another, and they can do so in an enjoyable and nonthreatening manner, because each person is "controlling" the information that is shared about himself or herself.

Time and again, university students have declared their pleasure at taking part in these activities. They enjoy writing about themselves and finding out about others. They have also commented that they plan to use these activities whether or not they have an advisory class, for they feel they are excellent icebreakers, and that young people, from middle school through high school, would likely enjoy them.

Positively Experiencing Advisor/Advisee

CHARLENE JOHNSON
University of Arkansas, Fayetteville

STRATEGY/ACTIVITY/ASSIGNMENT

This activity is used to introduce the concept of advisor/advisee to under-graduate and graduate students in my middle level principles course. Students are assigned a reading on advisory programs in preparation for this class. In class, each student is asked to pin a large (11" × 17") piece of white paper to their backs. Then, each is given a colored marker to write on the sheets. Each student is directed to write something positive about his or her peers on the sheets pinned to their backs. The instructor also takes part in this exercise.

Once everyone has had a chance to write on everyone else's backs, we return to our seats, remove the sheets, and read the comments. A discussion follows that centers on the feelings experienced when reading the comments, how middle level students may react to a similar strategy, timing of the exercise, and its embodiment of the focus/intent of advisor/advisee programs.

The nature of the comments, insights, and feelings evoked are a major part of the discussion. Some comments are superficial (e.g., "I like your hair") while others offer new insights into their persona. It is generally agreed that middle level students benefit greatly from this exercise and would find it enlightening and rewarding, given that it is structured in a meaningful manner. An important aspect of the effective structure is the timing of such an exercise with early adolescents. To ensure that this exercise is genuine and provides some meaningful insights for students, a level of trust and familiarity is needed so that the comments are less likely to be superficial. It should be noted that this exercise is done only after we have been together as a class for some time (advisory programs are usually covered later in the semester) and that it would probably be wise to avoid such an exercise at the beginning of the year or at the initiation of the program.

Lastly, in class we discuss how this exercise exemplifies the connection between affect and cognition in the classroom. We discuss how the positive feelings generated by this exercise may affect student reaction to and involvement in school/instructional activities throughout the day. It is expected that early adolescents will be energized by such an experi-

ence. The importance of these types of experiences for positive development of early adolescents and effective operation in the classroom is also
discussed.

COMMENTARY

Student teachers often remark how this activity's positive effects were
felt throughout the day after the class session. Its effect underscores the
positive experience of advisory programs. Following this initial activity,
we review the different types of programs and their uses throughout the
nation. Many students are convinced that the programs have merit and
remark that they are amenable to implementing an advisory program.

"Hands-On" Advisor/Advisee Activities for Preservice Teachers

HAROLD L. SORKNES
Northern State University, Aberdeen, SD

STRATEGY/ACTIVITY/ASSIGNMENT

When I teach my "Middle Level Issues" class, I introduce the preservice
teachers to the concept of advisor/advisee programs, the role of the
teacher in an advisor/advisee program, and the advantages of such programs for middle level students. I begin the unit on advisor/advisee by
discussing the objectives of advisor/advisee programs. I point out that
for middle level students their social-emotional needs are at an all-time
high at a period in their educational career when they have been moved
from a relatively secure elementary school environment to a new middle
level program. For middle level students, an advisor/advisee program
may be the most developmentally responsive part of the middle level
program. The advisory program provides a time for middle level students
to become known well by at least one significant adult as well as a time
to form a sense of belonging to a smaller group of peers who are experiencing similar changes.

What I have found to be extremely valuable for introducing and discussing advisory programs is to use *Treasure Chest: A Teacher Advisory
Source Book* (Hoversten, Doda & Lounsbury, 1991). This book includes

120 classroom-ready activities for an advisor/advisee program and is divided into first-year, second-year, and third-year categories. The activities in the source book address topics such as goal setting, knowing oneself, self-esteem, listening skills, group skills, problem solving, peer pressure, nonverbal communication, partners in community, and feelings. In addition, the book provides an excellent introduction to advisor/advisee and offers helpful ideas in getting ready for advisor/advisee and getting advisor/advisee off to a good start.

Students in the "Middle Level Issues" class are divided into small groups (usually composed of two or three students), and each group presents an activity to the rest of the class. The class members actually perform the activity as if they were a group of advisees in a middle school. The reactions from the preservice teachers have been extremely positive. They state that they now have a much better idea of what advisor/advisee activities entail due to their experiences with the activities.

COMMENTARY

I have used this assignment for the three semesters that I have taught this course, and on course evaluations this activity has been rated by students as one of the most beneficial aspects of the course. I am convinced that one of the reasons for such excitement on the part of preservice teachers is the opportunity to connect theory to practice. The opportunity to actually do several advisor/advisee activities gives teachers and preservice teachers the confidence to serve as an advisor in middle level programs.

REFERENCE

Hoversten, C., Doda, N., & Lounsbury, J. (1991). *Treasure chest: A teacher advisory source book.* Columbus, OH: National Middle School Association.

Planning an Advisor/Advisee Program

SAMUEL TOTTEN
University of Arkansas, Fayetteville

STRATEGY/ACTIVITY/ASSIGNMENT

A key assignment in my graduate course, "Middle Level Principles and Methods," is the development of a plan for creating a new advisor/advisee program (a/a). Prior to undertaking such a project, the students are immersed in an in-depth analysis of the focus, purpose, and implementation of an a/a program.

Initially, the students individually brainstorm possible topics/concepts for an advisor/advisee program to be developed in the school in which they currently teach or, if they are not currently teaching, in a prospective school. These ideas are to be typed and submitted at the next class session.

Next, during class the students meet in groups of three or four and combine and hone their ideas. Every effort is made to form groups composed of members who teach in similar settings. Thus, if three or more students in the class teach at the same school, they are encouraged to form their own group. If two students teach at the same school, then they are encouraged to form a group along with one or two other individuals. If teachers are from rural areas, or, conversely, more suburban or urban areas, they are encouraged to form a group with those from similar geographical areas. In this way, the focus and/or topics of their a/a program are more likely to be somewhat similar and relevant for their schools. This group effort is typed up and submitted to the instructor.

Next, the students are presented with a list of concepts and topics brainstormed by the instructor. We discuss the differences between the instructor's ideas and those the students have come up with individually and in their respective groups. Once again, the students get in their groups to make any adjustments, if needed or warranted, to their list on the basis of this discussion.

Subsequently, the students develop a simple questionnaire to be used with middle level students for the purpose of gleaning the type of topics, subjects, and concepts that middle level students would be most interested in addressing in an a/a class. If at all possible, each group is to poll students in the exact geographical area (or, at least, one that is similar to their area) for which they are creating their plan. It is strongly suggested that they poll at least two to four classes in order to obtain diverse opinions and insights. Prior to administering the survey, this project is submitted to the College of Education's Internal Research Board to gain permission to conduct the study.

Once the poll is completed, the students are required to succinctly write up and report their findings to the class. We discuss whose ideas (each individual class member's, the various group's, the instructor's and/or the middle level students') merit consideration in developing an a/a program. We always discuss why it is imperative that the middle level students' voices and concerns be taken into serious consideration when developing such a program. We also discuss why and how a faculty should go about selecting topics and concepts for the express purpose of developing a developmentally and culturally appropriate program for a specific group of middle level students

During the course of the semester, each group is required to develop a tentative a/a curriculum. This is to be based on their additional readings about advisor/advisee programs, the findings from their survey of the middle level students, and pertinent class discussions.

Periodically throughout the semester (four pre-agreed upon times are established) each group shares its progress with the rest of the class. During this time (which totals no more than a half-hour in the three-hour course per week), the rest of the students in the class posit questions about various aspects of each group's work and also play the devil's advocate. Following each of these discussions, each group must turn in a three- or four-page progress report (two pages of which is a discussion of the tentative curriculum) to the instructor, which delineates the following: (1) a succinct discussion of the type of work engaged in since the last report; (2) additions, deletions, and alterations made in the tentative a/a program and a rationale for the major changes; (3) articles, chapters, a/a curricula, research, authors, and so forth that have influenced their latest efforts; (4) overall progress made since the last report; and (5) the focus of their next round of work and a rationale for that decision.

At the conclusion of the semester, each group submits its tentative a/a curriculum to the instructor. A short report (5 to 6 pages) must accompany each curriculum. The latter must, at a minimum, address the following: (1) a rationale for the focus and composition of the curriculum; (2) a solid discussion of the various articles, chapters, a/a curriculum, research, authors, and so forth that influenced their thinking in developing their a/a program; (3) a discussion of any additional changes they plan to make in the program prior to possibly implementing it (here the instructor is looking at the students' understanding that an a/a curriculum must meet the actual needs of an actual group of students and that no prepackaged curriculum is ever going to meet all the needs of a specific group of students); and (4) each individual's own statement as to what he or she gleaned from the project.

COMMENTARY

This assignment is generally well received by students as it involves a good mix of activities, including reading, small-group work, ascertaining the opinions/insights of middle level students, creativity, and authentic work (products that are likely to be implemented in one's classroom).

For some students, the most difficult aspect of the project is figuring out how and when they will meet with their fellow group members outside of class. This problem can be ameliorated to a certain extent by periodically allowing a half-hour or so during class for students to meet and work. To make maximum use of this time, though, students need to be informed prior to the actual work sessions that such time will be allocated.

At the end of the semester it is imperative that the instructor, both orally and in writing, remind the students that the programs they designed are not ready for immediate implementation. Rather, each teacher must consider the composition of his or her class and implement a program that is germane to the needs of students. This may involve using certain aspects of the newly developed program and/or developing an entirely new one. This admonition generally generates a discussion that revisits key research and practical concerns vis-a-vis the purpose and focus of outstanding and effective a/a programs.

Some students invariably comment that the major drawback of this activity is that they have no opportunity to "test" out their ideas/activities in a middle level setting. That is true, and the author is currently wrestling with this issue in an attempt to figure out how to address that concern effectively.

CHAPTER 14

Exploratory

Designing an Exploratory Wheel Program

TONI SILLS-BRIEGEL

Southwest Missouri State University, Springfield

STRATEGY/ACTIVITY/ASSIGNMENT

Working together in an interdisciplinary team to brainstorm and block out ideas for an exploratory program provides preservice teachers with the opportunity to develop an understanding of the range of subjects suitable for exploration. It also helps them to identify personal interests appropriate for use as a basis for planning their own exploratory classes. The following activity may be completed in a philosophy of middle level education or a middle level methods class as: (1) a brainstorming exercise in a 50-minute format to introduce the exploratory concept; (2) an extended block class that includes an overview of exploratory curriculum and initial development of model lessons; or (3) a formal unit to be completed and added to the preservice teacher's repertoire of strategies and materials.

Students are required to work together to design an exploratory curriculum for their hypothetical students using a wheel format (see diagram on page 354). Each team creates a wheel of minicourses suitable for use in 5th- to 8th-grade middle schools. The three-week minicourses should contain information and activities of high interest for both teacher and students. The purpose of each minicourse is to provide a quality exploratory learning experience for middle school students outside of regular classes.

Exploratory Course Wheel for Your Team

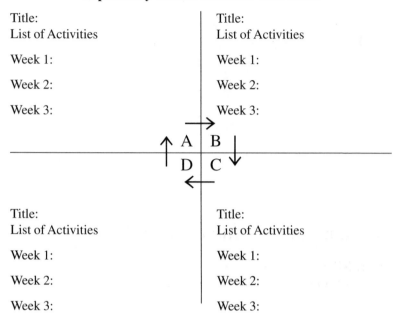

Title:
List of Activities

Week 1:

Week 2:

Week 3:

Title:
List of Activities

Week 1:

Week 2:

Week 3:

Title:
List of Activities

Week 1:

Week 2:

Week 3:

Title:
List of Activities

Week 1:

Week 2:

Week 3:

Teams are encouraged to be creative and to feel free to use guest speakers, field trips, special videos, hands-on practice with materials or tools, arts and crafts, and personal skills to design an engaging learning experience.

Although typical exploratory wheel-design courses last nine weeks (one quarter) in the middle school, in a middle level college course intended to be a survey of essential middle school elements, it is recommended that preservice teachers create three-week courses, with each exploratory class meeting three times a week for about 30 minutes. This allows the preservice teacher ample time to develop a personal understanding of the concept of exploratory courses.

Students may be invited or required to share their exploratory designs in a variety of ways—from simply sharing their ideas in class to teaching a sample plan to their college class or to a class of middle level students.

Extended plans require students to prepare full lesson plans with supporting materials. Students are encouraged to limit the costs of their exploratory, both to themselves and to their students, and are required to modify material to meet their own course design. References for all materials used must be duly noted.

The format to be used for option 1 (brainstorming exercise), option 2 (extended block lesson on exploratory classes), and option 3 (complete minicourse design) should begin with the following six items:

1. Course title
2. Brief, formal description of the course
3. Brief, captivating description of the course suitable for inclusion in a course guide for use by students in course selection
4. Enrollment limit, grades allowed to enroll, other restrictions
5. Location of the class
6. Materials needed by students. Note whether materials are provided or whether the students are expected to purchase books and/or supplies.

COMMENTARY

Preservice teachers enjoy this activity because it gives them a supportive environment to brainstorm and test their ideas about exploratory curricula. Students are able to visualize the "turning of the wheel" and develop an understanding of this method of designing exploratories. The one-page "Exploratory Wheel" handout focuses their attention on the idea that this is a team activity. This is particularly true when students work together to brainstorm exploratory ideas within their team. The last part of class is spent sharing ideas as a whole group and discussing the feasibility of each team's wheel.

An extended version of this activity requires students to take the results of their team design and class discussion and complete a formal series of lessons for future use.

As a quick brainstorming activity, students acquire a list of ideas for creating future exploratory classes. If more time is available, students work together in groups to fully develop the wheel concept and outline individual courses with a model lesson plan. Ideally, students will develop the wheel design into a full nine-week exploratory curriculum with complete lesson plans, teaching strategies, and resources.

Exploring Beyond the Core

TONI SILLS-BRIEGEL

Southwest Missouri State University, Springfield

ASSIGNMENT/STRATEGY/ACTIVITY

As an exercise to help preservice students design academically oriented exploratories in a middle level methods class, the professor should initially assist his or her class in designing a lesson plan in a core area. After working through the steps of a basic Objectives/Materials/Method/Evaluation (OMME) plan, the class should break into pairs or into groups of threes to generate topics related to a core subject of their choice—with the proviso that doing so will enhance the learning of that subject. After selecting one exploratory topic, each team should prepare a lesson plan on that topic. At the end of class, students should take turns placing their plans, which should be written on a transparency, on the overhead projector and sharing their results. A discussion follows that focuses on the merits of each exploratory plan and how it supports the learning of the core subject area.

Further discussion leads students to consider the development of a complete exploratory class linked to a core subject. Although academically based exploratory classes may provide students with additional outlets for learning and personal expression, it is emphasized that "traditional" exploratories must still serve the purpose of exploration. Designing exploratory classes to support core instruction should be just one facet of a comprehensive exploratory program in a middle school program.

COMMENTARY

Preservice teachers enjoy this activity. They appreciate the modeling of a lesson plan by the instructor. "Thinking out loud" techniques help students understand the thought process of a teacher as he or she works through planning for instruction. The design of the activity forces students to consider the importance of quality academics in a middle level program while bearing in mind the needs of early adolescents to explore both their lives and their environment. One student commented, "All I've heard from my professors was that there is never enough time to get everything taught." She went on to explain that designing an exploratory program that offered extended learning experiences in core areas seemed to be a way to " . . . find some more time to teach. We're getting several things done at the same time." Discussion among preservice teachers results in an understanding of the broad scope of an exploratory program, while making the point that exploration need not exclude academics. Exploratory class ideas keyed to core subjects have included: "Literary Magazine," "Word Play" (based on riddles, jokes, and humorous poetry)—language arts; "Our Community," "Manners and Proper Etiquette," "History in the Making"—social studies; "Art and Math," "Number Games," "Sports Stats"—mathematics; and "Rock Hounds," "Indoor/Outdoor Gardening," and "Quirky Inventions"—science.

CHAPTER 15

Response to Readings

Response Cards

LINDA R. MORROW
University of Arkansas, Fayetteville

STRATEGY/ACTIVITY/ASSIGNMENT

Strategic readers are actively engaged in reading text by using such strategies as activating prior knowledge and writing responses. Writing can be used to make learning personal, to create and explore thinking, to solve problems and struggle with difficult learning, and to consolidate learning. For each chapter or article assigned as class reading in my middle level methods courses at the undergraduate and graduate levels, students are asked to choose at least four specific points to list and to write a personal response. Students are asked to use 8" × 5" index cards to encourage succinctness and to facilitate grading.

These response cards provide students with an agenda for discussion and the instructor with insight into student understanding of the texts being read. During class, the cards are used for small-group discussions and then summaries from each group are shared with the whole class. The cards are turned in once a week and assessed for students' understanding of concepts, personal connections, and issues that need to be addressed in subsequent class meetings. Students can earn up to ten points per card based on the degree of participation in the assignment. More specifically, they earn ten points for a thought-provoking response that goes beyond the knowledge level; eight points for a knowledge-level response, which may include connections with personal experiences; and six points for a mere surface-level response with no attempt at application to experiences. To date, I have not received a response that warranted fewer than six points—with the rare exception of a student failing to turn in the response card.

COMMENTARY

I have found response cards invaluable not only as catalyst for class discussions, but also as windows into individual student thinking. Very often students will write questions and comments that they do not feel comfortable verbalizing. This assignment is a very nonthreatening means of involving everyone in the discussion of a particular topic. As I read the cards, I make a list of questions asked, misconceptions that have been formed, and connections made between research and practice. These items become the opening agenda for the next class session.

Constructivism in Practice

CHARLENE JOHNSON
University of Arkansas, Fayetteville

STRATEGY/ACTIVITY/ASSIGNMENT

Believing in a constructivist philosophy, activities and assignments in my undergraduate and graduate middle level principle courses are designed to reflect such a belief. More specifically, I share with my students that:

> Constructivism is not a theory about teaching. It's a theory about knowledge and learning. Drawing on a synthesis of current work in cognitive psychology, philosophy, and anthropology, the theory defines knowledge as temporary, developmental, socially and culturally mediated, and thus, non-objective. Learning from this perspective is understood as a self-regulated process of resolving inner cognitive conflicts that often become apparent through concrete experience, collaborative discourse, and reflection. (Brooks & Brooks 1993, p. vii)

In my syllabus I note that:

> A constructivist approach is employed in class whereby students are expected to actively involve themselves in their learning. The class will engage in a variety of classroom practices to address the different ideas and issues presented. Class discussion, an important component of the course, will be the primary method employed to examine the various dimensions of these issues and ideas. Students are expected to attend class regularly with assigned readings completed so that they can participate fully in the discussion and other exercises.

During the course, the definition (Brooks & Brooks, 1993) is shared again via transparency and/or assigned readings as well as in the assignments. Two of the major areas where student work reflects a constructivist approach is in journals and class discussions.

In their journals, preservice teachers are expected to summarize the readings and classroom discussions, record their reactions, and provide analyses (pro and con) of the issues discussed. The summary is to cover the readings and class activities of the week (one to two paragraphs). Reactions and analyses of events must include the preservice teacher's perspectives and thoughts on the material presented regarding its significance to them as future educators, to middle level programs, to early adolescents, to education in general, to society, and so forth. With the exception of the directive on the summary (in one to two paragraphs), definitive limits and specifications on content are not provided. For many, there is uncertainty about what is meant by analysis. Thus, it is emphasized numerous times that analysis involves thoroughly dissecting the issues and examining them for their singular impact, as well as in combination, in addressing the differing educational needs of contemporary learners. Students are also tentative as to why they need to summarize when I was in the class and obviously know what was covered. The point is consistently made that the summary allows me the opportunity to see how they incorporated the material into their schema and how they constructed an understanding of it.

Class discussions often cause considerable distress among the preservice teachers because of the variety of methods used to convey information, assess understanding of material and the lack of direct instruction, and/or the lack of direct answers to questions. Indeed, they are often poised with pen waiting for something to be written on the board or presented on a transparency so they can commit it to paper, thus having something to "show" for what they learned that day. However, my questions often center on how the information was incorporated into their schema and how it affected their views on education or their understanding of the concept under discussion. When preservice teachers ask my opinion on a strategy or idea, I often respond by asking them their thoughts on this issue. I try to move out of the role of "knowledge provider" and into the role of knowledge facilitator.

Strategies that require few or no words or demand formal writing are also employed in class. For example, preservice teachers are placed in groups and asked to depict the different dimensions of adolescent development (social, emotional, intellectual, and physical) on a large piece of paper. When the depictions are completed, each group presents their depictions and explains why it represents/reflects the dimension they were assigned. These illustrations are displayed and referred to often during the course.

During another class the preservice teachers used different size and shape blocks to delineate the different levels of curriculum and their relationship as outlined by Goodlad (Messick & Reynolds, 1992).

> John Goodlad offers five separate conceptual levels: (1) the ideal curriculum is that which a group of specialists proposes as desirable; (2) the formal curriculum is that which a state department of education prescribes; (3) a perceived curriculum is that which teachers do to attend to the needs of their preservice teachers; (4) an operational curriculum is what really happens in the classrooms; and (5) an experiential curriculum is that which students perceive is being offered them and to which they relate. (p. 56)

This was done after several discussions on the different levels and their relationships as outlined by Goodlad were reviewed, and it was obvious that preservice teachers remained uncertain of this concept. As a result, the preservice teachers were placed in groups, given different shaped blocks (math manipulatives I borrowed from a colleague), and directed to "build" or design a figure that depicted the relationship among the different conceptual levels. Within each group, the preservice teachers debated, discussed, and came to some consensus on what was meant by these concepts. As they struggled to depict these concepts with the shapes, they began to construct their meanings of these concepts and understand them better. As the students worked, I continually moved about the room, working with them by asking leading questions in order to assist them to address some of their misunderstandings. After completing this exercise/activity, preservice teachers were more cognizant of the levels, concepts, and importance of what Goodlad was discussing.

COMMENTARY

Initially, some preservice teachers have a difficult time with the analyses expected in their journals. They tend to regurgitate the information, comment on it in very vague or obtuse terms, and/or glibly reflect on their own experiences without fully exploring the implications of these reflections. I am constantly encouraging them to "dig deeper," look beyond the surface for meanings, and not to rely on my opinions/ideas for their thoughts and/or meanings. As one preservice teacher remarked after asking my opinion on a subject and I referred the question back to her and the rest of the class, "This class is just one big question!" Her frustration, while understandable when one is accustomed to having "cookbook" replies, was part of the learning experience of the course.

The different exercises/activities require preservice teachers to utilize different intelligences/modalities to explain their ideas. Although the initial reaction to these activities is frustration as students attempt to figure out "what the teacher wants," eventually preservice teachers become involved in them and produce very creative, insightful models that reflect the concept being studied. Many have commented that the exercises/activities caused them to really grapple with the concept and present it in an understandable manner.

REFERENCES

Brooks, J. G., & Brooks, M. G. (1993). *In search of understanding: The case for constructivist classrooms.* Alexandria, VA: Association for Supervision and Curriculum Development.

Messick, R. G., & Reynolds, K. E. (1992). *Middle level curriculum in action.* New York: Longman.

Responding to Readings:
A Paper Assignment With "Voice"

SAMUEL TOTTEN
University of Arkansas, Fayetteville

STRATEGY/ACTIVITY/ASSIGNMENT

Students in my undergraduate and graduate "Middle Level Principles and Methods" classes always read James Beane's *Middle Level Curriculum: From Rhetoric to Reality* (Columbus, OH: National Middle School Association, 1992). Prior to doing so, they are presented with the following directions for a related assignment:

Please read the following scenario and directions, and then complete the assignment:

The Situation: You have heard that the school board is seriously thinking of endorsing the ideas espoused by James Beane in his book entitled *A Middle School Curriculum: From Rhetoric to Reality.* Assume the role of either a parent of a young adolescent, a middle school teacher, or a young adolescent, and take a stance in favor of Beane's proposal, against his proposal, *or* as one who can see both the pros and cons of it. In regard to seeing the pros and cons, one might be in favor of Beane's integrated approach but argue that without also changing from a traditional to a block/flexible schedule such a program might be difficult, if not impossible, to implement in an effective manner.

Your reaction can take one of two forms:

1. In the voice of either a student, parent, or teacher, write a letter to the school board arguing in favor of your stance. The letter, which must be between 4 to 6 pages in length (double-spaced, typed), should delineate your position in regard to whether Beane's ideas vis-a-vis middle level curriculum should be implemented. When addressing Beane's points, make a point of focusing on the major issues espoused and do not emphasize or concentrate on peripheral or minor concerns. Be sure to support your argument(s) with key theory and research, both from Beane's book and other sources. When quoting Beane or others be sure to use complete and correct citation procedures. Since this is a letter, be sure to set it up in letter format. That is, include the date, a salutation, and a closing.

Finally, remember, because you are taking a stance, be clear, passionate, and support your argument as well as you possibly can. While being academic and professional in tone, also have some fun in designing the letter. Let your own voice and opinions shine through!

2. Assume that you are either a student, a parent, *or* a middle school teacher and that you are at a school board meeting. There is an open forum (which includes school board members, a superintendent, a middle school principal, middle school teachers, lots of parents of middle school students, and a few middle school students) to discuss Beane's curricular ideas.

In your paper, which should be between 4 to 6 pages (double-spaced, typed), take a position as to whether Beane's suggestions vis-a-vis middle level curriculum should be implemented. Set up your paper in a discussion format. In doing so, be sure to include the various voices of the participants, many of whom have various and radically different perspectives and opinions. Do everything in your power to convince the board and other people of your stance. Since you are taking a stance, be clear, passionate, and support your argument as well as you possibly can. Have fun with this, and let your own voice and opinions shine through!

COMMENTARY

This assignment avails the students of Beane's perspective in a way that is more innovative, more meaningful, and, it is hoped, more enjoyable than a typical term paper. It encourages and allows the students to experiment with different perspectives and voices that, in turn, result in their grappling with Beane's ideas in an original manner. Ideally, it also raises a host of questions that they might not have confronted if they had written the paper in a more traditional format.

Many students have commented on how pleasurable it was to have the "freedom" to break from the traditional mode of writing a paper. In doing so, they asserted that the format encouraged them to "play" with the ideas more than they would have otherwise; and this, in turn, allowed them to dig deeper into and wrestle more ardently with the subject matter.

REFERENCE

Beane, J. (1992). *Middle level curriculum: From rhetoric to reality*. Columbus, OH: National Middle School Association.

Responding to Readings: Role-Playing a School Board Meeting

SAMUEL TOTTEN
University of Arkansas, Fayetteville

STRATEGY/ACTIVITY/ASSIGNMENT

Students in my undergraduate and graduate "Middle Level Principles and Methods" classes read James Beane's *Middle Level Curriculum: From Rhetoric to Reality* (1992). Upon completion of the book, they are required to complete a paper in which they take on the persona of an individual (teacher, early adolescent, or parent) who has a vested interest in the curriculum of a middle level program and is addressing the local school board. (See "Responding to Readings: A Paper Assignment with Voice," pp. 364–365.)

After completing the paper, a class session is dedicated to the discussion of the ideas inherent in Beane's book. However, instead of simply conducting a typical class discussion of the ideas, the class session becomes a school board meeting in which the issues are addressed. The week prior to the "school board meeting," each student draws a strip of paper out of a hat that describes the particular role he or she will assume. On the strip is the "title" of the individual and a succinct description of his or her stance in regard to middle level education: a supportive parent; a disgruntled and aggressive parent; a young teacher excited about the prospect of teaching in a middle level program; an outstanding and highly respected teacher with twenty years experience who is very ambivalent about the new program; a junior high teacher with three years experience who is totally dedicated to his or her subject matter and wants no part of the middle level program; a board member who has children who are 11 and 12 years old and very much likes the idea of middle level programs; a school board member who argues that the traditional program was good enough for him and his family and can't see why something like Beane's program is needed; a school board member who is extremely conservative and perceives Beane's program as radical and dangerous. (Each of these roles was developed by the instructor.)

One role not included in the hat is that of the moderator. This is the individual who introduces the session, explains the rules of the session, and runs the meeting. The student selected to be the moderator is generally a person who is confident and at ease in a "take charge" role. This role should be given to an individual who the professor thinks will hold the rest of the group members responsible for their roles and keep the session focused.

At the outset of the session, the moderator announces that the school board is conducting a special meeting to decide whether to consider seriously the possibility of opening two new middle level programs. He or she states that the school board has studied the issue, sent information to concerned parents, and that this board meeting is being conducted to air the ideas, concerns, and questions of interested parties.

The key rules of the session are: (1) everyone is expected to take part, and the moderator is free to call on those who don't readily take part in the discussion; (2) everyone must take on the persona of his or her character, and if they switch out of it and become themselves, the moderator will gently prod them to remain consistent within the role; (3) the board members will have the initial say and discuss the ideas among themselves and then open the discussion to the guests; (4) everyone must practice active listening; and (5) a single individual must not dominate the discussion.

After the students have randomly selected a slip from the hat, they are informed that they may switch roles with other students if they wish. Ultimately, each student's task is to prepare for the actual role he or she is going to play. Students need to review Beane's ideas, jot down notes on what their characters wish to say at the meeting, and be prepared to assume the persona of the individuals that they are playing. The students are informed that if the strip states the person is "argumentative," then the student playing that role must be argumentative. If the strip states that the person is adamantly against the middle level program and sees it as dangerous, then he or she must adhere to that stance. All are informed that not only must they play the part, but they must use their new knowledge based on reading the book and the initial assignment (e.g., the paper) in arguing their position. It should be stressed that although the session should be entertaining, it should not be viewed as fun and games. Key ideas should be hotly and seriously debated and done so in a good amount of depth. Again, it is the role of the moderator to assure that this happens. If need be, the professor can always step in and refocus the class.

The "school board meeting" is generally held for two of the three hours of class time. In the last hour, a debriefing session is held to discuss what was learned. During the debriefing we discuss the fact that schools are close to the hearts and minds of individuals, and how differences of opinion and philosophy are to be expected when it comes to changes in school programs. Concomitantly, we examine the ramifications of these realities for new and experienced teachers, parents, and students.

COMMENTARY

Of all the activities the students take part in during the course of the semester, this role-playing session is generally one of their favorites. Most of the students really "get into" the roles they are assigned. There is a lot of laughter, but at the same time the ideas inherent in Beane's book are thoroughly examined and contested. At the conclusion of the activity, students often comment that this session constituted one of the best discussions they've had in a university classroom, that they're amazed at how many different ideas and positions were examined, and that this would be a perfect activity for use in middle level classrooms.

REFERENCE

Beane, J. (1992). *Middle level curriculum: From rhetoric to reality*. Columbus, OH: National Middle School Association.

Ascertaining the Research Base for Middle Level Concepts/Components/Programs

SAMUEL TOTTEN
University of Arkansas, Fayetteville

STRATEGY/ACTIVITY/ASSIGNMENT

A major goal in both my undergraduate and graduate middle level principles and methods courses is to assist my students to develop a strong interest in and an ability to use research for the purpose of strengthening their pedagogical efforts. A key effort along this line is to engage students in an in-depth study of the knowledge base of a single aspect of middle level education (e.g., interdisciplinary teaming, school climate, advisory programs, flexible scheduling, or student transition to junior high), which is followed up with a "research day" in which the students/teams present their research via a poster session.

The requirements for the project are as follows: (1) conduct a thorough and exhaustive search of the literature on the topic of choice; (2) develop a detailed, annotated bibliography of the pertinent research; (3) analyze the findings in a paper of between eight to twelve pages, double-spaced, typed. In your analysis be sure to discuss the strength of the research base, any gaps that exist, key findings you've discovered, and recommendations for future study; (4) delineate the most significant findings on a poster board; (5) take part in a "research day" during a class period by displaying the poster board and discussing your findings with those individuals who stop and examine and inquire about your findings; and (6) prepare a short (one- to two-page) handout that succinctly delineates the key findings of your study.

Prior to having the students develop a poster board for delineating/highlighting their research findings, we hold a class session on poster board sessions. During that time, the purpose of poster board sessions is discussed, numerous poster boards prepared by professors for poster board sessions are shared and discussed, and a short set of directions for developing a poster board are provided. The directions for the latter are as follows: Use an actual piece of poster board, not butcher paper; use a trifold poster board that can stand freely on a table; use graphics, schematic diagrams, photographs, etc., to illustrate key concepts; delineate your main concepts; and provide a comprehensive overview of your study but avoid "busyness" (that is, avoid including so much that the poster board is difficult to read). Use the following headings to organize your poster: Introduction, Review of Literature, Implications for Practice, Recommendations, References. The poster should be readable by someone standing three feet away.

COMMENTARY

Although many aspects of this activity (developing a detailed and scholarly annotated bibliography, developing a poster board delineating one's research findings, and taking part in a poster board session) may be new to students and the amount of work involved might seem demanding, most students find at least one or two aspects of the assignment extremely worthwhile. Interestingly, the part that most students dread initially but find the most enjoyable and enlightening in the end is the actual poster board session. They are generally delighted that others are interested in their findings, and they are fascinated by the findings of others. For the first time, many actually begin to feel comfortable discussing research, and, for many, it is the first time they actually begin to see the real value research could have on the development and/or improvement of an educational program or one's teaching.

Journal Article Review

CHARLINE J. BARNES
University of Northern Iowa, Cedar Falls

STRATEGY/ACTIVITY/ASSIGNMENT

General description: All content areas in education have professional organizations and journals devoted to improving the profession. In the field of literacy, the two major organizations are the International Reading Association (IRA) and the National Council of Teachers of English (NCTE). The middle level journals published by IRA (*Journal of Adolescent and Adult Literacy*) and by NCTE (*Voices from the Middle*) focus on various topics in literacy, and the articles are usually contributed by university professors and classroom teachers. This review assignment is an effort to expose students to these journals in hopes that they will continue to read them throughout their teaching career.

Objectives:

1. To become acquainted with major professional journals in the field of literacy for early adolescents
2. To document learning acquired by the reading of professional journal articles
3. To learn to use APA bibliographic style appropriately

Procedures:

1. Read, summarize, and respond to three articles drawn from three separate journals. Focus on professional education organizations that produce monthly or quarterly journals that use a peer-reviewed format. Peer reviewers are educators who evaluate the content and provide insights on an article's potential usefulness to literacy professionals. Check the editorial section (sometimes found on the inside cover or the first page) of the journal and read the guidelines for selection of articles.

2. Select articles written within the last two years. Selection should be based on interests, class readings, and discussions made about various issues and topics within literacy education.
3. The content of each review should adhere to the following format:

Journal Article Review # _____

Your name, section, and date

APA bibliographic reference

Summary of key ideas

Reaction or response (no less than 1/2 page)

4. Length should be approximately 1 to 2 pages (double-spaced/ typed)
5. There are two options in format: A traditional typed paper *or* an e-mail entry sent to the professor
6. Provide a photocopy of the article for the professor

Evaluation:

1. Follows procedures and format
2. Punctuality in turning in the assignment
3. Concise summary of key ideas
4. Written clarity, reasoning, and insightfulness in responding to article's content
5. Copy of article

COMMENTARY

In the beginning, most students have difficulty with this assignment owing to their lack of knowledge regarding journals. Therefore, it is wise to have a model of the review and a list of journals for all content areas on reserve at the library. Another area of concern is the ability to do a bibliography, especially in regard to using the correct format. Many students believe that this format is just for researchers and university professors, not for classroom teachers. Therefore, class time should be allocated for students to learn to use the APA style, using their first article for this task.

Time should also be given during class for students to share their articles with their peers. Each student should provide the title and author, summarize the key ideas, and share his or her reaction to the article. A student's reaction or response to the article's content can range from no knowledge of the topic to affirmation of the subject. In responding, students can ask questions, share ideas, or comment on how the topic is being used in school.

Great, thought-provoking discussions have resulted from this exercise. Students have said that this was a good time to bring up controversial topics not listed on the syllabus, but pertinent to teaching and learning (e.g. dealing with schoolwide violence, teaching second-language learners, and implementing the middle school concepts in rural areas). Some have used the strategies or activities from the articles in their field experiences. Overall, they learned to connect theory with practice as a result of reading and responding to journal articles.

CHAPTER 16

Reflective Experiences

"Picturing" Our Own Early Adolescence

SAMUEL TOTTEN

University of Arkansas, Fayetteville

STRATEGY/ACTIVITY/ASSIGNMENT

Early on in both my undergraduate and graduate middle level principles and methods courses I devise ways for my students to reflect on their days as an early adolescent. One of the most powerful—and often the most disturbing as well as humorous and insightful—moments occurs when I have everyone bring a photograph of himself or herself as an early adolescent (between the ages of 10 and 14). I inform them that I will bring in a photograph of myself as well.

Upon the initial request, many students—men and women, young and old—groan and ask, "Do we have to?" I nod my head and tell them they are free to bring a photo that they like or dislike, one that causes them to recall their early adolescence with fondness or not, and so forth. Invariably, one or more students will continue to complain that those were tough years, and they can't recall a single photo they like or would be willing to share with the class. I explain that this is one of the many reasons why we have this assignment—to reflect on how we felt about our looks and how we perceived ourselves at that time. Over and above that, this activity allows us to reflect on the importance that such concerns have for the young people that they are preparing to teach, or, in the case of current middle level educators, currently teach.

However, being sensitive to the fact that some of my students may truly dread bringing in anything that deals with their early adolescence, I give them an "out." If they are adamant about not bringing in a photo of themselves as an early adolescent, then they may bring in a photo from a period in their lives when they felt good about themselves. I know from past class experiences that such photos as these will elicit a great amount of fascinating and insightful discussion about how certain individuals felt about their years as an early adolescent versus the time when their favorite photo was taken.

The next class session is always an exciting one. Initially, many are tentative about sharing their photos or talking about themselves as an early adolescent, but as soon as one person breaks the ice, there is an avalanche of sharing, discussion, laughter, groans and moans, and verbal pats on the back. As a rule, students begin by holding up their photo and describing their "look" to the class. From there, various students go off on various tangents but, in the end, most students end up addressing a number of the following topics: how they felt about their looks (e.g., style of hair, their skin, height, weight); their sense of being underdeveloped, overdeveloped, or "just right"; their impression of how others perceived them; the clothes they wore and how they felt about them; their personalities and their moods; the "group" they were in or not a part of, and their feelings about that; how they were treated by their peers because of how they looked or dressed; and their likes and dislikes in regard to classes, subjects, extracurricular activities, school in general, teachers, parents, siblings, friends, and people who were not their friends.

Participation in the discussion is voluntary, and some students opt not to take part. However, all are extremely attentive. After everyone has had his or her "say," a class discussion focuses on the ramifications of what we've just talked about and the insights gleaned from one another in regard to interacting with, teaching, and meeting the needs of young adolescents.

COMMENTARY

There is always a certain excitement in the air, from start to finish, during the session when we look at and discuss each person's photograph. There is just something about sharing one's own photograph (and ultimately, story) with others that proves extremely engaging. These stories about their years as an early adolescent generate genuine pleasure, laughter, and, in some cases, pain, and great empathy. No matter what the emotion, all agree that the ultimate result is an extremely worthwhile learning experience, one that many claim they will make a point of remembering as they interact with their young charges in the classroom.

Reflecting on Our Lives as Early Adolescents

SAMUEL TOTTEN
University of Arkansas, Fayetteville

STRATEGY/ACTIVITY/ASSIGNMENT

During an examination of socio-emotional issues germane to young adolescents, I have the students in both my undergraduate and graduate "Middle Level Principles and Methods" courses write an in-class description of themselves as young adolescents. I ask them to address such issues as how they felt about themselves as a person; what they looked like and how they felt about how they looked; how they felt about friends, parents, and siblings; how they felt about school in general; what they liked (if anything) most about school and what they disliked (if anything) most about school; greatest interests in those years/days; and favorite or least favorite class. I inform them that since they will be sharing their stories in small groups, they should not reveal anything they do not want to share. There is no specification as to how long or short the piece must be.

I always make a point of writing my own story as well. As I tell my students, if a teacher expects students to be open and reveal personal stories about themselves, then it is incumbent upon him or her to be willing to do the same. Thus, prior to asking the students to share their stories in small groups or with the entire class, I always share my account of being a young adolescent. In doing so, I do not hold back in regard to sharing my "loves" (e.g., surfing and the Boy Scouts), pains and tribulations (being too shy to approach girls, a difficult home life, having 48-days of detention in the eighth grade, running away from home), and successes (earning a load of merit badges in the Boy Scouts).

Upon the completion of the pieces, the students initially share what they've written in small groups of three or four. During this time, it is important for the instructor to circulate among the groups in order to glean the issues being discussed. This knowledge will be useful when he or she is conducting the large-group discussion. After sharing in small groups for about five to ten minutes, the class comes together as a whole. Students are invited to read their pieces or comment on key points made in their small-group discussion. During this time, the instructor should address those key issues he or she overheard in the small-group discussions for the purpose of corroborating what individual class members are sharing. Also, since the instructor is privy to what all the small groups discussed, it is helpful if he or she periodically points out that more than one group addressed a particular topic or theme (e.g., the issue of cliques, the importance of such issues as hair or clothes to young adolescents, what aspects made for a favorite or least favorite teacher). Not only is the latter likely to generate avid discussion about such issues, but it also illuminates the shared experiences and insights of the group.

COMMENTARY

This activity prompts everyone to return to a time that they may have forgotten or given little consideration or thought to for a good number of years; and in so doing, it brings back a host of memories—"the good, the bad, and the ugly." This sets the tone for examining the unique characteristics and needs of young adolescents and, as a rule, it encourages students to have more empathy for the age and the developmental group they are now studying. This simple but powerful activity sensitizes university students to the reality of young adolescence and encourages them to be more reflective about what they are reading, studying, researching, and discussing.

Generally, this is an activity that most students seem to enjoy. While not everyone takes part in the general discussion, the looks on each person's countenance during these sessions are telling in regard to the value that they place on the stories being told. Quite often, the stories elicit knowing nods, ample laughter, and sometimes tears. Each session seems to always result in at least one or more remarkably personal, and often painful, stories about an individual's experiences during early adolescence.

Everyone Is a Child of His or Her Past

MARY ANN MANOS
Bradely University, Peoria, IL

STRATEGY/ACTIVITY/ASSIGNMENT

Each student in a class studying the characteristics of early adolescents completes an autobiographical paper in which he or she describes his or her own years as an early adolescent. This paper constitutes part of their contribution to a "gallery" describing their own adolescence. The organization of the paper follows a past-to-present orientation and is composed of four parts.

Part 1 focuses on reflections of their early adolescence and *must* include a discussion of the following: (1) family organization; (2) birth order; (3) moral, religious, character-building experiences; (4) quotes from people who knew them during this time; (5) favorite food, clothes, music, TV shows, books; (6) extracurricular activities; (7) career aspirations; (8) friends; (9) creativity (i.e., special talents they developed); and (10) a description of a vivid memory (this should be something they feel confident and comfortable putting into print).

Part 2 is a theoretical explanation of their adolescent experiences, and this must include: (1) a minimum of three key learning theories and/or major proponents of learning theories (e.g., B. F. Skinner, S. Freud, M. Mead, A. Bandura, L. Kohlberg, T. Sullivan, K. Lewin), and (2) a discussion of the selected theories in light of personal life experiences during early adolescence.

By encouraging preservice teachers to connect well-known learning theories to their personal lives, they begin to see, perhaps for the first time, a dynamic interplay of theoretical tenets. A shallow, bookish analysis of human behavior is supplanted by one that involves the students in a reflective study of early adolescence.

Part 3, the conclusion of the paper, is "future-oriented" in that students must discuss: (1) how past experiences affect their understanding of the middle level student, and (2) how they will correlate theory and practice in their teaching.

Part 4 is an attachment to the paper. This attachment is to include: a *copy of a picture* of themselves during early adolescence (ages 10 to 15), quotes from people who knew them during this time, and a self-description of fifty words or less. This attachment "A" becomes the center of the "gallery" exhibit. Students do not identify themselves by name for this part of the project.

Completing the exhibit is a three-step process. First, several class periods prior to the actual exhibit, an "icebreaker" activity is completed in class. Each student is given a plain white paper plate on a string lanyard. They are to place the lanyard around their neck with the plate across their back, so that they cannot see what is being written on it. All students make their way around the class simultaneously. Each student will write *only positive statements* on the plates of five classmates. The anonymous positive comments could be about the classmate's character, personality, and/or leadership within the class. This is an enjoyable activity that generates laughter and openness. After all the plates are filled with positive comments, students write their name on the plate and each is given to the professor. This plate will in turn become part of the autobiographical exhibit.

Second, when the papers are turned in for evaluation, all "Attachment A" sheets are each labeled with a number, separated from the body of the paper, and posted around the room. The class then circulates trying to match past pictures with present classmates. Only about ten minutes are allowed for matching. One by one, each paper plate is claimed by the owner and is placed by their childhood picture, connecting the past to the present. Allow one more short session for students to view the final exhibit. Students enjoy viewing the "adolescent past" and "adult present," which illustrate the range and intensity of physical growth, personality development, and cognitive ability within a decade of growth.

The final activity involves students in a class discussion of the following questions:

1. Is early adolescence a "staging" for adulthood and/or a definitive look at future personalities? Explain.
2. Which theorists seemed to be most accurate in their explanations of the early adolescent experience? Why is that the case?
3. Growth is ongoing and problematic—could you have imagined yourself a decade later? In what ways, yes? In what ways, no?
4. Are early adolescents solely products of their historical times, their family organization, their culture, or their genetic inheritance? Explain. The discussions are often deeply insightful and highly personal, expressing the perspective of mature teachers.

COMMENTARY

Reactions to the assignment are mixed. Smiles appear when we discuss favorite TV shows, food, and music during their early adolescence. Groans resound when they must choose a picture of themselves for presentation in front of their classmates. Uneasy glances are shot about when they need to include quotes of those who knew them during their early adolescent years. Often the vivid memory element causes concerns about privacy. As a result, the paper is evaluated only by the professor. On the other hand, Attachment A becomes an exciting, important part of an all-class exhibit.

Understanding early adolescence as a "journey" may be most effective as university students reflect on their progress in moving from early adolescence to adulthood. Reflective practice begins with introspection. Interviews with adults, parents, and friends from their own adolescent years add accuracy and greater depth to the university student's personal reflection. The memories that well up are often eclectic. For example, our favorite teenage activities and friends may remind us of the faddish, transitory attachments of early adolescence. The serious concerns of early adolescence may often seem silly today, but by reflecting on how one felt and reacted to such concerns provides us with a degree of understanding of the nature of early adolescence. Describing their successes in extracurricular and/or academic activities may also remind each student of the tremendous creative effort put forth in early adolescence. The vivid memory section may also bring to mind a respected adult who provided care and/or guidance. Each reflective step retraces a memory from the past.

The journey is completed as the students finish the paper plate activity. The comments often describe capable adults, respected by their peers and confident in their abilities. The gallery then provides visual closure for the reflection activity. The differences and/or similarities between their past and present appearances are often startling. The child has become an adult through the tireless efforts of excellent teachers and the guidance of supportive adults and friends. This assignment brings educational theory alive in a way unlike detached, clinical case-study research.

The needs of early adolescents often dictate unique educational methods. Effective middle level teachers strive to identify and meet their students' instructional and interpersonal needs. Regardless of whether the journey is one of storm and stress or relative calm, it is an important journey for both child and future educator to fully appreciate, analyze, and experience.

"Story-Telling Sessions" as Impetus for Reflection: Implementing Peer Feedback in the Reflective Process

DAVE S. KNOWLTON
Crichton College, Memphis, TN

RENEE E. WEISS
Federal Express Corporation, Memphis, TN

STRATEGY/ASSIGNMENT/ACTIVITY

This reflective experience could be especially valuable in a graduate-level course in which students are already full-time teachers; however, it also could work in an undergraduate course with preservice teachers. Since one of the main purposes of this activity is to help students "make meaning" out of their own experiences and connect those experiences to theory and course concepts, this activity is used best in a course that is designed to help students understand the relationship between the theory and practice of middle level education.

At the beginning of the semester—prior to studying course content—students are asked to write five stories about their real-life experiences as teachers or students. These stories should be no more than two pages each, and they should describe situations that the students consider to be significant to their own understanding of the educational process. (For example, students might remember the first time they were disciplined by a teacher. What's more, the student might remember delivering a lesson plan that worked extremely well. The point is that the stories ought to focus on situations that were significant to their lives.) These stories should be far more than matter-of-fact accounts of events; they should include intellectual and emotional reactions to those events.

Five times during the semester, course time is dedicated to "sharing" the stories in small-group "story-telling sessions." Students are placed into groups of four or five. Students take turns reading their own story aloud to the rest of the group. After each story is read, the students each have the opportunity to ask a question of the storyteller. The purpose of these questions should be to help extend and deepen the storyteller's thinking about his or her own experiences. Then, each of the listeners makes one comment about the story. The comments that they make should help the storyteller ground the story in course concepts and theoretical frameworks that are relevant to middle schools and the theory and practice of teaching.

After each of the five story-telling sessions, students are instructed to add a page of commentary to the story that they read. This commentary should be based on revelations that they had regarding their piece and new understandings that developed as a result of the session.

There is intrinsic and immeasurable value in participating in story-telling and sharing these five stories with classmates. Therefore, it may be advisable to grade students only on the basis of their participation in the story-telling sessions. However, in other cases, additional evaluation might be necessary. Each of the five stories can be graded on the basis of the following criteria questions: (1) Did the students write five original stories regarding their own experiences as teachers and students? (2) Did the students participate fully in the story-telling sessions by sharing their own stories and providing oral feedback to their classmates? (3) Did the additional page of commentary reflect a sincere effort to connect the story to course theory and new understandings that emerged as a result of the story-telling sessions?

COMMENTARY

This assignment provides a valuable reflective experience for students. The value is increased when students are encouraged to invest a fair amount of time and thought in selecting and writing their stories prior to studying the course material. It is critical to assure students that the *quality* of their experiences will not be graded. Instead, they will only be evaluated on the basis of a sincere willingness to comprehensively and accurately share their experiences. To reassure them, it might be valuable to share with students the criteria outlined above.

Specific criteria for each story might further enhance the possibility for a meaningful reflective experience. For example, perhaps one story might be specified as a story dealing with an ethical dilemma. Another story might be designated as an experience that could be defined as "successful." It is important, though, not to assign too rigid criteria to these stories, as it will squelch the creativity of the process.

The value is also increased when a classroom milieu of openness and trust is established early in the semester. Sometimes it is even useful to establish an ethic of confidentiality in the classroom. Students might

be more likely to share a broader range of experiences if such confidentiality were guaranteed.

Initial reactions to this assignment are often mixed. Students are
sometimes skeptical about opening themselves up to the vulnerability of
sharing their feelings with colleagues. It can be intimidating to share
feelings—as opposed to academic observations—about past experiences. After sharing the first few stories, however, students have a
stronger understanding of the purpose of story-telling. They see that their
experiences and the feedback that they receive can inform their practice.
Students regularly comment that peer feedback provided unique perspectives about their experiences. Other students have said that the sound
of their own voice reading their stories has helped them "hear" their experiences in a more objective light. As a result, understanding the related
theories and frameworks became easier.

Favorite/Least Favorite Middle Level Teacher: A Reflective Exercise

SAMUEL TOTTEN
University of Arkansas, Fayetteville

STRATEGY/ACTIVITY/ASSIGNMENT

To encourage students to begin to reflect on the type of teachers they valued and the type they didn't value during the middle level years, I have
them write two papers, one each on their favorite and least favorite middle level/ junior high teachers. The directions are as follows: Write separate pieces (they need not be polished) on both your favorite and least
favorite teachers at the middle level/junior high level. In writing each
piece, address the following: physical description of the teacher (no
names, please!!!), subject taught, why you liked/disliked the teacher as a
person or the person as a teacher. Be specific and thorough.

The pieces are written in class, and generally it takes most students
no more than about fifteen to twenty minutes to write both pieces. Once
the pieces are written, the students share their pieces in small groups of
three or four students. This session always produces a lot of laughter,
nodding of heads, and groans. Once the small groups have had ample
time to share and discuss the pieces, a large-group discussion is held.

During this time students may read one or more of their pieces for the class, but the major focus of the discussions is on what has been gleaned from writing the pieces, listening to the other pieces, and the small-group discussions.

Ultimately, we focus on and list those characteristics that have been noted in both the favorite and least favorite teachers. As a general rule, there are few discrepancies in students' assessments, but when the qualities of favorite teachers are broached we address them in some detail. A discrepancy in one class, for example, arose when one student asserted that she preferred teachers who possessed and shared their wealth of knowledge and said she didn't care that much about a "friendly climate," whereas other students claimed that a creating a friendly climate was one of the key reasons they deemed a teacher a favorite.

COMMENTARY

This activity is frequently moving and enlightening for the students. It prompts the university student to think about his or her days in middle school and/or junior high and recall those teachers who they thought really cared for students (in academic and/or social realms). This sets the tone for examining the unique characteristics and needs of young adolescents as well as the unique characteristics of the "ideal" middle school teacher. This activity also encourages students in the course to ponder what it means to be a middle school teacher, e.g., the sort of qualities that best lend themselves to truly meeting the unique needs of young adolescents.

Have Journal, Will Travel

WARREN J.DIBIASE
University of North Carolina at Charlotte

STRATEGY/ACTIVITY/ASSIGNMENT

Reflective journaling is a major requirement of the middle level methods class. Each student is asked to keep a journal of his or her thoughts and reflections as well as any questions for which answers are sought. In addition, the students share what meaningful learning, major concepts, and/or insights they are developing. The students' reflections generally focus on assigned and outside readings, field experiences, class activities, and class discussions; however, the students often use the reflective journal to share their concerns and vent their frustrations. Issues of concern and frustration for the students include, but are not limited to, the following: discipline; the ability to modify instruction to meet the needs of all learners; issues of accountability (in which the teacher is held responsible for student performance on state-mandated testing); teacher feelings of inadequacy and low self-confidence; and ways to motivate students to learn.

The journaling process is normally a two-way communication between the instructor and the student. In this class, however, sets of traveling journals are used. The journals not only travel between the students and the instructor but among the students in the class. The traveling journal process is explained to the students during the first class meeting.

Students write one journal entry during the period between subsequent class days. Journal entries travel in pocket folders that are supplied by the students. Each journal entry is written on a separate sheet of paper. Entries can be either handwritten or typed. The students either place their names on each entry or mark the papers in such a way that they will be able to identify them at a later date. The students deposit the folders in a designated place upon entering the classroom. After class, each student leaves with another student's folder. The students place their next journal entry into this "new" folder. In addition, the students are encouraged to read and comment on all the other entries traveling in the folder. As such, the methods students have an opportunity to read and comment on each other's thoughts, questions, ideas, and insights. The students repeat this process, in similar fashion, all semester long.

The instructor collects and reviews the journal entries three times during the semester: one-third into the semester, two-thirds through the semester, and again at the end of the semester. The folders circulate through the class prior to collection of the journal entries. At this time, the students retrieve and collate all their journal entries, identify them if necessary, and clip them together. In this way, the instructor is able to assess each student's progress when reviewing his or her entries. Before leaving class, the students place the latest, uncirculated entries into the folder and exchange it with another student. The traveling process begins anew. This whole procedure, except for initiating the journal traveling, is repeated one additional time during the semester.

COMMENTARY

In the traditional two-way journal, the only feedback the student receives is from the instructor. Yet, all classes are composed of diverse individuals, each having their own expectations, perceptions, and experiences. As such, we all have much to offer and learn. The traveling journal provides an opportunity for students to receive feedback from both the instructor and the other students in the class. In this way, the students are exposed to views, beliefs, and insights from a number of diverse and unique perspectives. As a result, the students are given the opportunity to critically assess their own beliefs, views, and perceptions.

The students have a bit of a problem understanding the logistics of how the journals travel at first. However, after two classes, they fully comprehend the process. Initially, the students are reluctant to comment on other students' journal entries. As the semester progresses, however, they become more comfortable with commenting on each other's work.

The reflective journal is one component of a portfolio developed by the students. The journal's last entry is a self-assessment, and it contains a series of questions to which the students respond. These questions include the following:

1. What meaningful learning, major concepts, and/or insights about middle level teaching and learning have you developed this semester?
2. How might you use these concepts and insights in your student teaching or teaching?
3. As you enter your student teaching experience, what do you feel are your strengths and weaknesses?

Individual exit conferences are scheduled with the methods students during exam week. At this time, the students turn in their portfolios and discuss what meaningful learning, major concepts, and/or insights they have developed. The reflective journal is "graded" on a four-point rubric, with respect to criteria such as completeness, "depth" of reflection, and timely submission.

The Thinking Journal

KAREN B. FREDERICKSON

Queen's University, Kingston, Ontario, Canada

STRATEGY/ACTIVITY/ASSIGNMENT

To engage teacher candidates in techniques pertaining to metacognition, a thinking journal is kept for the intermediate music education course (grades 6 to 9). The journal is designed to assist students in thinking about their thinking and to help them in preparing thought-provoking lessons for middle school pupils. It is collected each week, and the professor writes a reply in each student journal. The students are encouraged, but not required, to include one or more of the following in their journals:

1. **The search for meaning in the activities undertaken during the class sessions:** (*Note:* Sample lessons are frequently presented with the teacher candidates playing the roles of the middle school students.) The journal entry could include an analysis of the lesson, reflecting on its assumptions and biases; recalling the parts of the lesson; recalling feelings that they experienced during the lesson; and addressing other pertinent points.
2. **The attempt to become adventurous in one's thinking:** The students are encouraged to pose "what if" questions and to think about alternatives to the content, methodology, or process experienced in the class sessions. In these cases, they should also reflect on their own assumptions and biases.
3. **A personal understanding of what reasonable thinking is:** The students are encouraged to use evidence to support their statements or claims. They are routinely urged to define what is important to them, particularly the goals of middle level education and the goals of music education. They are encouraged to identify multiple points of view and to present potential consequences of each.
4. **A reflection on one's own thinking:** Each student is encouraged to become more aware of his or her own thinking, or lack thereof (i.e., mindlessness—"blindly follow[ing] routines . . . acting like automatons . . . " —Langer, quoted in Barrell, 1994, p. 4). They are encouraged to acknowledge the feelings that are

experienced when reading material that is either consistent or incompatible with their own beliefs. They are encouraged to perceive various ways of solving teaching problems as well as personal problems that may occur in small-group work, personal study, and lesson planning.

There is an expectation that all students will receive a grade of A for the project if a journal is submitted every week. At the beginning of the course, the journal project is discussed with the class, identifying the importance of personal knowledge for becoming an effective teacher of middle level pupils. The concepts of evidence, assumptions, bias, point of view, reason, and so forth are explored and discussed. They are examined continually throughout the course, in class sessions as well as in the journal experience.

COMMENTARY

This has been both a source of great satisfaction and a great challenge for the instructor. When the class size is large, many hours are required to read and respond to each student. Many students have recognized this as a significant experience in their preparation for teaching and are interested in adopting the project for use in their future classrooms.

REFERENCE

Barrell, J. (1991). *Teaching for thoughtfulness.* New York: Longman.

Early Adolescent Literature

LINDA R. MORROW
University of Arkansas, Fayetteville

STRATEGY/ACTIVITY/ASSIGNMENT

As a means of activating memories of early adolescent experiences and of opening a window to the thinking of early adolescents, I read aloud from *Middle School Blues,* a novel by Lou Kassem (1986). I use this novel in both undergraduate and graduate middle level methods classes.

After the reading of a chapter, students are invited to respond either verbally or in a five-minute written reflection. The experiences of the protagonist, Cindy, elicit memories of early adolescent experiences as well as connections with material previously read and discussed regarding the physical, social, emotional, and intellectual characteristics of early adolescents. As I continue reading aloud selected chapters in subsequent class meetings, students articulate parallels between Cindy's experiences—the death of a grandparent; relationships with peers, siblings, and teachers; and self-identity issues—with the characteristics of early adolescents described in the assigned readings. It should be noted that generally I do not read the entire book. I use excerpts from the book to illustrate examples of early adolescent characteristics and to demonstrate the power of using such literature with university as well as middle level students. The time needed to include a wide array of middle level materials is also a factor in not being able to read the entire book.

Other ideal titles include *Reluctantly Alice* (1991) by Phyllis Reynolds Naylor, and *The Friendship Ring* (1998) by Rachel Vail.

COMMENTARY

I read this novel to my students when I taught seventh grade because it paralleled their experiences of moving to a new school in which they were often separated from their elementary school friends. Not only are the experiences of the protagonist typical of this age group, but her focus is on writing a survival guide for success in seventh grade. The reading of this novel jogs memories in the minds of university students, as evidenced by the nodding of heads as I read and by comments in responses written at the close of the class session. Thus, students make connections between early adolescent experiences and how middle school practitioners can best serve these students. Reading this novel aloud also models a literacy strategy to be used in middle school as well as the critical place of early adolescent literature in the middle level curriculum.

CHAPTER 17

Field Experiences—Preservice

Site Visits

LINDA R. MORROW
University of Arkansas, Fayetteville

STRATEGY/ACTIVITY/ASSIGNMENT

Each semester in my undergraduate and graduate middle level methods courses, I arrange a site visit to an area middle school that includes a tour of the building and a description of the school program by the principal. Because these courses are taught in the evening or during a summer session, middle school classes are not in session during the tour and program. Thus, the focus is on the building/facility and its relevance and use for middle level learners. All three schools visited at this point have been in operation from one to three years and were constructed to address the specific needs of young adolescents. As the principal explains each area of the building (e.g., pods, common team-meeting areas, health services, media services, exploratory classrooms, cafeteria, and so forth) and the daily schedule, the university students are given an opportunity to review how recommendations made from middle level experts are being operationalized.

In addition to the building tour, middle level teachers often describe and discuss their advisory program, teaming practices, and interdisciplinary studies.

COMMENTARY

This site visit is a powerful strategy for the integration of theory and practice. Students are always amazed at the school plant and how it is specifically constructed to address the needs of middle level students. The professionalism and enthusiasm exhibited by the middle level educators lends credibility to the middle level program and its advocates, resulting in most students expressing a desire to teach in just such a school.

Middle School Investigation

SANDEE SCHAMBER
Black Hills State University, Spearfish, SD

STRATEGY/ACTIVITY/ASSIGNMENT

This assignment takes students into the field to investigate the current practices of local middle schools. Students are required to interview middle school teachers or administrators to determine the extent to which the practices of effective middle school program are being implemented in the local school which they have chosen to investigate. Prior to being sent into the field for this investigation, the students are introduced to the characteristics of effective middle schools as delineated by Schurr (1992) in *Evaluating Your Middle School.*

For the assignment, students are told to select any ten characteristics and question the interviewee relative to the presence or absence of those particular characteristics. If a particular characteristic is present, the students are to describe its implementation; if the characteristic is absent, they should question the interviewee relative to the underlying cause of the absence. A final report is then submitted which includes a discussion of each of the chosen characteristics and a summary that addresses the overall strengths and weakness of the middle school based on the information gleaned from the interview. These written reports also serve as a basis for class discussion.

COMMENTARY

This assignment serves two purposes. First, it provides students with the opportunity to get out into the field to see what is happening in the "real world" of middle schools. In this respect, it serves to bridge the gap between the ideal and the real, between theory and practice. In addition, the students experience a certain excitement when they are able to observe in the field the practices that have been discussed in class. Second, the interview serves as a reminder to those who are already in the field of the characteristics of effective schools. It also provides the opportunity for analysis and reflection by the interviewees relative to the current state of their middle schools.

The reactions of the students to this activity are invariably bipolar. They exhibit genuine excitement as they discover that the characteristics of effective middle schools that have been discussed in the classroom in a theoretical context are actually being implemented in the field. Conversely, however, they demonstrate both surprise and dismay as they discover that many of these characteristics are not being enacted by local middle schools.

REFERENCE

Schurr, S. (1992). *How to evaluate your middle school.* Columbus, OH: National Middle School Association.

Focusing in on Young Adolescents

SAMUEL TOTTEN
University of Arkansas, Fayetteville

STRATEGY/ACTIVITY/ASSIGNMENT

An optional assignment open to both the undergraduate and graduate students in my "Middle Level Principles and Methods" course is to spend half a day at a middle school taking photographs of the students. The purpose of the assignment is to encourage the university students to take a closer look at the middle level students in regard to the great diversity in their sizes; the groups with which they associate (e.g., whether the groups are mostly composed of boys or girls, the number of friends and acquaintances); activities they engage in during recess; the similarities and/or differences in dress; classroom seating, including how many sit in their chairs (which may provide clues to physical comfort or discomfort of their bodies and/or the type of seating provided); what they eat during nutrition break and at lunch; the type of activities they engage in during class; and so forth.

The directions for the assignment are: (1) prior to conducting the project, outline or map out the various situations in which you wish to photograph students and provide a succinct rationale as to why you are interested in those particular shots; (2) obtain permission from a site administrator to spend half a day taking photographs of young adolescents for your project; (3) once in the school, take photographs of those situations you've already delineated as well as any others that might be revelatory in regard to understanding the school life of young adolescents; (4) either immediately after shooting the photographs or upon having the film processed, write a short (2 to 4 page) report that addresses the following points: an introduction, the name and location of the school, the grade levels in the school, your initial ideas as to what you planned to photograph and why, additional situations photographed and why, and what you learned about young adolescents from this experience. In regard to the latter, include a discussion as to how this experience either corroborated or called into question information about young adolescents that you have gleaned from the assigned readings and discussions thus far in class, and offer a solid conclusion; (5) mount the photographs on poster board and under each write a short description (several words or no longer than a single sentence) of what the photograph is about and the rationale or purpose for taking the photograph (e.g., "This photograph illustrates the vast difference in height and weight among young adolescent boys in grades seven and eight."); (6) bring the poster board with the mounted photographs to class to share with the rest of the class. (*Note:* Instructors may need to submit a description of this activity to their college/university research and human subjects committee in order to gain permission for their students to carry it out.)

COMMENTARY

This assignment provides students with a different "take" and perspective on young adolescents. Initially, many students select this optional assignment because it gets away from the observations they are accustomed to doing. Following the assignment, they appreciate the unique type of information and insights they've gleaned from planning, taking, and analyzing the photographs.

Among the comments students have made about this assignment

are: "Talk about all sizes, shapes, and interests! The photographs really do tell the story"; "This assignment literally made me look at young adolescents in a new way"; and "We need more assignments like this. Not only is it fun and creative but it made me see things that I would've never gotten from the text."

Food for Thought: Having Lunch with Middle Level Students

SAMUEL TOTTEN
University of Arkansas, Fayetteville

STRATEGY/ACTIVITY/ASSIGNMENT

One optional assignment that the students in my undergraduate and graduate "Middle Level Principles and Methods" courses can select is to have lunch with middle level students. The purpose of the assignment is twofold: First, it provides university students with face-to-face interaction with middle level students; and, second, it provides the former with unique insights into the diverse thoughts, interests, maturity, and physical size of young adolescents.

The directions for the assignment are:

1. Contact a site administrator and ask permission to have lunch at least three times with middle level students. One may choose to have lunch with the same group of students each time or a different group of students.
2. Once permission is given, bring or purchase a lunch and sit down with a group of middle level students, introducing yourself as a university student who is currently enrolled in a middle level education course. You may also wish to inform them that you are considering the possibility of eventually teaching in a middle level program.
3. During lunch, observe, listen, and speak with the students. While doing so, reflect on the following: their language, tone of voice, topics of discussion, interactions with one another, clothing, and so forth.

4. Following each observation write a 1- to 2-page report that addresses each of the areas for reflection listed in instruction 3, adding any additional insights/information that you wish. Each report should include an introduction and conclusion and use proper grammar, spelling, and sentence structure. In addition to the report, write a one- to two-page summary of the experience in which you discuss the following: whether this assignment was of value to you in regard to gleaning additional insights into young adolescents, and why that was so; the most important insights you gained from this assignment; at least one surprising or new insight you gleaned about young adolescents by completing this assignment; and any suggestions you have for making this assignment more valuable or useful.

COMMENTARY

It is surprising how many students enjoy this assignment. Many return to class and share unsolicited comments with their peers and instructor. At the same time, many who have had lunch with young adolescents urge their peers to consider doing so as well. Most comment on how funny, bright, and open the young adolescents were. They also comment on the type of humor (ironic, cutting, self-deprecating) the young adolescents are prone to use, the immense variation in topics found between groups of girls and boys, the range of issues the young adolescents discussed (teachers, various classes, assignments, the latest "couples," clothing, music, music videos, singers, actors, sitcoms, sports, and so forth).

Among the comments the university students have made about this assignment are: "It never ceased to surprise me how open these munchkins were with a total stranger"; "I forgot how much fun kids this age can be"; "I don't think my peers and I were talking about stuff like that when we were that age"; and "This should be a required, not an optional, assignment. It is nothing short of revelatory."

Interviewing Middle Level Students

GERT NESIN
The University of Georgia, Athens

STRATEGY/ACTIVITY/ASSIGNMENT

At the outset of their junior year of college, students who are accepted into the Middle Level Education program at The University of Georgia begin courses whose focus is specifically middle level. The first of these classes, "Introduction to Middle School Education," explores such topics as the history of junior high and middle schools, components of effective middle schools, and the characteristics of young adolescents.

Before formally discussing young adolescent development, the preservice teachers prepare for an experience at a local award-winning middle school. Issues related to the social, emotional, cognitive, physical, and moral growth of young adolescents are introduced in a single class session prior to this field experience. Methods during this introductory session include a mix of the instructor sharing illustrative classroom teaching experiences and class recollections of adolescent development and issues.

The activity discussed here is conducted as a whole-group exercise. Initially, the preservice teachers brainstorm a list of questions they would like to ask middle level students. The questions are based on the previous class session and their own questions and concerns. A common class list of questions is compiled, and three copies are made for each preservice teacher.

Because the university has a long-term, collaborative relationship with the cooperating school system, parental permission for interviewing is not required. This interviewing does not go through the university's internal research review board since the interviews are for classroom use and not for publication purposes. Anonymous interview responses are also shared with the cooperating teachers for their reference.

For the next class period, preservice teachers and the instructor visit the middle school. Arrangements are made in advance so that each preservice teacher spends about 20 minutes each with a sixth-, seventh-, and eighth-grade class. To begin, all of the preservice teachers visit one grade-level class, where they are briefly introduced. Preservice teachers and middle school students then randomly form pairs for interviewing. To ensure that all the middle level students in the class participate, some of the preservice teachers interview two students simultaneously. The interviewing groups stay in the class or find an area in close proximity and spend 10 to 15 minutes together. The preservice teacher makes a mental note of the gender, age, and physical description of the young adolescent for later recording. The preservice teachers then proceed with the list of questions. Upon completing the interviews, the middle level students return to class, and the preservice teachers, as a group, proceed to the next grade. The same procedure is followed with the other two grade levels.

Prior to the next class, the preservice teachers reflect on the interviews and prepare a written summary. They return to the university for the next class session to discuss the interviews and summaries, first in small groups and then as a whole class. Looking at the middle level students' responses to the questions, they form some common themes about young adolescent development and effective teacher responses to that development. For example, one theme might be the need for peer interaction, and a teacher response might be collaborative grouping. With the guidance of the instructor, comparisons and contrasts are made between grade levels, with an emphasis on understanding the growth and development of the middle-grade students.

The one-week interviewing activity has provided a concrete experience on which to build further knowledge. Following this activity, several class periods are then devoted to more formal exploration of young adolescent development.

COMMENTARY

Instead of just talking about young adolescent development in the abstract, this activity gives faces and personalities to put with characteristics. In addition, this activity allows preservice teachers the opportunity to see the differences in adolescent development across the middle school years. They become excited and animated when preparing for and conducting these interviews. By spending time with young adolescents, these future teachers can reaffirm or reconsider middle level careers.

Many students commented on the positive outcomes of this experience. Following are several statements taken from reflections about the course:

> We learned what actually makes up a young adolescent. We did this by
> looking at their five characteristics: physical, emotional, moral, social,
> and intellectual. We have now learned what these children are experi-

encing in all the different phases . . . . Everything that we will be teaching to middle school students is developed around these five characteristics . . . . We were able to get first-hand experience with some of these
issues by going out into a middle school and interviewing the students.
This was a great experience that I think we all learned a lot from.
Sandy (Pseudonym)

I really benefited from interviewing the three kids at the . . . middle
school. I really thought I wanted to teach sixth grade—now I'm not so
sure. Pat (Pseudonym)

I especially gained a lot from going out to the middle school and interviewing the students. It really helped me learn about that age group
and their beliefs and ways of thinking. Tracy (Pseudonym)

Studying the Young Adolescent in His or Her Natural Environment

MARY L. SNYDER
Central Missouri State University, Warrensburg

STRATEGY/ACTIVITY/ASSIGNMENT

Students enrolled in my middle school strategies course complete a
unique research project on early adolescents that brings both parties face
to face. The class brainstorms ideas and devises a questionnaire (see next
page) to use in learning more about today's early adolescent. Care is
taken in the planning of the questionnaire in order to eliminate any identifying information about the interviewees. An area shopping mall is
used as the research site (Logan, 1996). It is advisable for the instructor
to receive written permission from mall management ahead of time for
students to survey mall patrons. Copies of the document should be provided to each student. It should be noted that this project was *not* routed
through the university's Human Subjects Committee because the research involves survey procedures in which the human subjects "cannot
be identified directly, the subjects' responses could not reasonably place
the subjects at risk, and the research does not deal with sensitive aspects
of the subjects' behavior" (Central Missouri State University, 1997).

The preservice students take an after-school trip to a mall, where the makeup of its customers often mirrors the diversity found in many school populations. While there, students work in teams to interview middle schoolers about their plans for the future, interest in current issues, involvement in extracurricular activities, and so forth. The university students later tally their results, describe their findings in a reaction paper, and give an informal presentation to the class.

Questionnaire: Questions to Ask Students at the Mall

1. What grade are you in?
2. What do you do after school?
3. What is your favorite music?
4. What are your plans for the future?
5. Tell me about your family.
6. What is your favorite subject in school?
7. What exploratory subjects can you take?
8. What current event/issues concern you (abortion, president, drugs, gun control)?
9. How much time do you spend a day watching TV? Doing homework?
10. Do you like middle school/junior high, and why?
11. Are you in any extracurricular activities?
12. What do you like about school?

COMMENTARY

This project generates lively class discussion. Students discover firsthand that although young adolescents demonstrate diverse interests in music, personal and societal issues, sports, school, and so forth, most share similar hopes and plans for the future (Elkind, 1994) and a common admiration for teachers who respect and care for their students (George, Stevenson, Thomason, & Beane, 1992; George, Lawrence, & Bushnell, 1998).

REFERENCES

Beane, J. A. 1993. *A middle school curriculum: From rhetoric to reality* (2nd ed.). Columbus, OH: National Middle School Association.

Central Missouri State University Faculty Guide 1997. *Procedures for human subjects review.* Warrensburg, MO: Central Missouri State University.

Elkind, D. (1994). *A sympathetic understanding of the child* (3rd ed.). Needham Heights, MA: Allyn and Bacon.

George, P., Stevenson, C., Thomason, J., & Beane, J. (1992). *The middle school—and beyond.* Alexandria, VA: Association for Supervision and Curriculum Development.

George, P., Lawrence, G., & Bushnell, D. (1998). *Handbook for middle school teaching* (2nd ed.). New York: Longman.

Logan, L. (1996) "Want to teach? First go to the mall." *Phi Delta Kappan, 77* (5), 383–384.

Field Experiences Integrated into an Introductory Middle Level Education Course

NORMA J. BAILEY
Central Michigan University, Mt. Pleasant

STRATEGY/ACTIVITY/ASSIGNMENT

Throughout the semester of our introductory middle level education course, students participate in four field experiences that are integrated with the course content to help them develop a deeper understanding of the needs and characteristics of young adolescents and various aspects of middle level education. These field experiences include: a shadow study of a middle school student, engagement in an extracurricular activity with young adolescents, observation of an interdisciplinary team meeting, and a field trip to three middle schools (one urban, one suburban, and one rural).

Each activity requires a thorough explanation to prepare the students for the experience and to place it in context of the course content. Students write a two- to three-page reflective paper after each field experience, based on specific guidelines given by the instructor. Each is geared to the experience and gleans the students' thoughts as to how the experience will help make them better middle level educators. Examples of such guidelines are: (1) What differences did you observe between middle school students in a classroom setting and middle school students in an extracurricular activity? Incorporate in your answer your knowledge of the characteristics of young adolescents. (2) Analyze the meeting you observed in relation to what you have learned about the discussions, top-ics, and activities that occur during effective team meetings. (3) Explain how this experience helped you to better understand the needs and char-acteristics of young adolescents and how it will help make you a better middle school teacher.

It is always important to have a group debriefing time during which *all* the students share with one another their most surprising insights, and concerns, and have a chance to interact with one another and with the in-structor regarding them.

After students have learned about the needs and characteristics of young adolescents, their first field experience is a half-day *shadow study* of a young adolescent in our local middle school. Students are given a week to complete this, with one of our class periods canceled to provide students with the time to conduct the study. Each university student is ar-bitrarily assigned a middle school student to shadow, and at ten-minute intervals they record the behavior of their student and the environment at that time. (In our particular situation, there has been no requirement from the school administration for parental permission to shadow nor from the university's internal research review board to conduct the shadow study; however, these concerns need to be considered when planning this field experience.) After the shadow study, our students assess the behavior of their student as best they can, given the short contact time, in terms of the developmental characteristics (physical, cognitive, social, and emo-tional), using the Student Development Profile (see next page). In the re-flective paper for this first field experience, the students provide evidence from their observations to support their assessment of the behavior of the student and describe how this experience helped them better understand the needs and characteristics of young adolescents.

At any time throughout the rest of the course, on their own time, stu-dents are required to participate in an *extracurricular activity* with young adolescents (not necessarily their shadow study student), for at least 2 to 3 hours. Students are given the key names and phone numbers of people to contact in regard to helping with sports teams, student council, lunchtime tournaments, after-school minicourses, or student activity nights. Students are free to arrange their own activities with their home schools. For this reflective paper, students are to describe the differences they observed between middle school students in a classroom setting and middle school students participating in an extracurricular activity, incor-porating their knowledge of the characteristics of young adolescents. They are also expected to discuss the aspects of this experience that were most significant to them.

Student Development Profile

Observer: _____ Date: _____ Time: _____

Assessment	Evidence
Physical Pre Pub Early Pub Pub Late Pub Adol _____ _____ _____ _____	
Cognitive/Intellectual On Set Con Con On Set Abst Abst _____ _____ _____ _____	
Social Isolate Interactive Highly Interactive _____ _____ _____	
Emotional/Psychological Low Self-Concept Med Self-Concept _____ _____ High Self-Concept _____	

Once students have had a thorough explanation of interdisciplinary team organization with all its aspects and variations (purposes, rationales, schedules, team roles, use of common team planning, flexing the schedule, regrouping students, benefits, etc.), the entire class observes an interdisciplinary team meeting (some students are able to attend two) at our local middle school. Using the Team Meeting Observation Guide, which includes questions to frame the observation (see next page), we basically observe the meeting(s). However, depending on the team and the circumstances, the students are sometimes given the opportunity to ask questions of the team members to gain further information about the team and its functioning. The guidelines for this reflective paper are to analyze the meeting(s) they observed in relation to what they learned in our class about the discussions, topics, and activities that occur during a team meeting, to discuss the aspects of this experience that were most significant to them, and to delineate what their questions, concerns, fears, hopes, and/or aspirations are in regard to working as a team member on an interdisciplinary team.

Team Meeting Observation Guide
(Questions, Observations)

(in no particular order!)

Instructions: Take notes during the observations. These will be used to help you write your reflective paper. (You won't be able to answer all the questions.)

How many team members are there? What subject areas do they represent? What subjects do they teach?

How was the team formed? Who selected the membership?

How was their schedule determined? Is it flexible? If so, how do they flex it?

What is(are) the purpose (s) of the meeting? What specific things do they talk about during a team meeting?

Is there an agenda? How is the agenda determined?

Do they keep minutes? Do they have to report them to someone?

How do they communicate with others: the principal, the counselor, the exploration team, the special education teachers, the media center persons, etc.?

Do they meet with other people during a meeting? Who? How much time do they spend on this? Is it regularly scheduled? How do they arrange for these times?

Is there a team leader? How was he/she determined? What are the other roles on the team?

What are the tasks and responsibilities they share? How do they determine who does what?

What decisions were made? How are decisions made? How do they keep a record of their decisions?

How do they handle differences, conflicts, and feedback in the functioning of their team?

What kinds of things do they do to create a team identity for their students? In what areas are they consistent across the team of students? In what areas have they decided not to be consistent across the team?

What do they feel their accomplishments are as a team? What are they most proud of?

What do they see as their areas of need for growth as a team?

What are the advantages they see to their teaming? The disadvantages?

What were the advantages you saw to their teaming? The disadvantages?

The last field experience, which is conducted near the end of the semester, is an all-day field trip to three different middle schools. Its purpose is to afford the students the opportunity to see various middle schools in urban, suburban, and rural settings "in action." We speak with the principals, teachers, and students of these schools regarding the various aspects of developmentally responsive middle level education. These are not exemplary middle schools but, rather, schools that are trying to become more effective places for learning. We spend about an hour-and-a-half at each school, conversing with the principal and/or teachers for about 45 minutes and then touring the school and conversing with student guides. Our students use the School Visitation Checklist from the *Handbook for Middle School Teaching* as a guide for framing their observations (George, Lawrence, & Bushnell, 1998, p. 235). The guidelines for this reflective paper are much more flexible, allowing the students to reflect and comment on anything at all that is significant to them regarding this experience.

COMMENTARY

Without question, these field experiences are an incredibly important and valuable part of this introductory course. They give reality and practicality to the theory, or, as one student said, they "gave us a much clearer understanding of what we were talking about in class." As with middle school learners, these college students learn better with hands-on activities in which they can actually integrate the ideas they are learning with real life. However, the students also indicated that these experiences would not have been nearly as valuable without writing the reflective papers ("Sometimes I do not realize how much I have learned until I have done the reflection") and without having the time to process the experiences orally with their colleagues ("It was a great help to know that others have the same thoughts and fears about the same things that I have").

REFERENCE

George, P., Lawrence, G., & Bushnell, D. (1998). *Handbook for middle school teaching* (2nd ed.). New York, NY: Longman.

Elementary Setting/Middle Level Focus

CHARLENE JOHNSON
University of Arkansas, Fayetteville

STRATEGY/ACTIVITY/ASSIGNMENT

This field experience is part of an undergraduate introductory middle level principles course, and it takes place in an elementary school setting with fifth- and sixth-grade students. The school has a partnership with the university, and the instructor has served as liaison for this partnership for three years; thus, there is an ongoing relationship among the instructor, the faculty, and the administration. The experience was designed to allow preservice teachers firsthand observation of early adolescents; their differing developmental rates; and their classroom behaviors/interactions with peers, teachers, and learning materials.

Students are assigned to a supervising teacher, usually in groups of four or five depending on the number in the university class. Students spend a minimum of ten hours in the classroom working with the teacher and the students. The purpose is to ensure that preservice teachers have opportunities to observe early adolescents and the instructional process for this group of learners.

A field experience notebook is to be submitted to the instructor at the end of the ten hours with the following items included:

Field notes

Preservice teachers are to maintain a record of their classroom visits and the activities observed. The focus is on early adolescents and the classroom environment—specifically, what middle level instructional practices are employed and students' reactions to these and other classroom practices. References to middle school philosophy and the developmental, curricular, and instructional theories studied should be included. For example: Where are the students in terms of physical, social, intellectual, and emotional development? What middle level practices are observed? How do students react to the instructional process and how do they interact with their peers in class? What effects do these reactions and interactions have on the classroom environment? How do you know these things? Include evidence for your assertions of phenomena noted (i.e., behaviors, interactions, etc.).

Group meeting

The assigned group of preservice teachers for each supervising classroom teacher are to set up meeting times (a minimum of two) in order for all of them to meet and discuss the different activities observed in the classrooms, the relationship of these activities to the course material, and their interpretation and evaluation of the various activities. Reactions and insights from these meetings are to be written and included in the field experience notebook.

Summary of lesson/experience

Preservice teachers are to provide a summary of the classroom environment that describes the students, the instructional unit(s) implemented during the field experience, and the relationships observed. The summary should include the following elements: class demographics (number of students, ethnicities represented, gender distribution); general information concerning development within the class (ages, sizes, social interactions, etc.); objectives of lessons (general, cognitive, affective, socialization, etc.); method(s) of evaluation; and number of student-teacher and student-student interactions.

In addition, the class will visit a middle school in the area. Students are to compare and contrast the middle school environment with that of the elementary school environment in terms of structure, practices, and students.

Student profiles

Each preservice teacher will choose two students, a male and a female, and provide a developmental profile on each. The two students are observed throughout the ten hours of the field experience. The profile includes assessments of the students' physical, emotional, social, and intellectual development based on observations and feedback from the supervising teacher and peers. The preservice teacher is to first give his or her general impressions of the student's developmental stage based on his or her observations and/or interactions with the students. After formulating a perspective, preservice teachers interview the supervising teacher concerning the students' development and discuss his or her reasoning for the assessment of the students.

Additional questions of a more sensitive nature that the preservice teacher would like to ask the students concerning their feelings about the classroom and the instruction received should be provided along with a rationale for the questions. *These questions will not be asked. Reflection:* (The following questions are to be addressed: As a middle-grades teacher, how would you use this information [answers to student questions] for designing and implementing instruction? What classroom practices seemed to work the best for these students? Why? How do you know these practices affected them in a positive manner?)

Formulating questions for the students is part of the reflection and inquiry process. Because of the preservice teachers' inexperience and the fact that they have not received parental permission to question the students, the proposed questions are not asked of the students. Rather, the questions are an indication of the preservice teachers' inquiry skills and talents for gathering student information to inform/benefit their instruction.

The experience has been designed to foster and encourage reflection on practices and perceptions. A major focus of this assignment is that preservice teachers reflect on their perceptions of students and engage in a process of comparing and contrasting those perceptions with different individuals. They are encouraged to form their perceptions about the students first, discuss these perceptions with the teachers, and further discuss their perceptions with their peers.

In addition, cooperating teachers are asked to evaluate the preservice teacher that they supervised on the basis of the degree to which he or she exhibited responsibility, initiative, and professionalism in carrying out the assigned duties. The evaluation is used in determining the student's final grade for the field experience.

COMMENTARY

The preservice teachers consider the field experience one of the highlights of the course. Incidents from their field experiences are shared as they relate to concepts or ideas being studied during class discussions. The discussions are enriched by these experiences when we review how students and classroom practices operate in reality and how they are portrayed in textbooks. Differences between the book and students observed are questioned. This inquiry is always thought-provoking and provides substantive background for a better understanding of the theories.

The teachers' evaluation provides additional reality to the experience. Students have commented that this evaluation has illuminated areas of concern related to responsibility, professionalism, and initiative. As preservice teachers, they reflect on the teachers' perceptions about them in relation to these areas and how they will address these concerns.

Because this experience takes place in a school that has a very diverse student population (low socioeconomic status, 67 percent qualify for free or reduced-price lunch, 12 percent are students of color, and the population is very transient), preservice teachers are also exposed to some of the precepts and ideas regarding how diversity affects early adolescence and its progression. The realities of these sometimes depressing statistics are viewed firsthand, thus providing a better understanding of the reasons behind them.

Logging the Field Experience

WARREN J. DiBIASE
The University of North Carolina at Charlotte

STRATEGY/ACTIVITY/ASSIGNMENT

The methods students complete fifteen hours of clinical or field experience at one or more area middle schools. During this time, the students observe, tutor, co-teach with the support of a clinical instructor or cooperating teacher, or teach a lesson on their own. As part of this experience, the students keep a log describing their participation and observations as well as any insights, questions, or concerns that they may have. The students are asked to pay particular attention to how a number of practices, issues, and strategies discussed in methods class play out in the various classrooms they are observing. To assist them with this task, the students keep a log of their field experience. The log contains a detailed description of the following:

1. Level(s) and grade(s) observed and taught. (The methods students do not provide the name(s) of the teacher(s) they observe.)
2. Physical layout of the classroom(s) (seating arrangement, location of teacher's desk, etc.).
3. Class content and method(s) of instruction (lecture, demonstration, hands-on activity, group work).
   (a) *Subject/topic*—Curriculum area, what was taught?
   (b) *Rationale/purpose*—Why should this material be taught? What is the value to the learner? (Align with district, state, and national standards/goals and objectives.)
   (c) *Objectives*—What did the learners understand or were able to do after the unit was completed?
   (d) *Content*—What major concepts, questions, investigations, or skills were emphasized?
   (e) *Strategies and activities*—What was done for, by, and with the learners in order to achieve the objective(s)?
   (f) *Materials*—A checklist of the items needed for the strategies and activities (include copies of handouts, etc.).
   (g) *Plans for individual differences*—How was the unit adapted to meet the individual needs of various learners in the class?
   (h) *Evaluation*—How was learner progress assessed?
   (i) *Unit critique*—What revision(s) would you implement if you were to use this unit again?
4. Learner interest, motivation, and participation (relate to method of instruction, questioning techniques, etc.).
5. Nature of assignments given.
6. Use of textbook(s), resources, computers, or other learning technologies (laser disc, CD-ROM, etc.).
7. Types of questions asked by the teacher(s) and how the learners responded.
8. Classroom management techniques (discipline, materials management, record keeping, etc.).
9. How the learners were assessed and evaluated.

The methods students usually receive their clinical placements during the third week of the semester. Most of them have logged a handful of hours at their respective schools by the end of the fourth week. From this point on, considerable class time is allotted for the students to share and discuss their observations and perceptions as well as the connections they see between theory and practice. Most of the initial discussions are instructor-initiated and take place at the beginning of each class. It does not take long, however, for students to come to class eager to share an experience and spontaneously initiate the discussion. In addition, a discussion is oftentimes sparked by a class activity or a comment made or question asked in class.

COMMENTARY

This class is the sole methods course, and it is generally taken the semester prior to student teaching. Although the students have completed a number of clinicals or field experiences as part of other classes in their professional sequence, the methods course marks the first time the students are asked to keep a log and critically reflect on teaching and learning in such an in-depth manner. When the particulars of the log are first presented, the students are confused and concerned over what seems to be an arduous task. When writing their first few entries, the students are more concerned with recording what they believe the instructor wants to see. This perception changes when students realize that their log entries function as field notes, forming the basis for both critical reflection and class discussions.

A four-point rubric is used to assess the log. Point values are based on the following criteria: 4 points—the student has provided a complete, detailed description of the field experience, addressing all nine major areas; 3 points—the student has provided a detailed description, addressing a majority of the nine major areas; 2 points—the student has described the field experience, including no more than five of the nine major areas; 1 point—the student has described the field experience, including fewer than five of the major nine areas.

The clinical or field experience is perhaps one of the most valuable experiences of any methods class because it usually marks the first time the students perceive what happens in a classroom from a teacher's perspective. Also, it is during this time that the methods students begin to make connections between content knowledge, content pedagogical knowledge, and the realities of the classroom. It is also at this point that the students are in the initial stages of crafting their teaching style and formalizing perceptions of teaching and learning.

Preservice Field Experiences at Old Dominion University

LEE MANNING
Old Dominion University, Norfolk, VA

STRATEGY/ACTIVITY/ASSIGNMENT

Prospective middle level educators at Old Dominion University in Norfolk, VA, participate in preservice field experiences designed to provide firsthand perspectives of young adolescents and essential middle level school concepts. The students and instructor in this field experience meet twice weekly for a total of four hours. The major areas of emphasis are: working with young adolescents, teaming with another preservice middle level educator, working with seasoned professionals on an interdisciplinary team, and gaining experience in a middle level school that is committed to essential middle level school concepts.

Prior to placing students, university personnel evaluate each school to determine its commitment to middle school concepts—mainly, the extent to which it has adopted the characteristics espoused in *This We Believe* (National Middle School Association, 1995) and the recommendations proposed in *Turning Points* (Carnegie Council on Adolescent Development, 1989). If the school is not taking an active stance to achieve characteristics such as "adult advocates for all young adolescents," "positive school climate," "comprehensive guidance services," "flexible organization structures," "communities of learning," "reengaging families," and "connecting schools with communities" (just to name a few representative examples from *This We Believe* and *Turning Points*), university personnel withdraw their request to place students at the school. Without exception, to this point, the district has agreed to placement requests.

All prospective middle level educators in the practicum select a team member (e.g., another student in the practicum) with similar subject matter expertise (e.g., mathematics and science) and with a similar grade-level interest. Other requirements for these preservice middle level educators during their eight-week field experience include:

1. Serving as a functional member of an interdisciplinary team and learning collaborative techniques required in effective teams, e.g., using appropriate communication and cooperation between

and among teachers, administrators, and other school staff. Each prospective middle level teacher is evaluated by her or his preservice team member, other members of the interdisciplinary team, and the team leader to determine whether she or he has the motivation and ability to work as an effective team member.

2. Diagnosing, prescribing, planning, implementing, and evaluating developmentally responsive instruction that is based, whenever possible, on young adolescents' actual physical, psychosocial, and cognitive developmental characteristics. Prior to beginning their school placements, prospective middle level educators learn about young adolescents' physical, psychosocial, and cognitive developmental characteristics. They also practice writing lesson plans and designing specific educational experiences that reflect developmental characteristics. During the field experience, the students and university supervisors insist on educational experiences that reflect young adolescent development (e.g., providing different physical activities for early and late maturers; allowing friends and peers to socialize during small-group learning activities; and providing higher-level thinking experiences for formal operational thinkers and concrete educational experiences for learners in the concrete operational stage).

3. Teaching a minimum of four lessons using a variety of effective instructional strategies and organizational patterns; being evaluated during each lesson by a middle level educator (or more than one) on the interdisciplinary team.

4. Developing, evaluating, and adapting instructional materials and technology to young adolescents' developmental needs.

5. Teaching a minimum of one lesson for a university supervisor to observe.

6. Videotaping three teaching lessons for self-evaluation, using a detailed teaching evaluation instrument as well as critique from the university supervisor.

7. Evaluating the teaching of the other practicum student on the interdisciplinary team using a "peer-observation" instrument.

8. Maintaining a journal that focuses on two major aspects. First, this daily journal focuses on young adolescents' physical, psychosocial, and cognitive developmental characteristics, and cultural and gender diversity. The preservice middle level educators are provided with a detailed observation guide of young adolescent characteristics and behaviors to observe. Second, in their

journals, the prospective teachers look for and offer comments on specific middle level concepts such as integrated curriculum, advisor-advisee programs, exploratory programs, interdisciplinary teaming, positive school climates, and other recommendations put forth in *This We Believe: Developmentally Responsive Middle Level Schools* (National Middle School Association, 1995) and *Turning Points: Preparing American Youth for the 21st Century* (Carnegie Council on Adolescent Development, 1989).

COMMENTARY

The preservice field experience for middle level educators at Old Dominion University has sought to take advantage of actual experiences with young adolescents and seasoned middle level professionals. Both prospective teachers, members of their interdisciplinary teams, and their university coordinators see a difference in professional training as well as attitudes toward middle level teaching as a profession as a result of the experiences.

Satisfaction with the middle level field experience has been high. Prospective educators finishing this field experience feel well versed in young adolescent development and middle level school concepts and philosophical beliefs. They feel "middle level trained" because their field experience included interactions in an actual middle school and with educators genuinely committed to middle level concepts. Most participants have offered positive comments such as feeling prepared to teach at the middle level, feeling more positive about teaching young adolescents, and feeling secure and comfortable working on an interdisciplinary team. Approximately 10 percent of the approximately 300 students who have taken part have indicated a desire to teach at another school level. Reasons included wanting to teach younger or older students, disagreeing with the middle school philosophy, and feeling uncomfortable with advisor-advisee programs. Overall, however, the middle level field experience has received high ratings by both prospective and inservice teachers.

REFERENCES

Carnegie Council on Adolescent Development. (1989). *Turning points: Preparing American youth for the 21st century*. Washington, DC: Author.

National Middle School Association. (1995). *This we believe: Developmentally responsive middle level schools*. Columbus, OH: Author.

Program Development Plans

SAUNDRA BRYN
Arizona State University West, Phoenix

STRATEGY/ACTIVITY/ASSIGNMENT

What are program development plans?

Program development plans are an opportunity for undergraduate and graduate students enrolled in Middle School Curriculum and Organization to develop plans to address the implementation of various aspects of a middle level program. These plans, developed in collaboration with practicing teachers/administrators for an actual middle level program, are designed for implementation at a local school. Depending on the needs of the school, the focus of the plans varies from school to school.

Major objectives:
1. The students will plan the implementation of a middle level program that is congruent with the middle level characteristics and components addressed in *This We Believe* (1995) and *Turning Points* (1989).
2. The students will operate as a team.

What is the process for the program development plans?
1. The instructor contacts an administrator and/or teacher at a local school to determine the receptivity to collaborating with university students to develop or expand a program area identified by the school. In the past, the program areas have ranged from developing an advisory program or a student success (student prep) program to planning a family involvement program or investigating the implementation of looping.
2. The instructor then secures the commitment from the school faculty in regard to:
   (a) hosting a site visit for the students;
   (b) attending at least two university class meetings, one to establish the parameters for the project and one to serve as an audience for the presentation of the final project; and
   (c) serving as a resource for the students, answering their questions, providing direction, and giving feedback on the draft of the project.

3. The instructor provides directions to the students, supplying models as well as criteria for evaluation. The criteria includes the following:
   - The plan is appropriate for the developmental needs of early adolescents.
   - The plan reflects research-based best practices for middle level programs.
   - The plan is consistent with the needs of the school's middle level program.
   - The plan contains a statement of purpose consistent with the mission statement of the school, a program rationale appropriate for teachers, parents, students, and administrators; program outcomes and measurements as well as activities to support the achievement of the outcomes; an overview of the program organization; the role and functions of the stakeholders; and plans for a "feedback loop" to facilitate monitoring and evaluation of the program.
   - The plan may include scheduling information and resource documents and/or citations.
   - The plan follows format specifications and is mechanically error-free.

4. Students indicate their preferences in regard to (a) the classmates they wish to work with as team members and (2) their choice regarding the project assignment.

5. The instructor assigns teams and projects.

6. As a class, students visit the school site and obtain information from the school staff about the community, student population, and school setting.

7. Working as a team, students research the critical attributes of their program, consult with school staff to ensure congruency with their direction and parameters, then draft the plans for the program. All the program plans share similarities, but the specifics of the program also dictate differences in the content of the plans.

8. Each team obtains feedback on their draft from another team, school staff, and the instructor.

9. Teams revise their plans on the basis of the feedback given and determine which sections of the final document should be presented to class members. The school staff receives one complete copy. Teams provide the instructor with the final copy prior to the presentation session.

10. Teams present their findings and their plan to the class and to members of the school staff.

COMMENTARY

One student commented in the end-of-course reflections: "I think that students often forget the professional aspects in education. I may be way off, but I believe many students are more interested in learning cute ways to teach a lesson and forget the 'other stuff' in education. This project forces students to examine the needs of the middle level student and develop a structural framework for the learning process. . . . It was great to create a program for an actual school and not a fictitious one."

As indicated by the comments of the student above, this semester-long activity provides an excellent opportunity for students to gain a thorough understanding of how to develop a program that is congruent with effective middle level practices. While students have developed many different programs (health and wellness, service learning, advisory, student success, looping, accommodations for special education students in regular classes), those most commonly requested by the schools are the advisory program and the family involvement program.

Students are extremely enthusiastic about the activity, and they constantly express their appreciation vis-à-vis its relevance. As one student said in her end-of-course reflections, "Most of the time we are asked to write lengthy research papers in our classes, knowing that they will then be shelved and never used again. . . . The opportunity to actually develop programs for a real school was an incredible experience."

School staff appreciate the assistance in program development. Teachers often express their frustration with wanting to develop a program but feeling that they don't have the time to do it well. One team leader related that a teacher had said, "You mean, they [the university students] will research and develop the program to fit what we need?" After one set of presentations, which was attended by both school staff and the district superintendent, a teacher requested that the university students present their plan to the entire school staff during a staff development day. Moreover, the superintendent requested that the students present the plan to the district governing board. One of the students in the group reflected: "I absolutely loved working on the Student Success piece for the program development plan because I really believed in the program we designed. I had fun working with my partners, designing the curriculum, and making the PowerPoint presentation. The icing on the cake was that we were asked as a group to present this to the governing board for the school. It felt really good to be recognized by the superintendent when I have never even taught before."

While the benefits to both the school and to the university students are rather obvious, another major benefit occurs in the word-of-mouth praise generated by the project. Teachers talk with one another, and their good words prompt volunteers for school sites to surface. Students talk with one another, too, and their good words prompt other students to enroll in the course.

Still, inconveniences do occur. In one instance, several parents from the school indicated great interest in assisting the students but did not follow through with their commitment. Another time, the school staff's vision did not include the most current knowledge of best practices, and the university students had to learn tactful ways of guiding the teachers. Still another time, the staff's vision for the product conflicted with the instructor's vision, and the instructor had to modify her expectations. None of these problems was insurmountable.

One student summarized many students' feelings about the project:

> The Program Development Project was a true learning experience. It provided useful information about the parts of a developmental program as well as what is involved in setting up such a program. The four programs . . . gave a useful framework for developing a successful middle school. It required a great deal of research and group work. It also allowed for creativity which made it more interesting. I was relieved when you told us it was fine if our program did not follow the outline you gave us exactly. I was also glad when you required only the first section to have the same voice. Thanks for being flexible.

Contrasting Middle Level Settings

CHARLENE JOHNSON
University of Arkansas, Fayetteville

STRATEGY/ACTIVITY/ASSIGNMENT

In my undergraduate middle level principles and methods class, the point is made that the middle level is not a building or a schedule but a philosophy about early adolescents and their unique developmental needs.

Based on this belief, effective middle level practices are designed to meet the needs of this age group appropriately. To exemplify this principle and examine its significance for educating early adolescents, comparisons are made between an elementary setting (fifth and sixth grades) where the university class is held and local middle level schools that are visited during the semester.

The methods course meets in a room within the school that is designated for university classes. As a class, we are enmeshed in the school milieu and experience many of the nuances of a school day, e.g., fire drills, public address announcements, public school students, etc. These experiences contribute to the authentic learning espoused for field-based classes by introducing preservice teachers to many of the realities of a school day. The two fifth- and sixth-grade classes within the school are used for the twelve-hour field experience requirement for the class. Preservice teachers are assigned to a class with the classroom teacher as their supervisor. They interact with the students (i.e., tutor, work with a reading or math group, assist with a lesson, etc.), as designated by the supervisor, and complete course assignments based on these interactions. Another assignment for the field experience—not directly related to interactions in the class—is to compare the elementary school to a local middle school that is visited during the semester.

Area middle level schools are visited to highlight differences between the middle level setting and that of the elementary school. These setting differences are examined for their implications for effective instruction at this age. Two visits to middle level schools are arranged with one-half of the class visiting each of the sites. A tour is arranged with the principal of the school, and it takes place when classes are in session. The principal and/or a designated guide from the school conducts a tour of the following: the team pods, media room, health facilities, cafeteria, physical education facilities, and other areas of interest. Faculty and students address the questions of the preservice teachers. The students are usually observed while engaged in some type of physical activity, e.g., physical education class, intramural sports, etc.

A major emphasis of the visits is how the facilities differ in regards to teaming, health concerns, physical education, and other areas in which early adolescents interact (e.g., the cafeteria). There is no formal observational instrument provided. Preservice teachers are encouraged to take notes during and after the tour to help them remember any specifics that they wish to remember. The school often provides literature on the school regarding its mission statement, student body, and when the building was built.

COMMENTARY

Initially, students resist taking a class that is held at a school because of the distance from the university campus and the inconvenience this causes. But as the semester proceeds and they are enmeshed in the school milieu, students recognize the value of their experiences in this environment. As a result of being in such an environment, our discussions are often engaging and thought-provoking in their combination of theory and practice as they center around the realities of the educational experience.

Observational experiences are often shared during class discussions, and similarities and differences in settings, materials, and instructional approaches are noted. Preservice teachers are often amazed at the differences between the two settings (elementary and middle level), including the faculties, resources, and facilities. How middle level practices are operationalized in the two settings are examined for their effectiveness and developmental appropriateness. Preservice teachers often note that although the elementary school teachers are very effective in recognizing the developmental uniqueness of this age and making accommodations for it within the classroom/building, the middle school—by its design—seems most relevant for early adolescent needs.

Preservice teachers have also noted the differences in provisions between the middle schools that are in more affluent neighborhoods and those available at the elementary school that is in one of the lowest socioeconomic areas of the district. Many comment that they will be more aware of these conditions in the future and also express a desire/commitment to address them as educators. The discussions concerning these field experiences and their relationship to the material being studied often refer to middle level precepts, societal concerns, how the two converge in schools, and their implications for the educational experiences of early adolescents.

Exploring Early Adolescence Through Observational Research

DAVID K. PUGALEE
University of North Carolina at Charlotte

STRATEGY/ACTIVITY/ASSIGNMENT

This activity is part of the "Adolescent Learner" course, which focuses on adolescent development and learning. The course includes a field component designed to familiarize the preservice middle level educator with the early adolescents' learning environment. It was developed to provide a structured experience for the student as he or she begins to consider the complexity of early adolescent development, particularly how various factors affect student learning. The activity involves conducting some basic qualitative research as part of a ten-hour minimum observation.

First, some class time must be devoted to providing students with some essential information relative to conducting observational research. This is imperative in order to ensure that the experience involves some type of systematic process for observing, instead of simply "visiting" a school site for ten hours. We begin with characteristics of good observations adapted from Best and Kahn (1993). Some of these characteristics include:

- carefully planned, systematic, and perceptive observations
- awareness of the wholeness of what is observed (holistic perspectives)
- objectivity through the recognition of personal biases
- separation of fact from interpretation
- verification through repetition and comparison
- carefully recorded notes

We then spend some time discussing field notes. Students are presented with the advantages of dividing their paper into two columns, so that a space of approximately two inches is left for follow-up notes and notes made during analysis. This space provides students with room to make comments as they begin searching for patterns and relationships as they analyze their data. We also spend time discussing how the notes should reflect a detailed account of the behaviors, events, and the contexts of the targeted students. We do a short, five-minute practice session of taking field notes by viewing a videotape of a classroom episode taken from an actual classroom lesson. Emerging themes and patterns provide a beginning point for developing a characterization of the early adolescent experience. This provides students with an opportunity to see how important detailed notes are in the interpretation of data. This process acquaints the students with how homogeneity and heterogeneity of data are utilized in the analysis of narrative observational data. Students analyze their notes several times, classifying and categorizing data based on similar themes and ideas (homogeneity) as well as noticeable differences (heterogeneity).

Students complete their observations midway through the course. Schools used as observation sites are part of a collaborative university-school partnership. One of the benefits of the partnerships for the university is the availability of field sites for extended clinical experiences, including student teaching. School administrators, teachers, and university faculty work together to structure productive clinical experiences that will prepare them for student teaching. With the observations scheduled midway through the semester, there is class time to develop a framework for the study of adolescence. This framework is developed by studying the interrelationship of variables in five domains: biological/physical, psychological, social, cultural, and cognitive. These domains provide a focus for the observations the students complete in the schools. When students are in the schools doing their observations, they focus on two or three students. If logistics permit, the observations involve the same students throughout a typical school day. In situations in which scheduling problems arise, the observations are done in the same classroom for an entire day, but may focus on a different group of students for one or more classes. Detailed notes of the events and behaviors of these students are collected and analyzed. During the observations and analysis of the resulting data, particular attention is given to factors in the five domains of development that we have been studying. Once students complete their observations and analysis, they write a brief (approximately three pages) synopsis of their findings.

COMMENTARY

This assignment accounts for 25 percent of the student's grade. That said, it is difficult to put a score on this experience. The quality of the notes and evidence of a concerted effort to analyze and understand the data is taken into consideration in determining the quality of the work. I average all other grades for this course before considering this project. Typically, the quality of the student's project is in line with the average of his or her other grades. When this occurs, I can look at the observation experience without being forced to reduce it to a numerical grade. This process of grading generally works for the majority of my students.

This activity provides preservice teachers with an opportunity that emphasizes the complexity of the early adolescent experience and the multifaceted nature of the school experience. It also gives students an opportunity to develop systematic approaches to observing students and events. Such experiences are important in light of the emphasis on action research and reflection as key factors in the professional development of teachers.

Students find this experience valuable to their growing knowledge of teaching and learning, particularly as they relate to the multifaceted needs of the early adolescent. One student commented that she learned a lot as a result of this clinical. She went on to add that she wished she "could have helped Mr. J_____ see the goodness in R_____." In these comments, she demonstrates an understanding of the importance of teacher and student perceptions. Several students come from the experience seeing how teacher behaviors affect students. This leads some students to the conclusion that "I'm not going to teach like that." The majority of the students come to a realization that being an early adolescent is a complex experience.

Further, schools involved in the observations are composed of diverse student populations. Since some of our students come to us from relatively homogeneous school experiences, this activity gives them an opportunity to interact with students from diverse backgrounds. Because of this clinical experience, several students expressed a need to broaden their multicultural perspectives. There has not been a student who did not demonstrate enriched insight as a result of this experience. The experience is invaluable for providing students with a context for information gleaned from class and for broadening their understanding of the issues and experiences of early adolescence.

REFERENCE

Best, J. W., & Kahn, J. V. (1993). *Research in education.* Needham Heights, MA: Allyn and Bacon.

Field-Based Investigation of Some Aspect of Middle Level Education

SAMUEL TOTTEN
University of Arkansas, Fayetteville

STRATEGY/ACTIVITY/ASSIGNMENT

In both my undergraduate and graduate "Middle Level Methods and Principles" courses, I have the students develop and complete a major field-based project on some aspect/component of middle level education. Each student or team (which must be limited to three people) is required to complete a project in which he/she/they examine a key aspect of middle level education that has been implemented in a local middle school (*Note:* A list of local exemplary middle level programs/schools is provided to the students.)

The philosophy, theory, and research on middle level education and on the specific component under study must be used to frame the project. Thus, they must cite key research to corroborate their assertions and findings.

The students may approach and complete the project in several ways. For example, they can develop observation guides, conduct observations, and then analyze the data collected; develop, conduct, and analyze surveys; take and analyze photographs of students engaged in different activities or programs, e.g., advisor/advisee, exploratory, on the playground; collect and analyze key documents, such as school-developed plans, school board minutes, steering committee minutes, etc. To complete the project, some students may elect to pursue a combination of these and/or other approaches. Results must be written up in a paper.

To help frame the project, it is suggested that students consider setting their paper up in the following manner: (1) the rationale for selecting the topic under study; (2) a succinct but thorough discussion of the topic; (3) the theory and research vis-à-vis the middle level topic under study; (4) the process(es) used to conduct the study; (5) the major findings of the project; and (6) the most valuable insights gleaned from the study, and a discussion as to why they were so important. Key documents, tools, and other artifacts collected during the course of the project may be included in the report under a separate series of appendices.

Students are informed that a good starting place to locate information on theory and research related to a specific issue is the journal, *Re-*

search in Middle Level Education, and the book, *Middle Level Education: An Annotated Bibliography,* by Totten, Briegel, Barta, Digby, and Nielsen (Westport, CT: Greenwood Press, 1996).

If a team of two or three people is formed to carry out the project, then a separate section in the paper should detail what each person did to assist in the development and completion of the project. This must be composed of two distinct parts: (1) a detailed and personal statement of each person's contribution, which must focus, in part, on the quality and quantity of effort, thought, and creativity that he or she contributed to the project; and (2) a detailed comment by each person regarding the effort, thought, and creativity that each of the other individual(s) put into the development and implementation of the project. The latter should identify each person by name and then provide the details. This process serves as a check and balance concerning individual effort. If a group member has not carried his or her weight, then that will be reflected in this report. Prior to the start of the project, the students are informed that if a problem appears at any stage of the process regarding another individual's participation, then the concerned team members ought to consult with the professor so that it can be addressed as soon as possible. Each team member will receive the same grade as all the other team members *unless* a team member is totally remiss and contributes little during the course of the project.

The actual body of the paper is generally about ten to twelve typed pages. The accompanying documents (e.g., copies of the surveys, interviews, photographs) and the documentation regarding team effort are in addition to the aforementioned 10 to 12 pages.

COMMENTARY

This project moves the study of the middle level from written materials in a university classroom to the real world of the middle school that is peopled by students, teachers, administrators, counselors, parents, and other key players. It also enables the university student to see the middle level component they are studying "up close," thus providing them with a view that they could not get from afar.

Most of the students find the project to be a great deal of work. Those, however, who "really get into" the project, walk away with a feeling of pride in their newfound knowledge and expertise. Many undergraduates comment that as a result of the field-based work they feel more comfortable about the prospect of teaching in a middle level program.

Concomitantly, many comment that they feel much more confident about interviewing for such a position because of the in-depth knowledge they have acquired of various facets of middle level education.

Parent-Teacher Conferences to Build Confidence

MARY L. SNYDER
Central Missouri State University, Warrensburg

STRATEGY/ACTIVITY/ASSIGNMENT

In order to reduce the anxiety novice teachers face in conferencing with parents, instructors work collaboratively with area Parent Teacher Associations (PTA) to host an evening of "mock" parent-teacher conferences.

Once a semester, preservice teachers enrolled in elementary or middle school methods classes convene at a designated school to have scheduled conferences with parent volunteers. The local PTA organizes the parents, room arrangements, and refreshments, and the university is responsible for making initial contacts with PTA leaders in the chosen community, establishing conference schedules, creating scenarios, and assessing evaluations of preservice teachers.

Several days before the conference, preservice teachers and parents receive short scenarios providing some information concerning their shared "student." However, the scenarios vary slightly, so that the teachers know some things about the child that the parent isn't aware of (perhaps of a troubling behavior or of performance difficulties in an academic area), while the parent has information to which the teacher isn't privy. This, of course, makes the conference interesting and realistic.

On conference night, a brief meeting is held for parents before they meet with the preservice teachers. At that time, university faculty explain the parents' roles, encouraging them to do some role playing, such as asking difficult questions or being somewhat defensive, but not to the point where they won't work with the teachers.

Each conference lasts between 10 to 15 minutes, and preservice teachers work in pairs, participating in one conference, then observing a peer in the second. Each parent is asked to "attend" two conferences and is provided background information on two different children.

The parent rates the preservice teacher on his or her performance at the end of the conference.

COMMENTARY

At the end of the evening, preservice teachers and parents meet as a group to share feedback on their experiences. Students' reflective journals and follow-up class discussion indicate that preservice teachers find this activity very valuable in providing them with a better understanding of the kind of dynamics involved in parent-teacher conferences. This activity has provided a means for parents to contribute input on how future teachers are prepared. This, in turn, strengthens the university's relationship with the community and provides insight for preservice teachers and university faculty on current issues in area schools. This has served as a positive experience for all who participate.

Field Preparation for Successful Student Teaching

MARY L. SNYDER
Central Missouri State University, Warrensburg

STRATEGY/ACTIVITY/ASSIGNMENT

As a result of a Professional Development School (PDS) partnership, my middle school strategies course is held on-site at the local middle school. Students enroll in this class the semester immediately prior to the student-teaching semester. Working with the building principal, an attempt is made to pair each preservice student with a teacher in the same content area. Each student is responsible for a minimum of 25 hours of observation with the assigned teacher and is encouraged to visit the school during various times in order to experience a wide range of activities. The student will then student-teach with the same teacher the following semester. This arrangement has obvious benefits for the student teacher, as he or she becomes familiar with the teacher, routines, students, physical layout of room and building, and social climate of the school before starting the student-teaching semester.

Several assignments and outcomes are related to this two-semester sequence. Highlighted here are some of the components of the field experiences that occur during the first semester, or what we term the "internship."

Field trip: Although this class is site-based, one or two days per semester are spent visiting other middle level schools that reflect different philosophies than those found in our regular PDS location. This is an opportunity for interns to observe that there are differences in school climate and culture among schools.

Unit: Interns work in teams to prepare an integrated unit based on an authentic document dating from 1900 or before. I have two reasons for using authentic documents. First, it allows middle level students to make personal connections to people and events through materials from the last century (Massich & Munoz, 1996), and, second, it obligates the university student to conduct some research and build a lesson from "scratch" instead of using prepackaged materials. This requires the teams to determine a history-based unit that has relevance for today's students. Working with the classroom teachers' cooperation and approval, the team members develop the unit and then teach part of it to the class in which they're interning. Each group provides a copy of its unit (complete with bibliography) to other class members.

Legacy: Interns work as a group in surveying stakeholders to determine and establish a "legacy" based on the perceived interests and/or needs of the students, faculty, parents, or administration of the PDS site. One semester, interns worked with middle level students in planting hundreds of red and white tulips at the newly built school, and the next semester birdhouses were built for outdoor classroom study. Other possibilities include organizing a science fair, starting an ecology club, or creating a time capsule. This experience provides opportunities for students to organize and work together as a group in order to accomplish a common goal.

Classroom/student teachers: Approximately once a week a classroom teacher volunteers to spend 20 to 30 minutes with the interns at the beginning of our class in order to discuss and field questions on a variety of topics (teaming, counseling services, technology, transition activities, etc.). Their visits are scheduled ahead of time and topics are taken from the course syllabus, so there is a close relationship between theory and application. Student teachers (who interned in the building the previous semester) also meet with the interns throughout the semester to share their experiences.

COMMENTARY

The interning experience has led to strong, more confident student teachers. Interns are introduced to many of the teachers in the building, observe middle level students in a variety of settings, and realize that schools vary in their interpretation of "the middle school philosophy." Interns also gain a sense of the give and take needed for successful teaming through their units and legacy project. The school and the community see the value of having interns in the building because of the interactions with middle level students and the legacy they leave behind. Too often field experiences are perceived as being beneficial only to the university. The legacy is one way of expressing our thanks to the PDS site.

REFERENCE

Massich, M., & Munoz, E. (1996). Utilizing primary sources as building blocks for literacy. *Social Studies Review, 36,* (1), 52-57.

Hands-On Experience for Preservice Teachers in Middle Level Education Courses

HAROLD L. SORKNES
Northern State University, Aberdeen, SD

STRATEGY/ACTIVITY/ASSIGNMENT

This past semester, the students in my "Middle Level Issues" course were able to participate in a "Directed Study Program" class at a local middle school. The principal at the middle school was looking for tutors to assist students with their homework assignments, study skills, test reviews, etc. I had been looking for an opportunity to place university students in a middle level setting so they could observe and work with students of this age. I felt this was especially important in our teacher education program since our students major in either elementary education or secondary education. As a result, they do their Junior Field experience and their student-teaching experience at one of those two levels. Elementary majors are always placed in a K-6 school, and even though some of our secondary majors do get placed in a junior high setting, the majority of our secondary student teachers are placed in a senior high setting and end up teaching only in grades 9–12. As a result, it is possible for our teachers to graduate from our program, have a middle level endorsement (based on the coursework taken), but not actually have taught in a middle level program. In our program at the present time there is not a field experience required for the middle level endorsement. Our graduates often get jobs that involve teaching seventh or eighth grade students, and because they do not have actual teaching experience at this grade level, they do not feel as well prepared as they would like to be. Preservice teachers have expressed concern about this situation and I, too, felt that this was an important issue that needed to be addressed.

The opportunity to tutor seemed to be one possible solution. Students enrolled in the "Middle Level Issues" course this past semester (Fall, 1997) were very receptive to this assignment. Student reactions following their first visits were extremely positive. Several students indicated that they were enjoying it so much that they planned to put in additional time with extra visits. Needless to say, the teachers at the middle school did not object! Our preservice teachers were getting an opportunity to see "real, live middle-schoolers." The list of characteristics of students of that age level that I had provided during our first class session became quite apparent as our preservice teachers observed and worked with these students.

Students kept a journal of their experiences and observations during their twelve visits to the middle school. Based on the journal entries it was apparent to me that the preservice teachers saw the types of things we had discussed in class—the range of differences in physical appearance, the swings from mature to immature behavior, the social aspects of middle school students' lives, student reactions to various teaching strategies, and so forth. The preservice teachers were able to observe students' reactions to a "barrage" of worksheets, for instance. Preservice teachers were also able to observe some students' lack of organizational skills, lack of study skills, and lack of skill in the basics. Being able to work with students on a one-to-one basis allowed preservice teachers to experience the satisfaction of helping students achieve success. That was an important aspect of this assignment as evidenced by their journal entries.

COMMENTARY

A concern that I had with regard to preservice teachers was whether they would be able to make an "informed decision" about whether they would like to teach, or even wanted to teach, at the middle level. Based on the comments from student journals, this assignment helped students decide about middle level teaching. Some students indicated that they had always thought they would like to teach at the middle level and this experience affirmed that feeling. Other students indicated that they were not sure they wanted to teach middle level students, but after this experience they changed their mind. They actually preferred teaching at this level. I was pleased with this reaction! I thought this was an extremely valuable benefit of this assignment.

All of the students who were enrolled in the issues class during fall semester and were enrolled in the methods class during the spring semester indicated that they wanted to be involved in the tutoring program again. Since they were not yet in student teaching, scheduling was not a problem. Having university students actually look forward to an assignment is a novelty! Based on the preservice teacher suggestions, and with the approval of the middle school administration and teachers, I am going to have the students who were involved in the tutoring program in the fall semester do a few additional activities during their visits in the spring semester. One assignment they will have, for instance, is to make a presentation to the "Directed Study" class of middle level students on study skills, test-taking skills, note-taking skills, or another suitable topic. Another assignment for the "returning" preservice teachers is to observe middle level teachers in their particular content area.

I believe that these assignments will benefit our preservice teachers in several ways. First, it will give them an opportunity to work with middle level students and teachers before they do their student teaching (or their Junior Field experience). Second, if they don't have the opportunity to do either their Junior Field experience or student teaching at this grade level, they will at least have had the chance to work with middle level students. When they begin their search for a teaching position, they will feel more confident in applying and interviewing for teaching jobs in a middle level setting.

Project Co-Teach

TONI SILLS-BRIEGEL
Southwest Missouri State University, Springfield

STRATEGY/ACTIVITY/ASSIGNMENT

Area teachers are very agreeable to opening their classes to our preservice teachers for observational purposes and, to some extent, providing opportunities to work with middle school students during on-going lessons. Project Co-Teach endeavored to take the interaction between teacher and professor one step further. Exemplary middle level teams from area schools were invited to function as co-lecturers in the middle school program. Teams were specifically invited to assist in the development and co-teaching of the new course, "The Middle School Teacher" (MID 539), and to provide instructional assistance in other middle level courses. MID 539 is generally designed to be an investigation of the roles and responsibilities of middle school teachers. Preservice teachers assess their personal attributes and abilities as they relate to quality middle level teaching, then strive to develop an awareness of the ways in which teachers and students communicate in middle level classes. This course is taken immediately prior to student teaching.

In other middle level courses, select middle school team members provide opportunities for preservice teachers to observe their classes, serve as discussion leaders, and act as resources for a variety of activities. They also allow themselves to be videotaped with the understanding that the tapes would be used in future college lecture classes.

Evaluation forms from graduates of education programs consistently contain phrases such as: "More preservice experiences," and "Student teaching was the most valuable course I took." To meet this documented need, MID 539 was designed as a part of Project Co-Teach to be a field-based course for middle level preservice teachers. MID 539 students were assigned to middle school teams in order to acquire on-site experiences that would generate questions and enable participants to gain an understanding of effective middle school strategies. The observation experience was taken a step further by creating an interactive, interdisciplinary seminar series co-led by the university professor and the cooperating middle level teams.

The purposes of Project Co-Teach were many. First, of paramount importance was the provision of an intense interactive learning experience for middle level certification students before they enter into the schools as student teachers. Second, was the offer to practicing educators in area middle schools to acquire university teaching experience and to be recognized as an important and respected link in the educational process of preparing our nation's teachers. Third, was the opportunity for the university professor to create and maintain a network of exceptional middle school teachers as co-instructors and resource people for the future. Fourth, was to pilot a program to be used as a model for other faculty in the college of education as more collaborative activities are encouraged among public school and university educators.

Area middle school interdisciplinary teams were identified as models of exemplary practices in middle level education. These core teams included subject area specialists (normally mathematics, science, language arts, and social studies). Exemplary teams were identified through recommendation by the school principal, college student recommendations (based on observations from previous field experiences), and/or peer teacher recommendations. Teams were selected from different schools, different grade levels, and different school districts.

COMMENTARY

At the end of the semester, a 10-item survey was administered to the cooperating middle school teachers (see below). On a five-point scale, with five being most positive, all responses averaged above 4.47. Eight responses scored above 4.67, and four responses averaged above 4.86. Forty-four preservice teachers were involved in the program. MID 539 students placed on-site in the middle school teams were effusive in their comments about the program, rating this experience during class discussions as one of the best. Previous concerns about readiness for student teaching were eased and they declared their eagerness to return to the classroom on an extended basis. Students in philosophy and methods courses voiced their appreciation for the co-teacher presentations in their comments on the teacher evaluation forms filled out at the end of class.

Eventually, it is our intention that exemplary classroom teachers in the region will be identified in every certification area and invited to serve as co-lecturers. Project Co-Teach has proven its worth in providing preservice teachers with on-site experiences while providing an inexpensive way to bring practicing teachers into the college classroom.

End of Project Survey/Co-Teach
Classroom Teachers

	Strongly Agree			Strongly Disagree		n = 15
1. I thought Project Co-Teach was a success.	5	4	3	2	1	4.50
2. I believe that public schools and universities should form partnerships to help educate preservice teachers.	5	4	3	2	1	4.87
3. I would like my school to be a part of a continuing school/university partnership in some manner.	5	4	3	2	1	4.73
4. I think Project Co-Teach was a positive professional experience for me personally.	5	4	3	2	1	4.67
5. I felt I contributed to the education of preservice and serving teachers.	5	4	3	2	1	4.67
6. I felt my team's presentations in middle school courses were informative and useful to preservice students.	5	4	3	2	1	4.86
7. I felt I was treated as a respected partner in the education of future teachers by the professor.	5	4	3	2	1	4.94
8. Middle school preservice teachers should spend time observing and working with a middle school team before their student-teaching experience.	5	4	3	2	1	4.87
9. I provided my MID-539 student with a variety of valuable classroom experiences.	5	4	3	2	1	4.47
10. I was pleased with the quality of the preservice teacher assigned to my team.	5	4	3	2	1	4.67

A Field Experience for Preservice Middle Level Teachers

LAURA C. STOKES
University of North Alabama, Florence

JOE W. WILSON
University of North Alabama, Florence

STRATEGY/ACTIVITY/ASSIGNMENT

At the University of North Alabama, field experiences for future middle level teachers provide an opportunity to strengthen pedagogical skills while gaining insights into young adolescent students and the community in which they reside. Upper-level undergraduates observe and work with teachers in public schools to implement and reflect on tutoring lessons. These preservice teachers also plan, implement, and reflect on a lesson for at-risk preteens who live in a group home, which is part of the Department of Youth Services for Alabama.

"Principles of High School Education," a required course for those who plan to teach middle level or high school, focuses on learning theories and effective teaching strategies. An overview of the characteristics of adolescents and preadolescents, as well as the steps in planning and implementing sound lessons that achieve specific educational objectives, are emphasized in the course. These preservice teachers are provided opportunities to apply the knowledge gained through four application activities: (1) observation/ reflection, (2) tutoring, (3) designing/ implementing/ reflecting on a lesson, and (4) preparing educational materials.

Observation

With the consent of the principal and the classroom teacher, the preservice teacher observes teacher/learner behaviors in a public school middle level classroom for a total of two hours. Prior to the arrival of the preservice teacher, the classroom teacher receives an explanatory letter and evaluation sheets (see Tables 17.1 and 17.2). Using a cue sheet with particular behaviors to observe (see Table 17.3), the preservice teacher circles the teaching methods and procedures demonstrated by the classroom teacher. After the observation, an analysis report is written about the observed behaviors and possible strategies/methods that might have proven to be more effective. The report is then turned in to the professor and evaluated on the basis of the reflection demonstrated in the written analysis.

Volunteer work

In return for the opportunity to observe the class, the pre-intern does volunteer work for the classroom teacher. The amount of volunteer work varies according to the student's grade aspirations: A = 5 hours; B = 4 hours; C or below = 3 hours. Although the exact nature of the volunteer work is determined by the classroom teacher and the pre-intern, instructional design is stressed. Designing and preparing an educational bulletin board, an advanced organizer, or an educational mobile are all possibilities. Developing an educational game, such as "Jeopardy," in the content area is another popular project. In addition, the education major may help the teacher grade or file papers, photocopy materials, or do record-keeping chores.

Tutoring

Tutoring a middle level student is also a course requirement. The number of hours required are, again, contingent upon the student's grade aspirations: A = 4 hours; B = 3 hours; C = 2 hours. Tutoring may be done in the public school for students of the cooperating teacher to whom the preservice teacher is assigned, but this is in addition to the volunteer work mentioned earlier. Tutoring sessions must be conducted in the classroom so that there is a certified teacher present. Reflection, an integral part of a teacher's growth, is included in the pre-intern's report of the tutoring sessions (see Table 17.4).

Tutoring middle level students may also be done after school. The Boys and Girls Clubs in the local area have after-school care, and some education students volunteer to tutor the sixth-, seventh-, and eighth-grade students there. Other preservice teachers tutor young adolescents at their church. Occasionally, education majors and art majors use their talents to tutor middle level students who are taking part in activities at the YMCA. Tutoring is also conducted at the North Alabama Girls' Group Home, a 24-hour facility that houses ten or fewer girls (age 12 to 18) who have been adjudicated to this facility for four to six months.

Enrichment lesson

The population of the North Alabama Girls' Group Home provides students an excellent opportunity to work with at-risk students. Working in teams of two or three, education students design and implement an enrichment lesson for the girls. The lesson does not have to be related to a specific content area but it must have an educational objective, such as recognizing the obstacles faced and overcome by Helen Keller and other physically challenged individuals. Since the intent is to help these girls realize that learning can be fun and helpful, preservice teachers often teach them nonacademic material or teach them about academic subjects in a nontraditional way.

Preparing this enrichment lesson challenges these preservice teachers to learn about and utilize community resources. When materials are needed for the lesson, education students seek donations from local merchants. Often they get materials from several sources. For instance, a group who wanted to teach T-shirt painting had a local manufacturer donate T-shirts, and Wal-Mart donated the paint. Often local tourist attractions are used as teaching sites. A group composed of history and music majors used W. C. Handy's home to teach the girls about the history of jazz. The Alabama Music Hall of Fame also helped integrate the knowledge of music and history by showing the contributions of various Alabama musicians. Education students were surprised to find that both these establishments often donate tickets if asked. Natural community resources, such as Indian Mounds and the Tennessee River and the dam, have proven to be excellent educational sites. Because the North Alabama Girls' Group Home has a van and driver, a mini-lecture for background information can be given at the home and then the girls can be taken to the site for hands-on experiences.

As with the previous components, the enrichment lesson must be reflected on. Often this reflection includes quotes from those who were taught (see Table 17.5).

COMMENTARY

Field experience brings relevancy to educational theory, allowing preservice middle level teachers to observe teacher-student interactions and to work with practitioners. It is intended to prompt students to compare educational theories with real practices and reflect upon strategies that might be helpful. Allowing education students to work with middle level teachers encourages networking, the sharing of ideas and resources, a stronger partnership between the university and local schools, and an opportunity for the fledgling teacher to experience various phases of teaching while enjoying the safety net of a seasoned teacher.

Tutoring enables the preservice teacher to work closely with a middle level student. Many preservice teachers have reported that the tutoring experience enabled them to understand the early adolescent more fully. In addition, by working with one student at a time, they are able to recognize when a teaching strategy is effective and when it isn't. Students frequently comment that different learning styles become evident during the course of tutoring.

The enrichment lesson enables the student to not only plan and execute a lesson but to develop one that often integrates several subjects. The team approach used in the enrichment lesson also prepares individuals for teaming in actual middle level settings.

Comments have been very positive from preservice teachers, public school teachers, and community leaders whose populations have benefited from tutoring or enrichment lessons. All agree that the youth served have benefited and future teachers have gained much insight about community organizations. The most common remark from preservice teachers is, "Why didn't I get to do this earlier?"

Table 17.1. Letter to Middle School Teacher

Date

Dear Teacher:

Thank you for allowing an Education 382 student to observe your class. This actual classroom experience is very helpful to education majors, many of whom have not been in secondary schools for many years. We hope this observation will be a win-win situation for everyone involved, since the pre-intern student is to do volunteer work for the participating teacher. This may include an advanced organizer of either a video or film that you plan to show or a lecture that you plan to give. An educational bulletin board that the student designs and displays in the classroom is also an option. If a bulletin board is not appropriate, an educational mobile, educational game, educational crossword puzzle, etc., may be substituted. The pre-intern is learning to develop materials and, in the process, design/create helpful materials that you may not have time to develop yourself. These should be original products rather than copies from another source or copies supplied by you. Also, volunteer work must be done on the student's own time, not simultaneously with observation time.

Tutoring is part of the assignment for the Ed 382 student. Tutoring should be conducted in the same room with a certified teacher since the student is not yet an intern. Tutoring may be done one-on-one or in small groups. The content area must be the one in which the student is getting certified. Since the number of tutoring and volunteer hours that the student must do varies according to the grade he or she is striving to earn, please note these hours stated on the forms that you will need to sign. After the student has completed the observation and the volunteer and tutoring work, please complete the evaluation form and return it to me in the self-addressed, stamped envelope. Should you have questions, please feel free to call me at (256) 765-4686 or (256) 765-4575. Again, thank you in advance for your help.

Sincerely,

Laura C. Stokes, Ph.D.

Table 17.2. Observation/Evaluation Sheet

Volunteer work: I am working toward a/an _____ and, therefore, I
have done _____ hours of volunteer work and _____ hours of tutoring, _____ of which was done in the public school. With my volunteer
hours, I did/created:

I did not copy any of these materials. _____

                                                    (signature of student)

==

To Be Completed by the Cooperating Teacher
_____ hours of tutoring were completed in my class and the following was performed for volunteer work (list products and services):

_____

**Please mark the following to indicate the quality of the work that was
done.**
   5 = superior; 4 = good; 3 = satisfactory; 2 = poor; 1 = not done

A.   Completion of product(s)/service(s)
            1   2   3   4   5

B.   Degree of work quality
            1   2   3   4   5

C.   Level of professional judgment used
            1   2   3   4   5

D.   Interpersonal relationship skills used
            1   2   3   4   5

E.   Positive attitude in relation to work ethic
            1   2   3   4   5

F.   Dependability
            1   2   3   4   5

                              _____
                                                    (signature of teacher)

Table 17.3. Classroom Observation Cue Sheet

Student: _____

School: _____

Directions: Circle the effective teaching methods and procedures demonstrated by the classroom teacher.

Teacher

Lecture	Demonstrates critical thinking	
Seat work	Groups students	Motivates
Presents objective	Monitors	Questions
Restates/emphasizes	Evaluates	Prompts
Uses examples	Questions	Neg. response
Makes material relevant	Disciplines	Pos. response
Relates subject to other subjects	Discusses	Neut. response
Relates subject to previous material		

Other: _____

Students

On Task

Individual work

Group work

Listening/following text

Participating

Violence

Other _____

Off Task

Talking

Writing notes

Daydreaming

Disrupting

Other _____

Table 17.4. Tutoring

Date	*Times*	*Personal Signature*
_____	_____	_____
_____	_____	_____
_____	_____	_____

Activity: (Briefly report the names of the students you tutored, the subject/content in which you tutored them, what techniques you used and reflections on the session.)

Reflections:

(Date): _____

_____

_____

_____

_____

_____

Reflections:

(Date): _____

_____

_____

_____

_____

_____

Table 17.5. Reflections for Enrichment Lesson

On the basis of the lesson that you presented at the group home, discuss what you learned and what you would change (if anything) by deleting, enhancing, amplifying, adding, or altering your strategies in future teaching.

_____

_____

_____

_____

_____

Times and dates that you taught:

_____

Number of students involved: _____

Please attach your lesson plan, which includes **intent, objective, activities, resources, and evaluation.**

Adventures Beyond the Classroom

KATHRYN REINKE
Oklahoma State University, Stillwater

STRATEGY/ACTIVITY/ASSIGNMENT

As part of their methods classes, middle level preservice teachers participate in a program called "Adventures beyond the Classroom." This is an interdisciplinary outdoor education activity involving sixth-grade students. For an entire day the sixth graders, their teachers, parents, and the preservice teachers go to a campground near a lake. While at the campground, the students learn about plants and wildlife and relate their experiences to mathematics and language arts. The preservice teachers assist the parents and classroom teachers as well as take charge of a specific group of students.

The activities are many and varied:

1. **Water Ecology:** Concepts of conservation and water usage are taught on the shores of the lake. For the first part of this activity students are told that it takes about seven gallons of water to flush a toilet, 30 to 35 gallons to take a bath, 10 to 15 gallons for a 10-minute shower, and 25 to 50 gallons to wash a load of clothes. Preservice teachers and students then form a bucket brigade and pass buckets of water from the lake to large 55-gallon barrels. At some point in the process, a teacher stops the line of buckets and says that someone needs to shower. The teacher then throws out 15 gallons of water and starts the line again. Soon the teacher again stops the line and says that a toilet is being flushed. Seven gallons of water are taken out of the barrels. As this continues, students become aware that the water is being used faster than they can generate the amount of water, thereby causing a water shortage. A discussion about the importance of conservation follows this part of the activity.

    The second half of this activity is spent near the water with the preservice teachers assisting the students in the collection and identification of living organisms. Concepts such as the water cycle (evaporation, clouds, condensation, transpiration, etc.), which are part of classroom discussions, are related to this real-life environment. There are discussions about the ability of animals to adapt to their environments. The interrelationships among the water organisms are observed and discussed by the students. Following the activity, questions are asked:

- What happens to organisms if the water level of the lake drops?
- Where does the water come from? What evidence is there to support your answer?
- What are some sounds associated with the water?
- What are the smallest and largest organisms found?
- What signs of pollution were found?

2. **Plant Ecology:** This activity is led by a plant expert who teaches the students to classify common prairie plants. Preservice teachers assist the students with the collection and labeling of a variety of specimens. Edible plants and their use in wilderness survival are explored.

3. **Metric Olympics:** The students are divided into groups of five or six with one or two preservice teachers assisting. Each group moves through a series of stations that allow the students to discover metric estimation and measurement. Before each activity, students must give an estimate to the preservice teachers. After the activity, measurements are made, and the difference between the estimation and the actual amount is calculated.

- *Station 1,* Cotton Ball Shot-Put—Students throw a cotton ball. Measurement is in centimeters.
- *Station 2,* Javelin Throw—Students throw a plastic drinking straw. Measurement is in centimeters.
- *Station 3,* Sponge Squeeze—Students squeeze up as much water as possible in a sponge. Measurement is in milliliters.
- *Station 4,* Standing Long Jump—Students jump as far as possible from a standing position. Measurement is in centimeters.
- *Station 5,* Weight Lifting—Students lift as many paper clips as possible with a magnet. Measurement is in grams.

In addition to participating in this program, preservice teachers also reflect on their experience. The reflection consists of answering the fol-

lowing questions in a paper turned in a week after the "Adventures beyond the Classroom" experience:

1. What experiences were the most valuable for you? Why?
2. Explain how you would assess what students learned during the
   day.
3. Describe how the day was organized, how the activities were developed, and the reactions of the students.
4. What suggestions do you have to improve the program from the
   standpoint of the middle level student?
5. What have you learned about the middle level child?
6. Based on your observations, discuss how middle level students
   learn.

COMMENTARY

This field experience is a valuable one for students who are interested in
teaching upper-elementary or middle level students. The opportunity to
interact with students is repeatedly mentioned as a valuable part of the
activity. Many of the preservice teachers do not realize how verbal, curious, mature, and cooperative this age child can be. They also become
aware of the challenges that teaching the middle level student can present.

Field Experiences—
Student Teachers/Interns

Student Teachers: Issues and Concerns

ELIZABETH D. DORE
Radford University, Radford, VA

STRATEGY/ACTIVITY/ASSIGNMENT

Student teachers, especially those trained in middle level teacher preparation programs, need to be aware of the unique developments of the students with whom they will be working. Likewise, student teachers need to be conversant with and able to implement effective teaching strategies that are appropriate for use with middle level students. Prior to embarking on their student-teaching stint, the preservice students are trained in middle school concepts, including flexible block scheduling; integrated, thematic, and interdisciplinary subject organization; advisor-advisee programs; interdisciplinary teams; and intramural athletic programs that emphasize participation by all students. However, once they start student teaching they often discover very traditional classrooms with few, if any, "real" middle level components in place. Approximately once every two weeks, the student teachers come back together for a seminar in which they not only discuss classroom strategies and techniques but also talk, compare notes, and realize they are not "alone."

One of the most interesting and thought-provoking as well as settling activities/assignments for this seminar is the issues/concerns cards. As students enter the meeting room, before they have had a chance to begin "catching up" with each other, they are handed a 3" × 5" index card and instructed to write one issue/concern or "great happening" on the card. The writer of the card remains anonymous. The last hour of the seminar is spent discussing what was written on the cards.

COMMENTARY

What the class often focuses on is the fact that many cooperating teachers have not been taught the "middle school concept" and, therefore, are not comfortable using strategies such as cooperative learning, interdisciplinary units, and addressing the issues of multiple intelligences. In many cases, they are convinced these strategies will not work anyway— so why let the student teacher try them? Other issues that have arisen are:

- "Why does this parent have so much power in this classroom?"
- "What do I do about a student who is highly unmotivated?"
- "I feel my cooperating teacher is trying to turn me into a 'carbon copy' of herself."
- "I am bothered by teachers who try to talk you out of teaching because they are frustrated with their profession."
- "When my teacher doesn't agree with my methods, it makes me feel like I'm not a good teacher."
- "My cooperating teacher wants a whole week's detailed lesson plans on the previous Thursday!!"
- "How can I find the time to get materials together for my lesson plans?"

These are only a few of the myriad questions haunting student teachers as they experience teaching firsthand. It is extremely important they are given the opportunity to vent their frustrations and discuss their concerns with others who are in similar circumstances. The results of the issues/concerns assignment have been extremely positive. Although some student teachers leave the seminar with new methods of dealing with some of their questions, others realize that other student teachers have many of the same concerns. Also, when a particularly "great happening" has occurred, it becomes a cause for celebration. In essence, student teachers become their own community—caring, assisting, and showing concern for each other as they go through the student-teaching experience.

Mentor Associate Teaming Program

JERRY J. ROTTIER
University of Wisconsin–Eau Claire

STRATEGY/ACTIVITY/ASSIGNMENT

During the spring semester of 1995-96, a pilot program was begun in which two groups of student teachers were each placed with a team of teachers in a middle school. Because of the positive response to the initial activities of this program, it was continued in order to learn more about this arrangement for a student-teaching/intern-teaching field experience. After five semesters, students have been placed on twelve teams in three middle schools. One team has participated in this program for three semesters, attesting to their belief in and success of the program.

The traditional procedure of assigning a student teacher to one cooperating teacher was replaced by assigning a group of two or three student teachers (associates) to an interdisciplinary team of teachers (mentors). A major purpose of the program was to challenge the mentors to utilize the talents of the three associates to help with instructional practices that may be unwieldy for one teacher in a classroom of 25 to 30 students. For the associates, the goal was to not only develop their skills of planning, teaching, evaluating, and managing a middle level classroom but also to involve them in activities within all the disciplines represented on the team. It was believed that involvement across disciplines would help to break down the barriers between disciplines and encourage these prospective teachers to seek ways to provide interdisciplinary opportunities for students in their future classrooms.

While being assigned to a team of teachers, each associate was aligned with a mentor on the team that coincided with their major/minor area of preparation. The mentor served the traditional task of the cooperating teacher, providing students opportunities to establish themselves in the classroom along with supplying feedback on their performance.

During the first week of the semester, the associates visited the classes of all mentors on the team and shadowed one student for an entire day to gain a sense of life as a student on the team. Associates spent about one-half of the semester in the discipline of their mentor, learning and practicing the skills of planning, instructing, evaluating, and managing middle level students. The amount of time that associates were "in charge" of one or more classes varied depending on the desires of the associate and his or her mentor.

The associates were involved in a variety of activities throughout the semester. Below is a list of activities that demonstrate the nature of this unique program. The associates are identified by their major/minor to indicate that they were involved in activities outside their major/minor area of concentration.

Interdisciplinary units were planned and taught by three different teams of associates on the topics of diversity, elections, and environment:

- An English associate and a social studies associate collaborated on a research project in social studies requiring students to research countries in Europe. They developed the evaluation rubric, helped teach the unit, and graded the projects.
- A team of associates participated in a week-long environmental simulation activity in science.
- A team of associates worked with a science mentor on an orienteering activity.
- A math associate assisted a reading teacher for four weeks, helping with an interdisciplinary unit on travel.
- A math associate and English associate team taught a drama unit in English.
- An English associate taught two classes in social studies for six weeks.
- A science associate teamed with a teacher of learning disabled (LD) students for two weeks, helping with reports in science.
- A science associate and English associate worked together on reading strategies for science and participated in an interdisciplinary unit on the Titanic.
- An English associate taught a unit on spread sheets with the math mentor.
- A math associate assisted the English mentor in the computer lab.
- A social studies associate observed and assisted in science classes for several weeks.
- An English associate taught a unit with the media specialist.
- A team of associates participated in a math stock-market game.

Units ranged in length from four days to twelve days. In addition, the associates were involved in numerous field trips and student social activities.

The author has served as the university supervisor for the majority of the associates in this program, allowing for the continuous monitoring of the program. Each student in the program was required to keep a list of activities in which they were involved as a means of determining the effectiveness of their experience. During the third semester, a more formal assessment procedure was initiated by inviting the principals, mentors, and associates to an evening of reflection. Many comments were expressed that will help to determine future directions of the program.

Program Findings

On the basis of five semesters of implementation, we have learned the following about this program:

1. The program has allowed mentors to implement new units of instruction and modify others due to the assistance provided by the associates. Not all mentors on the team found ways to utilize the talents of the associates. This has been a learning process, with a great deal of exploration taking place. As more teams become involved and as teams become involved for a second or third time, this aspect of the program will improve.

2. Associates worked with the mentor in their major/minor area of concentration for a minimum of half the semester. Reports from the associates and mentors indicated that this amount of time was adequate to develop their skills of planning, instructing, evaluating, and classroom management. We need to keep in mind that these skills continued to be practiced in their instructional responsibilities throughout the remainder of the semester. In one case, the amount of time the associate was involved in team activities was reduced to provide more time to focus on planning and instructional skills.

3. In one instance, an associate with certification in math and physics was a member of the team. This caused some difficulties when the associate left to teach physics at the high school. We learned that the program works best when the associates can stay in the middle school for the entire semester.

4. Several teams consisted of associates with 1 to 9 and 6 to 12 certification. Associates and mentors both agreed that having a combination of associates from both 1 to 9 and 6 to 12 certification areas generated some interesting ideas as they worked together on activities.

5. On one occasion, a special education student was assigned as an associate on a team. The special education associate and one other associate team taught one class for the entire semester, along with being involved in a variety of other activities on the team. This arrangement was very effective and will continue to be used whenever possible.

6. In two instances, an intern (a student teacher who has a provisional license and is paid to teach two to three classes) was one of the three associates on a team. Scheduling problems were encountered when the intern was required to teach classes at a specified time. It appears this arrangement can work effectively, but it does place some restrictions on the program.

7. With three associates on a team, the issue of potentially overloading middle level students with students from the university was recognized. When associates were teaching in their major/minor areas, they were all scheduled during the same two periods to prevent their students from interacting with three different associates in one day. This turned out to be less of a problem than was originally thought.

8. In several instances, the mentors and associates were freed from their teaching duties for an afternoon in order to review the major topics to be taught during the semester and determine those topics and times that the associates might work with one or more mentors. This was very profitable for both mentors and associates and both groups recommended that this be a staple feature of the program.

9. During one semester, each associate was assigned to two mentors. At the midterm and final conferences, both mentors, the associate, and I met to discuss the progress of the associate. It seems to work well, but this item will need more study. For a large team, it drew more teachers on the team into the mentoring role.

10. During the first semester of the project, associates were involved in this project with no previous notification. Since then, students are informed of this opportunity and allowed to volunteer for this type of field experience. As a result, students entered willingly into this arrangement, which has been very beneficial.

COMMENTARY

Below are some student testimonials of the program:

"I feel I have gained a wealth of confidence and ability in all areas due to the understanding, support, and flexibility of the team."

"Even though I spent most of my time in English class, there were several teaching projects that were done in collaboration with other subjects areas. It felt good to apply my English skills and knowledge to these projects in order to enhance their results. Experiences like these helped to 'break down the walls' that exist between the discipline areas. I believe that spending time outside the English classroom has made me a more confident, creative, and versatile teacher both inside and outside the English classroom."

"I thoroughly enjoyed team teaching with a fellow student teacher (English and special education). The companionship in the classroom was comforting and confidence-boosting. Because of this arrangement, I was able to more efficient and accurately adapt lessons to all different levels."

"My most valuable experience was teaching the integrated unit on diversity. Through this experience, I was able to completely plan and execute lessons in the other disciplinary areas. The feeling of ownership and success at the end was very rewarding."

"One very valuable experience was being able to see several different kinds of teaching styles. I did not compare styles but simply observed how each teacher organized his/her class."

"The interdisciplinary unit was a valuable experience for me because it showed how much work we could get done as a team compared to an individual."

"It was especially nice to be working so closely with two of my peers. Having the opportunity to be able to go to them was comforting."

"I felt the whole semester was worthwhile and I cannot find a single thing that was not satisfactory and/or valuable."

Below are some testimonials to the program from the mentors:

"All three associates were involved in a big early civilization research project assignment. It turned out well and was an assignment I would have never tried on my own without help. Much of the credit for the quality of the research papers and the oral reports is due to the fact that I had the assistance of the associates."

"I think these three associates forced our team to reevaluate some of our methods and ideas. They inspired us to look at our teaching in new ways. I am grateful for that opportunity."

"They have experienced the middle school concept in action. They understand shared decision making and planning. In addition, they had opportunities to view a variety of discipline and organizational approaches. This will help them as they set out to establish a comfortable style for themselves."

"The program provides a real 'jump-start' on all aspects of teaming."

This project is a work in progress. We have learned that our student teachers enjoyed and believed they profited from this experience. Teachers on the teams were grateful to be able to utilize the talents of all associates for certain instructional units. Principals were extremely positive about this type of experience for prospective teachers. We are very pleased that almost all students who have completed the program are employed full time as teachers. Two students who are in their second year of teaching are team leaders in their middle school.

This program requires a paradigm shift from the traditional procedures of the student-teaching program. Universities interested in this program need a strong advocate for this type of experience, one who is willing to spend a large amount of time introducing the idea to principals, teachers, and university students and then nurturing the program once it is implemented. Going slowly in the beginning is urged in order to make the initial experience successful. Once rooted within a building, other teams will ask to become involved because they will see the advantages of having a team of students assigned to a team of teachers.

Author Index

453

Subject Index

About the Editors

Charlene Johnson is director of the Center for Middle Level Education, Research and Development, and an associate professor in the Department of Curriculum and Instruction at the University of Arkansas, Fayetteville. Working with the Center, Charlene has codirected the annual Middle Level Summer Institute and the Trainer of Trainers program. Both are instrumental in educating teachers throughout the state in middle level concepts and practices for the purpose of more effectively meeting the needs of early adolescents. She has taught undergraduate and graduate middle level methods and principles courses and has chaired the committee for the development of middle level degree programs (undergraduate and graduate) at the University of Arkansas, Fayetteville. Working with adolescents, she was a guidance counselor in the United States Virgin Islands in which her primary emphasis was on fifth, sixth, and seventh graders. She was also a program administrator for a youth (ages 14 to 19 years) summer employment program. She is a member of the Steering Committee for the Foundation for Mid South's Middle Start (MS2) initiative and the Board of Directors for the Arkansas Association of Middle Level Education.

Linda R. McElroy Morrow is currently an assistant professor of middle level education in the Department of Curriculum and Instruction at the University of Arkansas, Fayetteville. She has over twenty years of public school teaching experience at the middle level. She teaches preservice and graduate-level courses in middle level principles and methods and participates in the University of Arkansas' Center for Middle Level Education, Research, and Development as a Senior Fellow and Codirector of the Middle Level Summer Institutes. She also serves as a liaison in the Northwest Arkansas University/Public School Partnership.

Toni Sills-Briegel is currently an assistant professor of middle level education at Southwest Missouri State University in Springfield. She began her career as a junior high school teacher in Russellville, Arkansas. After earning her doctorate at the University of Arkansas, she accepted a position as visiting assistant professor at Tulane University, in which her research and teaching centered on middle level education. During that period she worked closely with Live Oak Middle School, an inner-city school. A move to Murray State University in Kentucky allowed her to work across grade levels and develop an understanding of the early adolescents' place in the scope of human development. Then, appreciating the fact that fourteen years of teaching junior high school did not adequately prepare her to teach true middle level concepts, she left higher education for two years to serve as a core team teacher in two middle schools in Las Vegas, Nevada. She now cocoordinates the Middle Level Program at Southwest Missouri State University. Dr. Briegel has written and published extensively on middle issues and currently co-edits *The Transescent,* the state journal for the Missouri Middle School Association.

Samuel Totten is currently a professor of secondary and middle level education in the Department of Curriculum and Instruction at the University of Arkansas, Fayetteville. From 1992 through 1997 he served as one of the founding Directors of the Center for Middle Level Education, Research and Development at the University of Arkansas. Before entering academia, he taught students in grades 7 through 12 in California, Washington, D.C., Australia, and Israel, and served as a K–8 principal in northern California.

Among the publications he has co-edited/co-authored on middle level education are: *Middle Level Education: An Annotated Bibliography* (Westport, CT: Greenwood Press, 1996), *Social Issues and Service at the Middle Level* (Needham Heights, MA: Allyn and Bacon Publishers, 1997), and "The Current Status of Middle Level Education Research: A Critical Review" (*Research in Middle Level Education,* Summer 1995).